D0875746

NATIONAL MANAGEMENT OF THE INTERNATIONAL ECONOMY

Also by M. Panić

PRODUCT CHANGES IN INDUSTRIAL COUNTRIES' TRADE, 1955–68 (*with A. H. Rajan*)
THE UK AND WEST GERMAN MANUFACTURING INDUSTRY, 1954–72 (*editor*)
CAPACITY UTILISATION IN UK MANUFACTURING INDUSTRY

National Management of the International Economy

M. Panić

St. Martin's Press New York

First published in the United States of America in 1988

Printed in Hong Kong

ISBN 0–312–01294–2

Library of Congress Cataloging-in-Publication Data
Panić, M.
National management of the international economy/M. Panić.
p. cm.
Bibliography: p.
Includes index.
ISBN 0–312–01294–2 : $49.95
1. International economic relations. 2. International economic integration. 3. Energy policy. I. Title.
HF1411.P2935 1988 87–18764
337–dc 19 CIP

Contents

Acknowledgements

This book would probably never have been written but for the help which I have received from two people. Wynne Godley, Professor of Economics and Director of the Department of Applied Economics in the University of Cambridge, encouraged me to undertake the project and helped arrange my return to Cambridge. David Sainsbury, Finance Director of J. Sainsbury plc, helped secure financial support for the project and took great interest in its development. My debt to both of them is very great indeed.

I am equally indebted to the trustees of the Sainsbury Family Trust without whose generous and continuous support my research in Cambridge, of which the present books forms only one part, could never have been undertaken.

Most of the ideas in this book were developed over a number of years. I have had a chance, therefore, to discuss them with many economists and policy makers in the UK and abroad. Some of them subsequently read various chapters and commented on them, too many unfortunately for me to be able to express my gratitude here to each individually. There are, however, several economists to whom I owe a special debt. Brian Reddaway read most of the text; and Charles Kindleberger and Tadeusz Rybczynski read the whole of it. Phyllis Deane found both time and energy, while convalescing from an operation, to check my interpretations of economic history and the history of economic ideas. Michael Landesmann listened with patience as I kept reworking some of the analysis in Part II and then fired more awkward questions. Barrie Stevens supplied me with OECD data and publications which were of great help in drafting some of the chapters; and Stephen Potter and his colleagues at the OECD very kindly allowed me to quote at length from one of the OECD papers in the penultimate section of Chapter 2. None of them is, of course, responsible for any remaining errors and omissions, and not all of them would necessarily agree with every detail as it stands.

Anne Mason and her colleagues provided excellent service typing and retyping, with great patience and efficiency, various drafts of the book. Ann Newton read the whole manuscript and suggested stylistic improvements.

Finally, work on a book covering a wide range of subjects and issues, completed over a relatively short period of time, may easily strain family relationships as the author is either frequently away from home or inaccessible in his study. I was fortunate to receive nothing but understanding and encouragement from my wife, Marianne, and son, Alexander. To the two of them, I owe the most special debt of all.

M. PANIĆ

Introduction

By any criterion, the world economy has, over the last decade and a half, been going through one of its most serious crises.

The international economic order that was developed in the 1940s collapsed at the beginning of the 1970s. It has been replaced by a series of short-term, hastily improvised measures which can in no way provide solutions to what are basically long-term problems. Thus the highly successful international financial arrangements of the 'Bretton Woods System' have disintegrated into what has been called, unimaginatively but correctly, the international financial 'non-system'.

The deep-rooted belief in industrial and developing countries that their interests are diametrically opposed added a new dimension to international instability with the two 'oil shocks' and the subsequent collapse of energy and other primary commodity prices. With neither surplus nor deficit countries ready to co-operate, it was inevitable that the mass redistribution of world income, and widespread stagnation which it brought about, would result sooner or later in an international debt crisis. It duly appeared in the early 1980s, threatening many banks with insolvency and, in this way, the viability of national financial systems.

Apart from a few exceptions, it has now become virtually impossible even for industrial economies to reconcile low unemployment with low inflation rates, and the two with a sustainable balance of payments. Not surprisingly, 'creeping protectionism', with threats of even more serious trade restrictions, has been increasingly in evidence. Many of these threats have come from the United States, which is going through yet another phase of economic nationalism. Far from helping developing and other countries with major adjustment problems (as it did for a long time after the Second World War), the world's largest and wealthiest economy is making these adjustments virtually impossible by sucking in a very high proportion of international investments, partly in order to finance a huge rearmament programme.

The most notable thing about this list of problems is that, with the exception of the energy crisis, it contains nothing that is really new. Similar problems have occurred in the past and for basically the same reason: the integration of national economies at significantly different productivity and income levels – unaccompanied by any serious attempt to evolve long-term arrangements for reconciling these differences. As a result, conflicts of interest proliferate. Growing global economic interdependence turns national problems into international problems – yet each country is left to deal with them in isolation, as best it can. It is hardly surprising, therefore, that major international economic crises usually end with a disintegration of the world economy and, occasionally, with wars.

I have tried in this book to analyse the reasons behind these conflicts – their origin, consequences and policy implications. I have also attempted to suggest at least some answers to what is probably one of the most important economic and political questions at the close of the twentieth century: what conditions have to be satisfied to ensure short-term stability and long-term progress in a highly integrated and continuously changing world economy?

Although the international community has never been able to evolve a lasting economic order, there have been several periods of relative stability and sustained progress since the early nineteenth century. Invariably, however, they have been followed by equally long periods of great international instability, costly 'beggar-my-neighbour' policies and widespread stagnation. What has been the cause of these profound changes in national behaviour?

It is extremely difficult even to begin to answer these and similar questions without adopting a rather different analytical approach from the highly compartmentalised method traditionally employed in international economics. International production, trade, investment and finance are usually treated separately. As a result, policy prescriptions in any one of these areas are seldom related to policy prescriptions in the other areas. The problem with this approach is that the dynamics of international integration, its effects and policy requirements are the result of changes which are taking place continuously and simultaneously over a wide range of economic activities. In the circumstances, partial analysis can be at best inadequate and at worst dangerously misleading.

To avoid these shortcomings, I have treated international production, trade, investment, finance, institutions and policies as an integral part of the process which shapes long-term international economic relationships and which is, in turn, influenced by them. Consequently, the book covers a wide range of issues – combining economic theory, empirical research and history. The issues covered include: changes in the character and organisation of international production, trade, investment and finance (Part I); the origins and elimination of short and long-term ('fundamental') international economic instability (Part II); the long-term evolution of national commercial policies and the international economy (Part III); the origin and long-term effects (economic and financial) of the energy crisis (Part IV); and adaptations in international relationships and policies required to cope with long-term changes in the world economic environment and unequal national capacities to respond to them (Part V).

I hope, therefore, that the book will be of interest to economists specialising in different areas of the subject, economic historians, historians of economic ideas, and policy makers, as well as to a much wider audience.

M.P.

Part I
International Economic Integration

The process by which the world has, since the early sixteenth century, undergone an increasing, apparently irreversible and often violent political, economic and cultural integration has produced probably one of the most significant transformations in history. In the words of an eminent historian: 'there has never been a time when world civilisation has been more of a reality. Mankind is now tied together by some common experience as it has not been tied together since it was liberated from the simplest and most crushing restraints of environment'.[1]

Not surprisingly, economists have devoted a good deal of attention over the last two centuries to different aspects of economic integration. The term itself is, however, of very recent origin, at least in the analysis of international *economic issues. According to Machlup, it was used for the first time in this context in the 1940s.*[2]

In the 1950s and 1960s, inspired by attempts of European and other countries to create customs and economic unions, the literature on the subject proliferated, dealing mainly with problems of regional integration. Since the early 1970s, however, the concept of international integration has come to be used increasingly to explain the growing interdependence of national economies, irrespective of whether it is brought about by acts of governments or by the independently conceived and executed actions of the various micro-economic agents.

At the same time, the increasing importance and interaction of different aspects of economic integration seem to have caused a certain degree of confusion in the concepts currently in use, as well as in the treatment of the origin and development of these extremely important phenomena. The two chapters in Part I therefore analyse in some detail the meaning, causes and extent of international economic integration.

1 The Process of International Economic Integration

I

In common use, 'integration' normally describes either the process of unifying diverse parts into a harmonious whole, or the stage which such a process has reached. The first represents, obviously, a dynamic and the second a static concept.

Exactly the same notions are also employed in economics in order to define a number of different phenomena. At the micro-economic level, the concepts of 'vertical' and 'horizontal' integration are used to describe the spread of a firm's production and ownership relationships over different stages, or forms, of economic activity. At a more aggregate, national, level economic integration 'is taken to denote reducing social or geographical differences in the distribution of income and wealth and/or increasing national control over the means of production, raising the local content of goods and services, forging a closer correspondence between a country's production and its consumption, etc'.[1] Finally, at the international level, the concepts have 'traditionally been used to describe' government actions which lead to a reduction in 'barriers to trade in goods and services and to the mobility of factors of production, and also [to a harmonisation of] national economic policies'.[2]

This chapter will concentrate on the last of these three forms of integration.

II

There is a tendency to use 'openness', 'integration' and 'interdependence' interchangeably, as if they were all describing exactly the same phenomenon. In fact, the three may refer to different processes as well as to different degrees of international involvement.[3]

To describe an economy as *open* should, normally, imply that it has relatively few barriers – legal, social, political, geographical or cultural – to international trade and factor movements. Over a period of time, an economy will become more open, therefore, if such obstacles to international exchange are reduced; and less open when they are erected or increased. This means that, although the description is frequently used to refer to changes in commercial policy (such as reductions in tariffs, quotas, exchange controls and subsidies), improvements in transport and communications can have a similar effect. Changes in tastes can also increase significantly a country's receptiveness to foreign influences and, in this way, its exchange with the outside world.

In other words, there are a number of important determinants of the openness of an economy: government regulations, technical and institutional changes, participation in supranational institutions and international treaties which commit governments to a more internationalist attitude, and the behaviour of private and other enterprises.

However, the fact that an economy is 'open' does not necessarily mean that it is 'integrated' into the world economy. The expression *international integration* is meaningful only when it is used to describe an active participation in the international division of labour. That is, it should refer to close links between the economies whose specialisation has resulted in productive and financial structures which are significantly interrelated. Similarly, changes in international integration should refer to changes in the participants' production, trading and financial relationships with each other.

Clearly, although 'openness' may be synonymous with 'integration', this need not be always the case, especially if the former is used predominantly, as most economists tend to use it, to describe nothing more than a change in commercial policy. Attempts to promote international integration by reductions in barriers to trade and capital flows do not always achieve the desired result. In other words, *de jure* integration is not the same thing as *de facto* integration.[4] An economy may be subject to very few regulations against exchanges with other countries. However, its geographical location, culture, tastes, factor endowments and income may be such that it has a very limited scope – at least in the short to medium term – for international specialisation.

On the other hand, government measures designed to reduce the extent to which their economies are integrated internationally, by decreasing their openness, may produce exactly the opposite result. For instance, the creation of common barriers to trade with the rest of the world by the European Economic Community was one of the factors which encouraged the United States and other countries' transnational enterprises to establish their production facilities there – leading to a much tighter integration of industrial countries' productive structures. Similarly, the exchange controls imposed intermittently by US governments in the 1960s and 1970s, intended to reduce capital outflows from the country, contributed to the expansion of the eurodollar markets. As a result of this, the US money and financial markets became much more integrated with those of other industrial countries than they had been before.[5]

Moreover, even when there is very little direct link, formal or informal, between two sectors, regions or countries, they may become highly integrated through their economic relations with a third party. A good deal of global economic integration probably takes place now in this indirect form. Big increases in the price of oil may affect adversely employment and income levels in a country which is completely self-sufficient in energy, through their effect on its trading partners. Large-scale Soviet purchases of North American wheat – as a result of a major harvest failure in the USSR – may affect the livelihood of farmers and nutritional standards of consumers in countries which have few, if any, trading links with the USSR.

Finally, whether international economic integration is synonymous with international economic *interdependence* depends to a considerable extent on whether the former is defined in institutional (*de jure*) or economic (*de facto*) terms. To say that two or more economies are interdependent is to imply that they are linked to such a degree that economic developments in each of them are influenced significantly by policies and developments outside its borders. In other words, international economic interdependence is determined by *de facto* integration: the extent to which consumption patterns, production structures, money and capital markets of two or more countries are integrated either directly or through their links with a third country.

Consequently, institutional changes which create a greater degree of 'openness' in national economies will not increase international interdependence unless they give rise first to an increase in international integration. It is only in this case that the three concepts – openness, integration and interdependence – will be describing different aspects of the same phenomenon, irrespective of whether they are defined in static ('a state of affairs') or dynamic ('a process') terms.

III

The rather common practice in economic analysis and public debate of regarding 'international openness' as a precondition for 'international integration' is not difficult to understand when it is recalled that two of the most successful economic unions ever created, the German *Zollverein* and the European Economic Community (EEC), both originated in this way. In each case, governments of a number of independent, sovereign states reached a formal agreement to abolish restrictions on trade between them. This formal or *institutional (de jure) integration* provided, then, the desired impetus to a much greater degree of specialisation and trade between their economies.

However, as already mentioned, government efforts to create an institutional framework conducive to international integration need not always be successful. Most attempts made since the early 1950s to form regional economic blocs have, in fact, either failed completely or achieved very little, for the simple reason that the initiatives were incompatible with the economic and other conditions prevailing within the regions. Among the factors which have prevented successful economic integration over the period the following appear to have been particularly important: low levels of industrial and political development (the East African Community); too small an internal market to support more than a very modest industrialisation (the Central American Common Market); too great a dependence on countries outside the grouping for internal integration to proceed very far (the two already mentioned, the Caribbean Community and, to some extent, even the CMEA[6] and the European Free Trade Association); high transportation costs and poor communications (the Latin American Free Trade Association); and a highly centralised system of economic management which prevents spontaneous integration of production (the CMEA).[7]

Given the fairly high rate of failure of institutional integration one may begin to wonder how it is exactly that the world has achieved the unprecedented degree of cultural uniformity and economic interdependence mentioned in the introduction to Part I. After all, even the most successful economic union of sovereign nation states, the EEC, is regional rather than global in character.

The answer lies in the rapid growth of real incomes in many countries after the Second World War as well as in the enormous technical advantages in transport and communications. It is these unprecedented changes that have made possible a dramatic transformation in the character and pace of the integration process by breaking down the barriers to international specialisation imposed by the limited size of national markets, geographical distances and parochialisms in tastes, attitudes and organisational forms. The rapid extension of international markets, in turn, unleashed an unprecedented growth of the *spontaneous (de facto) or market integration*, brought about by actions of industrial corporations, banks and financial institutions, frequently without the knowledge and against the wishes of their governments.

Unlike the institutional attempts to integrate different economies, spontaneous integration is prompted by what the enterprises involved believe to be their corporate interest, not by considerations of national political and economic gains.[8] The speed with which it takes place will be determined – in the absence of changes in barriers to trade and factor movements – by the rate of technical and organisational improvement. The adjustment problems which their actions may create in the economies in which they operate will be of concern to the micro-economic agents only if they threaten to affect their long-term interests.

Spontaneously created integration and interdependence can evolve, therefore, at a rate which, once it gathers momentum, is outside the ability of any single government to control. During the last twenty-five years, transnational enterprises, to take one important example, have linked European countries closely, irrespective of the grouping to which they belong; European economies with those of countries outside Europe; and all of them with OPEC – often in spite of government efforts to prevent greater integration of these areas.[9] In some cases, spontaneous integration will be absorbed without serious costs. But, in others, it may impose on the countries concerned, for reasons to be discussed in Part II, a rate of change for which they are neither economically nor institutionally prepared.[10]

What exactly, then, is the process by which this form of integration comes to dominate international economic relationships?

IV

An increase in world-wide cultural uniformity is probably one of the most important preconditions for a greater degree of global economic integration and interdependence. Its importance lies in the fact that it gives rise to far-reaching changes in international patterns of demand, production methods and the behaviour of economic agents.

Technical advances in transport and communications play a critical role in this process for the very simple reason that international cultural integration depends on the development and spread of the mass media: films, television, radio, newspapers, magazines, books and records. As most of them are produced by the dominant industrial nations, they will inevitably reflect and idealise the lifestyles, beliefs and values held by these nations. Consequently, their values and patterns of behaviour will, in time, have an extremely strong influence on the values and patterns of behaviour of the rest of the world.

In this way a common, consumption-oriented value system will develop and come to permeate and drive all dynamic economies. The success, happiness and fulfilment of individuals and nations will be judged now according to the quantity and quality of the goods and services which they consume. Nor surprisingly, the advent of such a system is accompanied by the spread of an international demonstration effect, as people become aware of the superior standard of living available to the more affluent members of the world community.[11] This, in time, leads to a growing uniformity of international tastes and demand patterns, as those with similar incomes come to demand – irrespective of the country in which they live – similar (but not identical!) goods and services.

There is, however, much more to the international demonstration effect than the fact that it expands greatly the market for particular goods and services. As soon as an individual starts to aspire to somebody else's standard of living, the notion of his well-being is influenced not only by what is happening to his own level of income and consumption patterns but also by what is happening to the income and consumption patterns of his reference group. To the extent that comparative material acquisitions affect his social standing, his perceptions of prestige – even his self-respect – will be determined by how well or badly he comes out of these comparisons. Whether or not those with whom he compares himself have a greater influence on their destiny is something that will also influence the individual's behaviour. It is for this reason that in an integrated society *relative* income, status, influence and power become extremely important. Absolute improvements in any of them, though important and welcome, may still create a good deal of dissatisfaction if they are smaller than the improvements achieved by the reference group.

With the spread of information about the more affluent countries, the educated elites in the rest of the world are likely to use as the reference group their counterparts in industrial nations. In the countries where this happens, the rest of the population will then adjust its aspirations according to the level of material affluence and the pattern of behaviour of their educated elites.

An important consequence of international cultural integration will be, therefore, to sharpen the general sensitivity to changes in the standard of living. In particular, it will give rise to a very strong resistance to any reductions in either real or relative incomes. Individuals, groups and nations will increasingly use whatever power and influence they have in order to prevent changes in the economic environment which are likely to make them worse off. The result is the so-called 'downward rigidity of real wages' which has come to play such an important role in economic analysis and policy making.

The rigidity will be strengthened further by a number of other changes which take place in the process of industrialisation.

Once the citizens of a country begin to aspire to the lifestyle of the more affluent nations, the only way to realise these aspirations is to achieve the efficiency and income levels enjoyed by their reference groups abroad. This requires a restructuring of the country's economy in order to adjust its productive potential to the new patterns of domestic and international demand.

At a very low level of the division of labour, industrial change can be brought about, for reasons to be discussed in Part V, by a highly centralised form of organisation – a 'command economy'. However, as industrial progress gathers momentum, the growing complexity of running a modern economy will demand that decisions concerning detailed resource allocation become increasingly decentralised, irrespective of whether the means of production are privately or publicly owned. This is true of decision-making processes within countries, regions and corporations.

Decentralisation, in turn, requires an elaborate system of incentives if such an economy is either to generate continuous changes, or to respond to changes initiated abroad. Hard work, efficiency and high productivity are rewarded by higher incomes. Special rewards, in the form of quasi rents, await those enterprises which introduce successfully new products and production methods.

However, people will respond to the promise of such material gains only if they are encouraged to attach a very high value to them. Continuous economic progress comes to depend crucially, therefore, on the combined effectiveness of the competitive ethos and the aspirations gap.[12] That is, it depends on making people dissatisfied with their existing standard of living and on encouraging them to emulate the standards attained by more successful individuals and groups. Thus, individual decisions become more and more influenced, as already pointed out, by what other people are doing. At the same time, the division of labour increases interdependence and, consequently, the bargaining power of various occupational groups. In addition, to advance and safeguard their status more effectively, people with similar interests will tend to organise into trade unions, professional associations and other pressure groups.[13] This collective power will be used, in other words, to promote improvements and resist reductions in a group's absolute and relative real income, status and influence.

Finally, the nature of modern production methods also makes an important contribution to real wage rigidity. The methods are normally complex and involve careful organisation and long-term planning. In the circumstances, the last thing that modern managers wish to see is a world of continuously changing (perfectly flexible) costs and prices. Such fluctuations would create so much uncertaintly as to make the task of running an enterprise extremely risky and difficult. Stability of nominal wages comes to be regarded, therefore, as something that is in their interest as well as in the interest of their employees. This explains the ubiquity of contractual agreements concerning earnings and the conditions of work.

But the agreements are likely to do more, normally, than provide simply for the stability of nominal earnings. The performance of a modern enterprise depends as much on the competence, commitment and effort of its employees as on managerial excellence. It is essential for its success, therefore, that the two groups work in harmony. This is impossible if the employees are dissatisfied with their remuneration and working conditions, with a strong grievance against the management. The threat of failure will ensure that managers become sensitive to the employees' concern for maintaining their real incomes; and society as a whole will, in time, develop a collective notion of what constitutes a 'fair' or 'adequate' standard of living.[14] Consequently, a group whose living standards have deteriorated persistently, or whose income has declined noticeably relative to other groups, may receive considerable sympathy and support from the rest of the society in its effort to rectify this.

With increasing international cultural and economic integration, these concepts may themselves become relative, influenced by what other nations regard as 'fair' and 'adequate'. So long as the countries enjoy similar levels of efficiency and incomes the comparisons will create few problems at either national or international levels. The situation changes dramatically, as will be shown in Part II, when international harmonisation of tastes takes place in conditions of significant differences in international efficiency and income levels.

The other important aspect of cultural integration, mentioned earlier, is that in altering the behaviour of economic agents it stimulates sustained economic change; and it is a major characteristic of this change, or economic progress, that it involves a continuous division of labour. Incomes rise and markets expand, making possible a continuous increase in the degree of, first, national and, then, international specialisation. It is this process that generates in the long run the international division of labour analysed in the remainder of this chapter and in Chapter 2.

V

Unequal natural endowments and an awareness of the existence of desirable goods and services not normally available in a country provide the basic conditions for international trade and factor movements. Geographic distance can also play an important role in this. The outlying regions of a large country, for example, may find it much easier to establish close economic links with the regions from another state with which they share a common border than with the more distant parts of their own country.

However, the volume and character of these links will depend on a number of highly interrelated factors: the size and level of industrialisation of the countries concerned; the geographic distance between them and the level of development in transport and communications; and national commercial policies. The first factor will determine the size of the countries' markets as well as their capacity to engage in international trade. The other two factors will influence the way in which international trade and production are organised.

In a world of low income, subsistence economies – with rudimentary transport and communication facilities – the volume of international trade and factor movements is likely to be very small. Trade will consist mainly of exports and imports of primary products and simple manufactures (those with a high raw material content). Its size will depend on differences in the nature of production conditions, which will be determined largely by differences in the natural endowments of the trading partners. The more they are dissimilar in this respect the greater will be the difference in their comparative advantages and, consequently, the greater will be the volume of international trade. In contrast, as constant returns to scale will prevail at this level of development, two or more countries with identical resource endowments and production conditions will have identical comparative advantage and, consequently, no reason to trade.

The low volume of saving generated – together with primitive money and capital markets and an extremely limited knowledge of other countries – will ensure that international capital movements are negligible. The same will be true also of international labour mobility, discouraged by lack of information about working conditions abroad, as well as by the small difference in prevailing income levels. Moreover, the limited capacity for technical change will leave these patterns of international exchange unaltered over long periods of time.

This rather modest scope for trade is likely to be reduced further by restrictions on exports of goods, capital and skills (in order to avoid serious shortages at home), and by the prohibition of certain imports (in order to protect domestic output and employment). However, in the case of imports, the low level of development in transport and communications will provide natural barriers to trade, so that administrative protection need not be extensive.

The picture which emerges from this description resembles very closely, in fact, the world which existed before the Industrial Revolution. It is enshrined in economic analysis in the classical model of international trade developed by Ricardo and others. Not surprisingly, some of the basic assumptions of the model which make little sense today, such as the constant returns to scale, and the absence of technical progress and international capital movements, appear to be not so much the result of theoretical simplifications as a fairly accurate description of the world with which Ricardo and his contemporaries were familiar. It was, basically, a world of self-sufficient, agricultural economies in which foreign trade accounted for a very small proportion of economic activity.[15]

VI

The fundamentally insular nature of such economies is altered irrevocably once they begin to industrialise. By separating permanently large numbers of people from the land, industrialisation breaks the long-established tradition of self-sufficiency which characterises pre-industrial societies and countries. Moreover, the countries which make a determined long-term effort to industrialise will differ, often a good deal, in their size and natural resource endowments. To overcome these problems, industrial development will generate continuous improvements in transport and communications; and in achieving these improvements it will, among other things, alter the scale and patterns of both national and international specialisation and trade.

Providing that its culture and socio-political institutions are such as to encourage economic change,[16] this far-reaching transformation is most likely to start in a country in which the ratio of land to population is low – with countries in a similar position among the first to follow its example. As their ratio of land to labour is already unfavourable, further increases in population will make the problem of land shortage even more acute, intensifying the search for new and better methods of agricultural production. If the search is successful, it will, in time, create an agricultural surplus (a volume of food production in excess of the amount consumed by the agricultural sector), enabling some of the population to leave the land and become permanently engaged in manufacturing production.

In these early stages of industrialisation, manufacturing processes are relatively simple, making it fairly easy for those who wish to enter an industry to do so. The rate of technical change is also likely to be slow initially so that the techniques of production will be stable. This fact, plus the limited market for manufactures, will give rise to a large number of small enterprises, all engaged in the production of what are, basically, homogeneous products such as textiles, clothing, metal objects, building materials and so on.

As manufacturing output expands beyond the point needed to satisfy domestic demand, the surplus will be exported in exchange for imports of primary commodities from the countries which have a high land:labour ratio. In addition, the latter are likely to be assisted in the development of their agricultural and mineral potential with transfers of technical knowledge, capital and labour from the more industrialised countries. A large-scale increase in the supply of primary commodities is needed in order to reduce the price of food and raw materials – an important consideration at a level of development when food accounts for a high proportion of consumer expenditure, and labour and raw materials are by far the most important component of total costs in manufacturing production. Lower food prices enable manufacturers to pay lower nominal wages without reducing the workers' standard of living. Given the low rate of technical advances and, consequently, slow improvements in productivity, this is the quickest and most effective way to reduce unit labour costs, raise profits and, in this way, give a further impetus to industrialisation. (This surplus is, of course, essential for further economic development irrespective of whether the means of production are owned privately or by the state.)

However, with time, the process of industrial development will not be confined to the countries which started it. As their markets expand, through increases in population and incomes, the countries with high land:labour ratios will also begin to industrialise by copying the manufacturing processes which already exist in the more industrialised economies. There will be, however, one important difference: given that in these countries labour is scarce, they will use more capital per person employed. Hence, their comparative advantages will lie in the activities which are capital and 'land' intensive; while the older, densely populated countries will continue to specialise in the relatively more labour intensive production processes.

In some cases, the different factor requirements and endowments will give rise to new products and new industries. On the whole, however, most industries, though employing techniques with different factor intensities in different countries, will be turning out fairly homogeneous products using the existing production techniques, known and accessible to all. As more and more countries try to develop such products, there will be an increase in international competition. The emergence of competitive industrialisation, compared to the complementary nature of economic advances in the early stages of global industrial development, is likely to lead to an increased use of administrative controls on imports. First, the newcomers to industrialisation will try to prevent foreign competition from destroying their 'infant' industries. Then, as these industries mature and start to compete effectively with their counterparts in the older industrial countries – using the advantage of lower primary product prices and the more efficient, up-to-date production methods – it will be the turn of the latter to protect their long-established industries.[17]

The developments described so far correspond quite closely, in fact, to the growth and pattern of international trade and factor movements in the nineteenth and early twentieth century.[18] Some of them are encapsulated in the neo-classical, or the Heckscher–Ohlin, model of international trade: the importance of different factor intensities; identical production functions (in the sense that the prevailing production techniques were widely known and applicable); the absence of significant economies of scale; and the fact that some industries will always use more capital (or labour) whatever the relative movements of factor prices. While not universally applicable, these assumptions reflect reasonably well the main characteristics of the industries which dominated international trade during the first hundred years or so of world industrialisation. Nevertheless, by ignoring completely the extremely important role played during this period by international factor movements, the Heckscher–Ohlin model fails to provide a complete account of this particular phase in global economic integration.

VII

Perhaps the most interesting feature (largely ignored by economists) of this early phase in the international division of labour is that it would remain limited in scope – so long as production techniques were such that industrial organisation was determined by constant returns to scale, and international exchange depended chiefly on countries' basic resource endowments (such as the relative availability of land, labour and capital). After increasing rapidly as a result of *inter*-industry specialisation and trade, the ratio of foreign trade to output would reach a peak and then decline – even if there were no barriers to trade! This does not necessarily mean that the absolute level of international trade would fall. In a dynamic world economy, with persistent increases in population, it would continue to grow. But it would not grow as fast as output.

Several long-term developments are responsible for this. As incomes rise, the proportion spent on food declines. The relationship – observed already in the second half of the nineteenth century by Ernst Engel, a German statistician – has proved to be of such a general validity that it has become known as 'Engel's law'. Similar changes also take place on the production side. Industrialisation increases the share in total output of services and the manufactures with higher value added; and, in doing this, it reduces the relative importance of raw material inputs in production.

These developments would be sufficient, other things remaining equal, to reduce the share of imports of primary products in industrial countries' output and expenditure. As a result, the countries would need to export a smaller proportion of their production in order to pay for the imports. The relative importance of foreign trade would shrink even further if the primary producers reacted to these changes by increasing output, which would reduce their prices and turn the terms of trade in favour of industrial nations.

More likely, and partly in order to avoid such an outcome, primary producing countries will, as already pointed out, begin to develop their own industries. Given the simplicity of the available production techniques and the homogeneity of most industrial products, their industrialisation will have an import replacing bias. As a result, there will then be less reason for them also to increase, or even maintain, in the long run the share of exports in total output.

The combined effect of all these decreasing propensities to trade with other nations would be to reduce progressively the extent of international integration and interdependence. Protection of the industries vulnerable to foreign competition would reinforce these long-term developments.

It was considerations such as these that led Sombart to formulate, at the beginning of this century, his 'law of declining importance of foreign trade'.[19] Robertson expressed a rather similar view in the 1930s.[20] The same outcome is also implicit in Hicks' analysis, in the early 1950s, of the dynamic developments in international trade which had resulted in the dollar shortage.[21]

All this analysis of the declining long-term importance of international specialisation and trade is based on the assumption that there are no movements of labour and capital between countries. This is important because if the assumption is removed the scope for international specialisation becomes even more limited in a world from which economies of scale are absent and existing production methods are easily accessible to new entrants.

For instance, emigration of labour from the countries with low land:labour ratios to those with high ratios – as people become aware of their differences in wage levels – would, other things remaining the same, increase the self-sufficiency in food production of the former and, consequently, reduce their imports. At the same time, immigration would increase food consumption in the latter, reducing, other things being equal, their exportable surplus.

For similar reasons, movements of labour from the countries with low capital:labour ratios to those with high ratios, and movements of capital in the opposite direction, would reduce the comparative advantages enjoyed by the two groups of countries as a result of the original disparities in their factor endowments. Consequently, the volume of trade would fall as each country developed import substitutes.

In other words, under the relatively simple technical and organisational forms which characterised most of world production and trade in the nineteenth and early twentieth century, international factor movements would reduce the level of specialisation and trade between countries. Protection would increase these tendencies further. In the extreme case, as Mundell has shown, international factor movements could be a perfect substitute for trade.[22]

VIII

In fact, although influences of this kind may have contributed to the reductions in international economic integration observed in the closing decades of the nineteenth and the early part of the twentieth century, the world economy has followed a rather different path.

The main reason for this is that, if sustained over a sufficiently long period, economic progress tends to generate a number of fundamental changes in the character of world economic growth and international economic relationships. By increasing specialisation and living standards, it expands the size of international markets and, thus, the scope for a more detailed division of labour. By raising simultaneously the level of capital formation and technical knowledge, it gives rise to technical and organisational developments which differ radically from those prevailing in the early phases of world industrialisation. In the long run, it is these developments that, under certain conditions, come to link national economies closely and inextricably together; and international capital movements, far from arresting and reversing the process, come to play a major role in it.

Given that early phases of industrialisation are invariably accompanied (for reasons which are analysed at length in Part III) by trade restrictions, these changes are most likely to originate in a large country which has a high land:labour ratio – providing, of course, that its socio-political and economic institutions are conducive to economic progress.

The country's generous endowment with natural resources will ensure that it starts the process of industrialisation with per capita incomes which are noticeably higher than in countries less fortunate in this respect. The difference will attract foreign immigrants, usually people who attach great value to improvements in their standard of living and who are determined to work hard in order to achieve this. Nevertheless, a combination of the country's large size and a policy of controlling immigration, in order to preserve the accustomed standard of living, is likely to ensure that the land:labour ratio remains relatively high. The result is that the character of its industrialisation will be quite different from similar developments elsewhere. From the start, the country's production processes will have a strong labour-saving, capital-using bias giving rise to rapid improvements in labour productivity and the standard of living. Together with increases in the population, high incomes will create a large and continuously growing market, with great possibilities for a much more detailed division of labour.

The actual and expected opportunities for specialisation will give a strong impetus to technical progress. Given the shortage of labour relative to capital, the inventions and innovations will be of a predominantly labour-saving character, in both consumer and capital goods. (Technical progress in services will have exactly the same bias.)[23] The intensive use of capital will, in turn, be responsible for a major change in the character of world industrialisation and, in this way, also in the nature and extent of international exchange. By introducing a high element of fixed costs into production processes, it will favour the introduction of products and production techniques which give rise to increasing rather than constant returns to scale.

One consequence of the opportunities offered by increasing returns will be an ever greater product differentiation, as well as the separation of different stages of production made possible by the large size of the market. The other consequence will be a development of rapid, more efficient forms of transport needed to reduce costs, and thus enable the existing and new firms to exploit fully the potential for specialisation offered by the domestic market. Such improvements in transport are, of course, impossible without a corresponding progress in communications. Important improvements will, therefore, take place also in this area.

The effect of all these changes will be to make it possible to organise production on a large scale, spread over a wide area. In this way, highly specialised enterprises – each with important, internally developed skills – are able to keep full control of their specific advantages *and*, at the same time, exploit the opportunities offered by a large and growing market.

Other countries going through the process of industrialisation are likely to take longer to reach the stage at which similar developments also take place in their economies. However, providing that they sustain the growth and restructuring of their economies, eventually an increasing number of them will begin to experience shortages of labour relative to capital. It is at this point that they will also turn to the much more capital intensive techniques of production which will raise their productivity and income levels further. The result will be an increase in the size of their domestic market, enabling the enterprises operating in this market to utilise the economies of scale – most likely by importing (at least initially) production techniques and methods of organisation from the large country. In their case, however, the rate of growth of new industries is likely to become dependent at an earlier stage than in the large country on access to other countries' markets.

As this will become possible only if their own country offers similar access to enterprises of the countries whose market they wish to penetrate, small- and medium-sized countries will tend, *ceteris paribus*, to liberalise their commercial policies to a greater extent than large countries. The other important reason for this is that, as their scope for specialisation is limited, the pursuit of freer trade will enable small countries to reap the benefits of the economies of scale developed in other countries. A major contribution of these economies to economic progress is that by lowering unit costs and prices in the industry they will stimulate the subsequent expansion of the sectors which are either heavy users of its products or its major suppliers. The expansion will, in turn, enable these sectors to utilise the economies of scale, making possible the development of new industries which are dependent on them, and so on. The liberalisation will increase further the tendency of small countries to become much more specialised and integrated into the world economy than large countries.

The revolutionary character of the economies of scale and of the large-scale enterprises which exploit them lies in the fact that by altering fundamentally the dominant form of industrial organisation they will also generate changes in the nature of national and international economic relationships; and, in doing this, they will speed up the whole process of economic development described so far in this section.

The viability and success of highly complex, large-scale forms of industrial organisation depends on the care with which their numerous operations are planned and coordinated. As mentioned earlier, this would be extremely difficult in a world in which costs and prices were highly unstable, reacting to the smallest changes in demand. Considerable attention will be paid, therefore, to their short-term stabilisation. The preference for stability will be strengthened also by the fact that no large-scale enterprise can increase its share of the market by, simply, reducing prices, because its competitors will respond quickly with similar price cuts. They all have the power to influence the state of the market by manipulating, if necessary, either their output or prices. On the other hand, a unilateral increase in prices may reduce a firm's share of the market if its competitors do not respond in the same way.

With prices stable, at least in the short run, the emphasis in competition will switch to technical change, that is improvements in products, production methods and organisation. The result is an increase in product differentiation; and further development of the specific advantages accumulated, at considerable cost, within each enterprise – something that can be exploited fully only in even larger markets. The problem is solved, partly, by advertising and other forms of market creation; and, partly, by an intensive, continuous search for markets outside the home country. It is this search which gives rise in the long run to spontaneous international integration and interdependence.

IX

The sequence of events which leads to this at the level of individual firms and industries, and which is described below, will be particularly pronounced in small countries, for reasons mentioned earlier. But given the economies of scale and large-scale organisation, the expansion of many enterprises, first within their own country and then abroad, is not likely to be confined to any particular size or type of country. In fact, given the size of their domestic market and the opportunities which it provides for specialisation and growth over a wide range of activities, firms from large economies will inevitably play a very prominent role in the international economy.[24]

The ability of a new enterprise to survive and gain a permanent foothold in an industry depends critically, other things being equal, on the extent to which its founders guess correctly the need for a new product or production method. Initially, its output will be on a modest scale and for the domestic market only, as this is the market with which the enterprise is familiar.[25] If the original demand expectations prove to be correct – or, even better, if they are exceeded – the firm will expand its productive capacity either through internal growth or through mergers and acquisitions. As it does so, the economies of large-scale production (technical, marketing and financial) will be realised, generating further expansion.[26]

With increasing saturation of the domestic market, growth at current or higher rates of return on investment becomes possible only if the firm can sell its products to other countries. The most obvious markets to explore are those of the countries which have reached a similar stage of industrialisation, efficiency and incomes to that of the country in which the enterprise is located. The reason for this is simple: potential consumers in these countries are not only likely to have tastes similar to those in the firm's domestic market but also the purchasing power to satisfy them.

What happens now will depend on how diverse – despite their basically similar tastes – are preferences in the countries concerned. If they are sufficiently distinct to produce a good deal of international as well as national product differentiation, there is likely to be considerable pressure for trade liberalisation from the industries which are internationally competitive and have, therefore, the capacity to exploit the economies of scale globally; and, if the barriers are removed, this is precisely what they will do. Each country's enterprises will try to specialise in and export a certain range of products which, although functionally similar, are noticeably different in terms of quality, design or technical specifications from those produced by enterprises operating in the same industry in other countries. The result will be a rapid growth of intra-industry trade (exports and imports from the same industry consisting of differentiated products as well as parts and components) among countries with similar efficiency and income levels, and factor endowments.[27] Given the capacity of industrial countries to generate and absorb technical changes, the possibility for the international division of labour becomes almost limitless under these conditions.

Following a substantial expansion of intra-industry trade, the next step for the enterprises engaged in it will probably consist of either acquiring or developing a distribution network in the countries to which they export. Finally, demand in the export markets may reach a level at which it becomes simpler and more profitable for the enterprises to develop productive capacity on the spot, instead of exporting a large and growing share of their output. They will be able to do this because of the skills and resources which they have acquired in the course of the specialisation made possible by economies of scale. To operate successfully in foreign markets, an enterprise must have some 'ownership specific advantages' – technical, managerial, marketing or financial – which will give it a clear lead over the host countries' competitors who will have a better knowledge of their own economic environment.

Two important considerations, apart from that of a satisfactory (current and future) level of demand, will influence firms' decision when and where to locate their activities abroad. First, the management will have to be convinced that the advances in transport and communications have reached the level at which the enterprises can internalise across the frontiers, through both vertical and horizontal integration, the various activities essential for their growth. The importance of 'global' internalisation is that it expands the scale at which enterprises can maintain and utilise profitably their ownership specific advantages. Second, the management will have to be satisfied that the various activities external to the firms, but of crucial importance for their satisfactory functioning and long-term growth,[28] are developed in the host countries to the extent that they require. The existence of large markets and external economies will ensure that by far the largest proportion of the world's direct investment is located in industrial countries. This is true of the investments in both manufacturing and services – for instance, many banks and other financial institutions will usually follow their important domestic customers abroad. In this way, they will preserve their share of a rapidly growing world market by utilising also the advantages offered by economies of scale.

Greater factor mobility, far from representing its final phase, will, in fact, stimulate even more the process of international market integration. With production facilities spread over a number of countries, a good deal of excess capacity may appear globally. The next stage in the development of transnationals will consist, therefore, of a rationalisation of their numerous activities, followed by even more intense specialisation. The large size of the market internalised now within individual enterprises makes this possible. Different stages of production will be located in different countries in order to utilise more effectively their 'location specific advantages'. The result will be an increase in international trade among the subsidiaries of large enterprises, so that a growing proportion of world trade will consist not only of intra-industry trade but also (within this type of international exchange) of intra-firm trade.

It is for all these reasons that, so long as economic openness appears to make a positive contribution to their employment and income levels, there will be strong pressure in the countries which have achieved high levels of industrial development and specialisation to maintain a relatively free regime of trade and capital movements – mainly in so far as it affects their relationships with one another. As long as they succeed in this, the scope for international rationalisation of production and integration will remain virtually boundless in conditions of rapid technical changes and economies of large-scale production. In other words, in this particular case, 'openness', 'integration' and 'interdependence' really come to describe different aspects of the same phenomenon.

X

The preceding analysis provides, in very general terms, a highly simplified description of the most important characteristic and trends in the international economy over the last two centuries. Nevertheless, the main conclusion which emerges from this analysis is extremely relevant for an understanding of long-term developments in the world economy and the influence that they have on the welfare of individual countries. It is simply this: international integration and interdependence are an inevitable consequence of the cultural, technical and organisational changes which are taking place continuously in dynamic economies. The extent to which any one economy becomes involved in the process may vary, even in the long term, according to its size, location, level of industrialisation, and so on. None the less, the character of modern, dynamic economies and the changes which they generate are such that improvements in economic welfare come to be linked increasingly – even in large and distant countries – to developments in the rest of the world.

2 International Economic Integration and Interdependence in the 1980s

I

If international 'openness', 'integration' and 'interdependence' present conceptual problems, the difficulties associated with their measurement often seem to be almost insuperable. Given the sheer magnitude and complexity of the relationships involved in general economic integration (that is, integration covering a wide range of economic activities), no single measure employed to show the degree of integration appears to be entirely satisfactory.

Few indicators of this kind seem to be less adequate for the purpose, however, than the price criterion. The reasoning behind it, embodied in 'the law of one price', is straightforward enough: in the absence of barriers to trade and factor mobility, homogeneous goods and services will command in conditions of perfect competition exactly the same price (when adjusted for transportation costs) in all parts of the world. Or, to put it in a slightly different way, the greater the convergence of prices, or their rates of change, in different countries the greater is the degree, or process, of international economic integration.

One has only to define the price criterion to realise its limitations. Applied to a wide range of transactions, it is completely at odds with one of the most important characteristics of modern economies: the great diversity of goods and services in which they specialise. The specialisation, made possible by the continuous division of labour, leads to such a diversification and differentiation of products and production processes as to make the price criterion totally inappropriate as an indicator of *overall* economic integration.[1] In fact a number of studies covering export prices of a fairly wide range of manufactured goods produced in different countries found that 'the law of one price' did not hold at a more disaggregated level either.[2]

Attempts to quantify the growth of international financial integration according to the dispersion of different countries' interest rates have not been more successful.[3] This is hardly surprising, as financial assets are no less likely to be diversified than their real counterparts. Economic growth and the division of labour create a wide range of products and, at least in market economies, financial instruments. Investors, after all, have different preferences, needs and expectations. Borrowers differ also in their needs and creditworthiness. The differences explain why a wide range of interest rates coexist permanently even on national financial markets. Internationally, economies – including their financial structures – do not have to be perfectly integrated in order to feel significant external constraints on their ability to pursue independent policy objectives.

For all these reasons, the price criterion will be ignored in the rest of this chapter. Instead, a number of different measures of interntional economic integration and interdependence will be used in order to give a more comprehensive picture of the developments in this area over the last few decades.

II

The ratio of a country's trade to its total output of goods and services is one of the most widely used indicators of international integration: the higher the ratio the greater the country's involvement in the international economy.

The measure is not, of course, as precise as this interpretion implies. Two countries with exactly the same trade ratios may have quite different degrees of dependence on external developments, as the latter will be determined also by the extent to which their foreign trade is concentrated in a few commodities and/or markets. The economy whose trade is more concentrated in this way is likely to feel much more the effects of changes in external demand, production and prices – especially if they happen to affect the relevant sectors of the world economy. Nevertheless, 'one may accept the foreign trade proportion as a rough gauge of dependence of a country's overall performance upon material flows from and to the rest of the world…'[4]

Table 2.1 shows the ratios of the value of exports *and* imports of goods and services to GNP for a number of countries grouped, following the procedure adopted by international organisations, according to either their levels of industrialisation, or special characteristics (such as, for instance, 'oil exporters'). The years coincide with the peaks of the world's business cycles. This is important because the ratios can vary a good deal, especially in the case of the primary producers, according to the state of the cycle.

Table 2.1 Exports and imports of goods and services as a proportion of GNP

	Per cent			
	1955	*1964*	*1973*	*1979*
Major industrial countries				
UK	53.0	45.9	57.0	65.9
Canada	45.4	45.3	53.7	64.0
Italy	25.8	31.7	43.1	58.4
West Germany	43.1	39.6	45.8	57.9
France	30.4	30.9	41.0	49.9
Japan	22.6	21.4	21.1	26.1
USA	10.0	10.3	15.1	21.0
Other industrial countries				
Belgium	69.1	96.4	118.8	151.6
Netherlands	103.5	97.0	99.9	116.6
Iceland	68.2	92.5	96.6	109.0
Norway	94.1	92.9	101.8	100.7
Denmark	75.5	74.1	68.8	89.1
Austria	48.5	57.5	77.4	87.6
Switzerland	56.6	62.2	64.5	72.2
Finland	46.2	47.4	59.9	72.1
Sweden	49.1	49.3	59.6	69.2
New Zealand	64.3	49.9	53.6	66.2
Australia	40.0	37.0	34.0	43.2
Newly industrialised countries				
Ireland	77.6	83.3	95.3	132.9
Israel	49.6	73.9	104.1	131.2
South Korea	n.a.	20.7	74.0	79.2
Portugal	44.0	58.6	60.1	68.6
South Africa	131.0	59.4	55.0	65.1
Greece	30.7	31.3	43.3	46.2
Spain	12.8	27.0	32.3	30.8
Argentina	11.8	17.5	16.6	18.4
Brazil	25.0	12.8	21.0	18.1
Oil exporting countries				
Iraq	106.3	76.4	71.2	106.9
Libya	n.a.	139.3	114.1	103.7
Algeria	62.0	51.2	69.7	92.7
Saudi Arabia	n.a.	76.1	129.5	89.3
Iran	n.a.	n.a.	n.a.	65.7
Venezuela	68.3	60.2	58.9	64.3
Nigeria	70.1	33.4	46.9	54.8

Table 2.1 *cont.*

	Per cent			
	1955	*1964*	*1973*	*1979*
Other developing countries				
Tunisia	n.a.	54.9	62.9	84.3
Egypt	n.a.	43.5	39.6	59.4
Thailand	39.5	44.4	45.8	57.9
Morocco	n.a.	45.4	47.4	49.4
Syria	n.a.	40.6	51.8	48.7
Chile	20.0	31.0	28.1	44.2
Peru	48.5	45.1	35.0	38.6
Mexico	n.a.	n.a.	n.a.	26.4
Pakistan	n.a.	15.9	23.0	25.2
India	n.a.	12.0	10.5	16.9
Turkey	16.7	15.5	21.3	11.3

Sources: OECD, *National Accounts of OECD Countries*; UN, *Yearbooks of National Accounts Statistics*; and IMF, *International Financial Statistics*.

What emerges clearly from the table is that, after a somewhat varied experience between 1955 and 1964, the proportion of trade in total output has increased substantially since the mid-1960s in all the groups. There are, in fact, only three countries whose trade ratios were lower in 1979 than in 1964; and only seven out of the forty-five countries experienced a decline in the ratios between 1973 and 1979. The international economic upheavals caused by the energy crisis appear, therefore, to have done little to reverse the continuous increase in the international division of labour which began in the early 1960s. This is confirmed also by the data analysed in Part IV. They show that trade has increased more rapidly than total output since 1979 in all the major groups of countries: industrial, centrally planned and developing (both oil exporting and others).

The variations in the absolute levels and changes in the trade ratios are influenced by a number of factors.[5] Among these, the distance from the main centres of international production and trade is still an important determinant of the levels of international integration, despite the enormous improvements in the means of transport. It is noticeable, for instance, that New Zealand, Australia and a number of Latin American countries are involved much less in the international division of labour than their European counterparts of similar size and income levels.

The character of a country's political system is another factor of considerable importance in this respect. Socialist revolutions usually seem to be followed by a self-imposed economic insularity. But a country may also become increasingly isolated as a result of political changes which meet with strong disapproval from the international community. The large drop in the importance of foreign trade in South Africa in the 1960s, or in the rate of growth of trade relative to that of GNP in Greece in the 1970s, coincided with political developments of this kind in the two countries.

The trade ratios are also likely to be influenced by countries' levels of protection. However, this factor appears to be overshadowed by what seem to be the two most important determinants of international integration: the size of a country and its level of economic development (as indicated, roughly, by per capita incomes).

As explained in Chapter 1, there are good reasons for expecting small countries to rely heavily on foreign trade. The small size of their domestic market would make development of many industries sub-optimal. Exports provide, therefore, the only way to expand these activities to the point at which they can realise economies of scale. At the same time, as they specialise in a fairly narrow range of industries they will require a large and fairly diversified volume of imports to satisfy domestic demand. Inevitably, the combined value of their exports and imports will be sizeable relative to their GNP; and, for exactly the opposite reasons, it will be small in large countries.

Kuznets' detailed analysis of the size and concentration of countries' trade in the 1950s showed that there was, as one would expect, a strong inverse relationship between their size and trade ratios.[6] Table 2.2 makes it clear that this was still the case at the end of the 1970s, especially if population is used as the indicator of size.[7] The extent to which countries control, or 'manage', their trade, on the other hand, does not seem to be related in a systematic way to size – though there appears to be a distinct tendency for the countries with medium-size populations to resort more heavily to this practice than either small or large countries.

'Managed trade' refers here to the proportion of a country's trade in goods 'that is subject to some non-tariff control, by exporter, importer or both, and therefore not determined entirely by market forces'.[8] Among the controls included in Page's estimates are 'quotas, anti-dumping duties, licenses, certificates of origin or other administrative controls, price controls', voluntary export agreements and others.[9] At the same time, the estimates exclude all tariffs. There is a

Table 2.2 Size, trade ratios and trade 'management' in 1979

A. Size according to population

	Group averages			
	Number of countries in each group	*Population (millions)*	*Share of exports and imports in GNP (%)*	*Proportion of trade which is 'managed' (%)*
Group I	6	3.2	102.0	42
Group II	6	7.0	75.2	44
Group III	5	10.5	83.5	64
Group IV	6	16.3	67.5	60
Group V	6	31.7	53.9	60
Group VI	5	48.1	48.9	52
Group VII	5	68.0	44.5	27
Group VIII	4	284.3	20.5	42

B. Size according to total GDP

	Group averages			
	Number of countries in each group	*GDP (billion US$ at 1975 prices)*	*Share of exports and imports in GNP (%)*	*Proportion of trade which is 'managed' (%)*
Group I	6	12.0	102.7	58
Group II	6	24.7	64.0	56
Group III	5	36.2	70.6	68
Group IV	5	48.8	58.9	31
Group V	5	68.5	84.2	41
Group VI	5	94.5	50.8	77
Group VII	6	215.3	43.9	22
Group VIII	5	713.6	34.4	41

Sources: Table 2.1, Summers and Heston (1984), and Page (1979).

possibility, therefore, that the data may underestimate the extent to which these countries 'manage' their trade in those cases where both tariff and non-tariff controls are important and complement each other. Unfortunately, there are no comparable estimates for a similar number of countries of the proportion of trade which is subject to tariff barriers. However, where such data exist (see Part III), a comparison of the two types of protection indicates that non-tariff barriers to trade

Table 2.3 Per capita incomes, trade ratios and trade 'management' in 1979

	Group averages			
	Number of countries in each group	*Per capita income (in US$ at 1975 prices)*	*Share of exports and imports in GNP (%)*	*Proportion of trade which is 'managed' (%)*
Group I	6	7,063	58.5	26
Group II	5	6,243	95.3	27
Group III	5	5,613	73.7	30
Group IV	5	4,331	66.6	59
Group V	5	3,258	78.2	35
Group VI	5	2,366	56.1	75
Group VII	6	1,969	49.0	76
Group VIII	6	1,008	43.9	63

Sources: See Table 2.2.

are far more important and widespread now than tariffs. Consequently, to the extent that these comparisons are meaningful, the data in Tables 2.2 and 2.3 provided probably as good an indicator of the relative protection levels as it is possible to get at the moment.

While it shows little correlation with the size of countries, the proportion of managed trade does seem to be negatively related to the level of per capita income, as can be seen from Table 2.3. In other words, the higher the levels of efficiency and incomes the lower the levels of non-tariff barriers to trade. Although it is obviously very important for an analysis of international economic relationships, the relationship between income levels and protection, and its significance, will be discussed at some length in Part III, and therefore no more will be said about it in this chapter.

For the moment, the important relationship to observe is the one between average per capita incomes and trade shares for each group: as income increases so does also the proportion of trade in GNP. This is, of course, again something that one would expect, for reasons given in Chapter 1. Other things being equal, as incomes rise they expand the size of markets which, in turn, increases the scope for further specialisation and product differentiation. The capacity to produce and consume a wide variety of goods and services grows with productivity and income levels so that, as Kuznets has observed, even small countries become capable of producing and exporting a fairly wide range of products.[10]

The interesting thing about the data in Table 2.3 is that the positive relationship between income levels and the involvement in international trade emerges from the grouped data even though the figures have not been adjusted for the size of countries in each group. Kuznets obtained a similar relationship for the end of the 1950s only after making the appropriate adjustment. Admittedly, his sample of countries was much larger and the data more detailed. But perhaps the observed strength of the relationship – even without the adjustment – indicates the much greater degree of international integration and specialisation at the end of the 1970s compared with twenty years earlier.

III

International specialisation and trade have come to play a particularly prominent role among highly industrialised countries. Given the very high degree of industrialisation and division of labour that they have achieved, industrial nations are bound to feature prominently in international trade as both exporters and importers – though the extent to which this happens in practice will depend also, of course, on their commercial policies as well as those of other countries.

Table 2.4 confirms the key role played by industrial countries in international trade of all the groups, with the notable exception of centrally planned economies whose trade with the rest of the world is tightly controlled.[11] The energy crisis and other disturbances experienced by the world economy in the second half of the 1970s have made, apparently, very little difference to the broad direction of international trade. Most of it involves, as always, the seven major industrial countries listed at the top of Table 2.1. Moreover, the 'big seven' plus 'other industrial countries' continue to be each other's most important trading partners.[12]

This is, as already pointed out, exactly what one would expect. The high level of industrialisation that they have achieved has been reached thanks to a continuous process of invention, innovation and specialisation in both products and production methods. The result is a perpetual increase in product differentiation as well as in a growing subdivision of the existing production processes. There is a constant increase, therefore, in the number of operations that can be

Table 2.4 Direction of world merchandise trade in 1973 and 1979 (per cent of total)

	Major industrial countries		*Other industrial countries*		*Newly industrialised countries*		*Centrally planned economies*		*Oil exporting countries*		*Other developing countries*		*Total*	
	1973	*1979*	*1973*	*1979*	*1973*	*1979*	*1973*	*1979*	*1973*	*1979*	*1973*	*1979*	*1973*	*1979*
A. *EXPORTS*														
From/to:														
Major industrial countries	45.4	42.9	21.2	20.4	10.6	10.1	3.7	3.5	4.5	7.8	14.6	15.3	100.0	100.0
Other industrial countries	55.0	54.1	25.1	23.8	6.3	5.6	3.9	3.8	2.3	4.4	7.4	8.3	100.0	100.0
Newly industrialised countries	50.8	46.1	12.6	12.2	6.6	6.4	4.9	4.9	2.6	6.2	22.5	24.2	100.0	100.0
Centrally planned economies	14.3	15.2	6.1	8.2	3.1	3.9	56.6	52.8	1.5	2.0	18.4	17.9	100.0	100.0
Oil exporting countries	62.3	61.0	11.3	10.1	9.5	12.9	1.0	1.2	0.6	1.3	15.3	13.5	100.0	100.0
Other developing countries	51.5	55.2	8.7	8.7	7.1	10.1	11.5	5.7	4.8	6.5	16.4	13.8	100.0	100.0
B. *IMPORTS*														
Into/from:														
Major industrial countries	48.2	42.7	19.6	17.6	7.7	7.5	2.7	2.6	9.2	16.4	12.6	13.2	100.0	100.0
Other industrial countries	57.0	55.4	24.8	22.6	4.2	4.4	3.3	4.3	5.1	7.5	5.6	5.8	100.0	100.0
Newly industrialised countries	58.4	52.0	12.3	9.9	5.3	5.0	3.4	3.9	6.9	16.4	13.7	12.8	100.0	100.0
Centrally planned economies	18.6	20.7	7.6	7.8	3.5	4.4	55.7	53.2	0.8	1.8	13.8	12.1	100.0	100.0
Oil exporting countries	64.6	64.4	10.6	11.6	5.2	7.4	4.6	3.2	1.2	1.7	13.8	11.7	100.0	100.0
Other developing countries	61.7	56.5	10.9	8.8	5.7	7.3	6.2	5.3	5.8	12.2	9.7	9.9	100.0	100.0

Sources: UN, *Yearbooks of International Trade Statistics* and IMF, *Direction of Trade Statistical Yearbooks*.

undertaken – in order to utilise the economies of scale – either by different subdivisions of the same firm or by different firms, depending on the transaction costs which will determine firms' decisions whether or not to internalise their increasingly diverse operations.

Two factors will influence the extent to which this process assumes international dimensions: the number and size of the countries which have achieved a high level of industrialisation and their commercial policies.

Since the early 1950s developments in each of these areas have made a major contribution to the growth of international specialisation and interdependence. Increases in income levels plus the equalisation of incomes both within and between industrial countries expanded the size of the world market.[13] The trade liberalisation which accompanied this growth, especially in the 1960s, enabled these countries to exploit the economies of scale, that the expansion of the world market had made possible, by intensifying the process of specialisation.

Consequently, there has been a major change in the character of international trade in recent decades in favour of intra-industry trade. In other words, a growing proportion of world exports and imports consists now of an exchange of goods and services *within* rather than *between* industries.[14] As a result, there has been a decline in the importance of inter-industry trade.[15]

The combined effect of industrialisation and trade liberalisation has been, therefore, to give rise to two distinct types of international exchange, each reflecting different levels of the division of labour. One, intra-industry trade, is the outcome of increasing specialisation, product differentiation and exchange of parts and components within sectors. It takes place mainly among industrial countries. The other, inter-industry trade, is the result of specialisation between industries and involves chiefly an exchange of goods and services between industrial and developing nations. It is still the predominant type of trade in the case of developing countries.[16]

There is little doubt that, for reasons described in Chapter 1, intra-industry trade would have become more and more important with increases in the interntional division of labour. It is very doubtful, however, that it would have reached its current level of importance without the spread of transnational enterprises.

If increasing returns to scale are the cause of this type of trade, and product differentiation the form in which it takes place, then it is obviously no more than a manifestation of oligopolistic competition on a global scale. It is economies of scale which reduce competition in most sectors to a few major producers;[17] and it is improvements in products and production methods that, ultimately, represent the most important form of oligopolistic competition. It is not surprising, therefore, that the industries such as chemicals and motor vehicles in which oligopolistic competition is most prevalent also happen to be heavily engaged in intra-industry trade.[18]

Available evidence shows that as countries industrialise their sectoral patterns of development,[19] as well as the predominant forms of industrial organisation, become increasingly similar.[20] Hence, industrial countries in particular have not only the sectors capable of achieving a very elaborate system of specialisation but also the enterprises with the organisation and resources to undertake this on a global scale. It is these advantages which, as explained in Chapter 1, enable national enterprises to transform themselves into transnationals. They first exploit their ownership-specific advantages through trade; and then establish production facilities in different countries[21] –predominantly those which have achieved a similar level of development. This explains why by far the largest proportion of international direct investments, is located in industrial countries.[22]

A high degree of process and product differentiation requires not only a large potential market but also the removal of uncertainty and a reduction of the risks associated with a high degree of specialisation within a very narrow area. Anyone committing resources to highly specialised production processes risks ruin unless the market for his products is secured – at least until the resources sunk in production are safely recovered. This is precisely what transnationals can achieve by internalising different production processes and functions. Given the scale on which they operate, they can divide their production processes to a very high degree – not least by rationalising their operations in a way which enables them to locate different stages of production in different countries.[23] The rationalisation may lead to the disappearance of certain activities from some countries and their expansion elsewhere – the results of corporate strategies about which the governments and most nationals of the countries concerned may know very little.[24]

There is no doubt that these changes have been responsible for the increase in both intra-industry and intra-firm trade. The existing evidence indicates quite clearly that, as one would expect, these two forms of international specialisation and exchange tend to feature prominently in exactly the same types of industry.[25]

The problem is that it is still difficult to assess the real extent of intra-firm trade. The data are rather patchy and based mainly, with the exception of those for US imports, on sample surveys covering the largest transnational corporations. Nevertheless, the data show clearly that this kind of international trade is very important, though not equally in all countries or industries.

According to one estimate, intra-firm trade may have been responsible for as much as 20 per cent of industrial countries' exports in 1971.[26] An UNCTAD study published in 1978 suggested an appreciably higher figure: around 30 per cent of all world trade.[27] A sample survey of 329 of the world's largest industrial enterprises revealed that in 1977 one-third of all parent company exports consisted of intra-firm sales. The shares (expressed as percentages) varied from country to country: United States 45.5, Canada 39.3, West Germany 34.6, France 32.2, United Kingdom 29.6, Japan 17.0, and so on.[28] Moreover, many developing countries are also closely linked in this way with industrial countries.[29]

The data provided in an UNCTAD report indicate that a considerable volume of international trade may consist not only of exchange between the parent company and its affiliates but also between the affiliates themselves. For instance, a very high proportion of all exports by foreign affiliates of foreign firms owned by US transnationals is to other affiliates in third countries, rather than to the US parent: 58.2 per cent in manufacturing and 70.3 per cent for all industries.[30]

The much more detailed information for US imports from 'related parties' sheds further light on the nature of this trade. (A related enterprise is defined for this purpose as an enterprise in which at least 5 per cent of its voting stock is owned by the other enterprise.)

In 1977 imports into the United States from 'related parties' amounted to 48.4 per cent of the total.[31] There were, however, considerable variations according to the type of product and the country from which these imports came. In the case of broad product categories, the importance of imports in each category was as follows (per cent): petroleum 59.4, finished manufactures 53.6, primary products other than petroleum 47.3 and semi-manufactures 37.6. As one would expect, intra-firm trade features much more in US imports from industrial economies than in those from developing countries. The relevant percentages for the three broad categories of imports were (with developing countries shown first in each case): primary commodities (49.1 and 41.3), semi-manufactures (17.0 and 43.4) and finished manufactures (37.0 and 61.1).

Finally, it is difficult to establish how much of this trade consists of imports of a vertically integrated transnational enterprise to be used in further production; and how much of it covers the goods to be simply resold or rented outside the country of origin. According to Helleiner, as much as 36 per cent of total US imports from related parties may be of the latter kind.[32]

Intra-industry and intra-firm trade are both indicative of a very advanced stage in the international division of labour; and transnational enterprises appear to be largely responsible for both. This means, of course, that their corporate strategies are likely to have a major effect on the pattern of a country's trade both in the short and in the long run.[33]

IV

The analysis in this chapter has dealt so far only with 'real' integration; in other words, international integration of the productive structures as manifested in trade between countries. This section will explore briefly the extent to which international financial relationships show similar characteristics and trends.

Given the rather close long-term relationship between economic and financial developments,[34] it would be very surprising if the experience of the two spheres of economic activity over the last two decades differed significantly. It is only natural, therefore, that most people should take it for granted that international financial integration has been, at least among industrial countries, as great as the integration of their 'real' sectors, if not greater.

The enormous increase in international capital movements which has taken place since the restoration of currency convertibility at the end of 1958 seems to provide a convincing proof of this. The increase, accelerated subsequently by the phenomenal growth of the 'euromarkets', has, according to at least one writer, rivalled and perhaps even surpassed 'in significance the great growth of international trade'.[35] Whether this particular claim is correct or not, the simple fact is that the euromarkets have increased greatly investors' ability to acquire long-term bonds and short-term securities in different countries. Consequently, as in the case of production and trade, national insularity has been diminished greatly by the increasing ability of residents of different countries to trade financial assets. After all, as the same author points out: 'International capital mobility ... is required for international financial integration.'[36]

While none of this is disputed, the problem has been to find a reasonably reliable indicator of the extent to which different countries have participated in the process. Internationally comparable financial data have never been as readily available as those for production and trade. Hence, this important aspect of international economic integration has not been explored empirically to the same extent as the one indicated by trade flows.

Table 2.5 presents an attempt to get, at least partly, around this problem. It shows a number of 'gross' financial ratios on as comparable a basis to those for goods and services as possible. The ratios have been calculated using the procedure employed originally by Whitman[37] in her analysis of the period 1960–64, and for a similar reason: to see whether the financial flows show similar differences between countries as those already observed in the case of trade.

There are, however, two important differences between these ratios and those set out in Table 2.1. First, although all the data for capital flows are shown on a 'gross' basis, this means no more than that the credit and debit sides of the balance of payments accounts have been added up in each case. The difference, compared to the trade data, is that many of these items have already been 'netted out' for balance of payments purposes. In other words, the numerator does not really show, in this case, an aggregate of all international financial transactions involving the residents of a particular country. Second, the 'gross' capital flows are given, for each category, as a proportion of a country's gross national product (GNP) at current prices. The underlying assumption is that the estimates of GNP can serve as a reasonable proxy for the size of a country's domestic financial flows. The indicator of international financial integration used here is, therefore, no more than a crude substitute for the indicator that would be employed if the relevant data were available: the ratio of international to domestic capital flows.[38]

In Table 2.5, and the rest of this section, the following categories of capital flows are used: 'short-term private capital' (short-term assets and liabilities of commercial banks plus monetary assets and liabilities of central institutions); 'long-term private capital' (direct investments plus other long-term assets and liabilities of the private sector); 'official capital' (central and local government assets and liabilities plus allocation of the Special Drawing Rights); and 'all (or total) capital flows' (an aggregate of the three categories). The figures for 'official flows' can be obtained for each country in Table 2.5 by subtracting the shares of short-term and long-term capital flows from that for total capital flows.

The figures set out in the table give some idea of the relative importance of the major types of international capital flows in different countries by comparing the averages for the three sub-periods: 1958–60, 1971–73 and 1979–81. (It is advisable to calculate the averages for each of the periods because international capital flows can fluctuate widely from year to year.) The years have been selected in such a way that each period includes high as well as low levels of international economic activity. Moreover, each of the three short periods represents either the beginning or the end of a particular phase in international economic and financial relationships over the last quarter of a century: the position of individual countries immediately after the return to currency convertibility at the end of 1958; the period just before the outbreak of the energy crisis at the end of 1973; and the years following the second oil shock in 1979, but preceding the great debt crisis which has affected so many countries since 1982.

The most obvious difference between the broad trends revealed in Tables 2.1 and 2.5 is the absence of a steady increase in the ratio of international financial flows to GNP since the end of the 1950s – in contrast to the experience in international trade. Only ten out of the thirty-five countries included in Table 2.5 show an uninterrupted increase in their ratios of 'all capital flows' to GNP. Nevertheless, in twenty cases the ratios were higher at the end than at the beginning of the period.

It is difficult to say how far the difference reflects the fact, emphasised earlier, that the financial (unlike trade) data do not include all financial transactions. The process of 'netting out' may well understate seriously increases in certain types of international financial flows.

Apart from this, changes in the figures shown in Table 2.5 have, undoubtedly, been affected by variations in the severity of exchange controls pursued by different countries. In general, although there 'has been a gradual move towards liberalisation'[39] of international capital flows, controls over them have been more widespread than those over trade.[40] Moreover, balance of payments problems have often led, even in industrial countries, to the reintroduction or tightening of such controls. Successive US administrations employed this policy weapon on several occasions in the 1960s and 1970s. The apparent eagerness of EEC governments to abolish trade barriers within the Community has not prevented them from taking measures to slow down the pace of financial integration, especially when

Table 2.5 Average annual outflows and inflows of capital as a proportion of GNP (per cent)

	Short-term private capital			*Long-term private capital*			*All capital flows*		
	I	*II*	*III*	*I*	*II*	*III*	*I*	*II*	*III*
Major industrial countries									
UK	0.34	1.86	1.84	2.19	3.29	3.05	4.29	5.42	7.01
West Germany	0.78	1.32	1.10	2.49	2.11	1.86	4.76	3.97	3.87
France	0.73	1.78	0.61	1.07	1.60	0.99	3.23	3.53	3.46
Canada	1.99	1.99	0.98	2.94	1.78	1.03	6.40	4.56	3.05
USA	1.14	0.59	0.35	0.89	1.40	1.49	2.55	2.28	2.98
Japan	1.20	2.13	0.86	0.51	0.87	0.85	2.45	3.25	2.63
Italy	1.06	1.52	0.25	1.42	3.23	0.73	3.33	4.98	1.34
Other industrial countries									
New Zealand	1.20	0.91	3.78	0.53	0.90	4.32	4.11	2.29	10.80
Netherlands	3.06	1.32	2.92	6.88	5.63	3.61	11.63	7.22	9.37
Iceland	2.51	2.98	1.53	1.40	2.04	5.58	16.05	8.28	8.32
Belgium	n.a.	0.69	3.55	n.a.	4.28	2.60	n.a.	5.63	7.73
Austria	0.68	1.80	2.30	0.97	1.98	1.01	2.71	4.15	7.08
Norway	1.58	3.30	4.51	2.56	6.51	1.68	6.90	10.05	7.03
Denmark	2.52	1.65	1.90	0.67	2.74	3.60	3.89	5.49	5.94
Finland	1.08	3.02	1.92	2.20	3.35	1.21	3.23	6.90	4.33
Australia	0.25	0.36	0.82	3.32	3.01	3.36	4.91	3.77	4.32
Newly industrialised countries									
Israel	1.81	1.94	6.77	7.72	4.14	8.96	31.11	13.19	19.25
Ireland	1.23	2.47	0.35	1.75	5.93	10.47	4.44	9.69	14.98

South Korea	n.a.	1.87	2.17	n.a.	3.69	4.22	n.a.	8.07	9.81
Argentina	2.93	1.45	4.36	3.72	0.22	4.62	8.25	2.28	9.35
Portugal	0.81	1.13	1.85	0.15	2.06	3.37	2.30	4.57	8.15
Brazil	0.65	1.84	0.75	5.54	2.82	3.22	10.74	5.87	5.44
Spain	0.34	0.60	0.58	1.25	2.24	2.30	3.89	3.02	3.25
Oil exporting countries									
Venezuela	0.90	1.26	4.96	2.29	0.64	2.08	11.47	3.29	7.98
Algeria	n.a.	5.96	1.13	n.a.	2.69	4.22	n.a.	9.95	7.40
Nigeria	1.12	1.25	n.a.	2.29	2.78	n.a.	6.07	5.10	n.a.
Saudi Arabia	n.a.	1.73	n.a.	n.a.	2.98	n.a.	n.a.	4.93	n.a.
Indonesia	0.40	0.90	n.a.	0.13	1.30	n.a.	4.50	4.34	n.a.
Other developing countries									
Chile	1.14	3.88	2.84	2.69	1.20	6.05	6.57	10.28	15.61
Morocco	1.85	1.36	0.72	0.24	0.58	8.55	5.49	3.27	9.49
Tunisia	1.82	0.82	1.53	0.84	3.61	6.69	3.66	6.29	8.68
Thailand	0.53	1.10	1.16	1.61	0.74	6.02	2.94	2.29	8.08
Mexico	1.47	0.96	1.09	2.88	1.78	2.18	6.42	3.10	6.62
Peru	0.69	1.51	2.78	3.44	1.96	2.11	7.24	6.42	5.15
Turkey	0.67	5.21	1.04	0.27	0.69	2.25	5.06	7.15	3.81

Notes: I = 1958–60; II = 1971–73; III = 1979–81.
Source: IMF, *Balance of Payments Yearbooks*.

external deficits threatened to increase significantly the cost of internal adjustments.[41]

Finally, as Tables 2.5 and 2.6 show, considerable changes have also taken place since the end of the 1960s in the pattern of international capital flows. The importance of these changes for the long-term viability of internationally integrated economic relationships will be analysed later in this book. For the moment, it is enough to observe the most relevant aspects of the changes revealed by the indicator of international financial integration adopted here.

The general decline in the importance of official flows between 1958–60 and 1979–81 is one of the most noticeable changes. It has been particularly sharp (Table 2.6) in the case of the newly industrialised countries (NICs). The reliance on official rather than private capital flows, common in the 1950s, has been reversed, therefore, to a situation which resembles much more the position that had existed before 1914.[42]

Another important development since the end of the 1950s concerns changes in the relative importance of the short and long-term flows of private capital. As can be seen from Table 2.6, although the long-term capital flows in NICs and developing countries have increased over the period, they were insufficient to balance the basic balances of developing economies in 1971–73; and of, both, these countries and NICs in 1979–81. Long-term capital flows were also insufficient to cover the current account deficits of smaller industrial countries in 1979–81. Not surprisingly, the size of the short-term capital flows has become greater in all these groups of countries, for reasons that will be analysed in Part III and, especially, in Part IV.

Apart from these broad developments, the major characteristics associated with the 'financial ratios' are similar to those observed earlier in analysing trade ratios. This is hardly surprising given that, as one would expect, there is a positive correlation between the shares of trade in goods and services *and* international financial flows in GNP. The correlation coefficients for the countries included in Table 2.5 were 0.55 for 1971–73 and 0.50 for 1979–81, both of which are statistically highly significant. The relationship can be observed also from the grouped data in Table 2.7, though its strength is obscured here by the very high average ratio of the financial flows to GNP in Group V. This is caused entirely by the inclusion of Chile, which had exceptionally large private and official flows in 1979–81. (Three of the countries included in Table 2.5 – Indonesia, Nigeria and Saudi Arabia – are omitted from Tables 2.7, 2.8 and 2.9 because of the

Table 2.6 Averages of capital flows and balance of payments as a proportion of GNP for groups of countries (per cent)

	Short-term private capital			*Long-term private capital*			*Official capital*			*All capital*		
	I	*II*	*III*	*I*	*II*	*III*	*I*	*II*	*III*	*I*	*II*	*III*
Major industrial countries	1.03	1.60	1.27	1.64	2.04	1.43	1.19	0.36	0.78	3.86	4.00	3.48
Current balance										0.24	0.34	0.24
Basic balance										0.26	0.02	−0.61
Other industrial countries	1.61	1.78	2.58	2.32	3.38	3.00	2.75	0.82	1.63	6.68	5.98	7.21
Current balance										−0.16	0.56	−2.14
Basic balance										0.93	1.00	−0.91
Newly industrialised countries	1.30	1.61	2.40	3.36	3.01	5.31	5.46	2.05	2.32	10.12	6.67	10.03
Current balance										−0.77	−1.55	−5.95
Basic balance										0.51	2.14	−1.35
Developing countries	1.17	2.12	1.59	1.71	1.51	4.84	2.43	1.91	1.71	5.31	5.54	8.14
Current balance										0.46	−2.28	−6.22
Basic balance										1.60	−0.89	−1.11

Notes: I = 1958–60; II = 1971–73; III = 1979–81.
Sources: Table 2.5; IMF, *Balance of Payments Yearbooks*; and UN, *Yearbooks of National Accounts Statistics*.

Table 2.7 International trade and financial flows as a proportion of GNP in 1979–81.

	Number of countries in each group	*Trade in goods and services as % of GNP*	*Capital flows as % of GNP*			
			Short-term private	*Long-term private*	*Official*	*Total*
Group I	5	128.3	2.86	6.24	2.83	11.93
Group II	6	88.9	2.26	3.57	1.83	7.66
Group III	5	67.4	2.87	2.81	1.97	7.65
Group IV	6	56.2	0.80	3.20	0.88	4.88
Group V	5	36.6	1.62	3.20	2.17	6.99
Group VI	5	19.0	1.47	2.49	0.88	4.84

Sources: Tables 2.1 and 2.5.

lack of comparable data.) On the whole, however, a high degree of international integration in trade tends to be associated with a high degree of international financial integration.

Following this, it comes as no surprise to discover from Table 2.8 that the relative importance of total international capital flows will be inversely related to the size of countries – irrespective of whether this is measured in terms of population or GDP. The reasons are exactly the same as before: the small size gives limited scope for diversification. Hence, both their inflows and outflows of capital are likely to be relatively large.

The unadjusted (for size) financial ratios do not reveal as strong a positive relationship between per capita incomes and the relative importance of capital flows (Table 2.9) as do the trade ratios. There are probably two reasons for this: the widespread reliance on some form of control of capital flows; and significant differences in the development and sophistication of the financial markets even among industrial countries. Otherwise, there is on the whole a tendency for short-term private flows to feature more prominently in the countries with higher per capita incomes, indicating that the variety of financial institutions and instruments increases with the level of economic development.[43] The long-term capital flows, on the other hand, equal a larger proportion of GNP at lower income levels, as the countries borrow heavily abroad in order to industrialise. These flows tend to be very important, therefore, both in relation to their fixed capital formation and to their GNP.[44]

The figures used in this section include both capital inflows and outflows so that it is impossible to say anything about the two-way exchange of financial assets between countries and how far it resembles changes which have taken place in intra-industry trade. The few estimates of this kind that have been made indicate that the exchange is likely to be considerable, at least in the case of industrial countries; and that it has almost certainly increased, like intra-industry trade, over time.[45] The main reason for this is not difficult to find. As Goldsmith has shown, the variety and number of financial institutions increases over time, expanding the scope for a greater volume and diversity of both assets and their transactions.[46] Inevitably, 'the existence of a financial superstructure, and here particularly the operation of financial institutions, tends to increase the relative importance of foreign investment in both lending and borrowing countries'.[47]

All the indications, therefore, are that the importance of inter-

Table 2.8 Country size and ratios of capital flows to GNP in 1979–81

A. Size according to population

	Number of countries in each group	*Average population (millions)*	*Capital flows as % of GNP*			
			Short-term private	*Long-term private*	*Official*	*Total*
Group I	6	3.2	3.14	5.37	2.27	10.78
Group II	6	8.2	2.33	3.89	2.64	8.86
Group III	5	15.6	2.52	3.08	1.24	6.84
Group IV	5	28.9	1.76	4.14	1.09	6.99
Group V	5	51.3	0.98	2.61	1.15	4.74
Group VI	5	117.5	0.83	1.92	1.56	4.31

B. Size according to total GDP

	Number of countries in each group	*Average GDP (billion US$ at 1975 prices)*	*Capital flows as % of GNP*			
			Short-term private	*Long-term private*	*Official*	*Total*
Group I	6	12.0	2.52	6.71	1.23	10.46
Group II	5	26.1	2.37	4.17	2.38	8.92
Group III	5	42.8	2.62	2.96	1.27	6.85
Group IV	6	81.4	2.48	3.44	1.48	7.40
Group V	5	200.6	0.73	1.89	1.32	3.94
Group VI	5	706.6	0.95	1.65	1.39	3.99

Sources: Table 2.5, Summers and Heston (1984).

Table 2.9 Per capita incomes and ratios of capital flows to GNP in 1979–81

	Number of countries in each group	Average per capita income in 1979 (in US$ at 1975 prices)	Capital flows as % of GNP			
			Short-term private	*Long-term private*	*Official*	*Total*
Group I	5	7,169	0.99	1.79	1.08	3.86
Group II	5	6,121	2.67	3.37	1.31	7.35
Group III	5	5,402	2.14	2.09	2.14	6.37
Group IV	6	3,873	2.88	4.86	1.62	9.36
Group V	6	2,327	1.62	3.55	3.07	8.24
Group VI	5	1,589	1.46	5.52	0.78	7.76

Sources: See Table 2.8.

national financial integration and interdependence has increased considerably since the end of the 1950s.

V

Given the scale of increases in spontaneous, or *de facto*, international economic integration, the growth of international interdependence (in other words, the sensitivity of individual economies to outside developments) has been unavoidable. Unfortunately, the absence of reliable and consistent long-term data makes it impossible to estimate directly the strength of international economic linkages at different times.

However, there are a number of models which try to quantify the interaction of different, mainly industrial, economies in recent years. The results which these models produce can be criticised, like most econometric output, in terms of data coverage and adequacy, underlying assumptions and estimation procedures. Nevertheless, they perform a useful function by providing some, even though very rough, quantitative indicators of the extent of interdependence among industrial economies; and between them and the rest of the world.

One result which emerges clearly from all these estimates is that economic interdependence and integration reduce the effectiveness of national policies. Moreover, once individual countries synchronise their policies – either deliberately or in response to a common problem – the impact of policy changes becomes considerably greater than it would be had they remained insulated from external factors.

> The combination of open individual OECD economies with their relatively closed aggregate means that the OECD area policy multipliers are larger than those for most countries considered individually, possibly as much as double in some circumstances ... If a number of major countries are experiencing demand expansion at the same time ... the total effect can be unexpectedly large. Each country finds, in addition to the expected expansion of its domestic demand components, that its exports too are growing sharply. Overheating of the world economy can then arise. The equivalent effect, of inducing a greater than intended downturn, can just as readily occur in times of synchronised deflation.[48]

If countries pursue uncoordinated macro-economic policies, the effect of external policy changes will, invariably, depend on the size of the country, or countries, which initiate them. Not surprisingly, all the estimates show that economic policies which originate in the United States or West Germany will have a much greater global impact than similar policy changes in, say, Austria or Belgium.[49]

The size of the very broad global magnitudes involved can be illustrated with a few of the figures produced by the OECD Secretariat. In each case, the figures show, in terms of percentages of GDP, improvements (or deteriorations) following a specific change of policy compared with what would have happened without the change. All the estimates are obtained from a model which, appropriately for the world economic environment of the 1980s, is based on the assumption that there are no capacity constraints and production bottlenecks in any of the countries.[50]

The figures in Table 2.10 illustrate what will happen, according to the OECD model, if governments increase their expenditure (excluding the expenditure on wages) by 1 per cent of GDP under two alternative scenarios. In the first case, (A), all governments increase their expenditure by the amount specified, but it is assumed that their actions have *no* effect on other economies. In the second case, (B), all governments do exactly the same thing as before, but in conditions in which all the actions and economic developments within individual countries have international multiplier effects, as the economies are highly integrated and interdependent.

As one would expect, a large economy (United States) would grow faster in isolation (case A) than a small one (Sweden). But even US economic growth would accelerate appreciably over time in conditions of international economic integration and with all industrial countries introducing the same change in their fiscal policy (case B). The economic recovery in Sweden would, of course, be even faster under these conditions. Furthermore, the last part of the table shows that if the US government increased its expenditure in isolation, the country's current balance of payments would be much more unfavourable than if it did so in conditions in which other industrial countries were pursuing the same policy. The difference would be, again, even greater in the case of Sweden, for the very simple reason that it is much more integrated into the world economy than the United States.

The OECD aggregates in Table 2.10 show the difference that international integration and interdependence make to industrial countries as a group. For instance, if increases in government expenditure are taken by all countries in conditions of economic integration, the overall rate of growth and improvements in employ-

Table 2.10 Effects of a sustained increase in government expenditure (excluding wages) by 1 per cent of GDP*

		Per cent		
		1st year	*2nd year*	*3rd year*
Impact on GDP				
United States	A	1.5	1.8	1.7
	B	1.9	2.5	2.4
Sweden	A	1.0	1.0	0.9
	B	2.2	2.9	3.2
OECD	A	1.3	1.5	1.5
	B	1.9	2.7	2.9
Impact on prices				
OECD	A	0.2	0.4	0.6
	B	0.4	1.1	1.9
Impact on employment				
OECD	A	0.3	0.6	0.7
	B	0.4	1.0	1.3
Impact on current balance of payments (% of GDP)				
United States	A	−0.4	−0.4	−0.4
	B	−0.2	−0.1	−0.1
Sweden	A	−0.7	−0.7	−0.6
	B	−0.3	−0.2	0.1

Notes: *The estimates assume accommodating monetary policies (so that nominal interest rates remain unchanged) and fixed exchange rates.
A Each country takes the specified action, but under conditions in which this action has no effect on any other economy.
B Each country takes the specified action in conditions of economic integration and interdependence with other countries.
Source: Larsen, Llewellyn and Potter (1983, pp. 70 and 78).

ment achieved by the industrialised world will be twice as high by the third year (case B) than if they do exactly the same thing in conditions in which there is no interaction among their economies (case A). The only advantage of economic insularity, according to the OECD estimates, is to be found in relatively more stable inflation rates.

Taking all OECD countries together, the table shows that the overall effect on prices of simultaneous increases in government expenditure in member countries would be significantly lower if all the countries took this action in isolation (case A).

Table 2.11 Effects of a sustained 1 per cent increase in real GDP of OECD countries on the rest of the world (per cent)

	1st year	*2nd year*	*3rd year*
Non-OECD countries			
Exports of goods and services, volume	1.6	1.7	1.7
Imports of goods and services, volume	0.8	1.5	1.6
Current balance (billion US$)	7.7	1.0	−0.2
Trade prices (in US$ terms)			
Raw materials	2.5	3.4	3.8
Food	2.5	3.6	4.4
Energy	0.1	0.6	1.0
Manufactures	0.1	0.5	1.0

Source: Larsen, Llewellyn and Potter (1983, p. 85).

Table 2.11 illustrates another important characteristic of the world economy: namely the fact that the impact of a sustained increase in GDP of OECD countries on the rest of the world is very substantial.[51] Among other things, it will lead to a significant improvement in prices of primary products which feature so prominently in the production and trade of countries outside the OECD area. This is bound to raise the level of world income and trade – not least by reducing, especially in the short run, the external imbalances of developing countries.

Another way, not illustrated in the tables, in which faster growth in industrial countries assists in the adjustment process of developing economies is that it makes industrial countries willing to absorb some of the latter's surplus labour.[52] Moreover, the remittances from this labour help finance at least some of the countries' substantial current account deficits.[53] A sustained pursuit of deflationary policies in OECD countries reverses this process, as the experience over the past decade has shown, and in this way increases greatly the adjustment problems – especially in the case of the newly industrialised countries.

Table 2.12 Effects of a 2 per cent fall in non-OECD imports* on OECD and non-OECD countries (per cent)

	1st year	*2nd year*	*3rd year*
OECD countries			
Real GNP	−0.3	−0.3	−0.3
Exports of goods and services, volume	−1.1	−1.1	−1.1
Imports of goods and services, volume	−0.5	−0.6	−0.5
Prices	–	−0.1	−0.2
Current balance (billion US$)	−9.0	−8.6	−9.1
Non-OECD countries			
Exports of goods and services, volume	−0.9	−0.9	−0.9
Imports of goods and services, volume	−1.8	−1.8	−1.8
Current balance (billion US$)	9.0	8.9	9.4

Note: *Imports of goods and services (excluding investment income).
Source: Larsen, Llewellyn and Potter (1983, p. 86).

The impact of changes in economic policy is not felt, of course, in one direction only. The effect of a fall in imports of goods and services in the rest of the world on OECD countries, though considerably smaller, is not, as Table 2.12 shows, negligible. (The actual fall in non-OECD imports of goods and services is given in the table as 1.8 rather than 2 per cent. The main reason for this is that payments of investment income by non-OECD countries, amounting to 10 per cent of their imports of goods and services, are assumed to continue. This reduces the overall percentage fall in the volume of their current account payments to 1.8 per cent.) The fall is certainly sufficiently large to exacerbate the problems created by a deep recession and serious balance of payments difficulties, such as those which OECD countries have experienced in recent years. At the same time, and this is inevitable in condition of interdependence, the impact on OECD economies of a fall in world imports will have, as can be seen from the lower part of the table, a further – and stronger – deflationary effect on non-OECD countries.

Finally, the econometric estimates described briefly so far in this section have concentrated mainly on real 'interdependence', the international links which affect countries' output, employment and trade balances. However, as indicated earlier, financial integration has also made considerable progress over the last twenty years, increasing the extent of financial interdependence.

Table 2.13 gives, therefore, some of the OECD estimates of the size of the financial responses to changes in monetary policy under floating exchange rates.[54] The responses are produced by international capital flows which are regarded as the main channel through which the effects of a new policy in one or more countries are passed on to other countries. Each country's capital inflows and outflows, and the exchange rate changes to which they give rise, depend in this model on short-term interest rate differentials, the expected rate of currency depreciation or appreciation, and domestic and foreign current balances of payments. Furthermore, 'changes in the exchange rate, interest rates, and money supply for any single country feed via capital flows to other countries, affecting exchange rates and interest rates throughout the system'.[55]

Table 2.13 gives some indication of the size of these interactions for a number of countries. Once again the percentages show the difference between the outcome caused by the simulated changes in interest rates and the outcome that would have happened in the absence of these changes. The effects vary from country to country because the responses in their interest rates will depend on the extent to which their financial markets are linked with those of the countries which have altered their monetary policy. For instance, the impact of a cut in US short-term interest rates on Japan will be much greater than the effect produced by a similar reduction in European interest rates. On the other hand, the Deutschemark will move appreciably in both cases, and in the opposite direction from the US dollar, as the two currencies seem to be regarded fairly widely as very good substitutes. The highly developed financial markets in the UK, and their long-standing links with international markets, also ensure a high degree of sensitivity of the sterling exchange rate to policy changes at home and abroad. Moreover, all these changes will inevitably have some effect on the growth of individual countries' output; and, generally, their effect on domestic prices will be even more significant.

Table 2.13 Some financial and real effects of a sustained reduction in short-term interest rates (third year effects, per cent)

	*Reduction in US interest rates**					*Reduction in European interest rates**				
	Effective exchange rate	*Short-term interest rates (% points)*	*Long-term interest rates (% points)*	*Real GDP*	*Domestic prices*	*Effective exchange rate*	*Short-term interest rates (% points)*	*Long-term interest rates (% points)*	*Real GDP*	*Domestic prices*
USA	−6.4	−2.0	−1.5	0.8	1.0	8.0	−0.5	−0.2	−0.2	−1.0
Canada	2.7	−1.7	−0.9	−0.3	−0.6	−0.9	−0.8	−0.4	0.2	0.1
Japan	3.0	−1.4	−0.6	−0.2	−0.4	0.8	−1.0	−0.5	−0.1	−0.3
W. Germany	2.9	−1.2	−0.5	−0.4	−1.2	−4.9	−2.0	−1.1	1.4	2.2
France	−1.9	−1.0	−0.4	0.1	–	1.2	−2.0	−1.1	0.8	1.0
UK	3.1	−1.3	−0.6	−0.3	−1.2	−8.1	−2.0	−1.2	1.4	3.1
Italy	2.4	−0.6	−0.3	−0.4	−1.0	−1.9	−2.0	−1.6	0.7	1.2
Belgium	−0.5	−1.1	−0.4	–	−0.5	−0.9	−2.0	−1.0	1.4	2.0
Netherlands	1.0	−0.9	−0.3	−0.2	−1.4	−0.8	−2.0	−0.9	0.9	2.3
Sweden	−0.4	−0.9	−0.3	0.1	−0.2	0.2	−2.0	−0.9	0.9	1.0
Total OECD	n.a.	−1.5	−0.9	0.2	–	n.a.	−1.2	−0.6	0.3	0.2

Note: *A sustained 2 percentage point cut in short-term interest rates from baseline levels.
Source: Larsen, Llewellyn and Potter (1983, p. 80).

VI

All the evidence presented in this chapter points in the same direction: a substantial increase in international economic integration and interdependence over the last two decades. This has three important consequences for the economies of individual countries as well as for the world economy.

First, national economic problems become international economic problems. The close links of national production and financial structures ensure that a crisis of any kind (or a recovery) cannot be confined to the country in which it originates. *Ceteris paribus*, inflation or unemployment in one country will sooner or later cause increases in costs and prices, or reductions in a activity and employment, in other countries. This being the case, the effects of the policies employed by individual countries to solve these problems will be also felt widely. Economic instability is a highly contagious failing in conditions of economic integration and interdepedence; and economic problems which affect simultaneously a large number of countries inevitably require that they should pursue compatible policies. That is, each country should pursue those policies which help, rather than frustrate, other countries' attempts to achieve their national economic objectives. In contemporary economic conditions, this is not a matter of altruism. Given the degree of international integration and interdependence, each country's ability to achieve its own economic goals will depend, ultimately, to a significant extent on the success or failure of other countries. Hence, one major task confronting an integrated world economy is how to achieve 'compatible policies'.

Second, policies which are likely to attract most attention will be invariably those that can be easily associated with certain outcomes. In practice, this will normally mean those policies that are widely known to have a very rapid impact on one or more macro-economic aggregates. As nothing can match in this respect the speed with which actual, or even anticipated, changes in macro-economic policies can influence international capital flows (and through them exchange rates and prices) – this is the area of economic policy where the pressure for 'harmonisation' will be greatest. In an open economic environment, fiscal and monetary convergence is the only way to avoid financial instability. The snag is that, as the figures in Table 2.10 imply, if countries pursue identical short-term macro-economic policies their business cycles will become synchronised, increasing greatly the size of cyclical fluctuations in the world economy.[56] The much more pronounced volatility of the short-run demand for real resources may, in turn, have an adverse effect on the long-term growth of investment, output and employment. The second major task confronting policy makers in an internationally integrated economy is, therefore, to achieve compatible policies which avoid sacrificing long-term prosperity for the sake of the short-term stabilisation of their inflation rates and/or external balances.

Finally, unlike institutional integration, the process of spontaneous integration sooner or later engulfs countries at different levels of development, with different levels of international competitiveness and, consequently, with significantly different capacities for maintaining short-term external equilibria, or even for achieving long-term adjustments. This means that the nature and seriousness of the problem affecting individual nations and the world economy as a whole will depend increasingly on where they originate. The third major task confronting the international economic system – and the one on whose solution is likely to hinge its long-term stability – is to evolve an effective common approach to what are fundamentally different national problems. It is for this reason that it becomes extremely important to distinguish carefully between different types of external disequilibria, their nature and causes.

Part II
The Nature, Causes and Elimination of International Economic Instability

It is difficult to contemplate an effective course of action that might solve contemporary economic problems if ambiguities and uncertainties surround even some of the basic concepts used in formulating economic policies. Yet it is precisely disagreements of this kind which are at the root of a number of long-standing disputes and misunderstandings in international economics.

To take one important example, there are many definitions of 'balance of payments' – none of which is necessarily applicable in all circumstances. Similarly, there is no one definition of 'international economic equilibrium': an economic relationship between two or more countries which is sustainable. Moreover, it is often not clear whether problems which are analysed are temporary or of a long-term nature. Yet the distinction is vital because their causes will be different and so also, of course, will be the policies necessary to deal with them.

There is an important reason why these definitional ambiguities should be clarified. The way that basic economic concepts are formulated will determine the way in which economic problems are analysed; and this, in turn, will have an important influence on the policies employed to correct them. For instance, economic policies may differ significantly according to whether a government defines its objective of a 'satisfactory' balance of payments in terms of the current balance, the basic balance or an 'overall' balance; or whether its concept of 'external balance', however defined, incorporates some notion of 'internal balance' (a high level of employment and a low rate of inflation) or not.

To avoid these ambiguities, different types of international economic disequilibria and the policies required to eliminate them will be defined and examined in some detail in Part II.

3 The Concept of Fundamental Equilibrium

I

It is impossible to discuss international economic issues meaningfully without some idea of the conditions necessary for the relationships between two or more countries to be sustained over a period without – and this is the crux of the matter – changes in existing policies and, in some cases, institutions. In other words, it is essential to have a definition, no matter how broad, of 'international equilibrium'.

The world consists of a large number of independent, sovereign states – each with its own objectives, policies and policy instruments. For reasons explained in Part I, the way that a country sets about achieving its policy objectives will, inevitably, affect other countries when there is a good deal of international integration. These countries, in turn, will react and in the process either increase or cancel out the intended impact of the initial policies.

Two questions become highly relevant, therefore, in conditions of economic openness and interdependence: are all these actions and counteractions compatible and sustainable? And, if they are, for how long? Neither can be answered satisfactorily without some notion of international equilibrium.

That much has always been accepted in economics. Where the consensus starts to break down is when it comes to deciding what consitutes the most appropriate definition of such an equilibrium. Should it refer simply to countries' external balances, irrespective of the means by which they are achieved? Or should the definition also include these means? And while it is perfectly true that no country can run a balance of payments deficit for very long, can the concept of 'equilibrium' be applied seriously to external 'balances' that are achieved by methods which are equally unsustainable? Even when the first and, in appearance at least, the simplest of these three questions is answered in the affirmative, there are frequent disagreements about the most suitable measure of the balance of payments. Different circumstances, interests, problems and needs will ensure that the concepts favoured by some countries are regarded as inappropriate by others.

II

The balance of international payments can be recorded in a number of ways:[1] trade balance (goods only); current balance (goods, services and current transfers); basic balance (the current balance and long-term capital flows); balance on non-monetary transactions (the basic balance and short-term capital flows used to finance trade); or balance for official settlements (the basic balance and all short-term private capital). The problem is to decide which of these represents the most reliable indicator of whether a country's external position is sustainable or not.

In fact, although the choice is not always straightforward, it is easy to exaggerate the difficulties. What the disagreements boil down to, really, is whether the financing of external imbalances or their elimination should have a greater claim on the attention of policy makers.

Yet a rigid distinction of this kind is, of course, completely artificial. Short-term financing of external imbalances, to take one example, cannot realistically be expected to provide a lasting substitute for a reallocation of real resources where these are needed; and the adjustment process is unlikely to get very far – in conditions of economic openness and integration – in the absence of adequate provisions of external finance. Moreover, the relative importance of balance of payments financing and adjustment may vary from country to country and, within any one country, from one period to the next.

Consequently, those responsible for a country's economic management must be constantly aware of two things: (a) whether the country is capable of financing the level of its external transactions in the short term; and (b) even if it is, whether there are economic developments at work which may make this position unsustainable in the long term. Preoccupations of this kind tend to focus attention on the following measures of external balance: the balance for official financing, and the current or, alternatively, the basic balance of payments.

The financial requirements and obligations of governments and central banks provide good operational reasons why they need to follow closely what is happening to the overall financial flows which are outside their direct control. The appearance of unanticipated external imbalances will involve them in the sale or purchase of foreign exchange, including either borrowing from other authorities or lending to them. Moreover, by influencing the overall financial balance of a country, private flows of capital will also affect its monetary policy. The balance for official financing is not, therefore, something that the authorities can afford to ignore.

Of course, if all economic adjustments could be carried out instantly and painlessly, the authorities could let the exchange rate float freely – ensuring in this way that the overall balance of payments is always balanced. Although theoretically attractive, few governments and central banks have been willing to adopt this particular policy option in practice. Economic adjustments are complex, long-lasting affairs, especially in open, highly integrated economies. The shorter the period over which they have to be carried out the greater the risk that they may have undesirable social and political consequences. Even the most reluctant governments and central banks may have little alternative, therefore, but to participate in settling the overall external imbalances which cannot be financed autonomously; and in order to do this they must have an operational measure of their external financial obligations and transactions.[2]

They cannot rely entirely on such a single measure of the short-term financial position, however, for the simple reason that even an absence of serious imbalances on its overall financial flows does not necessarily mean that a country's external position is sustainable. For instance, a large and lasting deterioration in the current balance, or in long-term capital flows, can be masked for a time by short-term capital inflows – making the task of policy changes and real adjustment much more difficult when the inflows are suddenly reversed.

This means that apart from a financing aggregate, such as the balance for official financing, it is also essential to observe constantly some external indicator of the longer-term developments in an economy. While the choice of such an indicator will always remain somewhat arbitrary, the concept which comes closest to providing evidence of this kind is probably the basic balance of payments. As Cooper pointed out, 'it represents an attempt to measure the underlying trends, abstracting from such "volatile" transactions as short-term capital movements'.[3] Each of its two major components – current balance and the balance on long-term capital flows – makes, in fact, an important contribution towards understanding the present state and likely future development of an economy.

Current balance transactions perform this function by reflecting a country's cyclical and competitive position in the short run as well as any alterations in its relative economic strength in the long run. Changes in a country's activity levels, costs and prices, tastes, resource endowments and productive capacity relative to other countries will all influence the volume and composition of its trade with the rest of the world.

The importance of the long-term capital movements – both private and official – lies in the fact that they are likely to have an important effect on countries' future levels of employment, productivity and incomes. At the same time, net inflows of long-term capital can also play an important role in financing current account deficits not just in the short run but over long periods of time, while an economy is undergoing structural adjustments.

These characteristics, plus its relative stability,[4] all point to the basic balance as the most appropriate indicator of changes in a country's long-term competitive strength. The problem is that its measurement gives rise to a number of practical difficulties – the main reason why some countries such as the UK,[5] which had been using the concept for a time, decided eventually to abandon it.

Some capital flows which are nominally 'long-term' are influenced in fact by short-run considerations, such as actual and/or expected movements in interest rates, exchange rates and share prices. This is particularly true of long-term bank credits and portfolio investments. Even direct investment, normally the most stable component of the capital balance, includes a certain proportion of short-term flows. Moreover, the current balance may also contain some purely transitory elements (such as military exports or imports, or once-for-all transfer payments); and a certain, unknown, proportion of current and long-term capital transactions will always be recorded among the errors and omissions, in other words outside the basic balance.[6]

However, in periods like the 1970s and 1980s, when international short-term capital flows are large as well as highly volatile, the conceptual deficiencies of the basic balance become relatively unimportant. The fact that it is much less prone to fluctuations than other measures of external transactions makes it a useful indicator of the longer-term economic developments and trends in a country's position relative to the rest of the world. Without some understanding of these underlying changes it is impossible to comprehend the problems experienced by industrial nations over the past decade, and even less the perennial difficulties of developing countries. Consequently, as this study is concerned primarily with long-term adjustment problems, in what follows, unless stated otherwise, the balance of payments will always mean the *basic balance*.

III

If international equilbrium describes an economic relationship which nation states can sustain over a period without changes in their economic policies and institutions, it is essential to identify all those factors which either make this possible or, alternatively, create pressure for change. Moreover, as a condition, or development which is feasible in the short term may be unsustainable over a longer period, it is also important to specify whether the relevant relationships are of a temporary or long-term nature.

The state, or evolution, of national balances of payments with the rest of the world, has obviously to be taken into account in any definition of 'international equilibrium'. But that is not the only factor that matters. The pressure for change in economic performance, policy and institutions – all of which may have important international repercussions – can also come from within individual countries. This means that a definition of 'international equilibrium' would be seriously deficient if it ignored internal economic developments such as rising unemployment and/or an accelerating rate of inflation. Both can trigger off far-reaching changes in policy because of their effect on a country's economic welfare. Hence, equilibrium will be determined by the extent to which nation states can sustain balanced economic development within their borders as well as in their relationships with the outside world.

The size of a country's balance of payments deficits and the period over which they can be maintained will be limited by the size of its reserves and the willingness of other countries to provide the necessary finance. In practice, no open economy has sufficiently large reserves to sustain its external deficits for very long. The alternative is to finance the basic balance deficits by raising short-term loans abroad. The problem, as a number of countries discovered at considerable cost in the early 1980s, is that this particular option does not amount to a viable long-term solution. It does not usually take very long before foreign providers of this type of finance become concerned about the ability of deficit countries to repay their loans. Consequently, they may either refuse to 'roll-over' the loans unless the countries introduce major policy changes, or only agree to do so at much higher interest rates, making it impossible for deficit countries to continue borrowing on the same scale as before. Basic balance deficits are likely, therefore, to be sustainable only in the short term.

A surplus country is in a more favourable position, in the sense that it enjoys much greater freedom and flexibility in determining its own policy objectives. However, even in this case, long-term policy options of an open economy are limited, unless it happens to be very small. If a large surplus country is unable, or unwilling to invest abroad on a long-term basis, the effect on other countries will be such as to leave them, for reasons to be discussed in the chapters that follow, little alternative but to change their policies in a way which is bound to be detrimental to its own long-term interests.

Alternatively, a country may balance its external account, or even run a large surplus, by creating unemployment at home. The period over which such policies can be pursued will depend, however, on the extent to which the population of the country is prepared to tolerate them. Whatever the level of tolerance, the situation is fundamentally unstable and, therefore, unlikely to be sustained in the longer term without major changes in economic and social policies. For similar reasons, pressure on resources which leads to an acceleration in the rate of inflation beyond the levels to which the citizens of a country are accustomed is unlikely to persist for very long, even though there may be no external demand for a major reappraisal of policy.

Consequently, the only definition of long-term 'equilibrium' which is of relevance for economic policy in an open economy is that which incorporates notions of *both* 'internal balance' (a high level of employment combined with a low rate of inflation) and 'external balance' (a basic balance of payments which is neither persistently in deficit nor in surplus). This is, in fact, what *fundamental equilibrium* really means.[7] More specifically, *a country can be regarded as being in fundamental equilibrium only if it is capable of balancing its basic balance of payments in the long term at socially acceptable levels of unemployment and inflation*.[8]

The concept of 'socially acceptable levels' is unavoidably vague. It will vary from country to country and governments will have to judge it carefully in formulating their policies. The important point is that any major departure from these levels is unlikely to be sustained over a long period, either for internal or for external reasons.

Finally, it should be noted that this definition does nothing more than specify broadly a condition which has to be satisfied if a particular state of affairs is to persist. It does not say anything about the way in which the equilibrium is reached, nor that there is an automatic tendency towards such an equilibrium in national economies. Both these issues are discussed in the rest of this book.

It is also impossible to say how far the definition offered here corresponds to the 'fundamental equilibrium' mentioned in the Articles of Agreement of the International Monetary Fund. The term used by the founding fathers of the Bretton Woods System 'was not defined in the Articles and has never been officially defined'.[9]

IV

The conditions which have to be satisifed if a country is to achieve and maintain fundamental equilibrium can be described more precisely with the help of a simple graph, such as the one shown in Figure 3.1. In both the upper and lower parts of the graph, the horizontal axis gives the long-term rates of growth. The vertical axes depict basic balances of payments (upper part) and the rate of inflation (lower part). The assumption underlying the analysis that follows is, as before, that there are no radical changes in institutions and/or policies.

The rate of economic growth that this particular country has to sustain in the long term in order to maintain full employment is $\mathring{y}_l$. This is the rate of growth of its productive potential, determined by the growth of its labour force and technical changes reflected in the growth of its labour productivity.[10] In other words, providing that it starts with full employment, the economy cannot grow in the long term in excess of $\mathring{y}_l$, though it may do so in the short term if there are under-utilised resources.

On the other hand, any rate of growth which is persistently below $\mathring{y}_l$ will result in long-term losses of economic welfare, either in terms of employment or income. Suppose, for instance, that the economy is growing at $\mathring{y}_c$ while, at the same time, absorbing technical advances which would give it the rate of growth of labour productivity compatible with $\mathring{y}_l$. The result will be a continuously rising unemployment rate, something that is very difficult to sustain politically in the long run. Alternatively, suppose that the country maintains full employment while achieving a long-term rate of growth, $\mathring{y}_c$, which is well below $\mathring{y}_l$. It can do this only if it persists with, or changes to, products and production methods which result in a much lower growth of productivity, and thus real income, than would be obtained if its actual long-term rate of growth were equal to the growth of its productive potential ($\mathring{y}_l$). Whether or not this situation is sustainable in the long term will depend on how far people are aware of the difference and accept it.

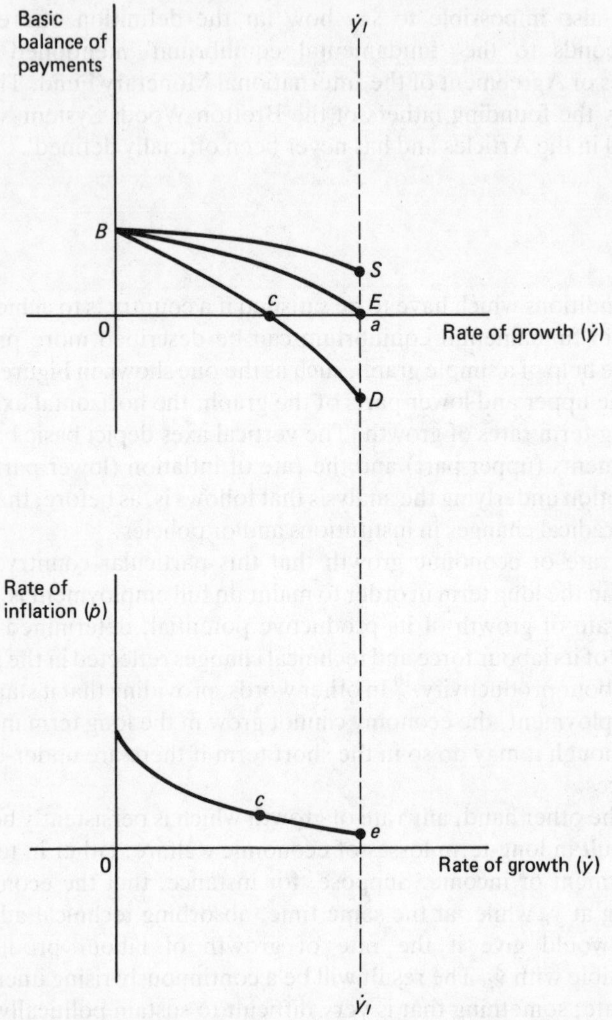

Figure 3.1 Fundamental equilibrium

There is another possible cause of the pressure for change in this case. The lower part of the graph is drawn on the assumption that the long-term inflation rate will be at its lowest at $\mathring{y}_l$. There are basically two reasons why, other things remaining equal, this is likely to happen. First, it is only if $\mathring{y}_a = \mathring{y}_l$ (actual growth equals potential growth) in the long run that firms will be able to utilise fully the best practice techniques, and the economies of scale available to them given the size of their markets. Second, as this would enable the country to sustain optimum increases in productivity and real income, the pressure for the growth of nominal wages in excess of real wages would also be smaller in the long run than it would be at lower rates of growth such as $\mathring{y}_c$. In other words, the advantage for the country in achieving and sustaining in the long term a rate of growth which is equal to that of its productive potential is that the pressure for increases in real incomes can be accommodated through continuous improvements in productivity, without affecting adversely either inflation or employment.

The achievement and maintenance of internal balance is a complex process involving a whole range of economic, social and political factors. There are, however, two rather 'simple' economic conditions which their interaction must fulfil if $\mathring{y}_a$ is to equal $\mathring{y}_l$ in the long term: the growth of investment has to be sufficiently high to sustain $\mathring{y}_a$, and increases in the volume of savings have to be of the magnitude needed to finance the required growth of investment. It is these conditions, in fact, which provide also the long-term link between internal and external balances – leading to fundamental equilibria or disequilibria.

An open, internationally integrated economy is inevitably 'leaky'. A certain proportion of its total income will be spent regularly on imports of numerous goods and services; and the terms on which these imports are exchanged for the country's exports of goods and services may have a significant effect, over time, on its ability to generate the required volume of savings. Moreover, for reasons described in Part I, its residents may also wish to invest abroad on a long-term basis.

For all these reasons, a country with an open economy has to ensure that the long-term growth of domestic *and* foreign investments within its borders is sufficient to generate $\mathring{y}_a = \mathring{y}_l$. This is possible only if the combined growth of domestic and foreign savings available to its population matches the required growth of investments. In other words, the country must ensure that in the long term its basic balance of payments is in balance: its net outflows (inflows) of long-term capital have to be equal to its current account surpluses (deficits).

In Figure 3.1, the country is in this position at point E. Its long-term actual growth ($\mathring{y}_a$) equals its potential growth ($\mathring{y}_l$); the long-term rate of inflation ($\mathring{p}_e$) is at its minimum; and the basic balance is in balance. The country is, therefore, in fundamental equilibrium. It cannot grow faster, and it would be quite irrational for it to pursue an economic policy which results in a long-term rate of growth that was below $\mathring{y}_l$.

Other things remaining equal, the country would be able to sustain this position (E) over a long period without the need to change significantly either its institutions or its policies.

The situation appears to be different at point S in the upper part of the graph. The country is now combining internal balance with a persistent surplus on the balance of payments. Yet, under certain conditions, this position is also compatible with fundamental equilibrium. For instance, a small country could combine basic balance surpluses with internal balance over a long period, using the surpluses either to accumulate its reserves or, more rationally, to lend on a short-term basis to the rest of the world. Either course of action would be possible because it would have no significant effect on the ability of other countries to reconcile their internal and external balances.

It is for precisely this reason that S would be much more difficult to sustain for long if the country were large. Its refusal to provide the rest of the world with long-term investments would have an important effect on economic developments and policies in other countries (as will be shown later). Sooner or later, this would alter the country's own external position also.

Finally, whatever its size, there is no ambiguity about a country's position at D: it is in fundamental disequilibrium. Internal balance could be achieved now only by accumulating large external deficits, something that cannot be sustained in the long term. On the other hand, keeping the basic balance of payments in balance would condemn the country to a long-term rate of growth, $\mathring{y}_c$, which would create serious internal problems of the kind described earlier.

Either way, the situation is unsustainable in the long term. The country will have to take measures to shift somehow the BD curve up to BE. Whatever the policies that it chooses for this purpose – and there a number of possibilities analysed in Chapter 6 – its economic relationships with other countries are bound to be affected. As pointed out earlier, stability of international economic relationships ('international equilibrium') depends on the ability of the countries concerned to maintain them without significant changes in their policies. An apparent inability to reconcile internal and external balances makes such changes imperative.

V

Definitions of 'equilibrium' in conditions of international openness and integration similar to that given in this chapter[11] have been criticised by at least one economist, Machlup, for bringing 'value judgements' and 'disguised politics' into economic analysis.[12] The most serious weakness of this criticism is that the need to reconcile internal and external balances is not so much a 'value judgement' as a recognition of the inevitable. The irresistible pressure for change – which can come either from the outside or from within a country – will ensure that no other outcome can be maintained in the long run.

In fact, twenty-five years after criticising Nurkse and Meade, Machlup was forced, by the behaviour of economic agents in the United States and elsewhere, to come to terms with reality. The result was a complete revision of his earlier view:

> To combat a deficit in the balance of payments by demand adjustment at a time of serious unemployment is politically impracticable. No government will nowadays consider such a policy, and advisers who recommend curing a payments deficit by demand deflation when unemployment is already a serious problem fail to understand some of the unalterable political facts of life.[13]

This led him to the conclusion that 'the "orthodox" adjustment mechanism [according to which external imbalances can be corrected without any regard for their internal consequences] no longer exists'.[14]

4 Short-term, or Cyclical, Disequilibria

I

The previous chapter described a number of important conditions that had to be satisfied if an internationally integrated economy was to enjoy long-term, or fundamental, equilibrium. This does not mean, of course, that such an economy will never experience temporary disequilibria. In fact, there are good cyclical reasons why it may be unable to reconcile internal and external balances in the short run. Some of the most important cases of this kind, together with the policy responses needed to correct them, are described briefly in this chapter.

In order to separate this category of problem from the more difficult one analysed in Chapter 5, it is useful also to specify some of the most important characteristics of a world in which *only* short-term external disequilibria are to be found.

First, in such a world all countries are in fundamental equilibrium. Hence, whatever the problems, they are temporary and can be corrected within a short period. Major policy changes are neither needed nor expected.

Second, the main reasons for this confidence in the existing order of things is not only that all economies are in long-term equilibrium but also that the period under consideration is too short to produce lasting changes in their relative position and performance. All those factors that can cause fundamental disequilibria are absent. There are no technical advances. The patterns of consumption and production are given. The same is true also of the labour force, capital stock and the maximum output obtainable at full employment.

Third, as the underlying economic conditions and competitive position of individual countries remain the same, there is no reason for international investors to alter their preferences. The long-term capital flows remain unchanged. This does not mean that *net* flows of long-term capital will be stable in the short run. They can and, normally, do fluctuate. The point is that, in the highly stable underlying conditions assumed in this chapter, there is no reason for the flows to be altered. They are influenced predominantly by long-term considerations rather than short-term economic developments and policies. If they occur, fluctuations in the long-term capital balance will tend to be temporary and random rather than of a permanent and systematic nature. This means that short-term changes in a country's external balance will come predominantly from variations in its current account, caused by temporary changes either in its own economy or in the rest of the world. It is for this reason, and in order to emphasise effects of the international transmission mechanism, that it will be assumed throughout this chapter that improvements, or deteriorations, in a country's basic balance are caused entirely by changes in its exports and imports of goods and services.

Finally, it is a world in which governments share similar policy objectives and, normally, pursue compatible policies. As a result, the volume of destabilising short-term capital flows is such that central banks can offset them and, in this way, preserve exchange rate stability. A system of fixed exchange rates, operated by all countries, strengthens further the underlying stability of international economic relationships and the prevailing confidence in existing institutions and policies.

In summary, it is a static world in which fundamental, lasting changes neither happen nor are expected to happen. Short-term disequilibria, on the other hand, can and do occur.

II

One reason why countries may run into temporary external imbalances in the course of a business cycle is that not all of them specialise in the same type of goods and services. Nor do they all have the same institutions and attitudes to changes in the economic environment. Hence, output and income may fluctuate much more in some countries than others; or they may have different income elasticities of demand for imports.

To illustrate the first case, suppose that there are two countries *A* and *B* with similar propensities to import. Both experience business cycles, but the variations in income are, normally, greater in *B*. For analytical purposes it may be assumed, therefore, that income and imports are stable in *A*. This means that the countries' external balances – assumed to be in balance over the cycle as a whole – will be determined entirely by changes in the two variables in *B*.

In the cyclical upturn, as *B*'s output and income increase, imports will rise with them, and they will do so faster than exports (as imports into *A* remain stable). Consequently, *B* will experience a deficit on its balance of payments while *A* will, in contrast, earn a surplus. Exactly the opposite will happen in the downturn. With its output and income declining, *B*'s imports will fall relative to exports so that it will have now a surplus on its balance of payments, while *A* will be in deficit. Over the cycle as a whole, however, both countries will be in external balance.

To illustrate the second case, assume that there are again only two countries, *C* and *D*, both of which balance their accounts over the cycle. They have similar income levels and business cycles of similar amplitudes. Their cycles also tend to be highly synchronised. The important difference this time is that they export goods and services with different income elasticities: *C*'s is greater than unity (predominantly 'luxuries'); and *D*'s is lower than unity (predominantly 'necessities'). As it is assumed that they trade only with each other, their income elasticities of demand for imports will be, of course, exactly the opposite of their export elasticities: *C*'s lower and *D*'s greater than unity.

As a result of these differences, *C*'s exports will increase faster than its imports in the upswing, so that it will have a balance of payments surplus (with a corresponding deficit in *D*). The positions will be reversed in the downswing because *D*'s exports will decline by less than its imports, producing an external surplus (with *C*, this time, in deficit).

What these two examples illustrate is not only the reasons why the balance of payments imbalances may be common in the short run but also the conditions which would prevent this from happening. In the latter case, the economies would have to be identical. This does not mean, of course, that they have to produce identical goods and services, only that their product mixes should be such as to ensure identical import and export income elasticities and cyclical fluctuations.

As for the countries' economic policies, there would be obviously no reason to change them in either case. All that is required for the system to function smoothly is for *B* and *D* to be provided with adequate short-term loans (private and/or official) in cyclical upswings; and for the two to generate adequate capital outflows in the downswing when *A* and *C* will need to borrow abroad.

III

The examples discussed in the previous section represent regular, anticipated, types of external imbalances. Given the productive patterns of the countries concerned, the imbalances are expected to occur during certain phases of the cycle and the system is prepared to deal with them. Policy decisions are always formulated in such a way as to take all this into account so that there will be no reason to alter them.

Rather different problems arise when external and internal imbalances are of an irregular, unanticipated, kind. This is the case which has received a good deal of attention in economic literature, usually in relation to changes that take place in a *small* country. It also happens to be the simplest and, in terms of economic policy, the easiest example that one can analyse, not least because there are no further complications caused by interactions with other economies. Hence, whatever disturbances and policy misjudgements take place, they are confined to one country. The problems are its own and so, also, are the solutions. Economic developments and policies in the rest of the world remain unchanged.

Figure 4.1 illustrates the two types of unanticipated, temporary internal and external imbalances that can arise in such an economy. Although they appear at first sight to be similar, it will be noticed that there are important differences between these (and other graphs) in the present chapter and the graph in Figure 3.1. The horizontal axis now shows different *levels* of output, with Q_f indicating the full employment volume of production. In the upper part, the vertical axis shows the basic balance of payments (BP). Following the assumption made earlier about long-term capital flows, the basic balance varies with changes in output – reflecting only short-term improvements, or deteriorations, in the current balance of payments, mainly through what happens to imports. As this is a small country, fluctuations in its activity levels will have no effect on the rest of the world. With policies and output levels in other countries remaining the same, its exports will be unaffected. Hence, changes in its output levels will influence the balance of payments through corresponding changes in imports. In Figure 4.1 it is assumed that the country is capable of reconciling, at E, full employment with a balance on its external account.

The lower part of Figure 4.1 is drawn in such a way as to reflect another important assumption: that at E the full employment level of output, Q_f, is compatible with a socially acceptable rate of inflation, $\mathring{p}_f$. The rate of inflation declines for a time as the economy recovers and higher utilisation of the productive capacity reduces unit costs. It reaches its lowest level at $\mathring{p}_m$, which is below $\mathring{p}_f$. In other words, $\mathring{p}_m$ is associated with a level of output and employment which is below Q_f, and it is this difference that is likely to prevent the level of activity from

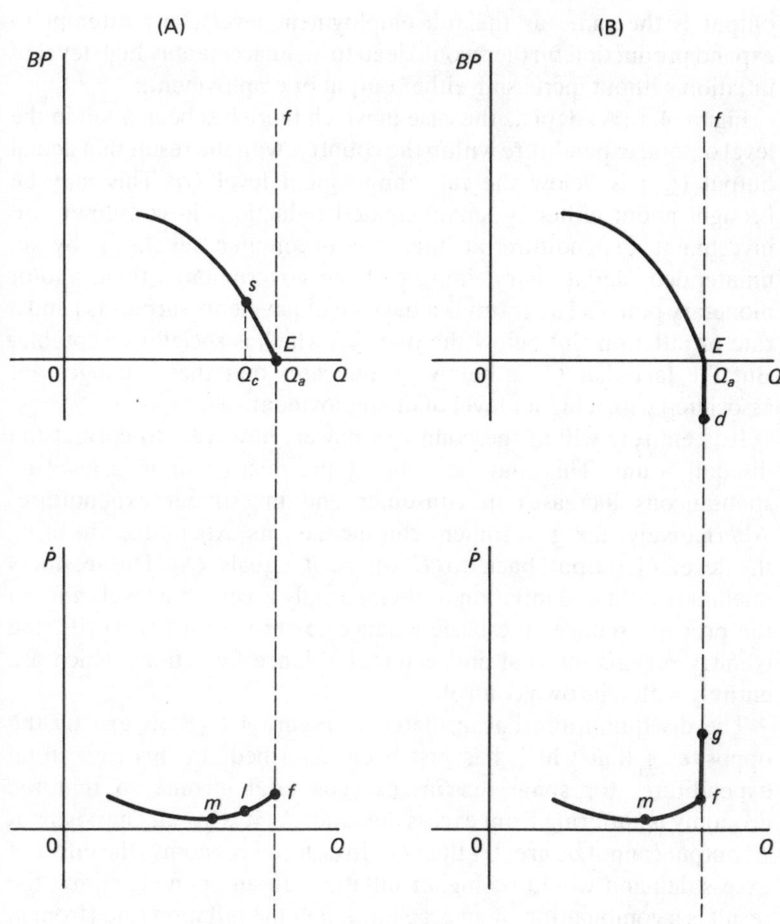

Figure 4.1 Short-term disequilibria in a small open economy

settling at Q_m. Once it is realised that output and employment can be raised to E – especially if, as assumed here, the increase would not be constrained by a deficit on the balance of payments – there would be strong political pressure to do precisely that. However, as the economy approaches E shortages and bottlenecks start to appear. Labour, especially skilled labour, becomes scarce and plant capacity inadequate in an increasing number of sectors. Consequently, the rate of inflation begins to accelerate until at $\mathring{p}_f$ it reaches the highest level that is socially acceptable. As at this point $Q_a = Q_f$ (actual level of output is the same as the full employment level), any attempt to expand production further would lead to an unacceptably high level of inflation without increasing either output or employment.

Figure 4.1 (A) depicts the case in which there has been a fall in the level of total expenditure within the country, with the result that actual output (Q_c) is below the full employment level Q_f. This may be brought about either by unanticipated reductions in consumer and investment expenditure at the micro-economic level, or by an unintended, deflationary, impact of the government's fiscal and/or monetary policy. The result is a balance of payments surplus (s) and a rate of inflation ($\mathring{p}_l$) below the one ($\mathring{p}_f$) which is socially acceptable. But the fact that Q_c is below Q_f indicates that these changes are associated with a higher level of unemployment.

It is entirely within the country's power, however, to correct the disequilibrium. This may be done at the micro-economic level by spontaneous increases in consumer and investment expenditure. Alternatively, the government can increase its expenditure to bring the level of output back to E where it equals Q_f. This restores unemployment and inflation to their socially acceptable levels and, in the process, reduces the basic balance to zero. In other words, the country regains internal and external balance by actions which are entirely within its own control.

The disequilibrium encapsulated in Figure 4.1 (B) is exactly the opposite of that which has just been described. In this case, total expenditure, for some reason, exceeds total income so that the economy is suffering from excess demand. As it is at full employment E, output cannot be greater than Q_f. In a closed economy, the effect of excess demand would be higher inflation. In an open economy, the result is a combination of an acceleration in the inflation rate (from $\mathring{p}_f$ to $\mathring{p}_g$) and a balance of payments deficit (Ed).

It will be noticed that the fact that neither the balance of payment-output nor the inflation-output curve has shifted indicates that there have been no underlying changes in the behaviour of either the micro-economic agents or the government. The excess demand and its consequences are the sign, therefore, of temporary errors which require correction, rather than of fundamental changes which would need adjustment to a new equilibrium.

Again, as in the previous example, such corrections are entirely within the country's control. They might be achieved either by spontaneous action at the micro-economic level, or by fiscal and monetary measures introduced by the government in order to eliminate excess demand.

The highly simplified examples analysed in this section yield two important conclusions. First, in conditions in which *all* economies are small and in fundamental equilibrium, and where there are *no* changes in economic policies and developments abroad, an unanticipated, short-term external deficit will always be the result of excess demand within the economy in which it originates; and an unanticipated short-term external surplus will be caused by deficient demand and under-utilised resources. Second, under these conditions, corrections of external and internal imbalances are, obviously, entirely the responsibility of the country which is experiencing them.

IV

The problem with the preceding analysis is that the assumption of a small country makes it uninteresting if taken literally; and, if not, it is unrepresentative of what happens in conditions of highly interdependent economies. In this case, partial analysis which concentrates on developments in one country and ignores everything else is of limited value for the simple reason that economic developments and policy changes in one country will affect other countries. Their reactions will then be felt in the country which initiated the changes, and so on.

All this was described in some detail in Part I. The question to be considered here is the origin and policy implications of the unanticipated, short-term disequilibria in conditions of international interdependence. What are their causes and where does the responsibility for taking corrective measures really lie in this kind of environment?

To answer this question, it is necessary to retrace some of the arguments developed in the previous section. This time, however, it will be assumed that there are two countries neither of which is small. In other words, whatever happens in one country will have a significant effect on the other country.[1]

Figure 4.2 shows the consequences of a contraction in the level of output in *A* on *B*, and the subsequent effect of this on *A*.[2] What has happened in this case is that total savings have increased in *A* more than total investment. As a result, Q_a is below Q_f (Stage I). The country is running a balance of payments surplus because its imports have expanded less rapidly than its exports, but this has been achieved at the cost of an increase in unemployment. However, unlike in the example of a small country, this is not where the problem stops. The fact that *A*'s imports have increased by less than before means, of course, that there has been a contraction in *B*'s exports and output so that Q_b is below Q_f.

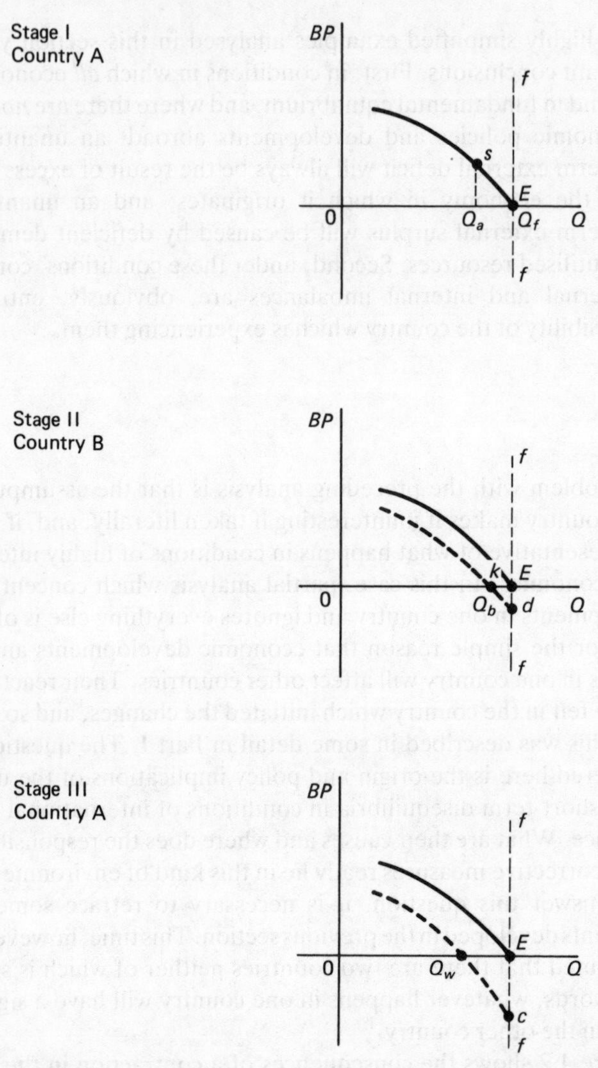

Figure 4.2 International transmission of short-term disequilibria: deflation

At this level of output B is in external balance (k), but its unemployment has gone up (Stage II).

If B now tries to correct its internal imbalance by increasing the level of output back to E, it will run into a balance of payments deficit (Ed) which can be sustained only by using its reserves (normally a very short-term solution), or by official borrowing from *A*. In other words, *A*'s disequilibrium has been transmitted to *B* despite the fact that no internally generated changes had taken place there either in economic development or policies. What is more, it is clear from this example that *B* cannot, under these circumstances, restore the equilibrium on its own. Unless it alters radically its economic relationship with *A*,[3] *B* is completely dependent on it for reconciling its internal and external balances. If *A* acts promptly to deal with the crisis, the whole thing can be resolved without lasting damage and complications. If it does not, the disequilibria created in both countries by the original contraction in *A* will become much more difficult to solve.

A successful solution still requires *A* to initiate the expansionary measures. But now, as the last diagram (Stage III) in Figure 4.2 shows, this would not be sufficient to return both *A* and *B* to the initial equilibrium. The reason for this is that *A* cannot expand now beyond Q_w without running into external imbalances unless *B* responds with appropriate reflationary measures. Moreover, even if *B* acts in this way, it will require the two countries to coordinate their actions very carefully if their policies are not to destabilise the system further by giving rise to an inflationary disequilibrium.

The most important problems that excess demand and inflation can create in the short run are illustrated in Figure 4.3. What has happened here is that, for some reason, total expenditure in *A* has become greater than total output. As the economy is operating at full employment, output cannot be increased in the short run to satisfy this expansion in aggregate demand. The result is partly an acceleration in the rate of inflation (from $\mathring{p}_e$ *to* $\mathring{p}_h$), and, partly, a deterioration in its balance of payments from a balance at *E* to a deficit *En* (Stage I).

While *A* is experiencing excess demand, there has been no change in domestic expenditure in *B* which is also at full employment and the actual level of output equals Q_f. But as the two economies are integrated, the inflationary pressure from *A* will spill over into *B* through greater demand for *B*'s exports. The snag is that *B*, also operating at full capacity, is in no position to increase the volume of its exports significantly. Instead, their prices go up, and if they increase by more than the prices of its imports it will earn a balance of payments surplus *Ez*. At the same time, the combined effect of higher import prices and greater demand for its exports gives rise to inflationary pressures in its own economy. The rate of inflation accelerates from $\mathring{p}_c$ to $\mathring{p}_i$ (Stage II).

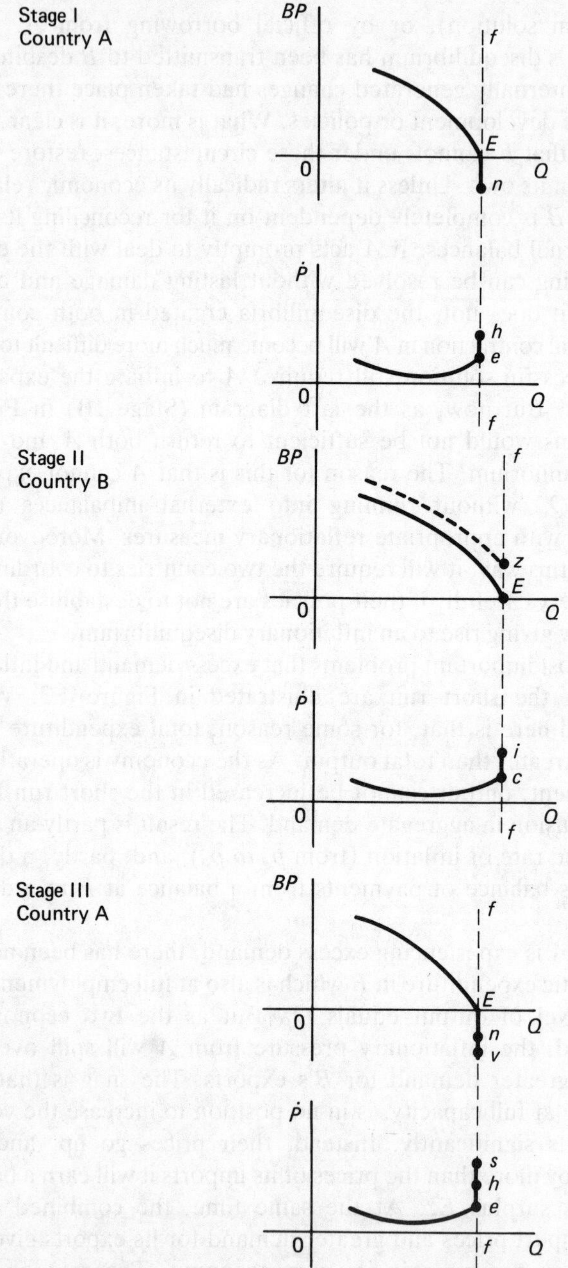

Figure 4.3 International transmission of short-term disequilibria: inflation

The increase in *B*'s export prices may reduce some of the demand for its products in *A*. But, as the two economies are highly specialised and integrated, the short-run price elasticities for imports (and thus for exports also) are likely to be low.[4] Hence, the result will be another round of inflation and balance of payments deterioration in *A* (Stage III), further increases in external surpluses and inflation in *B*, and so on. In other words, excess demand in one country has spilled over into another country – becoming an international rather than a purely national problem.

Even when this happens it is *A*, the country in which the problem has originated, that should take the initiative to regain price stability. As the two economies are integrated, *B* cannot stabilise its own prices so long as *A* fails to do something about its excess demand. Responsibility for taking the initiative rests, therefore, with *A*.

At the same time, the overall effectiveness of its action will depend on *B*'s reaction to imported inflation. If it is regarded in *B* as no more than a temporary disturbance which requires no change in existing policies then, by eliminating excess demand within its own economy, *A*'s anti-inflationary policy will also eliminate the cause of increases in costs and prices in *B*. Consequently, it will not be necessary for the latter's authorities to take any action themselves. Indeed, the combined effects of *A*'s and *B*'s anti-inflationary policies in these circumstances could easily lead to a contraction in their activity levels, creating problems of the kind analysed earlier in this section.

If, on the other hand, the transmission of inflation from *A* to *B* causes people in the latter to change their expectations about future increases in prices, giving rise to a strong inflationary spiral, it may become necessary for *B* also to take anti-inflationary measures in order to restore normality quickly by proving the expectations to be unjustified. Otherwise, *A*'s actions will either not be sufficient, or will take a long time to stabilise prices in the two countries, as the effects of the inflationary spiral in *B* will continue to be felt in its own economy. Hence, a speedy restoration of the equilibrium will require some sort of co-ordinated action in the two countries. However, once again, they will have to be careful that their actions do not lead to overshooting, creating the sort of problems shown in Figure 4.2.

V

The analysis in this chapter rests on a number of highly simplified and unrealistic assumptions. The world in which all countries are always in fundamental equilibrium is an analytical curiosity rather than a normal state of affairs. As a result, major policy changes are common; and their timing, 'packaging' and effectiveness are a matter of continuous uncertainty and concern. Inevitably, changes in the relative position and prospects of individual countries will also lead, over time, to changes in the volume of international flows of long-term capital, not necessarily in favour of the countries with the tendency towards persistent current account imbalances. To make things worse, governments do not always have similar short-term policy objectives, and they frequently pursue incompatible policies. In the absence of very rigorous exchange controls, all these uncertainties and problems will be reflected in incessant and highly destabilising flows of short-term capital, some of them of a precautionary nature, and others purely speculative.

Nevertheless, even in a world from which all these complications and uncertainties are absent, some countries may experience, as the preceding analysis shows, temporary disequilibria. This may happen either because of the structure of their economies or because of unanticipated, temporary changes (and miscalculations) in the behaviour of economic agents.

Moreover, it is also clear that the small country model – normally used in economics to analyse international disequilibria – can be seriously misleading if applied to a world in which national economies are internationally integrated as well as sufficiently large to influence economic developments in other countries. After the initial shock, it is far from clear in this kind of environment who exactly is responsible for perpetuating a particular problem. What is more, it may now become very difficult for a country to correct a disequilibrium on its own, even if it has originated within its own borders. Once the disequilibrium is transmitted to other countries it will tend to become an international problem, requiring in most cases an international solution.

This is even more true, as the next two chapters will show, when some countries begin to experience problems associated with fundamental disequilibrium.

5 Fundamental, or Structural, Disequilibria

I

The most important difference between the short-term economic disturbances analysed in the previous chapter and fundamental, or structural, disequilibria is that in the former the underlying conditions and behaviour of economic agents remain unchanged, so that the analysis is concerned entirely with movements along the balance of payments-output and the inflation-output (employment) curves. In contrast, structural disequilibria represent shifts either in these curves or in the rate of growth of the productive potential – all caused by fundamental changes in underlying economic conditions and behaviour.

A number of factors can cause these shifts: changes in tastes brought about by inventions and innovations made in other countries; trade liberalisation; improvements in international communications which make people aware of new, or superior, goods and services available abroad; technical changes in production methods; increases in population; bankruptcy, confiscation or nationalisation of a country's assets abroad which reduce the invisible earnings that have enabled its citizens to reconcile their existing patterns of consumption and production; the exhaustion of the soil or mines; rapidly growing scarcity of a key resource such as oil; destruction of productive capacity caused by war; a significant and lasting change in the terms of trade between primary and manufactured goods; and so on. The magnitude of these changes will often be increased further by the fact that in altering countries' location specific advantages they are also likely to alter the direction of international long-term capital flows.

In more general terms, structural[1] disequilibria can be said to arise as a result of some fundamental change either in demand (both domestic and foreign) for a country's goods and services, or in the volume and composition of its output relative to shifts in demand. Moreover, these shifts are likely to be reinforced, *ceteris paribus*, by movements of long-term capital away from the countries which are becoming less competitive.

It does not require much reflection to realise that most of these changes will take place over a longer period, mainly as a result of differences in the adaptability and performance of individual economies. Some economies will initiate structural changes, or respond quickly to similar developments in other countries, reaping considerable long-term benefits in high levels of employment, productivity and income. Others will fail to do so and, consequently, experience a cumulative deterioration in their economic welfare. Even when steps are taken to arrest and reverse this decline, the nature of a fundamental, or structural, disequilibrium is such that it is likely to take a long time to eradicate.

This chapter will analyse, both, the way in which persistent differences in national rates of economic development tend to give rise to fundamental disequilibria when combined with increasing international similarities in tastes and aspirations, and the extent to which these problems are to be found in four different groups of economies. Major policy options open to countries experiencing long-term disequilibria will be examined in the next chapter.

II

No country which begins sustained, extensive industrialisation is likely to remain unique in this respect for very long. Sooner or later an increasing number of imitators will first copy its pattern of development and then evolve their own brand of industrialisation. In some countries this will happen as a result of socio-political unrest and change, as it dawns on an increasing number of people that there is nothing 'natural' and 'inevitable' about poverty. In others, the impetus for change will come from powerful economic interests, determined to acquire the kind of wealth and power enjoyed by similar groups in other countries. Finally, industrialisation may be sparked off when those in power realise its political potential. A country with a strong industrial base will tend to enjoy military as well as economic advantages, enabling it either to play a major role on the international scene or, at least, prevent outside interference in its domestic affairs.

Whatever the reason, not all countries will start to industrialise at the same time; and some of the more isolated and traditionalist societies, or countries dominated by a foreign power, may not do so at all. Moreover, among the countries which embark upon the process of industrialisation, some will be much more successful than others. The rates of growth which they achieve over a long period will tend, therefore, to vary – in some cases a good deal. Eventually, it is the difference between the productive capacity, efficiency levels and incomes that individual countries have achieved and the levels to which they aspire that will give rise to fundamental disequilibria. The greater the gap the more serious the disequilibria are likely to be.

In order to trace the origin of these problems it helps to make a number of assumptions concerning the character of the international economy.

To start with, it will be assumed in what follows that a number of countries, all at a more or less similar level of development, begin to industrialise at roughly the same time. It will also be assumed that none of them is sufficiently large, or so perfectly endowed with natural resources, that it can develop in total isolation as an autarky. Hence, they all have to trade with one another, with the volume of trade rising (for reasons explained in Part I) with their levels of economic development. In addition, it will be assumed that all these countries import and export capital. Labour, on the other hand, is mobile within the countries but not between them. It will also be assumed that all these countries are bound by strong cultural bonds.

The only difference, which turns out to be of critical importance, is that for various reasons their economies do not develop at the same rate in the long term. To back this assumption up, it will also be assumed that whatever changes in institutions and policies start off the process of industrialisation, once it gets under way no similar changes will take place in any of the countries. The assumption is obviously not very realistic. But it enables the subsequent analysis to trace the long-term effects of the difference in performance and problems which appears between those economies that industrialise rapidly (referred to in what follows as *fast*) and those which do so at a lower rate (*slow*) – without the unnecessary complication of leap-frogging. In any case, historically, some economies have developed consistently faster than others.

III

A more rapid expansion in their productive capacity and absorption of technical advances will affect the composition of output in *fast* in a way which will make it much easier for them to satisfy changes in domestic and foreign demand. As explained in Part I, cultural integration leads to an international harmonisation of tastes and demand patterns. People come to desire goods and services which are similar in function, though they may be differentiated in many other respects. *Fast* not only develop the capacity to produce existing ('standard') products more rapidly than *slow*, but will also tend to introduce many new or greatly improved goods and services ('luxuries'). As demand for 'luxuries' increases faster than income – while demand for standardised products grows, in general, at a lower rate than income – and as output, technical change and income increase more rapidly in *fast*, the proportion of new goods and services will inevitably come to feature prominently in their total output. In contrast, *slow* will find themselves in the long-term producing predominantly standardised products.

The growing difference in their structure of output will inevitably come to be reflected also in their trade patterns. Increasingly, *fast* will export 'luxuries' and import standardised products, while *slow* will export standardised products and import 'luxuries'. As these changes are taking place, there will be also an important change in world income elasticity of demand for each group's exports, as well as in their own income elasticities of demand for imports. Income elasticity of demand for 'luxuries' is normally greater than unity. It is lower than unity in the case of 'standardised' products (necessities, lower quality or long-established ones).[2] This means that, in the long term, the rate of growth of imports into *fast* will become lower than the growth of their output and income, while, at the same time, the growth of their exports will become more rapid than the growth of world output and income. *Slow*, on the other hand, will find themselves increasingly in a situation which is exactly the reverse of that experienced by *fast*. (Each group's terms of trade are assumed to remain unchanged.)

As a result, it becomes impossible after a certain time, other things remaining equal, for *slow* to grow as rapidly as *fast*. At an equal rate of growth, *slow* will be running growing current account deficits, while *fast* will be experiencing increasing current account surpluses, a development which is unsustainable. Under the conditions described here, the only sustainable scenario is that in which *slow* grow at a lower rate than *fast*, with the required difference determined by the widening differential in income elasticities of demand for their exports and imports. The widening differential is inevitable, *ceteris paribus*, because disparities in their growth of output and fixed investments will ensure that *fast* expand their productive capacity and absorb new technical inventions and innovations more rapidly.

All these important advantages which *fast* are accumulating in the long term could be offset if they were accompanied by more rapid increases in their cost and prices compared to those in *slow*. This would not affect the ability of *fast* to trade among themselves. But it would put an increasing proportion of their exports out of the reach of *slow*.

More rapid inflation rates in *fast* could also encourage them to specialise less in standardised products and import them instead from *slow*. The problem is that such a development would not necessarily work to the latter's advantage. It would encourage *fast* to specialise even more in 'luxuries', with the result that the difference in income elasticities of demand for exports and imports of the two groups would increase further in their favour. It is for this reason that the improvement in the relative position of *slow*, as a result of persistently higher inflation rates in *fast*, would come mainly through a reduction in the growth of their imports relative to that of income.

Unfortunately for *slow*, long-term differences in international inflation rates are likely to work to their disadvantage rather than in their favour.

Other things being equal, more rapid economic growth in *fast* than in *slow* will ensure that the former absorb at an earlier stage of their development all their unemployed and underemployed labour. The actual and potential scarcity of labour will encourage widespread use in *fast* of capital intensive methods of production. The result will be a rapid growth in their productivity, real income and consumption. This, in turn, will have two important long-term effects on their costs and prices. First, rapid improvements in the standard of living will reduce the pressure on nominal incomes to increase faster than productivity. Second, as the size of their own markets is increasing more rapidly, *fast* will be able to exploit to a greater extent than other countries the economies of large-scale production. Combined, these two developments will ensure that inflationary pressures diminish in *fast* in the long term.

None of these advantages will be enjoyed by *slow*. Their low rates of growth of productivity, real incomes and consumption, combined with the international harmonisation of tastes and aspirations generated by *fast*, will tend to keep increases in their nominal incomes in excess of those in productivity. In addition, the relatively slower expansion of their markets will give them less scope for exploiting economies of scale fully. Consequently, far from falling relative to those in *fast*, their costs and prices are likely to increase more rapidly. It will, therefore, become even more difficult for them to compete internationally.

The long-term tendency of cumulative decline in *slow* relative to *fast* will be exacerbated further by one important factor not mentioned so far: in the absence of control on capital outflows, *slow* will tend to become net exporters of long-term capital.

As pointed out in Part I, international investments are attracted predominantly to countries with large and rapidly growing markets, invariably countries with the most advanced economies. They offer much greater scope for specialisation, both 'real' and financial, than economies at a lower level of development. Moreover, the fact that they have accomplished successfully a higher level of industrialisation than the rest of the world – combined usually with the greater social and political stability brought about by their economic success – makes them much less risky as a location for new investments.

It is for these reasons that investors from both *slow* and *fast* will prefer to invest in the latter and, in the absence of controls on international movements of capital, this is where most of the world's private savings and investments will tend to concentrate. The long-term outcome of this will be to widen significantly the gap in efficiency and income levels of the two groups. Unlike *slow*, fast will be able to sustain rapid growth of investment, technical improvements and output without experiencing balance of payments problems. The only constraint on the long-term rate of development of their economies will be the growth of their own productive potential.

IV

This widening of the gap between the two groups of countries need not lead to the appearance of fundamental disequilibria so long as it is accepted by *slow* as something which is beyond their power to alter. In that case, they must become resigned to low growth of productivity and income instead of trying to emulate the achievement of *fast*. This will leave a slow growing economy in fundamental equilibrium.

Some countries in the *slow* group may be forced to adopt this attitude. (In conditions of international cultural integration they would have to be *forced* by some means or other to persist with such an attitude over a long period.) Other members of *slow*, on the other hand, may do something that has been assumed so far as given: undergo political and institutional changes with the specific purpose of achieving in the long term the economic and other advantages enjoyed by *fast*.

However, in order to do this, they have to attain and sustain a rate of economic growth which is higher than that of *fast*. Potentially, they may be capable of this. The rate of increase in their labour force, combined with the absorption of technical advances made in *fast*, is likely to give the 'reformed' members of *slow* long-term rates of growth of productive potential in excess of those in *fast*. The problem is that their income levels and marginal propensities to consume will be such as to make them incapable of generating domestic savings on a scale sufficient to sustain the required investments; and without these investments they will be in no position, other things remaining equal, to achieve and maintain a long-term rate of growth equal to that of their productive potential. Every attempt to do this will lead to unsustainable balance of payments deficits. In other words, they will find themselves in fundamental disequilibrium, unable to reconcile and maintain their internal and external balances.

There is no reason, of course, why *slow* should be the only countries to be confronted with such a problem. *Fast* are unlikely to remain a monolithic bloc indefinitely either. Some of them, while achieving much higher levels of economic development than *slow*, may after a time become unable to match the rate of economic progress made by the more dynamic members of the group. Hence, gaps in efficiency and income levels, and international competitiveness, will appear among *fast* also – though not on the same scale as between *fast* and *slow*. Eventually, the choice facing the less successful members of *fast* will become similar to that facing *slow*: to accept the consequences of their relative decline, or to make the necessary changes which will enable them to rejoin the pace setters among *fast*. Moreover, by the time that they adopt the second alternative, they may discover that their relative decline has gone so far that they have become incapable of reconciling and maintaining their internal and external balances. In other words, they will find themselves in fundamental disequilibrium.

At any point of time, therefore, the world is likely to be divided into four broad groups of economies, with distinctly different capabilities for maintaining stable international relationships: 'subsistence' (those which have failed to make a sustained effort to absorb modern methods of economic organisation and production); 'developing' (substistence economies and those from *slow* which have broken with the past and made a major and sustained effort to industrialise); declining' (economies which, after a long period among *fast*, have failed to keep in step with technical and other developments in the more successful members of the group); and, finally, 'structural surplus' (leading members of *fast*).

As economic relationships among these (mainly the last three) groups of countries determine the character and stability of an international economic system, it is important to bear in mind the main characteristics and problems of each group when considering major policy options open to them. These problems can be illustrated with the help of a slightly altered version of the graph used in Figure 3.1.

V

The first group consists of *subsistence economies* (Figure 5.1) in which productivity and income levels are low and virtually static. The same is true also of their savings and investments. The rate of technical progress, either generated domestically or absorbed from abroad, is negligible. The rate of growth is very low. However, as most of the population is employed in agriculture, the apparent level of unemployment is likely to be low, though there may be a good deal of disguised unemployment. In addition, given a rudimentary system of education and very primitive means of transport and communications, the aspirations gap will be small. The consumers' wants and preferences are sufficiently insulated and traditional, therefore, for their limited productive capacity to satisfy them. Hence, the rate of inflation is likely to be low, except in periods of poor harvests.

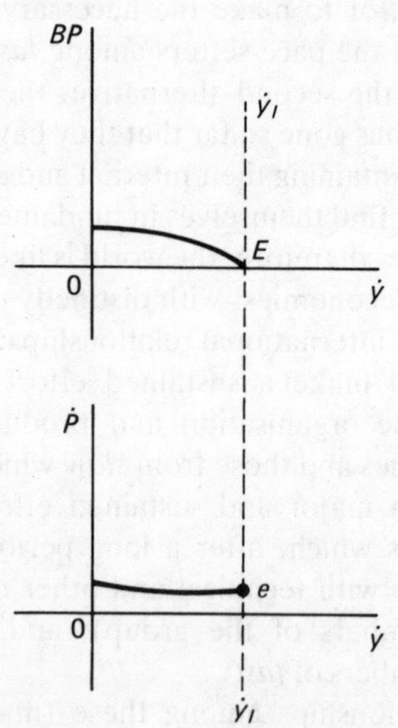

Figure 5.1 Subsistence economies

Subsistence economies will tend to be roughly in balance on their current balance of payments, except in periods of bad harvests, or of a large fall in world commodity prices. When this happens, the deficits will usually be financed with the help of aid and grants from foreign governments and international organisations. Assistance of this kind will be vital. These economies will normally attract very little private capital, unless they happen to be endowed with some primary product demanded by the rest of the world. Otherwise, their flows of long-term capital will be negligible. Lacking location-specific advantages they will be in no position to attract foreign investment; and their low levels of savings and development in general will make them incapable of exporting capital. On the whole, subsistence economies will be in fundamental equilibrium, just managing to eke out a meagre existence on the periphery of the world economy.

The situation is quite different in the structural deficit countries, countries which are incapable, other things remaining equal, of reconciling their external and internal balances in conditions of international openness and integration.

Unlike subsistence economies, *developing economies* (Figure 5.2A) are trying, as Rostow would put it, to 'take off into self-sustained growth'.[3] They are absorbing technical and organisational knowledge from the more advanced economies, with the result that there is an acceleration in the rate of growth of their labour productivity. In addition, they have a large reserve of unemployed and underemployed labour; and their population (including the working population) is growing rapidly as a result of improvements in nutritional and health standards. The combined effect of all these changes is to accelerate the rate of growth of their productive potential from $\mathring{y}_l$ to $\mathring{y}_{ln}$. This means, in effect, that $\mathring{y}_{ln}$ is now the minimum rate of economic development at which they can absorb technical and organisational improvements from abroad and, at the same time, achieve full employment in the long term. (Given the size of the technical gap which exists between them and highly industrialised economies, and the size of their labour force, developing economies can, of course, expand at much higher rates than this in the short to medium term.)

However, other things remaining equal, it is precisely this rate which is beyond their capacity to reach and maintain in the long term. As shown in Part I, most exports from developing countries go to industrial economies, the economies whose levels of productivity and income they are trying to equal in the long term. To achieve this,

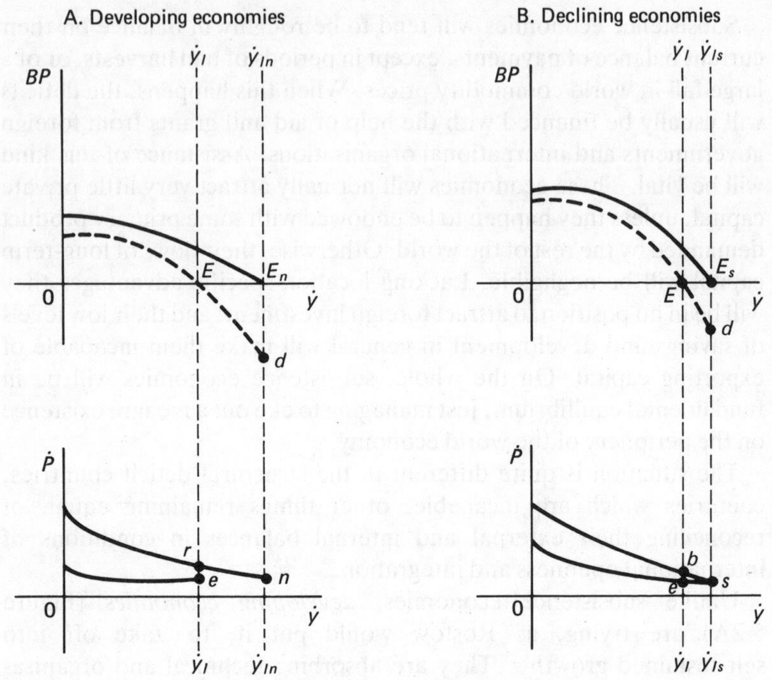

Figure 5.2 Structural deficit countries

developing countries have to sustain a rate of economic development which is higher than the long-term rate of growth of industrial economies. Otherwise, the gap between the two groups will widen. The problem is that developing (*slow*) countries' income elasticity of demand for imports is invariably higher than the world income elasticity of demand for their exports. This means that, with the terms of trade remaining unchanged, they will have a deficit on their current balance of payments even if their rates of growth are equal to those in the rest of the world. An acceleration in their rate of economic growth relative to the world's will make the imbalance larger and, consequently, even more unsustainable in the long term.

In addition, unless they happen to be rich in natural resources, developing countries will tend to find it very difficult to attract sufficiently large long-term investments from abroad to finance their current account deficits. *Ceteris paribus*, their markets will be smaller than markets in industrial economies of comparable size, because of the latter's much higher incomes per head. Moreover, industrial economies enjoy the advantage of a wide range of highly developed industrial and service sectors plus a highly skilled and educated labour force. Combined, the advantages give rise to important external economies which developing countries cannot match in the short to medium run. The fact that they will be widely expected to be incapable of sustaining as rapid a rate of economic growth as industrial countries, because of their balance of payments difficulties, will tend to make them even less attractive to transnational corporations and other international investors.

Hence, other things remaining equal, developing countries will find themselves in a vicious circle of relative economic stagnation: low rates of development (past and expected) lead to low investments, slow absorption of technical advances, low productivity and income levels, low propensity to save, inadequate capacity to undertake new investments, low rates of development, and so on.

Nor is this all. The cultural integration and the desire to imitate standards of living prevalent in the more affluent countries will create another important problem, also illustrated in Figure 5.2A: an upward shift in the inflation-growth curve. For reasons analysed in Part I, the competitive ethos and the aspiration gap will be strong in this case, with the result that demand for new goods and services is likely to exceed for many years the countries' limited capacity to produce or import them. For this reason also, the numerous investment opportunities will for a long time be well in excess of the countries' ability to generate sufficient domestic savings to finance them. Under such strong pressure of conflicting claims on scarce national resources, governments may be forced to pursue highly expansionary monetary policies in the hope of reconciling – at least in the very short term – some of these claims and, in this way, preserving political stability.

Consequently, *ceteris paribus*, developing countries will be prone to large deficits on their external balances *and* high rates of inflation. Inflationary pressures will be particularly strong if the lack of foreign exchange restricts the growth of imports and through them the countries' economic development in general. This is illustrated in Figure 5.2A by the fact that, with the upward shift in the inflation-growth curve, $\mathring{p}_r$ is not only higher than $\mathring{p}_n$ but also above $\mathring{p}_e$. In other words, a long-term rate of economic development below $\mathring{y}_{In}$ will tend to condemn a developing country to both rising unemployment and a higher rate of inflation.

The only way to avoid a progressive deterioration of this kind is to achieve somehow an upward shift in the balance of payments-growth curve so that it crosses $\mathring{y}_{ln}$ at *En*, enabling developing economies to balance their external account while growing at the rate of growth of their productive potential.

Exactly the same type of problem, though on a smaller scale, will be experienced by *declining economies* (Figure 5.2B), another group of structural deficit countries. The group consists of those economies which, having reached an advanced stage of industrial development, fail to keep at, or close to, the frontiers of technical and industrial advance. (In other words, these are the members of *fast* who, having reached a high level of industrialisation, fail to keep in step with the most dynamic economies in the group.) Consequently, their exports, output, productivity and income levels tend to decline, over a period of time, relative to those of *both* other industrial and developing economies.

This relative decline gives rise to a number of problems, all similar in character, though not in the scale, to those experienced by developing countries. To reverse such a decline, economies in this group also have to absorb technical and organisational advances made by the leading industrial countries. The result is an acceleration in the long-term rate of growth of their productive potential from $\mathring{y}_l$ to $\mathring{y}_{ls}$. The snag is that, *ceteris paribus*, they would be running at $\mathring{y}_{ls}$ a sizeable deficit on their basic balance of payments (*Esd*), something that cannot be sustained for long. The reasons for the deficit are familiar: a higher import than export income elasticity of demand, and the inability to attract sufficient net long-term investments from abroad. The latter will be influenced to a great extent by the relatively lower size and expected growth of declining economies compared to those of industrial leaders. The building up of inflationary pressures as aspirations are frustrated (indicated in Figure 5.2B by the upward shift in the inflation-growth curve), and increasing conflicts around income distribution, may give rise also to sizeable disinvestment by transnational corporations. This will, of course, make the fundamental disequilibria of declining economies even worse.

As a result of all these changes in its international competitiveness, a declining economy can also be caught in a vicious circle of relative decline, unless it can somehow push the balance of payments-growth curve up so that it crosses $\mathring{y}_{ls}$ at *Es*. A failure to do this will leave the economy with rising long-term unemployment (both actual and disguised) and a higher rate of inflation. In Figure 5.2B this is illustrated by $\mathring{p}_b$ being higher than $\mathring{p}_e$. Finally, the longer it takes a declining economy to arrest and reverse its relative decline the more serious will its problems become as the gap between $\mathring{y}_l$ and $\mathring{y}_{ls}$ widens.

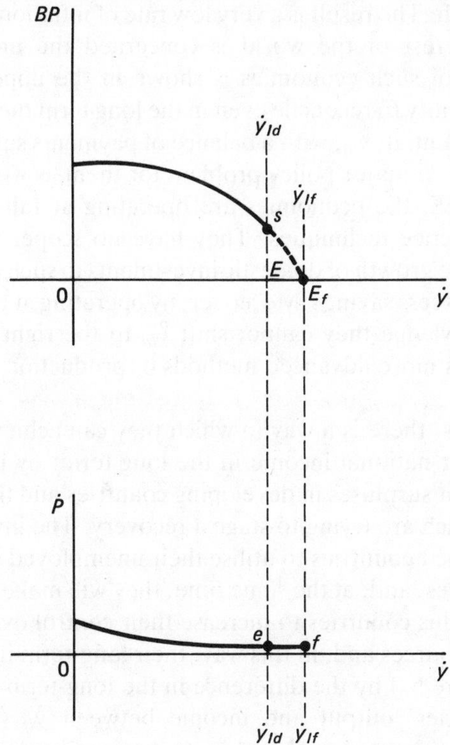

Figure 5.3 Structural surplus countries

The last group, *structural surplus countries* (Figure 5.3), consists of economies that are normally in the forefront of world technical development, enjoying high and/or rapidly rising productivity and income levels.[4] They tend to exert a strong influence, therefore, on international tastes and desired consumption levels and patterns. The growth of their domestic savings exceeds that of investment so that they tend to have very low rates of inflation and, other things remaining equal, can sustain balance-of-payments surpluses at full employment, even in the long term. Furthermore, what they do with these investible surpluses will determine, as will be shown later, the character of the international economy as well as the long-term growth of their own national wealth and income.

In Figure 5.3, structural surplus countries are growing at the rate of growth of their long-term productive potential, $\mathring{y}_{ld}$. As their levels of productivity, income and consumption are high, their propensity to save is also high. The result is a very low rate of inflation $\mathring{p}_e$. However, so far as the rest of the world is concerned the most important characteristic of such economies is shown in the upper part of the graph: their ability to reconcile even in the long term the growth of the productive potential, $\mathring{y}_{ld}$, with a balance of payments surplus, sE.

This presents a major policy problem for them as well as for other countries. At E, the economies are operating at full employment, using best-practice techniques. They have no scope, therefore, for accelerating the growth of domestic investments to such an extent as to absorb these excess savings. Moreover, by operating at the frontiers of technical knowledge they cannot shift $\mathring{y}_{ld}$ to the right by absorbing someone else's more advanced methods of production and organisation.

Nevertheless, there is a way in which they can achieve more rapid growth of their national income in the long term: by investing their current account surpluses in developing countries and those declining economies which are trying to stage a recovery. The investments will enable the deficit countries to utilise their unemployed and underemployed resources; and, at the same time, they will make it possible for structural surplus countries to increase their control over the world's productive resources and, in this way, their long-term income. This is shown in Figure 5.3 by the difference in the long-term growth of the surplus countries' output and income between $\mathring{y}_{lf}$ (generated by employing foreign resources) and $\mathring{y}_{ld}$ (generated by domestic resources).

Consequently, the long-term interests of structural surplus and deficit countries tend to be much closer than a superficial analysis of their characteristics might suggest. It is in the interest of the deficit countries to restructure their economies in order to raise productivity and income levels; and it is in the interest of the surplus countries that this should be done in conditions of international openness and economic integration.

In order to be able to undertake net investment abroad and reach $\mathring{y}_{lf}$ without disturbing internal balance, structural surplus countries have, first of all, to earn current account surpluses. The surpluses arise as a result of the imbalances experienced by structural deficit countries – which are their counterpart. This will occur only if the deficit countries try to restructure their economies in order to achieve productivity and income levels enjoyed by the surplus countries. If developing and declining economies restrict their growth to the rates (their respective $\mathring{y}_l$ in Figure 5.2) at which they have been able to balance their external accounts in the past, or if they accelerate their growth beyond these rates by restricting imports from the surplus countries, the surplus *sE* in Figure 5.3 will disappear. If this happens, structural surplus countries will also have to forego the additional growth of income ($\mathring{y}_{lf} - \mathring{y}_{ld}$) that they could have obtained in the long term.

It is in their interest, therefore, that developing and declining countries try to restructure their economies,[5] and that they do so without resorting to large-scale controls on imports. However, the deficit countries will, generally, be unable to do without such restrictions unless they receive sufficiently large inflows of long-term capital to finance their current account deficits. Investments of this kind can be provided only by structural surplus countries.

Not surprisingly, the latter will, invariably, tend to play a critical role in determining the character and the rate of development of the international economy. The deficit countries are under both internal and external pressure to undertake long-term adjustments – in other words, to modernise and restructure their economies. Whatever the nature of their economic system, they will have a number of external policy options open to them. Which of these is eventually adopted will depend on the speed at which they wish to adjust as well as on the policies of the structural surplus countries.

VI

Finally, it should be clear from the preceding analysis that the composition of each of the four groups is unlikely to remain unchanged in the long term. Some subsistence economies will shake off their conservatism and inertia and embark on a rapid and highly successful process of development. For similar reasons, some developing countries will acquire the status of industrialised, structural surplus economies. At the same time, certain structural surplus economies may undergo the process of relative decline – temporary in some cases, permanent in others. It is not inconceivable, in fact, that in the very long term some of the once highly advanced economies may regress back to subsistence level.

Ultimately, these changes will be determined by the way in which individual countries react to the appearance of a serious deterioration in their external and internal balances – in other words, on policies which they employ to deal with fundamental disequilibrium.

6 The Long-term Adjustment Process: Major Policy Options

I

Elimination of fundamental disequilibria is a complex long-term process invariably associated with wide-ranging economic, social and, in many cases also, political changes. Most of them appear to be predominantly domestic in character. Yet, whatever the original aim, they are bound – to the extent that they alter significantly a country's economic performance – to affect also at least some international economic relationships. The larger the countries involved the more likely this is to be the case.

It is beyond the scope of this book to analyse the innumerable changes in economic policy that might take place and their long-term implications. Consequently, what the present chapter will do is to examine a number of broad economic policy options frequently advocated by economists and policy makers as being particularly effective in eliminating serious and persistent international economic disequilibria.

Each option will be analysed on the assumption that countries in fundamental disequilibrium make no use of any of the other policy approaches. The assumption is obviously unrealistic. Most countries in this position will resort to a 'package' of measures containing many, or even all, of the policies considered here. However, looking at each option in isolation makes it easier to emphasise its individual advantages and problems, and consequently its feasibility and likely effectiveness.

II

The first policy option open to structural deficit countries is to restrict their long-term growth rates – irrespective of domestic consequences – to that level which has been consistent in the past with a sustainable, long-term balance on their external account. Expressed in terms of the analysis in Figure 5.2, this means that developing and declining economies would confine their long-term growth to $\mathring{y}_l$. Neither group would make a deliberate attempt to grow faster than this.[1]

The most serious weakness of this particular policy option is that it will lead to cumulative long-term losses in economic welfare in the form of growing unemployment, and/or falling real incomes and consumption relative to those in the rest of the world. Neither is likely to be acceptable to a population determined to improve its standard of living.

Growing pressure for change will be reflected in accelerating inflation rates and increasing balance of payments deficits. The pressure may be suppressed for a time, but not indefinitely. To make things worse, the combination of relative economic stagnation and instability will tend to encourage the emigration of skilled labour and capital,[2] intensifying the adjustment problems and, consequently, the general level of dissatisfaction.

The experience of many developing countries, as well as industrial countries with declining economies (such as the UK), provides ample evidence of the long-term problems involved in adopting this particular policy option. Economic dissatisfaction and frustration has also led in many countries to social unrest and violent political changes.

In a world in which countries experiencing fundamental disequilibria are prevented from adjusting their economies to higher efficiency and income levels, the only 'winners' appear to be structural surplus countries. The relative stagnation in the rest of the world preserves their international competitiveness and thus their economic and political pre-eminence.

Yet, prolonged stagnation in the rest of the world will diminish their own long-term welfare. In an integrated world economy no country is likely to utilise fully its long-term economic potential unless other countries do so also. Hence, from a purely economic point of view, the *status quo* option described in this section is against the long-term interest of all nations, with the exception of declining economies that have lost the capacity to adjust. It is for this reason that, although it may be employed with success over short periods, it will be unsustainable in the long term.

III

The second policy option open to structural deficit countries accepts the need for long-term changes and improvements. In doing this, however, it puts the burden of adjustment solely on these countries.

Expressed in purely macro-economic terms, the main problem of structural deficit countries lies in their inability to generate the growth of investment and exports needed to achieve full employment and higher productivity and income levels, even in the long term. This is caused by their inadequate propensity to save. Hence, to solve the problem, they have to increase the volume of domestic savings up to the level needed to achieve the required growth of investment and exports. The extent to which they have to do this will depend on two factors: the size of the initial gap in productivity and income levels between them and the surplus countries; and the rate at which they wish to eliminate the gap. The larger the initial difference or the more rapid the desired rate of development, the greater will have to be the increase in the propensity to save.

There is an important difference between this description of the underlying macro-economic problem and those (of the same problem) given in Chapters 3 and 5. There, it was assumed that the required savings could be achieved, in addition to increasing the domestic propensity to save, by borrowing on a long-term basis abroad. In contrast, the assumption behind the policy prescription in the previous paragraph is that structural deficit countries either cannot attract adequate foreign investments or deliberate refuse to rely on them.

The inability to raise long-term capital abroad is real enough and some of the most important reasons for this were given in Chapter 5. The unwillingness to do so is, of course, a matter of choice. The subsequent developments, however, will be identical, whatever the reason for the absence of foreign finance.

The apparent attractiveness of relying entirely on domestic savings in the long-term adjustment process is that it enables a country to choose its economic priorities and policies in accordance with its preferences, instead of having them imposed by foreign creditors. The danger with this approach is that the volume of investment and savings that has to be generated is normally so large, especially in the case of a developing country, that it will either restrict its economic development to a very low rate or impose immense social costs.

The success of this particular adjustment strategy depends critically on the ability to hold down the growth of real wages and consumption over a long period. Only in this way can the scarce domestic resources be released for new investment and exports, and the growth of imports be restrained.

The most obvious obstacle to achieving these objectives is that, in conditions of international cultural integration, people are likely to resist increasingly what will seem to them to be indefinite sacrifices, with little prospect that they will ever enjoy the benefits promised in the distant future.

Furthermore, the greater the sacrifices and the longer the period over which they have to be made the more centralised the economic and political life of the country will have to be. In other words, the reliance on the savings option is unlikely to be compatible with a decentralised, democratic, economic and political system.

The need for centralisation is bound to make it even more difficult for such a strategy to produce the desired results in the long term, despite the fact that it may lead to rapid economic advances early on. The more complex an economy becomes the more will its further progress require (for reasons described in Chapter 1) a good deal of liberalisation and decentralisation. The decision-making process becomes, quite simply, far too intricate for detailed decisions concerning resource allocation to be made at the centre.

There is a considerable risk, therefore, that the adjustment process may slow down significantly well before the country reaches the level of industrialisation enjoyed by the most advanced economies. If the system remains highly centralised, the deceleration will be caused by the inefficiency of the decision-making process. Alternatively, if the system is progressively decentralised it will become increasingly difficult to keep the growth of real wages and consumption low in order to generate the required level of savings. As a result, it will also become progressively more difficult to sustain the desired expansion of investment and output.

The problems of national acquiesence and economic management are serious enough. Yet even if they are overcome, there is no guarantee that the savings option will succeed in eliminating fundamental disequilibria in the long term. The ultimate result is not simply a matter of greater volumes of savings and investment. It will depend, among other things, also on a country's ability to acquire technical expertise as well as a wide range of goods and services from other, mainly more advanced, economies. Many of them cannot be produced at home. Moreover, even in some cases where this can be done, 'reinventing the wheel' will be a lengthy and costly process. It is much simpler and cheaper to purchase the products in question from those who already have the knowledge and the capacity to make them. However, in order to do this, a country must first be able to acquire foreign exchange by exporting to the rest of the world.

The ability to export will be of critical importance to countries of small or medium size for another reason. The size of their domestic markets is such that it is impossible for many of their industries to achieve optimum levels of production without access to foreign markets. This is not always easy. The ability to export depends on the economic policies of the countries in which the markets are located as well as on the exporters' own international competitiveness. Whatever the competitiveness, access to foreign markets may be limited because of the commercial and other policies pursued by the importing countries.

This obstacle, formidable though it is, is not the only one that firms from structural deficit countries have to overcome in order to survive and grow. A country which is successful in pursuing the savings option may ease its external problems by reducing its marginal propensity to import. However, so long as it remains open and integrated into the world economy, there is no guarantee that it will also be successful in channelling its greater volume of savings into investment projects which will enable it to adjust its productive capacity to the existing and new patterns of demand, either at home or abroad. Whatever the volume of investment, new firms and industries may not be able to survive under the competitive onslaught from the long-established foreign firms, especially transnationals. The more important economies of scale are in an activity, the more serious this problem is likely to be.

For all these reasons, the savings option is virtually impossible to sustain in the long term on its own.

IV

A country which is relying entirely on the savings option is expected to solve the problem of external disequilibrium without any change in its commercial policy. It makes no effort to insulate its economy from foreign competition – even during that phase of adjustment when its new firms and industries are trying to achieve the level of efficiency which will enable them to compete on equal terms with large, long-established foreign enterprises.

This deficiency can be overcome, at least in theory, by another policy option available to structural deficit countries: that of exchange rate depreciation. It tries to combine the main objective of the savings option (adjustment generated by greater domestic savings and investment) with restrictions on imports, and export subsidies.

The Articles of Agreement which in 1944 established the International Monetary Fund prescribed this particular policy option as the most appropriate remedy for eliminating 'fundamental disequilibrium', a belief which is still fairly widely held.[3] It is worth examining a little more closely, therefore, what exactly it is that exchange rate depreciation is expected to achieve, and why it has failed so consistently to fulfil expectations.

In theory, exchange rate depreciation (a fall in the price of one currency relative to others) leads to a reconciliation of internal and external balances through four important and interconnected routes.[4] (It is assumed in each case that all other things remain equal.)

First, it is a powerful protective device. It provides a subsidy to *all* exports and, at the same time, imposes a tax on *all* imports. Consequently, the rate of growth of exports accelerates while that of import falls, leading to an improvement on the current balance of payments.

Second, the long-term improvement in external balances takes place because the protection secured by depreciation ensures that profits and wages of those producing goods and services traded internationally improve relative to those earned in the sectors which supply only the domestic market. It is this change in relative incomes which encourages a reallocation, or 'switching', of resources from 'non-tradeable' to 'tradeable' sectors. That is, the long-term promise of higher earnings will lead to a movement of capital and labour into those activities which produce exports and import substitutes.

Third, the 'switching' is made possible also by a shift in income distribution from wages to profits (it does not matter in this context whether they are earned by private enterprises or by the state), caused by increases in export prices in domestic currency. As it is assumed that profit earners save a much higher proportion of their income than wage earners, the result is an increase in the propensity to save. The increase leads to a more rapid growth of new investments embodying the latest technical inventions and innovations. In the long-term, these changes will ensure that a country's productive potential becomes adjusted to the growth and patterns of international and domestic demand.

Finally, it is a major ingredient of the depreciation strategy that it depresses the growth of real wages, as a result of increases in import prices which are not offset by similar increases in nominal wages. This happens irrespective of whether wage earners continue to buy imports (because import prices are now higher) or switch to domestic products (which were more expensive than imports before depreciation otherwise wage earners would not have demanded imports). The subsequent reduction in the growth of consumer expenditure relative to those on investment and exports will adjust the external imbalance in the long term in two ways: it will reduce the growth of imports and, at the same time, accelerate the growth of exports by releasing productive resources for that purpose.

That is the essence of the argument for exchange rate depreciation.[5] One of the reasons why so many economists have found it attractive is that the whole process appears to be 'automatic'. It does not create any administrative problems and costs. Employed as an adjustment policy, however, it runs into a number of serious difficulties, which is why there is not a single industrial or semi-industrial country which has achieved its present status by relying entirely – or even mainly – on this course of action. The reason for this lies in the underlying assumptions on which the case for exchange rate depreciation rests.

First, it is assumed that all economies are normally in fundamental equilibrium. The disequilibrium, when it appears, is confined therefore to an isolated case and the whole problem can be treated, simply, as one of partial disequilibrium. It is hardly necessary to point out that such an assumption bears no resemblance to the current state of the world economy, when even most industrial countries find it impossible to reconcile their internal and external balances.[6]

Second, an important assumption in the whole argument is that the isolated example of fundamental disequilibrium refers, in fact, to a small country. Its exchange rate change will have no effect on the rest of the world, which can safely ignore it. But what happens if, instead, the country is large enough for its actions to affect other nations adversely, so that they retaliate by devaluing their currencies? The most likely outcome in this case will be either a return to the original position, with the depreciating country still unable to reconcile its internal and external balances, or a series of 'beggar-my-neighbour' depreciations. A similar effect can also be produced if a large number of 'small' countries let their exchange rates depreciate at the same time.[7] Other things remaining equal, in a world in which structural problems are widespread, depreciations by large countries *and* depreciations by a large number of smaller countries are likely to be so common that the small country assumption is totally inappropriate. Not surprisingly, the 1930s and the 1970s provide numerous examples of competitive exchange rate devaluations and depreciations.

Third, it is implicit in the argument for depreciation that there is relatively little international specialisation. The success of this particular policy demands that exchange rate depreciation does *not* give rise to significant increases in costs and prices – offsetting in this way most, or even all, of its beneficial effects. This is possible only if imports account for a small proportion of a country's total expenditure. The evidence in Part I shows that this is true now of very few countries. Consequently, once the increases in costs and prices have worked their way through the system, the expected increases in exports, reductions in imports and resource 'switching' will almost certainly be far too small and short-lived to correct the problem of a fundamental disequilibrium.

Fourth, for similar reasons, one of the key assumptions in the case for depreciation is that wage earners are either ignorant or indifferent to what happens to their real incomes. That is, they either suffer from 'money illusion' (confusing nominal with real increases in wages), or they are simply in no position to do anything about reductions in their standard of living. Again, the experience of so many countries since the early 1970s shows the ineffectiveness of any policy option based on such an assumption. Even if wage increases do not erode completely the expected advantages of exchange rate depreciation, the inflationary spiral to which they and prices give rise will go a long way – over a fairly short period of time – towards achieving such an outcome.[8]

Fifth, the absence of serious inflationary effects implied in the analysis also requires very high supply elasticities both in the depreciating country and abroad. Unfortunately, the fact that there is a good deal of unemployment in a structural deficit country does not necessarily mean that the supply of 'tradeables' can be increased easily. Excess capacity in the stagecoach industry is of little use when everyone wants to build railways! Moreover, changes in international trade flows may take some time to materialise even in the absence of such obvious maladjustments. Long-standing contracts with domestic and foreign customers and suppliers cannot be changed overnight. In addition, transnational enterprises will have to be convinced that exchange rate changes have altered the relative profitability of different markets permanently before they make significant changes in the sourcing of their activities and, thus, the pattern of their trade. Not surprisingly, short-term price elasticities of intra-firm trade tend to be very low.[9] The short-term supply rigidities provide another reason, therefore, why a fall in the exchange rate may generate serious inflationary pressures, making depreciation an ineffective policy instrument both in the short[10] and the long term.

Finally, the argument for using exchange rates to correct fundamental disequilibria completely ignores international financial integration and, consequently, the interaction between exchange rates and international capital movements. If those, such as transnationals, holding a portfolio of foreign currencies are absolutely certain that the existing policies and parities will not change, short-term capital flows will reflect nothing more than changes in the volume and pattern of international transactions. However, once exchange rates start to be used as a means for correcting macro-economic imbalances, international capital movements will be increasingly undertaken for precautionary and speculative reasons. Portfolio managers will react quickly now[11] not only to the actual but also to the expected state of a country's external balance.[12] Its expected ability – relative to other countries – to maintain an internal balance may have a similar effect. Consequently, expectations of exchange rate changes will, other things remaining equal, sooner or later bring them about.

However, even this may not stem the tide of capital flows if the 'markets' form the view that the changes have been 'inadequate'. It is, after all, impossible to determine with any degree of precision what an 'equilibrium' exchange rate is. This means that if, as at present, the degree of international integration is high and many countries are experiencing structural disequilibria, it is impossible to achieve, let alone maintain an international consensus on what exchange rates should be. Governments will become unable, therefore, to peg the rates at any particular level. The widespread awareness of this will ensure that there are frequent and, usually, sizeable movements of short-term international capital – almost invariably in response to purely short-run considerations.[13] This additional and very important element of uncertainly will do little to encourage the long-term adjustments without which the problem of fundamental disequilibria cannot be solved.

For all these reasons, exchange rate depreciation cannot by itself provide a sustainable long-term strategy for reconciling internal and external balances. As emphasised earlier, its success depends critically on a rapid, sizeable and long-term redistribution of income. Given the preoccupation with real and relative incomes in modern societies – and the bargaining power that different economic agents gain with the division of labour – this is impossible to achieve without either a widespread consensus or coercion. But, if either of these two solutions is available, exchange rate depreciation is unnecessary; and if neither of them is possible it is futile! To make things worse, the growing realisation of this fact increases the volatility of international financial markets[14] – making a deliberate resort to depreciation little more than an act of political impotence.

V

Although it is in theory an extremely potent protective device, in practice exchange rate protection has proved to be of little value in insulating an economy from external developments, as experience since the early 1970s shows. More rapid increases in wages and prices in the depreciating economy will normally ensure that the exchange rate changes have hardly any effect on its income elasticity of demand for imports. Implicitly, this means also that they are unlikely to be effective in protecting 'infant' firms and industries in a country's 'tradeable' sectors.

Not surprisingly, in order to achieve these aims nation states have traditionally resorted to administrative protection: direct controls on either some ('selective') or all ('general') of their transactions with other countries.

As it has played such an important role in the commercial policy of nations and, consequently, the character of international economic relationships, the dynamics of administrative protection will be considered at some length in Part III. The present section will concentrate, instead, on the most important advantages and disadvantages of this particular policy option.

What happens now is that in order to sustain the rate of economic development consistent with the long-term growth of its productive potential, a structural deficit country will impose taxes (tariffs) or quantitative controls (quotas) on either some or most of its imports. Similar quantitative measures will be used also to restrict capital flows, mainly investment abroad. Hence, if successful, administrative protection will achieve its objective of shifting the balance of payments-growth curve to the right by a combination of factors. It will reduce the growth of 'inessential' imports and, in this way, make it possible to use scarce foreign exchange for imports vital to the country's long-term development. At the same time, by reducing imports it will slow down the rate of contraction of the declining sectors so that the resources released from them can be absorbed elsewhere without giving rise to serious social costs. Adjustment costs will be minimised further if barriers to trade attract foreign direct investments which increase the production of import substitutes as well as develop new exports. Finally, in a dynamic economy, import restrictions can enable the new 'tradeable' sectors to reach the size and efficiency levels which are necessary if they are to compete effectively on the international market.

The advantages of this course of action, compared with exchange rate protection, are obvious. The controls, especially if applied rigorously in a quantitative form, will reduce imports into the country which imposes them and in this way its external imbalance. They will also decrease the uncertainty about future developments in the market: if potential demand for the 'protected' goods is to be satisfied they have to be produced on the spot. This should stimulate the output of import substitutes.

Given the extent to which transnational enterprises control international production and trade, even this approach does not guarantee total success, because they can use their internal trading and transfer pricing to get around at least some of the controls. Nevertheless, there is little doubt that administrative protection can insulate at least the most vulnerable sectors of an economy from external developments and shocks.[15] In addition, by being selective it need not give rise to a rapid inflationary spiral. Depending on a country's ability to produce them, a whole range of vitally important imports can be exempted from the controls: food, raw materials, intermediate products and even the finished goods (such as capital equipment) needed for the structural adjustment. (Exchange rate protection, as already pointed out, imposes a uniform tax on all imports, irrespective of their importance for long-term adjustments.) For similar reasons, investments abroad intended to increase the supply of any of these products can be also exempted from exchange controls.

The dangers are also fairly obvious.[16] The effectiveness of administrative controls can easily provoke retaliation.[17] However, the extent of retaliation, if any, will depend on how widespread and restrictive such controls are, on the size of the country which imposes them, and on the general economic environment. The last is particularly important. Experience shows that countries are much more likely to retaliate against restrictions placed on their exports in periods of economic stagnation than when world trade is growing rapidly so that they can easily find alternative markets. Naturally, if a large number of countries impose protective measures the scope for exploiting economies of scale will be reduced considerably – lowering in this way the rate of growth of their productive potential. As a result, they will all incur long-term welfare losses.

A similar outcome can be achieved also if, by creating a captive market, protective measures encourage inefficiency. However, if this happens, it will reflect more an inherent lack of economic dynamism than the fact that there has been an increase in economic insularity. Truly dynamic, successful economies will in the long run want to exploit economies of scale through international specialisation; and in order to be able to do this they will have to offer access into their own markets to foreign firms. The long-term survival of administrative protection is incompatible with a genuinely dynamic economic environment.

Whatever the dynamism, however, administrative protection will involve certain costs and problems which do not arise in the case of exchange rate protection. Import and exchange controls need an administrative apparatus to enforce them. Moreover, measures will also have to be taken to avoid the risks of illegal trading, corruption and blackmarketeering to which these controls may give rise.[18]

Nevertheless, in the absence of viable policy alternatives, the balance of argument is still likely to swing in favour of administrative protection. The reason for this is quite simple: by partly insulating an economy in fundamental disequilibrium such protection will reduce the size of the problem, making the adjustment process much more manageable during its most difficult, early phases.

VI

All the policy options considered so far share an important characteristic: the whole adjustment process is assumed to be of no concern to anyone except the country which is experiencing fundamental disequilibrium. It is, therefore, up to that country to decide whether to continue with the *status quo* or whether to adjust. Equally, if it opts for adjustment, it is entirely a matter of its own preference whether to do so within an internationally open and integrated framework, or in varying degrees of economic isolation. Other countries enter into the argument only if the protection introduced by a country in disequilibrium affects their own economic objectives and policies to such an extent that they retaliate. There is no indication in any of these arguments that actions by other countries, notably those running persistent balance of payments surpluses, might affect significantly the choice of policy options by structural deficit countries.

Yet this last factor may be of critical importance in conditions of international openness and integration. According to the analysis in the preceding chapters, there are three ways in which the surplus countries are likely to have considerable influence on economic policies and developments in the rest of the world: through their growth rates, their commercial policy and their attitude to international factor movements.

Ceteris paribus, it is reasonable to assume that their economies will grow in the long term at the full employment, or potential, rates. It is equally reasonable to assume that, given their international competitiveness, they will pursue a liberal commercial policy in order to encourage other countries to reciprocate. (Structural surplus countries, as pointed out in earlier chapters, need an access to international markets.) Both these factors will help the adjustment process in deficit countries. However, the size of the latter's problems, especially in the case of developing countries, is such that they will need more than this in order to shift the balance of payments-growth curve sufficiently to the right to sustain the long-term growth of their productive potential. This is where international factor movements can make a significant difference.

For instance, in theory, the problem of fundamental disequilibrium could be eliminated by labour migration from deficit (*D*) to surplus (*S*) countries.

The basic assumption here is that if all barriers to labour mobility are removed people will move from *D* to *S* which (as a result of, say, technical improvements and changes in tastes) are enjoying a world-wide increase in demand for their products. To satisfy this growing demand, *S* will need to expand their productive capacity; and one way in which this can be done is to absorb *D*'s surplus labour.

Thus, international migration could in the long-term eliminate *D*'s unemployment problems and, in the process, also adjust their external balances. As the population was reduced, the rate of increase in their imports would fall while exports, produced by those who could be absorbed into the labour force, would remain unaffected. Hence, *D* would not be required to generate and sustain a major increase in the propensity to save in order to reconcile their internal and external balances. *S*, on the other hand, would employ their excess savings for the purpose of creating new productive capacity and new infrastructure in order to accommodate their growing population. Moreover, over time the migration would increase the relative scarcity of labour in *D*, and reduce it in *S*. The result would be a reduction in the difference between their productivity levels and, consequently, an equalisation of international incomes.

That is the theory. In practice, all sorts of problems crop up. Labour mobility is far from perfect even within existing nation states, as their regional disparities and problems show.[19] Specialisation inevitably increases labour heterogeneity. The skill mix of new industries may be quite different from that of old industries and it can take some time to correct the imbalance. In other words, *D*'s surplus labour force may lack the skills required in *S*. Cultural, social and linguistic differences present even more serious obstacles to labour mobility. Besides, the information available to potential entrants is never perfect, and as the distance between two or more countries increases it will be even less so. For all these reasons, emigrants may incur considerable costs, both economic and social.

There is a serious risk, therefore, that migration from *D* to *S* may consist predominantly of the most skilled and dynamic members of the labour force attracted to *S* by their much brighter long-term prospects. If this happens on a sufficiently large scale, the so-called 'brain drain', instead of reducing, will increase *D*'s adjustment problem.[20]

However, costs associated with mass migration are not confined to *D* alone. Uncontrolled, large-scale immigration may create serious unemployment problems in *S* until the immigrants are absorbed into the labour force. It could also increase sharply the demand for housing, schools, hospitals and other forms of infrastructure, giving rise to inflationary pressure as these investments compete with those required to expand productive capacity in the sectors responsible for exports. Even more seriously, large-scale immigration can add significantly in the long run to the social costs created by urban problems such as congestion, pollution, noise, crime and so on – problems which, as experience shows, are capable of very rapid, non-linear, increases.[21] Finally, even in the absence of such problems, the population in *S* will resent mass immigration if it is likely to threaten the expected improvements in its own employment and income prospects.

Consequently, while those with rare skills are still welcome in most countries, and a small influx of foreigners prepared to undertake low paid, 'dirty' jobs continues to be tolerated, various restrictions now impose serious limitations on the international labour mobility, especially from countries in which structural problems are particularly serious. International labour migration cannot be regarded, therefore, as a major, practical option for correcting fundamental disequilibria.

VII

There is, however, an important alternative. Instead of moving labour from *D* to *S*, the needed adjustments can be achieved by exports of long-term capital and technical knowledge from *S* to *D*. Of course, to produce the desired effect, this policy option requires *D* to be ready and able to undertake the necessary adjustments and *S* to be capable and willing to invest on a large scale abroad.[22] Providing that these conditions are met, and that the flows are sufficient to facilitate the adjustment process, no international migration of labour is required.[23] Capital inflows will enable *D* to expand and restructure their productive capacity in line with the growth and changing patterns of international and their own demand. In this way, the changes will make it possible for *D* to achieve fundamental equilibrium, a transformation which also benefits *S*.

To illustrate the process involved, suppose that *S* start to export long-term capital and technical expertise to *D*. This supplements the latter's savings and enables them to increase their investment in 'new' goods and services for which both their domestic and world demand are increasing rapidly. The result is an acceleration in the growth of productive capacity, employment and income. Moreover, faster growth will also increase *D*'s demand for *S*'s capital and consumer goods, as well as for their technical and managerial expertise. By increasing *D*'s productive capacity and the levels of specialisation and income, *S*'s capital exports will generate further growth in their own output, employment and income.

These developments will cause a deficit on *D*'s current balance of payments for some time. However, so long as this is offset by long-term capital inflows, their basic balances of payments will remain in balance. In time, as *D*'s productive potential is expanded and restructured, and their income and savings rise, their current balance of payments will improve, reducing the need for imports of long-term capital.[24] In fact, for reasons explained in Part I, their own exports of such capital will increase.[25] Eventually, some of them will become structural surplus countries and *net* exporters of long-term capital, taking over this role from some of the older surplus countries which will become net borrowers abroad.[26]

The end result of these changes is that both *D* and *S* are now in fundamental equilibrium,[27] but at much higher levels of efficiency and income than before; and it is *S*'s participation in *D*'s adjustment process that makes such an outcome possible.

All this is bound to take a long time, though the length will depend also on the size of the prevailing fundamental disequilibria and the speed with which the necessary adjustments are carried out. The adjustment process, after all, depends on the success with which a country achieves economic growth, and this tends to vary a good deal.

An important element in all this will be the ability of *D* to attract foreign investment, as there is nothing automatic about the changes described above. Declining economies in the process of regeneration and developing countries which have some natural resource in demand abroad will usually find it relatively easy to attract foreign private capital, not just in order to expand their productive capacity but also, in the latter case, to develop the infrastructure needed to facilitate the growth of exports. The countries which do not enjoy such advantages will have to rely on official borrowing abroad, usually undertaken directly, or at least underwritten, by their governments.[28] Foreign private investments will move into such countries only at a later stage, when the infrastructure has been developed sufficiently and the size of the domestic market increased to ensure a satisfactory rate of return.

VIII

Although each of the six policy options has been described in isolation, it is, of course, unlikely that any one of them will ever be applied on its own. The emphasis may shift from one option to another in the short to medium term according to the nature of the problem and the extent to which other alternatives are available.

No country can hope to eliminate fundamental disequilibria without a significant increase in its domestic propensity to save. Inflows of foreign investments can help narrow the gap between actual and potential growth rates. It is most unlikely, however, that they will close it completely over long periods. There may be times when a country will be forced to grow below its productive potential; and there will be periods, even during fixed exchange regimes, when a country's unanticipated imbalances are so frequent and large that it has no choice but to alter its exchange rate. Furthermore, although mass international migration of labour is now out of question, there is always some movement across national frontiers.

However, the two policy approaches which have traditionally played the most important role in eliminating fundamental disequilibria have been those involving a combination of international investments and administrative protection. Indeed, for reasons to be analysed in the chapters that follow, the size of international capital flows and international resource transfers appears to have a major influence on the character of commercial policies pursued during any particular period. The easier it is for structural deficit countries to reconcile their internal and external balances with the help of long-term capital inflows the less need they have to impose administrative controls on their trade.

There is, consequently, an important difference between the responsibilities and methods for solving short-term and long-term disequilibria. While in the former case the responsibility for correction lies mainly with the country in which the imbalance originates, in the latter a successful solution is virtually impossible without policy co-ordination between structural surplus and structural deficit countries. In other words, when the problems are structural the burden of adjustment has to be shared between the two groups. Developing countries, for instance, may have the will to transform their economies. But they will invariably lack the resources and knowledge to accomplish this. If they fail, the cost of failure will be felt ultimately in the surplus countries also. In an integrated world economy, no country can enjoy prosperity in isolation. In the long term, this will be manifested in a general loss of economic welfare. In the short term, persistent inability of developing and declining economies to reconcile their internal and external balances will destabilise the economies of the surplus countries also – as the former try continuously to accelerate their growth rates beyond the levels which they can sustain.

For all these reasons, the efficiency with which countries organise the flow of international finance and resources required for eliminating fundamental disequilibria is likely to have a profound influence on the nature and progress of the international economy and, in this way, on the long-term viability of an open international economic order. Part III examines the extent to which this proposition is supported by historical evidence.

Part III
Phases in International Economic Integration since the 1820s

The neglect of fundamental disequilibria in economic analysis is reflected in the long-drawn and largely superfluous argument concerning the optimum commercial policy. For two centuries an enormous amount of energy and ingenuity has been devoted to restating and elaborating something that, with one possible exception, no economist of note has ever questioned: that under certain *conditions free trade is beneficial to all countries. The result of this preoccupation with proving the obvious (given the underlying assumptions no other outcome is possible!) has been to ignore almost completely the much more pertinent question: what exactly are these conditions which increase global welfare and how are they to be achieved?*

Part III examines, therefore, the extent to which a combination of changes in national economic strength relative to other countries and in the efficiency of the international financial system have influenced national commercial policies and, in this way, the character and progress of international integration. The analysis makes it possible also to consider another extremely important question: why is it that international economic system tends to work smoothly in certain periods but not in others?

This particular topic has again become of considerable relevance for economic policy. The world economy seems in the early 1980s to have reached one of those phases in its development when the existing institutions and policy instruments appear to be increasingly inadequate for ensuring even a temporary reconciliation of national internal and external policy objectives. It was in rather similar circumstances that there was a strong revival of economic nationalism in the 1930s, as governments tried to deal with the mounting problems of economic stagnation and political instability by insulating their countries from external disturbances. Was this an isolated incident, or a pattern of behaviour likely to be repeated again and again under similar circumstances?

Part III provides a broad description of the way in which economic developments, ideas and policies have tended to interact over the last couple of centuries.

7 The Doctrine of Free Trade: Internationalism or Disguised Mercantilism?

I

In its normative sense, as a statement of a general principle, a goal towards which mankind should aim, the case for free trade –developed originally by Adam Smith and then much more fully by Ricardo at the beginning of the last century and J. S. Mill in the 1840s – has never been refuted.

Adam Smith's argument is simple, logically consistent and persuasive. The wealth of nations is not necessarily given. On the contrary, it can be increased through the division of labour and specialisation in a way which is beneficial to all. As this process depends on the size of the market, the scope for adding to the existing wealth can be expanded greatly by reducing barriers to trade between countries.

International trade assumes, therefore, an important role in the wealth-creating process. In a world in which human wants exceed the capacity of scarce productive resources to satisfy them, each nation should specialise in the production of those goods for which it is best suited and exchange them for the goods that can be produced more efficiently in other countries. Consequently, there is no *need* for international trade to be an instrument of economic warfare, with each nation trying to increase its share of a static wealth at the expense of the rest of the world. The international division of labour will make it possible for all countries to gain through trade.

Ricardo turned this basic idea into the principle of comparative advantage. Even if a country is superior in all lines of production it will still benefit from concentrating on those activities in which its comparative advantage is greatest. The implication is that even low productivity countries can engage in international exchange by specialising in those goods and services in which their absolute disadvantages are least pronounced. Hence, international specialisation and free trade will secure gains from trade for all nations.

Moreover, the benefits will be spread widely within countries. Producers benefit from free trade through its 'production effects', as specialisation improves efficiency, lowers costs and raises profits. At the same time, there are also important 'consumption effects'. A more liberal commercial policy widens consumers' choice by increasing the volume and variety of goods available to them. In addition, by encouraging competition, it will reduce prices and in this way raise the general standard of living.

With the possible exception of Carey, a nineteenth-century American writer, no economist of note seems to have questioned the normative aspect of the doctrine of free trade:[1] that the international division of labour is a desirable state of affairs, a goal towards which all countries ought to aim. Hence, protection has always been advocated as a temporary expedient, a policy which should be employed until a country is ready to participate on equal terms in international specialisation and trade. Friedrich List, probably the best known critic of the claim that free trade is universally beneficial, was quite explicit about this. In his view, protection is justified 'only until [a] manufacturing [country] is strong enough no longer to have any reason to fear foreign competition, and thenceforth only so far as may be necessary for protecting the inland manufacturing power in its very roots ...'[2] In fact, according to Schumpeter, it would be incorrect to accuse even the mercantilists of recommending protection as a permanent solution to the problems confronting their countries.[3]

II

Given the apparent consensus, why is it that a system of free international trade has remained something of an utopian ideal, as even Adam Smith believed that it would? 'To expect', he wrote, 'that the freedom of trade should ever be entirely restored in Great Britain, is as absurd as to expect that an Oceana or Utopia should ever be established in it. Not only the prejudices of the public, but what is much more unconquerable, the private interest of many individuals, irresistibly oppose it.'[4]

What is intriguing about this observation is not so much the inaccuracy of Smith's prediction (it was, after all, almost a century after his death that Britain pursued for a time a policy of free trade) as his failure to analyse the reasons for such strong antagonism to free trade on the part of private interests. If private individuals are rational in the pursuit of their self-interest, as Adam Smith believed them to be, why should they resist a change in policy which, according to his analysis, promises to bestow all sorts of benefits on them – producers and consumers alike?

To understand this, it is necessary to look a little more closely at a number of assumptions implicit in the doctrine of free trade; and at the attitude of the main protagonists in the debate to the most suitable policy to be adopted when these conditions are not met. The most interesting conclusion to emerge from the analysis in the sections that follow is that, contrary to widespread belief, there seems to be, once more, very little disagreement among the most influential economists in this area.

III

To begin with, it is assumed that the economies liberalising their trade are in *fundamental equilibrium*, enjoying *full employment*; and that trade liberalisation will do nothing to alter this position. The classical and neo-classical models of international trade simply ignore all those shocks and dynamic changes, described in Chapter 5, which give rise to the problem of reconciling internal and external balances. It is recognised that an abolition of import duties will make it necessary to reallocate capital and labour. But the required adjustment is expected to be small and, consequently, relatively easy to carry out.

What happens, however, if trade liberalisation results in high unemployment and a drastic reduction in domestic income? It is their concern with problems such as these that led the mercantilists to advocate protection.[5] This is, of course, a fact which all students of economics learn in their first year. What they do not learn is that both Smith and Ricardo thought that this was the right policy approach in the circumstances. They did not believe in permanent protection. (As already pointed out, according to Schumpeter the mercantilists did not do so either!) Instead, they advoated quite explicitly gradual trade liberalisation in this case, in order to allow the country to adjust.

Adam Smith recognises, for instance, the possibility that a country may develop behind high protective walls 'particular manufactures' on such a scale that they 'employ a great multitude of hands'.[6] He did not think that even in this instance a sudden abolition of trade barriers would create as serious unemployment problems as opponents of free trade believed – thanks to a high degree of labour mobility within the country.[7] None the less, his policy prescription in this instance is not fundamentally different from theirs: 'Humanity may in this case require that the freedom of trade should be restored only by slow gradations, and with a good deal of reserve and circumspection.'[8] The reason for this is that if 'those high duties and prohibitions [were] taken away all at once, cheaper foreign goods of the same kind might be poured so fast into the home market, as to deprive all at once many thousands of our people of their ordinary employment and means of subsistence'.[9]

Ricardo used a similar argument in order to warn against a sudden abolition of the Corn Laws. Such a step would lead to a rapid increase in imports which would depress 'our price ... till the fall of price is ruinous to the interests of farmers ... To obviate, as far as is practicable, this enormous evil, all undue protection to agriculture should be gradually withdrawn'.[10] 'Gradually' in this case meant, in his opinion, that the duty on British imports of corn should be reduced over a period of ten years.[11]

IV

The belief in the existence of an *international harmony of interests* is another important assumption behind the argument for free trade. This is possible only if there is a good deal of global social and cultural cohesion. The cohesion, in turn, ensures that, although politically independent, nation states will nevertheless share similar values and goals.

The disappearance of restrictions on international trade creates, therefore, a world in which individual countries are economically integrated to an extent which makes them realise that the prosperity of each is determined by the prosperity of all. As J. S. Mill put it,

> commerce first taught nations to see with good will the wealth and prosperity of one another. Before, the patriot, unless sufficiently advanced in culture to feel the world his country, wished all countries weak, poor, and ill-governed, but his own: he now sees in their wealth and progress a direct source of wealth and progress to his own country. It is commerce which is rapidly rendering war obsolete, by strengthening and multiplying the personal interests which are in natural opposition to it.[12]

Few, if any opponents of free trade as a policy option would disagree with such a sentiment. What concerns them, however, is that there seems to be little indication in practice of such a 'harmony of interests'. On the contrary, the fact that they share similar values and aspirations appears to produce constant conflicts of interest, as each nation tries to exploit a particular advantage at the expense of the rest of the world.[13] There is an obvious danger that under these conditions the economic weaknesses of the less successful countries will be exploited ruthlessly by the more advanced nations. This was a major worry of the mercantilists[14] and of List;[15] and, in a milder form, it was expressed by Keynes in the 1930s when he suggested that, in the political climate of the time, the cost of national self-sufficiency was worth bearing.[16]

In fact, there is no reason to believe that the most ardent advocates of the free trade doctrine would have reacted differently in the circumstances. For instance, Adam Smith approved strongly of the Navigation Acts – the purpose of which was to build up the English merchant navy, at considerable cost, in order to destroy Dutch commercial supremacy – as 'perhaps the wisest of all the commercial regulation of England' because 'defence is much more important than opulence'.[17] In justifying the Acts, he points out that when they were introduced 'though England and Holland were not actually at war, the most violent animosity subsisted between the two nations'.[18] Moreover, he was in favour of protecting those industries which were 'necessary for the defence of the country'.[19]

V

The assumption of equality of opportunity, ensured by *constant returns to scale and perfect competition*, is also of critical importance in the argument for free trade. It implies the absence of any kind of discrimination, so that there are no barrier to the free movement of goods and factors of production. It is clearly impossible, under these conditions, for any one producer to reap the benefits of large-scale production and, in this way, prevent new firms from entering a particular industry. The equality of opportunity offered by perfect competition, combined with the rational pursuit of self-interest by economic agents, will enable all countries to achieve an optimum allocation of their productive resources – especially if there are no barriers to international trade. In fact, even if the factors of production are for some reason immobile between countries, international specialisation under free trade will ensure widespread benefits by equalising international incomes (within the limits imposed by transportation costs).

Clearly, in a world in which there is perfect equality of opportunity and all factors of production are homogeneous, state regulations in favour of a particular form of labour or a particular firm are unnecessary. More than that, they are positively damaging because they will tilt the finely balanced distribution of economic power unfairly, for the benefit of a particular national or sectional interest. In other words, government 'interference' in production and trade would produce sub-optimal results and was, for this reason, unwelcome – a not unreasonable view at a time of authoritarian, inefficient and corrupt governments! The argument for free trade formed, therefore, an important part of the wider case for *laissez-faire*.

The problem with this argument is that the eighteenth-century ideals of liberty and equality which had inspired it are rarely realised in practice. They were certainly not realised in the days of Ricardo and Mill. 'The common characteristic [of economic and social policies in the nineteenth century] is the consistent readiness of interest groups to use the state for collectivistic ends.'[20] Even in Britain, 'laissez-faire was a political and economic myth ... a slogan or war cry employed by new forms of enterprise in their politico-economic war against the landed oligarchy.'[21]

Consequently, the adherence to the principle of *laissez-faire* does not necessarily imply political neutrality. In conditions in which the balance of economic power is unequally distributed, government inaction can be as beneficial to an established vested interest as its intervention may be to an aspiring one. Considerations of this kind have become particularly important since the second half of the nineteenth century, as modern industrial processes have made increasing returns to scale – both internal and external to a firm and industry – possible. This means that, other things remaining equal, the already established, large, firms and markets enjoy an important advantage over newcomers, in terms of costs and prices, making it virtually impossible for the latter to compete on equal terms.

There is obviously no guarantee, under these conditions, that world resources will be optimally allocated, whatever the trading regime; or that private and social benefits from trade liberalisation will be equal – as money costs and prices will not reflect now social opportunity costs. Firms in countries which industrialise earlier may gain important advantages even in those activities in which the countries have no comparative advantage. If they can use their market power to prevent firms from countries in which such advantages exist from entering these activities, free trade can easily lead to a greater misallocation of the world's productive resources than protection! The likelihood of such developments is particularly strong in conditions of continuous technical changes which often alter national comparative advantages.

As these problems had become apparent in his lifetime, it is not surprising that J. S. Mill was the first prominent exponent of the free trade doctrine to take them into account. 'The superiority of one country over another in a branch of production', he observed, 'often arises only from having begun sooner.'[22] This led him to the conclusion that a country would be justified in protecting a new, 'infant', industry, though not 'beyond the time necessary for a trial of what they [the domestic producers] are capable of accomplishing.'[23] This is, of course, exactly the kind of argument for protection which had been put forward before him by Hamilton[24] and List.[25]

Similar considerations also prompted Marshall to criticise the English classical economists for making 'a grave error of judgement' by failing to take into account 'the needs no less than the potentialities of backward countries, and especially of new countries'.[26] For instance, it would have been wrong, in his opinion, for the United States to continue specialising in primary production and import manufactures, because in doing this it would forego the benefits which arose from 'the law of increasing returns' associated with modern industrial processes.[27]

More recently, the concern expressed by List, Mill and Marshall, among others, has received important theoretical support from modern developments in the analysis of the 'second best' optimum. If the existence of various departures from the classical assumptions makes it impossible to achieve a Pareto-type optimum – that is, to make someone better off without making anyone else worse off – a unilateral adoption of free trade will reduce a country's welfare; and, under certain conditions, such an action may reduce also the welfare of the whole world.[28]

VI

The existence of *an efficient international financial system* is another important assumption behind the case for free trade. What this implies is that the growth and distribution of international finance are such that they promote improvements in both national and global employment and real incomes.

The attitude of classical and neo-classical economists to international finance was influenced by the fact that they took for granted: (a) that the self-adjusting properties of a perfectly competitive economy would ensure that its external imbalances were only of a short-term nature; (b) that the tendency to automatic correction of such imbalances would be reinforced by international flows of gold and silver (from the countries with excess demand and deficits to those experiencing demand deficiencies and surpluses) for reasons described in the eighteenth century by Hume;[29] and (c) that gold and silver would always be acceptable as instruments for settling international debts because, unlike any other commodity, they were influenced very little 'by any of the causes which produce fluctuations of value'.[30]

Clearly, in the absence of fundamental disequilibria, and with an efficient international financial system, it would be irrational – given the advantages that can be derived from the international division of labour – for a country to pursue autarkic policies.

Unfortunately, it is precisely the absence of such ideal conditions which, as will be shown later, gives rise to serious economic problems; and the inability to cope with such crises forces countries into economic isolation. For those countries which desperately need imports in order to feed their population and industrialise, which have a limited capacity to export, receiving no assistance from a world in which international capital and money markets are either rudimentary or breaking down, and in which international conflicts rather than a 'harmony of interests' prevail, the worry of a seventeenth century writer cannot be dismissed lightly: 'if both war and dearth should come together ... how should we do? Surely we should be in a very hard case, and much in danger of strangers'.[31]

In highly unstable economic and political conditions it is only natural for governments, as for individuals, to accumulate internationally liquid assets for precautionary reasons. A country building up its stock of foreign reserves, in a world in which there is very little international investment, has to obtain a surplus on its current balance of payments; and the only way to do this – unless it happens to earn structural surpluses or is prepared to tolerate high levels of unemployment – is to impose restrictions on imports of goods and services as well as on capital exports. This is, of course, precisely what happened during the sixteenth and seventeenth centuries, the heyday of mercantilism.[32] Observing a similar crisis and responses to it in the 1930s, Keynes had no difficulty in understanding the reasons behind the mercantilist approach to economic policy:

> in an economy subject to money contracts and customs more or less fixed over an appreciable period of time, where the quantity of the domestic circulation and the domestic interest rate are primarily determined by the balance of payments ... there is no orthodox means open to the authorities for countering unemployment at home except by struggling for an export surplus and an import of the monetary metal at the expense of their neighbours.[33]

As one would expect, the importance attached by mercantilists to a favourable balance of payments diminished with the development of banking to channel credits needed for growth and, especially, with advances made in the eighteenth and, even more so, the nineteenth century towards a multilateral system of international payments.[34]

VII

There is, finally, one extremely important requirement which has tended to be ignored by most economists: if a policy of free trade is to be adopted by a large number of independent, sovereign states *the gains* from it will *have to be fairly evenly distributed* – assuming, as the classical economists did, that all countries start with fairly similar efficiency and income levels.

This is essential for two reasons. First, even if all countries gain from trade, if some gain much more than others the gaps in their economic performance will open up over time, leading eventually to changes in policy. The 'losers' will simply judge free trade to be against their national interest and, consequently, impose restrictions on imports. In an integrated, dynamic and competitive economic system, it is the *relative* performance that determines the long-term well-being of the competing units, be they firms, industries, regions or countries. In the last case, the process by which a structural surplus economy is transformed into a declining one may be generated, as explained in Chapter 5, by relative rather than absolute stagnation. Second, for reasons analysed in Part I, the greatest scope for international division of labour and trade exists in those countries which have already achieved a highly advanced level of specialisation. Hence, while an (upward) equalisation of international efficiency and income levels will accelerate the process towards a more efficient use of world resources, a growing international disparity in these levels may easily put the whole process into reverse, even if commercial policies remain unchanged.

Although the distribution of gains has important implications for the whole doctrine of free trade, it was completely ignored by classical economists. It was sufficient for them to prove that all countries would gain from international specialisation and exchange. That was enough, in their opinion, to convince everyone that free trade was more advantageous than protection. They realised, of course, that perfect international mobility of capital and labour would equalise incomes in all countries. But they also took it for granted that cultural and institutional factors would create formidable obstacles to such mobility. That led them to the assumption that the factors of production were mobile within but *not* between countries.

The classical indifference to relative gains from trade was not as unreasonable as it may seem, given that in the eighteenth and for most of the nineteenth-century international differences in productivity and income levels were small, rates of growth were low and international trade accounted for only a small proportion of total output.[35] However, by the early twentieth century the possibility of unequal gains and their influence on the losers' commercial policies could not be ignored, especially after the experience in the second half of the nineteenth century (which is described in the chapter that follows).

Not surprisingly, the neo-classical model of international trade, developed in the first quarter of the twentieth century,[36] tried to dispose of this particular obstacle to a liberal trading regime by showing that international incomes could be equalised through trade even when factors of production were completely immobile between countries. The argument was that free trade would enable a country where capital was abundant and labour scarce to export capital intensive products and import labour intensive products; while a country in which capital was scarce and labour abundant would do exactly the opposite. In this way, trade would make the scarce factor abundant and the abundant factor scarce, leading to an equalisation of their marginal productivities and incomes in different countries.

There is, however, one important qualification which was made quite explicitly by both Heckscher and Ohlin: the equalisation applies only to the factors of production which are of the *same* quality in conditions in which the *same* techniques of production are used in different countries.

It requires little reflection to realise that this is likely to happen only in trade between countries which: (a) enjoy similar levels of industrialisation, efficiency and incomes; and (b) manage to maintain this parity in conditions of continuous changes. Countries in such a group will have broadly similar economic structures, their factors of production will be of broadly similar quality – which is why they will tend to use similar techniques of production.[37] For all these reasons, they will also enjoy broadly similar income levels.[38] This qualification is crucial because, as Heckscher pointed out, if differences in factor endowments were large 'trade alone could not level out' the existing differences in factor incomes. 'Just as it is certain that, under free exchange, the same technique leads to the same prices for the factors of production in all countries, so it is equally certain that differences in techniques lead to differences in factor prices'.[39]

Once this qualification is taken into account, it is clear that the conclusion which emerges from the Heckscher–Ohlin model is not fundamentally different from that reached by Myrdal,[40] one of the most persistent critics of the proposition that free trade would reduce rather than increase international disparities in income levels. Heckscher and Ohlin are describing a world in which inter-country differences in productivity and income levels are small and narrowing. Myrdal, on the other hand, is concerned with long-term changes in a world in which these differences are not only large but growing.

Consequently, in the argument about income equalisation, as in the preceding arguments, the difference of opinion concerning the suitability of free trade as a policy option arises not out of a disagreement about the conclusions which stem from the same premises, but from fundamental differences in the premises themselves.

VIII

The intriguing question now is this: why have some of the most eminent and influential economists in history failed to emphasise in their analysis something of which they were perfectly aware: that different economic circumstances will almost invariably require different policy approaches? What purpose is served by the interminable debate concerning the relative merits of free trade and protection when there has been apparently little disagreement among economists that, as a policy prescription, free trade is universally beneficial and applicable only if a number of important conditions are satisfied?

To understand this, it is important to bear in mind that economists tend to consider the dominant policy issues of their time mainly in the light of the effect that a particular course of action is likely to have on the problems confronting their own country. After all, these are the problems which they understand best – a fact which will be reflected in their theoretical generalisations. Hence, there will inevitably tend to be a divergence of views among economists living and working under significantly different conditions. Moreover, the views of an influential economist are likely to alter if the circumstances of his country change noticeably during his lifetime – otherwise, he will, of course, cease to be influential!

Consequently, like the protectionist List, British classical economists advocated free trade for the simple reason that it was good for Britain at the time, and not out of their concern for the universal good. Contrary to the belief which has persisted, their views were far from cosmopolitan. According to Robbins,

> there is little evidence that they often went beyond the test of national advantage as a criterion of policy, still less that they were prepared to contemplate the dissolution of national bonds. If you examine the ground on which they recommend free trade, you will find that it is always in terms of a more productive use of *national* resources ... I find no trace anywhere in their writings of the vague cosmopolitanism with which they are often credited by continental writers ... [Consequently], we get our picture wrong if we suppose that the English Classical Economists would have recommended, because it was good for the world at large, a measure which they thought would be harmful to their own community.[41]

Adam Smith set an important precedent in this respect when he declared that: 'the great object of the political economy of every country is to increase the riches and power of that country'.[42] No matter how eminent they maybe, economists who forget this are likely to incur the great displeasure of their fellow citizens, as Marshall observed when he came, very discreetly, to the defence of John Stuart Mill.

Marshall appears to have sympathised with foreign economists, especially the Germans, for being 'irritated ... by what they ... regarded as the insular narrowness and self-confidence of the Ricardian school'.[43] He himself went so far as to accuse the nineteenth-century English classical economists of dogmatism and narrow-mindedness for refusing to admit that other countries had problems which were different from those of Britain. 'It was clearly to the interest of England', he wrote, 'that her manufactures should be admitted free by other countries: therefore any Englishman who attempted to point out that there was some force in some of the arguments which were adduced in favour of protection in other countries, was denounced as unpatriotic.'[44] Even the great John Stuart Mill was not spared. When he 'ventured to tell the English people that some arguments for protection in new countries were scientifically valid, his friends spoke of it in anger ... as his one sad departure from the sound principles of economic rectitude.'[45] Perhaps this is the reason why Marshall tucked all these critical observations in the appendices which few people usually bother to read!

IX

Nothing, probably, illustrates better the extent to which the relative economic strength of a country shapes the attitudes of its leading economists than the views on international factor movements expressed by five great British practitioners of the 'dismal science'. This is a useful test of economic cosmopolitanism because in the presence of perfect competition – assumed by all these economists – free movements of capital and labour between countries would equalise in the long run international levels of productivity and factor incomes. Adam Smith was familiar with this proposition, as indeed have been all his successors. But this has produced, as will be shown below, a far from uniform attitude to international factor movements.[46]

It was towards the end of Adam Smith's (1723–90) life that Britain embarked on what was to become known as the Industrial Revolution. Not surprisingly, the eighteenth-century British manufacturers were reluctant to share their knowledge and capital equipment with foreigners, fearing that in the long run this would lead to the loss of their markets. The hostility persisted well into the last century. Under such pressure, British governments prohibited emigration of skilled labour until the 1820s, and exports of the capital equipment which could be used to establish abroad industries that might rival British manufactures until the 1840s.[47]

Smith objected strongly to the restrictions placed on the emigration of skilled labour. This was 'contrary to the boasted liberty of the subject of which we affect to be so jealous'.[48] At the same time, his attitude to capital exports was much more ambiguous. He believed 'that the capital of the manufacturer should reside within the country'. In this way it 'puts into motion a greater quantity of productive labour, and adds a greater value to the annual produce of the land and the labour of the society'.[49] Moreover, it appears to have been his view that if capital was scarce it should be employed first in agriculture (where it was most productive), then in manufacturing and, finally, in trade where it had 'the least effect' on employment and output.[50] There was, however, an important exception here (advocated, incidentally, also by the mercantilists): a country could benefit from investing abroad in order to secure an adequate supply of raw materials.[51]

David Ricardo (1772–1823) saw Britain complete the first phase of its industrialisation, while at the same time fighting a series of costly wars. Capital was too scarce to be exported, even though this would obviously have increased the rate of return available to its owners. His attitude to capital exports was much more clear-cut, therefore, than that of Smith.

He appears, in fact, to have been pleased that the risks involved in operating in an unfamiliar environment as well as the reluctance of 'every man ... to quit the country of his birth and connections ... [will] check the emigration of capital. These feelings, *which I should be sorry to see weakened*, induce most men of property to be satisfied with a low rate of profit in their own country, rather than to seek a more advantageous employment for their wealth in foreign nations'.[52] His attitude to capital exports was expressed even more directly on another occasion:

> It can never be allowed that the migration of capital can be beneficial to a state. A loss of capital may immediately change an increasing state to a stationary state. A nation is only advancing whilst it accumulates capital. Great Britain is far distant from the point where capital can no longer be advantageously accumulated. I do not mean to deny that individual capitalists will be benefited by emigration in many cases, – but England even if she received the revenues from the capital employed in other countries would be a real sufferer.[53]

Britain's position changed dramatically, however, over the next fifty years, a transformation observed closely by John Stuart Mill (1806–73).

At the time of his death Britain was at the peak of its economic supremacy. It accounted for a large proportion of the world's industrial production and trade, and was also by far the largest exporter of capital. Most of the capital went, like British emigrants, to the newly colonised countries in North and South America and Oceania. The countries supplied Britain with cheap foodstuffs and raw materials and at the same time provided an important market for its manufactured goods.

It would have been surprising, in the circumstances, if Mill had expressed any doubts about the beneficial effects of international factor movements, at least so far as his own country was concerned. On the contrary, he was convinced that

> the perpetual overflow of capital into colonies or foreign countries ... [had] been for many years one of the principal causes by which the decline of profits in England [was] arrested ... It is to the emigration of English capital that we have chiefly to look for keeping up a supply of cheap food and cheap materials of clothing, proportional to the increase of our population; thus enabling an increasing capital to find employment in the country, without reduction of profit, in producing manufactured articles with which to pay for this supply of raw produce. Thus, the exportation of capital is an agent of great efficacy in extending the field of employment for that which remains: and it may be said truly that, up to a certain point, the more capital we send away, the more we shall possess and be able to retain at home.[54]

Labour emigration had, in his view, a similar effect in improving 'considerably' the standard of living of 'every labourer'.[55]

Although nobody could suspect it at the time, the decade in which Mill died represents an important watershed in Britain's economic fortunes. It was at about this time that the relative decline – so apparent now – set in, as the country failed to absorb important technical and organisational changes taking place in the last quarter of the nineteenth century and employed so effectively by the Americans and the Germans. Their new, high value added, products were already at the turn of the century challenging Britain's supremacy in international markets, as Marshall pointed out in a memorandum written in 1903: 'England rightly exports an ever-increasing proportion of machinery and implements which are of small bulk relative to their value ... but her imports of electrical plant and aniline dyes [that is, technically advanced products] show that her hold on leadership is not secure'.[56] Subsequent developments simply accelerated these trends and world industrial leadership soon passed from Britain to the United States.

Hence, when towards the end of his long life, Marshall (1842–1924) came to write about trade and industry his views were noticeably more nationalistic and defensive than those of Mill. 'A country's foreign trade', he wrote, 'is something more than a number of dealings between individuals at home and abroad; it is the outcome of the relations in which the industries that belong to her, that are part of her life, and embody much of her character, stand to the industries of other countries'.[57] This being the case, it was important that each country should look after its interests by developing, first of all, its own industries:

> it is becoming clear that this [Britain] and every other western country can now afford to make increased sacrifices of material wealth for the purpose of raising the quality of life throughout her population. A time may come when such matters will be treated as of cosmopolitan rather than national obligation: but that time is not in sight. For the practical purposes of the present and the coming generation, each country must, in the main, dispose of her own resources, and bear her own burdens.[58]

Finally, even in the early 1920s, when he was still 'a convinced Free Trader',[59] highly critical of those who suggested that protection might solve the problem of unemployment, Keynes (1883–1946) argued strongly against British exports of capital because

> there are many reasons for thinking that our present rate of foreign investment is excessive and undesirable. We are lending too cheaply resources which we can ill spare. Our traditional, conventional attitude towards foreign investment demands reconsideration ... Some foreign investments lead directly to the placing of orders in this country which would not be so placed otherwise. Whether or not they are desirable on general grounds, such investments do no harm to employment. As a rule, however, this is not the case. A foreign loan does not ... automatically create a corresponding flow of exports.[60]

Consequently, instead of being exported, he wanted the savings generated within the country to be used to create productive capacity and employment at home.

In fact, less than a decade later, Keynes was to go even further in his attack on 'traditional, conventional' British attitudes. With the country's economic stagnation deepening and unemployment rising rapidly, and with the whole international environment resembling increasingly the world of the seventeenth century which gave rise to the mercantilist concerns, Keynes shocked his contemporaries in 1931 by becoming the first eminent British economist to advocate openly protection.[61] A few years later he was to write approvingly of the mercantilist remedies – protection and direct state involvement in national economic management – recognising that 'mercantilist' problems (stagnation, unemployment, breakdown of the international financial system, threats of war) will tend to lead, regretably but inevitably, to mercantilist solutions.[62]

X

Three important conclusions emerge from this rather brief survey of the arguments surrounding the doctrine of free trade.

First, so long as the critical conditions on which the case for free trade rests are not satisfied completely it is impossible to generalise about the most 'appropriate' long-term commercial policy for any one country, let alone the world as a whole. In a dynamic international economy, the exact mixture of trade liberalisation and restrictions is likely to change, like everything else, according to changes in the underlying conditions affecting either individual countries or all of them collectively. When two diametrically opposed policy prescriptions, such as free trade and protection, continue to enjoy popular appeal for so long the unavoidable conclusion is that neither provides a satisfactory guide to policy, applicable at all times and places.

Second, those who passionately advocate free trade are not necessarily cosmopolitan in their outlook, with a deep concern for the welfare of the whole world. In conditions of significant differences in international efficiency and income levels, free trade can be used as effectively as protection to increase the wealth and power of a narrow national, or sectional, interest – at the expense of other nations, or sections of a community. As Sideri shows in his analysis of specialisation and trade between Britain and Portugal – the example actually used by Ricardo to demonstrate the gains that accrue to all concerned from the international division of labour – that trade was definitely to the long-term disadvantage of the Portuguese.[63] Hence, to advocate that countries at significantly different levels of development should pursue identical commercial policies is really tantamount to arguing for a further strengthening and continuation of the existing power relationships in the world economy, even when these may be patently sub-optimal from a global point of view. It is difficult to think of a more effective method for achieving a complete breakdown of an open, internationally integrated economic system!

Finally, the theoretical argument in favour of free trade has never been challenged. What has been questioned continuously is the extent to which the argument is relevant for policy purposes if the required underlying conditions are not met – again something about which, as emphasised earlier, there seems to have been little disagreement among the main protagonists in the debate. Economics would, therefore, have made, a far more important contribution towards creating a genuine 'harmony of international interests' had it concentrated on finding the most effective ways of bringing about the conditions required for the long-term survival and success of an integrated world economy, instead of restating *ad infinitum* the obvious: that a regime of free trade will maximise world welfare if these conditions are satisfied.

A major obstacle to such a genuinely internationalist approach to economic policy has been the tendency even among the great economists to generalise on the basis of their own country's specific experience and interests. There is, of course, nothing dishonourable about this, especially if the writers make no attempt to hide their fundamentally nationalistic approach to the major economic problems of the day. But this rather natural bias in the discussion of policy issues does mean that the origin and nature of economic ideas should be examined much more carefully before they are embraced by the profession as being universally relevant and applicable. As Schumpeter concluded his survey of the evolution of the doctrine of free trade: 'If Smith and his followers had refined and developed the "mercantilist" propositions instead of throwing them away, a much truer and much richer theory of international economic relations could have been developed by 1848 – one that could not have been compromised by one set of people and treated with contempt by another'.[64]

The most obvious way of avoiding an undesirable outcome is to ensure that the conditions which give rise to it never reach such proportions that the outcome becomes inevitable. The resilience of mercantilist attitudes and policies, as an economic historian has pointed out, 'must be sought in the disturbing tendency of international trade to revert to conditions which in some ways resemble those of the seventeenth rather than those of the nineteenth century.'[65]

8 Changes in International Competitiveness and National Commercial Policies

I

Arguments concerning the most desirable form of commercial policy have dominated discussions of international economic relationships for so long that it is easy to exaggerate both the contribution of these policies to the overall economic performance of individual countries, and the influence of economists on national commercial policies.

Trade policy, after all, is only one of a wide range of policy instruments employed by a country in the process of its economic development. The eventual success of a country's growth strategy will depend on the combined effectiveness of *all* these instruments. This is why similar commercial policies can often be associated with quite different economic outcomes.

Nevertheless, given the passion and disagreements which the doctrine of free trade has generated over the last two centuries, there has been a tendency to overlook the rather obvious fact that it is a country's economic performance relative to other countries that is likely to determine its commercial policy, rather than the other way round. Few ideas in economics are likely to be applied in practice – and even fewer will succeed – unless they reflect the interests and aspirations of some powerful economic group; and what course of action such a group believes to be in its interest will depend largely on its relative economic strength. Keynes' assertion that 'the power of vested interests is vastly exaggerated compared with the gradual encroachment of ideas'[1] is widely off the mark. On the contrary, as J. S. Mill observed: 'A good cause seldom triumphs unless someone's interest is bound up with it.'[2]

II

Nothing illustrates this better, probably, than the time that it took for

Adam Smith's and List's ideas to be applied in their own countries, and the way in which this was done.

There was a growing undercurrent of opinion in favour of freer trade in the eighteenth century well before the Physiocrats and Adam Smith produced coherent arguments in its favour.[3] Hence, it was not so much his brilliant exposition of a completely novel idea that made Smith influential, as the fact that he articulated convincingly something that the rising commercial and industrial classes desired because it was in their interest. Moreover, what these classes were clamouring for was not simply a greater freedom to trade with other nations. In many cases, considerable obstacles to trade existed at the time of Smith and Ricardo even within individual countries. Hence, there was clearly a strong case for arguing that the wealth of a country could be increased significantly through greater domestic specialisation and exchange.

For instance, although economic union between England and Scotland was established at the beginning of the eighteenth century, the customs union between England and Ireland was not completed until 1826. In the United States, individual states were not barred from levying separate duties on exports and imports until the 1780s. Internal barriers to trade within France (there were over 5000 internal tolls at the end of the seventeenth century) continued to be a serious obstacle to the country's economic integration until they were abolished by the Revolutionary Government in 1789–90. Prussia did not eliminate internal tariffs until 1818, and the customs union among German states came into effect in the 1830s. A customs union among Italian states was not established until after unification in the 1860s. And the Swiss cantons could not agree on economic union until 1848.[4]

Most of these changes followed political unification of the countries concerned. As nothing comparable was happening internationally, liberalisation of external trade usually had to wait either for a sudden change in a country's economic conditions; or for developments which eventually convinced its powerful interests that lower, even zero, barriers to trade would be to their advantage.

The repeal of the British Corn Laws in 1846 came seventy years after the publication of *The Wealth of Nations*. This major change of policy was brought about not by 'the gradual encroachment' of Adam Smith's ideas but because of the country's growing inability to feed its population, culminating in the diastrous Irish famines of the 1840s.[5] It took another thirty years, that is almost a century after Adam Smith's eloquent plea for freer trade, before Gladstone completed the liberalisation of Britain's foreign trade. By this time the country had become the world's dominant industrial power, with only a relatively small proportion of its population still engaged in agriculture.

The success of List's protectionist ideas, to take another example, owed more to economic conditions in the second half of the nineteenth century than to the brilliance of his analysis of the needs of a developing country. During most of his life (List died in 1846) Prussian customs duties appear to have been low even by British standards.[6] Powerful agricultural interests wanted to encourage imports of British manufactured goods 'in order to sell Britain more grain'.[7] When the Germans turned in earnest to protection in the last quarter of the nineteenth century the conversion owed little to List and a good deal to the impact which the flood of cheap agricultural products from America and Russia had on the livelihood of those engaged in what was still a large and important sector of the German economy: agriculture. Consequently, although the Germans increased the level of protection offered to their 'infant' industries, the duties on agricultural products were even higher – a rather different ranking of priorities from that which List had advocated.[8]

What these two examples show is that one should not overestimate the power of economic ideas to influence a country's policy significantly, irrespective of economic conditions. Economists do no more than provide a set of analytical tools and policy prescriptions. Which of the prescriptions will be used by policy makers at any particular time, or over any particular period, will depend on the type of problems confronting them.

Even the known ideological predilections of those in power are not necessarily a reliable guide to how they are likely to react in a major crisis. In Britain, it was a Tory Government dominated by landowners which had no alternative but to repeal the Corn Laws in the 1840s, despite the fact that the measure was against the landowners' interests. Almost a century later, in the early 1930s, the National Government abandoned the gold standard, devalued sterling and turned to protection. Yet most members of the Government were convinced Free Traders, and many of them had been responsible for the reintroduction of the gold standard in 1925 at an unrealistically high exchange rate.

In both cases, the changes were prompted by a clear recognition that to ignore the highly adverse effects of existing policies on the majority of the population was to risk the collapse of the existing socio-political institutions, something that those in power are expected to prevent rather than promote with their policies.[9]

III

The two examples in the preceding section describe, among other things, the reasons behind specific changes in the character of commercial policies pursued in the nineteenth century by Britain and Germany. Are these examples exceptional? If not, what is it exactly that determines long-term changes in a country's commercial policy?

There are a number of possible explanations. One of these, put forward by Bastiat, relates the character of a country's commercial policy to changes in its form of government. Thus, according to him, free trade is caused by the spread of democracy.[10] This appears to have been the British experience in the nineteenth century. However, as subsequent developments in Britain and elsewhere have demonstrated, democracy can as easily turn a country towards protection.

More recently, Helleiner has described differences in the various nineteenth century commercial policies in rather different terms.[11] Free trade was in the interest of the industrial and commercial middle class in Britain and of the landed aristocracy on the Continent. On the other hand, middle-class manufacturers on the Continent and the landed aristocracy in Britain argued for protection.

The reasons behind these differences are not difficult to explain. The groups which were so competitive internationally that they stood to gain significantly from free trade (British manufacturers and Continental landowners) were in favour of trade liberalisation, while those who were in a relatively weak competitive position (British landowners and continental manufacturers) demanded protection. The relative strength of these groups in the end determined their country's commercial policy.

Pincus, in his study of United States commercial policy in the 1820s, treats tariffs as a collective good. Their existence in representive democracies is caused by the failure of certain interest groups to obtain rents. (In contrast, the groups which can earn rents in conditions of free trade will not press for protection.) This does not mean, however, that all activities affected adversely by imports will succeed in persuading the government to impose tariffs. The chance of success will depend on the extent to which the industries involved are controlled by a relatively small number of powerful producers. In other words, the more diffuse the interests the smaller the likelihood of success.[12]

What these and similar theories have in common is that they give a fairly accurate description of the reason behind the commercial policies actually implemented by a particular country (Britain, the United

States) or a continent (Europe) during certain periods. But these policies do not remain unchanged in the long run. It is clear from available evidence that individual countries often pursue liberal trading policies during certain periods in their history and erect all sorts of barriers in others. Why?

Ignoring the protection of strategically important industries, or barriers to trade imposed in retaliation against similar policies introduced abroad (both of which are fairly common at all levels of development), there are a number of reasons why countries tend to resort to administrative protection more in certain phases of their industrialisation than in others. The most important are: (a) to raise government revenue, usually because the administrative apparatus is not sufficiently advanced to impose effectively other forms of taxation; (b) to protect new, rapidly growing industries in the early stages of their development – especially those in which economies of scale are important; (c) to enable the (declining) industries in which a country has ceased to be competitive internationally to adjust without imposing too great a social cost on the rest of the community; and (d) to economise in the use of the scarce foreign currency reserves by reducing 'unnecessary' imports, particularly of those products which have high income elasticities of demand.

It is clear from this list that, *ceteris paribus*, similar commercial policies may be associated with different rates of growth, even if one ignores the fact that, as already pointed out, trade policy is only one of a wide range of policies implemented by a country in the course of its economic development. A slow growing economy is likely to rely heavily on administrative protection for the third and fourth reasons. But a rapidly growing economy may be equally protectionist for the second and fourth reasons. As a result, the relationship between a country's rate of economic growth and its level of protection will tend to be weak, which is precisely what Capie discovered in his analysis of the experience of a number of countries before 1914.[13]

The relationship will be particularly weak if one ignores comparative levels of development. For it requires little reflection to realise that the higher the level of development that a country reaches relative to the rest of the world the less need will it have to rely on barriers to trade for any of the reasons listed above. Its fiscal system will become sufficiently advanced for the government to raise the required revenue by methods other than import controls; its new industries will become increasingly competitive internationally; and the structural adjustments that it has already achieved will ensure that declining industries account for a relatively small proportion of total output and employment. Moreover, technical improvements which take place in the course of these changes will reduce, by developing domestic substitutes, the proportion of imports for which domestic income elasticity of demand is high, raising at the same time also the proportion of exports for which the world income elasticity of demand is high. The result is an improvement not only in the country's long-term international competitiveness but also in its ability to expand economic activity in the short term without running into an unsustainable balance of payments deficit.

In other words, the achievement of a high level of economic development relative to the rest of the world diminishes the constraint which the availability of foreign exchange imposes on a country's economic policy by reducing the need to use the reserves for short-run stabilisation purposes. Eventually, the country may be in a position to maintain fundamental equilibrium with relatively few barriers to trade and capital exports. What is more, there will be a strong inducement at such an advanced stage of development to reduce these barriers. As explained earlier, if the country is to utilise fully its growing advantages it will need access to the global market; and it will be able to obtain this only by allowing other countries entry into its own market.

Hence, as their competitive strength and confidence increase, various interest groups within the country will press the government to negotiate with other nations a more liberal trading regime. Employers will favour the change because larger markets will enable them to utilise economies of scale, reduce costs, increase profits and, thus, finance easily further growth. Employees will support them in the confidence that cheaper imports will not threaten their jobs – an essential factor if they are to enjoy full benefits from trade liberalisation. Finally, consumers will welcome such a change of policy because it will increase their choice.

With economic success, these three interest groups will come to constitute a powerful majority; and as continuous, widely diffused economic progress tends to bring about a more responsive, democratic form of government, the preference of the majority will be reflected, eventually, in the official policy of the country. By contrast, exactly the opposite is likely to happen, in the long run, in a declining economy which fails to arrest the process of its relative stagnation.

For all these reasons, genuinely independent, sovereign states will favour a liberal trading system only when a majority of economic interests within them is confident that it will gain rather than lose from such a change in policy.

IV

One way to test this proposition is to compare protection levels in a number of countries during a particular period with their per capita incomes, using the latter as a rough indicator of their relative levels of development, efficiency and international competitiveness.

If the earlier analysis is correct, other things being equal, the two should be negatively correlated. On the other hand, the relationship between the countries' incomes and current balances of payments should be positive – implying, according to the analysis in Chapter 5, that in a fairly integrated international economy the correlation coefficient between either incomes or current balances and net long-term capital flows should be negative.[14] In other words, the higher (lower) is a country's per capita income relative to the rest of the world the more favourable (unfavourable), *ceteris paribus*, will be its current balance of payments, the greater will be its outflows (inflows) of long-term capital and the lower (higher) will be its level of protection.

The data available on a reasonably comparable basis for most of the countries listed in Chapter 2 can be used to test in a simple but nevertheless adequate manner whether or not these relationships can be observed in practice. When this is done, the tests reveal that, as one would expect, there is a positive and statistically significant correlation between per capita incomes and current balances of payments (normalised for the size of each country's GNP) for both 1971–73 ($r = 0.40$) and 1979–81 ($r = 0.58$). At the same time, the correlation coefficients between per capita incomes and net long-term capital flows (also normalised for the size of each country's GNP) have the expected signs in both 1971–73 ($r = -0.21$) and 1979–81 ($r = -0.57$), but only the latter is statistically significant. Exactly the same is true also of the coefficients between current balances and net long-term capital flows, which were -0.34 and -0.75 respectively.

The last result is important because it indicates that, although there is a tendency for long-term capital to move from surplus to deficit countries, there is no certainty that it will always do so, and even less, of course, as the analysis in Chapter 2 shows, that it will be of sufficient size to offset current account deficits. In the circumstances, and given the wide disparities in international levels of development and incomes, it is hardly surprising to find that the figures for broad groups of countries given in Table 2.3 suggest a fairly strong inverse relationship between per capita income and non-tariff protection levels.

The important question to consider now is whether this is a freak result, something that is characteristic of our time only (the data in Table 2.3 refer to 1979), or a relationship that can also be observed when using different data for different periods? To answer this question, levels of income and protection will be compared in the tables that follow for a number of countries, using whatever reasonably comparable indicators of protection are available for as many countries as possible. Given the paucity of internationally available data in this area, the choice is very limited. Fortunately, the years for which data of the kind required here exist are representative of three quite distinct periods in the development of the international economy over the past century.

Table 8.1 shows levels of per capita incomes and nominal tariffs in 1913, the last year of the 'golden age' of relatively free trade which existed before the First World War.

The data on per capita incomes, though not without problems,[15] are straightforward enough. The figures for tariffs represent weighted average levels of import duties on foodstuffs, raw materials, semi-manufactures and finished products. Their main shortcoming is that they show the level of *nominal* duties. There is a risk, therefore, that the figures may understate, or in some cases overstate,[16] the degree of *effective* protection because they do not take into account variations in tariffs at different stages of production. However, it is easy to exaggerate the problem. Most studies which employ both these measures agree that, although effective protection seems to be generally higher than the levels indicated by nominal tariffs, the ranking of countries appears to be virtually identical, irrespective of which of the two measures is used.[17] This means that for 1913, at least, there is a very good chance that these figures give a reasonably accurate ranking of the countries according to their protection levels. Before the First World War tariffs were the dominant form of administrative protection, exchange rates were fixed (at least among the countries included in Table 8.1) and, according to Bloomfield, there were only two instances of countries using exchange controls, though in a rather limited form: the United States in 1895 and Russia in 1905–6.[18]

Table 8.1 Levels of per capita income and nominal tariffs in 1913

	Per capita income	*Tariffs*	
		All trade	*Manufacturing*
USA	1,749	33	44
Australia	1,408	17	16
Canada	1,363	18	26
UK	996	0	0
Switzerland	963	7	9
Belgium	894	6	9
Denmark	862	9	14
Germany	757	12	13
Netherlands	754	3	4
France	695	18	20
Austria	681	18	18
Sweden	680	16	20
Czechoslovakia	524	18	18
Argentina	500	26	28
Italy	441	17	18
Hungary	372	23	18
Spain	367	33	41

Notes:
Rank correlation coefficients:

	All trade	*Manufacturing*
(a) All countries	−0.36	−0.28
(b) Excluding USA	−0.61*	−0.54*

*Statistically significant.
Sources: Per capita income – Bairoch (1976b). The figures for USA, Australia, Canada and Argentina were taken from Rostow (1978) and scaled to Bairoch's estimates for European countries. Tariffs – League of Nations (1927).

It is clear even from a visual inspection of the data in Table 8.1 that the countries in the lower half of the table had, on the whole, higher nominal levels of tariffs in 1913 than those in the upper half. The most notable exceptions were Australia, Canada and, especially, the United States – the three countries with protection levels above the average even though their incomes were already appreciably higher than in the rest of the world. The main reason for this is that although these countries were enjoying, thanks to their very favourable ratio of natural resources to population, very high per capita income they were still in the process of developing their industrial potential. Protection of some of the industries with standardised products (textile, metal manufactures) or those in which economies of scale were important (steel and chemicals) was one of the policies used to achieve this end. Moreover, two of the three countries were running persistent deficits on the current balance of payments.[19]

Taking all the countries in Table 8.1 together, the rank correlations between per capita income and protection levels have the expected (negative) sign but are statistically insignificant. However, if the United States is excluded, the correlation coefficients are significant, as the foot of the table shows, both for all trade and for manufacturing. The rank correlation is even higher ($r = -0.86$) if the four non-European countries are excluded.

Fifty years on, an inverse and statistically significant relationship between per capita incomes and protection levels could still be observed, as Table 8.2 shows, even though the countries and the measure of protection are somewhat different. The year, 1965, for which these data are available, is interesting because it falls well within the period of 'economic miracles' of the unprecedented economic expansion which took place beteween 1950 and 1973. At the same time, it reflects also the relationship between income levels and protection just before these countries felt, in the second half of the 1960s, the full impact of trade liberalisation, following agreements reached in the early part of the 1960s and the establishment of the EEC, EFTA and other customs unions. Moreover, 1965 is to some extent similar to 1913 in the sense that, although exchange controls were now fairly widespread, exchange rates were fixed and most of the quantitative controls on trade had been abolished by the majority of the countries included in the table. Consequently, the figures in Table 8.2, like those in 8.1, probably give a fairly accurate picture of the relative protection levels in OECD countries in the mid-1960s.

By 1980, however, the situation had changed a good deal. It is impossible now to obtain a statistically significant relationship between income and protection levels in a cross-section analysis of *individual* countries, irrespective of whether one uses the data on customs and import duties as a percentage of imports, or the non-tariff barriers to trade of the kind used in Chapter 2. (These figures, as pointed out in Chapter 2, refer to the proportion of 'trade that is subject to some non-tariff control, by exporters, importers or both'.)[20]

Table 8.2 Levels of per capita income and protection in 1965 and 1980

	1965		1980	
	I	II	I	II
USA	6,178	6.75	7,986	3.08
Sweden	5,190	6.26	6,779	1.72
Switzerland	5,065	6.93	6,480	1.57
Canada	4,846	7.95	7,451	4.62
Denmark	4,748	2.84	6,336	1.02
Australia	4,465	9.62	6,188	10.13
W. Germany	4,386	4.64	6,876	1.81
France	3,964	6.05	6,679	1.07
Norway	3,925	4.03	7,026	0.86
UK	3,906	5.97	5,145	2.17
Netherlands	3,893	5.72	5,715	1.40
Belgium	3,854	3.79	6,084	1.38
Finland	3,600	9.97	5,657	1.37
Austria	3,328	8.57	5,861	1.70
Italy	2,898	5.94	4,636	0.78
Japan	2,630	7.55	5,735	2.46
Spain	2,582	16.56	4,179	9.46
Ireland	2,234	15.75	3,352	0.90
Greece	1,969	11.75	3,922	5.51
Portugal	1,498	11.72	3,047	3.41
Turkey	1,155	53.55	2,048	15.20

Notes: I: per capita income in US$ at 1975 international prices.
II: receipts of customs and import duties as a per cent of all imports.
Rank correlation coefficients between columns I and II:
1965: −0.55 (statistically significant).
1980: −0.17 (not significant statistically).
Sources: I – Summers and Heston (1984). II – OECD (1985).

There are probably two reasons for this. First, since the beginning of the energy crisis and the economic stagnation in the early 1970s even industrial countries have resorted increasingly to quantitative controls on trade, competitive devaluations and exchange controls. This means that no single measure of barriers to trade is now likely to provide a reasonably accurate ranking of individual countries according to their levels of protection. Second, there seems to have been a significant increase in the number of countries at different levels of income pursuing similar commercial policies. This is, partly, a result of the prolonged economic stagnation which has often affected unequally countries at the same level of development; and, partly, a consequence of the deliberate harmonisation of commercial policies by industrialised nations, especially those which belong to various customs unions. The EEC countries provide a very good example of this, with free trade within the Community and a common external tariff against the rest of the world.

Nevertheless, important differences in national commercial policies have not disappeared completely. They emerge clearly if countries for which the data are available are grouped according to their per capita income, as in Table 8.3. When this is done, the inverse and statistically significant relationship between income and protection levels reappears again. Commercial policies may be much more complicated (and their variations, therefore, more difficult to detect) now than before the First World War, or even than twenty years ago, but the underlying relationship between relative economic strength and trading policy is obviously still important.

Finally, the results in Table 8.4 indicate that when the ranking of countries changes in terms of their productivity and income levels there will also be a change in the ranking of their protection levels. The correlation coefficients of the two variables indicate a similarity in the relative positions of the fourteen countries (for which the data exist) in 1913 and 1965. In 1980 the relative position of the countries was similar in both these respects to that which they had occupied in 1965 but it was, clearly, different from the ranking of most of them at the beginning of the twentieth century.

V

The tendency of a country's commercial policy to change, *ceteris paribus*, over time with changes in its international competitiveness can be illustrated by a brief description of the experience since the late eighteenth century of two of the most industrialised countries in the world: Britain and Germany.

According to Rostow, Britain took off into self-sustained growth between 1780 and 1830.[21] Throughout this period it restricted imports, promoted exports and also, as already mentioned, prohibited exports of capital equipment and the emigration of skilled labour. The main purpose of all these controls was, of course, to enable the country to establish a firm industrial base which would give it an important

Table 8.3 Per capita income levels and proportion of imports subject to controls other than tariffs in 1979 (three country averages)

Groups	*Per capita income (US$ at 1975 international prices)*	*Proportion of imports subject to non-tariff controls*	
		All trade	*Manufacturing*
I USA, Canada, W. Germany	7,507	36	13
II France, Denmark, Sweden	6,640	37	14
III Norway, Switzerland, Australia	6,341	29	19
IV Iceland, Belgium, Netherlands	5,989	37	15
V Japan, Austria, Finland	5,707	40	7
VI UK, New Zealand, Italy	4,771	72	53
VII Israel, Spain, Greece	4,175	52	35
VIII Venezuela, Ireland, Iraq	3,443	48	39
IX Argentina, Singapore, Portugal	3,016	22	4
X Iran, Mexico, Taiwan	2,466	73	57
XI Chile, S. Korea, S. Africa	2,271	73	71
XII Syria, Turkey, Brazil	2,079	75	67
XIII Algeria, Tunisia, Peru	1,858	70	67
XIV Nigeria, Morocco, Thailand	1,296	74	67
XV Egypt, Pakistan, India	721	72	67

Notes:
Rank correlation coefficients between:
(a) Per capita income and all trade: −0.72 (statistically significant).
(b) Per capita income and manufacturing: −0.76 (statistically significant).
Sources: Per capita income – Summers and Heston (1984). Imports subject to non-tariff controls – Page (1979).

competitive advantage. For although the share of exports in Britain's GNP was small at this stage (it doubled from about 9 per cent in the early 1780s to 18 per cent in 1801[22]), it was very high in a number of key sectors and it was the development of these that the government was trying to assist. In accordance with this strategy, the duty on imports of cotton goods from India, to take one example, was increased on no less than twelve occasions between 1797 and 1819.[23]

Apart from promoting new industries, mercantilist policies were also intended to minimise the adverse effects of early industrialisation

Table 8.4 Rank correlation coefficients between countries'* income and protection levels in different years

	1913	*1965*	*1980*
A. Per capita income levels			
1913	–	0.60**	0.49
1965	0.60**	–	0.85**
1980	0.49	0.85**	–
B. Protection levels			
1913	–	0.64**	0.37
1965	0.64**	–	0.70**
1980	0.37	0.70**	–

Note: *USA, Australia, Canada, UK, Switzerland, Belgium, Denmark, W. Germany (Germany in 1913), Netherlands, France, Austria, Sweden, Italy, Spain.
**Statistically significant.
Sources: Tables 8.1 and 8.2.

which in Britain (as in so many countries afterwards) 'greatly increased the problems of unemployment, distress and the threat of disorder'.[24] These policies, plus the fact that by industrialising first it had gained important competitive advantages, probably explain why Britain, unlike so many countries which started their economic development later, had no balance of payments problems during the early phase of its industrialisation.[25]

By the middle of the nineteenth century Britain had acquired, thanks to its early start, an unparalleled industrial supremacy and, with it, the ability and confidence to put the doctrine of free trade into practice. The immediate cause of the abolition of the Corn Laws was, as explained earlier, the fear generated by a serious economic and social crisis in the 1840s. However, there was also a strong belief at the time among the influential business interests that the country's unilateral 'acceptance of free trade would persuade her competitors in Europe and the United States to shift factors back into agriculture by offering them the attractive bait of an open British market'.[26] In other words, it was confidently expected that the policy would work to the country's long-term advantage.

The idea that other countries would give up the desire to industrialise proved, of course, to be no more than wishful thinking. Yet the arrogance is perhaps understandable given that no other country, with the exception of the United States, has ever dominated the world economy to the same extent. 'In 1870 Britain's share of world industrial production was 32 per cent and her share of world trade 24 per cent. The United States came closest to this but a long way behind, the respective figures being 23 per cent and 8 per cent.'[27] No wonder that for several decades after 1870 Britain pursued a policy of free trade to an extent unmatched in any other part of the world.

However, it was from about this time, the 1870s, that Britain began to encounter increasingly effective foreign competition both at home and abroad. Many factors were, of course, responsible for this change, so that it would be wrong to attribute the development entirely, or even chiefly, to the country's commercial policy. At the same time, there is little doubt that the combination of rapid industrialisation and increasing protection abroad and free trade at home made a significant contribution to the sizeable deterioration in Britain's balance of trade in the last quarter of the nineteenth century.[28] For while imports continued to grow fairly strongly, the growth of exports slumped to less than 0.5 per cent a year during the last thirty years of the century and the share of exports to GNP fell from 24 per cent in 1870 to 17 per cent in 1900.[29] Export performance improved in the decade before the First World War – thanks to the growth of the captive markets outside Europe and the United States – but the growth of output continued to lag behind that achieved abroad, especially by other industrial nations.[30] Not surprisingly, during the same decade British investments abroad were equal to 6.8 per cent of its GNP, compared to only 5.2 per cent going to domestic fixed capital formation.[31] The relative stagnation accelerated further during the 1920s.

Nevertheless, a number of attempts to reverse the policy of free trade – in the 1880s, 1900s and 1920s – failed to make much impact. The reason for this is fairly simple: although Britain's international competitiveness was weakening rapidly, mainly under the challenge from the United States and Germany, those affected adversely by free trade were still in the minority. The protectionist argument finally won in the 1930s[32] when unemployment reached unprecedented levels and the balance of payments turned into a deficit, with the result that the country was confronted for the first time with the problem of fundamental disequilibrium. To make things worse, an increasing number of its trading partners were turning their backs on free trade. The subsequent British response was no different from the reaction of other countries in similar circumstances before and since: tariffs went up, quantitative controls were introduced on certain imports, sterling was devalued and, finally, exchange controls were introduced at the outbreak of the Second World War.

Since the war, Britain has participated in the general trend towards trade liberalisation among industrial countries. There is no indication, however, that it has ever again been in the forefront of the countries with very liberal trading regimes.[33] On the contrary, with the continuous weakening of its international competitiveness, its levels of protection appear to have increased to an extent which makes them higher now than the levels prevailing in most OECD countries.[34]

VI

Rostow puts the date of the German take off into self-sustained growth between 1840 and 1870, several decades after Britain.[35]

From the start, German productivity and income levels, already slightly above the European average, increased rapidly relative to those of other countries.[36] In fact, few of the industrialised countries appear to have been more successful in this respect in the early stages of their industrialisation.[37] Most of the German population was engaged in agriculture, producing a surplus at a time when Britain was finding it increasingly difficult to feed its population. This opened up a large and rapidly growing market for German exports, making it possible for the country to exchange its agricultural surplus for British manufactures. The fact that they were competitive internationally in what was still, predominantly, an agricultural world strengthened the landowners' position and had an important influence on the country's commercial policy.

As the pattern of Germany's foreign trade was advantageous to them, the attitude of powerful agricultural interests in Germany was very similar to that of British manufacturers: they were in favour of free trade not only because of their competitive strength at the time but also because there was the possibility, mentioned earlier, that it would encourage Britain to continue specialising in manufacturing, instead of developing its agriculture which would reduce the demand for German exports. This explains why, despite some increases in tariffs on manufactured goods in the 1840s, the level of protection adopted originally by Prussia and, subsequently, by other members of the *Zollverein* remained low throughout the early phase of German economic development.

The attitude to free trade changed abruptly at the end of the 1870s and, even more so, in the 1880s when, as a result of large increases in agricultural output in America and Russia, and a rapid reduction in transport costs, imports of corn flooded Europe and there was a sharp fall in prices and agricultural incomes. With no prospect that these developments would be reversed in the long run, improvements in agricultural efficiency and industrialisation provided the only way out of the ensuing crisis.

German agriculture underwent considerable transformation in the period up to the First World War.[38] But it was German industrial growth which really took off during the last quarter of the nineteenth century, increasing more rapidly than industrial output in the UK and most European countries.[39] The rate of industrial investment was so rapid that the sector was able to absorb a good deal of surplus labour from agriculture.[40] The outcome was a major structural change in the economy. In 1913 industry and construction accounted for almost twice as much of the GNP (45 per cent) as agriculture (23 per cent) – virtually a complete reversal of their relative importance in 1870 (28 and 40 per cent of GNP respectively).[41] The success of the structural adjustment is also reflected in the fact that by 1913 the Germans had become the world's largest exporters of engineering and chemical products;[42] and that after 1890 emigration from Germany fell sharply, while there was a significant increase in immigration.[43]

As the Germans were able to generate sufficient savings to run current balance of payments surpluses and to invest abroad,[44] protective measures were introduced during this period primarily for the other three reasons mentioned earlier in this chapter: to raise government revenue, to slow down the contraction of declining activities (such as agriculture and textiles), and to promote development of new industries (especially chemicals, engineering and steel). The last two were prompted by the intense international competition which developed towards the end of the nineteenth century, as world productive capacity increased rapidly and industrial prices and profits (like those in agriculture) plummeted. The combination of selective protection and cartelisation secured markets of sufficient size for the growth of large companies, capable of utilising economies of scale and generating adequate internal funds for further growth.[45] Together with other social and economic developments, these measures were responsible for the fact that by 1914 'German manufacturers were by far the most efficient ... in Europe'.[46] From 1890 on, this success made it possible for the country to relax some of its tariffs.[47]

After the First World War, German output increased rapidly until the end of the 1920s and the level of unemployment was, on average, lower than in most industrial countries[48] – despite the traumas of socio-political upheavals, hyperinflation and the burden of reparations. This was reflected, as one would expect, in the level of protection which, although slightly higher than in 1913, was still lower than at the turn of the century.[49]

Commercial policy became much more restrictive only at the end of the 1920s, when Germany was forced to adopt highly deflationary measures in order to correct its external deficits. The change 'was caused by the halting of long-term lending [by creditor nations such as the United States] and its replacement by short-term loans that could readily be cut off or withdrawn'.[50] As a result of these deflationary measures, the level of output was 15 per cent lower in 1932 than in 1930, the level of unemployment became one of the highest among industrialised countries[51] and there was a noticeable increase in trade restrictions.[52] These restrictions reached exceptionally high levels during the 1930s when the Nazis set about restoring full employment and preparing for the war.[53]

The trend was reversed sharply only in the course of the German 'economic miracle' after the Second World War which made it possible for West Germany to liberalise its trade much more rapidly than most countries.[54] By the 1960s the Germans had not only regained their industrial strength but had also become extremely competitive internationally, outperforming the United States and earning large surpluses on the balance of payments at full employment. Not surprisingly, their commercial policy became very liberal, with relatively few restrictions on international trade and payments. However, even in Germany restrictions started to reappear from the second half of the 1970s, as the energy crisis and the world-wide stagnation slowed down the growth of the economy, increased unemployment and turned the balance of payments into deficit at high levels of activity.

VII

In conclusion, the British and German expeience,[55] as well as the cross-section analysis, all point in the same direction: other things remaining equal, the lower the adjustment problems that a country expects to face if it liberalises its external trade and payments the more active it will be in the international division of labour. Hence, anything that increases adjustment problems of individual economies is also likely to contribute to the breakdown of the international system, as a growing number of economic agents discover that, for them at least, the losses incurred by operating in an open economy exceed significantly the gains foregone in conditions of economic insularity.

9 Historical Parallels in the Evolution of International Economic Relationships

I

The readiness of sovereign states to open up their economies and encourage a greater degree of international economic integration will be influenced by two important developments: changes in their competitiveness, as just described; and changes in the world economic environment,[1] analysed in the present chapter.

It is hardly necessary to point out that a country will be more willing to accept a greater degree of economic dependence on the rest of the world if it expects the existing international economic order to promote rather than hinder the achievement of its major policy objectives. This being the case, its commercial policy will rarely remain the same if global economic conditions and/or generally accepted rules of international economic behaviour alter. Not surprisingly, since the early nineteenth century the process of international integration appears to have gone through a number of phases, all of which have coincided with certain, clearly distinguishable, periods in the long-term development of the world economy. The important question, considered in this chapter, is whether the phases reveal any systematic similarities or differences.

II

The six major phases in the evolution of the international economy since 1820 are shown in Table 9.1.

Given such a long period of time, the data are bound to vary a good deal in both their coverage and quality. Nevertheless, it is possible to get some idea of the effects of changes in economic developments and policies over the period on the character of the world economy by observing differences between the growth of world output and trade, all measured in volume terms. The periods during which trade is

Table 9.1 The long-term trends in international economic integration (per cent, per annum)

	Growth of world GDP	*Growth of world industrial production*	*Growth of world trade*
1820–60	2.2[a]	3.2	3.8
1860–80	2.6	3.1	4.5
1880–1913	2.9	4.1	3.5
1914–50	2.2	2.9	0.7
1920–29	3.8	7.7[b]	2.2
1929–38	1.1	2.0	−0.7
1938–50	2.8	4.1[c]	2.2[d]
1950–73	4.9	5.6[e]	7.5
1973–84	2.2	1.8	3.3
1973–79	2.7	2.4	4.8
1979–84	1.7	1.2	2.9

Notes: [a]1820–70; [b]1921–29; [c]1938–48; [d]1938–53; [e]1948–71.
Sources: World GDP – Maddison (1982) and OECD, *Economic Outlook*. World industrial production and trade – Rostow (1978) and National Institute of Economic and Social Research, *Economic Review*.

growing faster than output indicate, generally, an increase in international economic integration and interdependence; and those in which output is expanding more rapidly than trade tend to be associated with the spread of economic nationalism and insularity, and the break up of the world economy.

The picture of the long-term trends which emerges from the table can be substantiated further with qualitative and quantitative information about actual changes in commercial policies and other developments during each of these periods.[2]

The world economy was still, basically, semi-mercantilist between 1820 and 1860. It was in the second half of this period that Britain abolished the Corn Laws and also removed most of the restrictions on its trade and factor movements. A number of smaller European economies followed the British example, though not to the same extent. Elsewhere, some countries became more protectionist (for instance, France in the 1830s and 1840s, Germany in the 1840s), while in others (the United States) trade liberalisation was interrupted occasionally by increases in tariffs. Most of the now industrialised countries, however, shared one characteristic during this period: a growing determination to dismantle major obstacles to economic progress, such as the special privileges granted to guilds and other interest groups, inherited from the mercantilist era.

It is probably these changes and the beginnings of industrialisation outside Britain that account for the apparent increase, according to Table 9.1, in international economic integration at a time when, apart from administrative trade restrictions, there was still a good deal of natural protection. Despite considerable improvements, the existing means of transport and communications were far too rudimentary to break down the widespread cultural and economic barriers to economic integration.

This was still basically true of the second phase, between 1860 and 1880 (and, indeed, until after the First World War). Nevertheless, this was a period of very rapid growth of world trade caused partly by an acceleration in the rate of expansion of the world economy, and partly by widespread reductions in administrative barriers to trade in Europe and to a lesser extent outside it.

The unprecedented liberalisation of commercial policies started in 1860 with the Cobden–Chevalier Treaty between Britain and France. Britain undertook to abolish all duties on manufactured goods, irrespective of their origin. France liberalised only trade with Britain. Nevertheless, the Treaty set a precedent, inspiring many similar agreements between other European countries over the next few years. Japan and China also participated in the general move towards freer trade when they were forced to grant concessions to Britain and the United Staes.

On the other hand, Canada increased its duties on manufactured goods by 20 per cent in 1859, the United States raised the level of protection during and after the Civil War, and some of the Australian states, New Zealand and South Africa also introduced and/or tightened trade restrictions.

Overall, however, the treaties ensured a period of unusually free international trade and factor movements. They achieved this by creating 'a stable world, in which traders were free to come and go, to organise and invest abroad, almost as freely and safely as in their own countries'.[3]

The trend was reversed in the 1880s, at the beginning of the third phase (1880–1913), when most European countries either reintroduced or raised tariffs. Trade relationships deteriorated further after

1890, as the countries at the receiving end of higher tariffs retaliated so that increases in import duties became competitive. The United States followed a slightly different pattern: tariffs declined for a brief period in the 1890s before being raised to even higher levels than those at which they had been originally. Only Britain and, to a slightly lesser extent, Holland resisted the pressure to abandon their policy of free trade.

The growth of economic insularity produced, in fact, different patterns of protection within and outside Europe. In Europe, barriers to trade were erected, first, in favour of agriculture and, then, industry. In North America and Australia tariffs were directed mainly against industrial products, as the countries were highly competitive in agriculture.[4]

The duties, which were applied very selectively, seriously restricted trade in certain sectors.[5] Nevertheless, the general impression has always been that they were, on the whole, so low, especially in effective terms,[6] that they made very little impact on the growth of world trade and integration.[7]

The figures in Table 9.1 raise considerable doubts about the accuracy of this long-held view. The rate of growth of world trade relative to that of output appears to have been less favourable during this phase than at any other time except in the period 1914–50. In other words, what the figures indicate is that the pace of international integration slackened sharply during the thirty years just before the First World War – with a definite disintegration of the world's industrial production and trade.[8]

This conclusion is supported by Maizels' data which give the relevant series by broad commodity groups.[9] The data show clearly that in the case of primary commodities world trade expanded faster than output during this period, an indication that international integration continued in this area in spite of the proliferation in trade barriers. The rapid growth of population and improvements in the standard of living were the main reasons for this. In manufacturing, on the other hand, production increased more rapidly than trade, implying a reversal of the trend towards greater international specialisation apparent during the preceeding two periods. The most likely cause of this reversal was probably a combination of two factors: the predominance of textiles and other products with constant returns to scale and relatively simple technical requirements – easy to copy, develop and, thus, substitute for imports;[10] and trade barriers behind which such products, as well as the new ones demanding large markets in order to exploit economies of scale, could be either developed or saved from rapid extinction.

The tendency towards an increase in the international division of labour suffered its greatest reversal during the next phase which lasted from 1914 to 1950.

With the outbreak of the First World War most countries introduced wide-ranging controls on their international transactions. Many of these persisted after 1918, as the countries which had developed import substitutes during the war were unwilling to give them up, while the combatants needed time to readjust their economies.[11]

The process of global economic disintegration intensified in 1929–38, when the multilateral trading and financial system built over the previous century crumbled. Tariffs were raised and exchange controls introduced or tightened. Moreover, the large fall in prices during the Great Depression induced a number of countries to turn to quotas, a much more effective way of protecting domestic output and employment than tariffs.[12] The effectiveness of quantitative trade controls also made them attractive in another sense: as a powerful bargaining weapon in trade negotiations with other nations. Finally, many countries resorted to competitive devaluations which, according to one contemporary observer, proved to be the least helpful policy instrument to those who employed it and most harmful to the rest.[13]

All these controls remained during the Second World War and the immediate post-war years. The exception was the United States which reduced its import duties substantially during the 1940s.[14] Furthermore, this time, unlike in the 1920s, the Americans persisted with their more liberal policy after the war and, what is more, actively assisted and encouraged other industrial nations to adopt a similar attitude to trade.

The result was a period, 1950–73, of extensive liberalisation of international trade and payments, particularly remarkable as this time there were very few natural barriers to international integration left.

The opening up of national economies started in earnest in the 1950s, with the end of the post-war reconstruction. Quantitative controls virtually disappeared in the industrialised world during the decade; and by 1955 tariffs were already below their 1937 levels.[15] The momentum continued in the 1960s with the Dillon and Kennedy Rounds of trade negotiations and with the creation of customs unions such as the EEC and EFTA. Moreover, although these changes mainly affected trade among industrial nations, developing countries were not, for once, ignored. Rapid growth and accute labour shortages in many industrial economies made them willing to import labour-intensive products in order to be able to move their own unskilled labour into the more productive sectors. In the course of this phase, most industrial countries relaxed, or even abandoned, their exchange controls; and virtually all of them adhered rigidly to the system of fixed exchange rates developed in the 1940s.

The exchange rate regime has altered significantly during the current phase (1973–), but there have been no radical changes in trading policies. Reductions in nominal tariffs have continued. They appear to be lower now than ever before, though this is probably not equally true of effective tariffs.[16] There has, however, been an increase in non-tariff barriers to trade and subsidies, as well as in the occasional reintroduction and/or reinforcement of exchange controls by both capital exporting and importing countries.

Most of these trade restrictions are highly selective, concentrating heavily on sectors such as clothing, textiles, footwear and, to a lesser extent, automobiles and steel. They have been used predominantly to restrict imports from developing countries which, because they are so labour intensive, might add to the already serious unemployment levels in industrial countries. Industrial countries have been very careful so far to avoid significant restrictions on trade with one another, except for 'voluntary' agreements to limit exports from Japan.

It is obviously still far too early to assess the extent to which these and other changes since the mid-1970s have affected permanently the process of international integration. As pointed out in Chapter 2, there was no evidence of a fundamental change in the second half of the 1970s. The figures in Table 9.1 confirm this. They also indicate that the trend towards international integration and interdependence continued in the 1980s. The importance of this conclusion is discussed later, in Parts IV and V.

One way to get at least some of the most likely future developments in the world economy is to isolate a number of important factors common to all the phases of international economic integration, or disintegration, described in this section. When this is done, the six broad phases fall, very roughly, into one of two larger groups: 'internationalist' (those in which policies were changed in order to increase international economic integration); and 'isolationist' (those during which commercial policies moved in the opposite direction). According to this criteron, 1820–60, 1860–80 and 1950–73 fall into the first group, while 1914–50 and the period since 1973 belong to the second category. The remaining phase, 1880–1913, falls somewhere between the two: strongly internationalist in finance and factor movements, but increasingly restrictive in trade. 'Semi-internationalist' is probably the most accurate description of what happened during this period.

III

If one compares histories of the 'internationalist' and 'isolationist' phases, the absence of major shocks to the established economic order in the former and their strong presence in the latter is one of the major differences which soon becomes apparent.

The importance of shocks such as wars and rapid technical or political changes is that, as explained in Chapter 5, they invariably increase the incidence of fundamental disequilibria – and, thus, the need for major structural adjustments – by creating significant imbalances in the world economy. A large proportion of the existing productive capacity suddenly becomes unusable either through physical destruction or because of a significant change in relative prices within and between primary producing and industrial sectors. The most serious and direct consequence of this is a large-scale increase in unemployment, with the risk of socio-political upheavals if alternative employment opportunities cannot be expanded rapidly.

There were no global shocks of this kind during the three periods characterised by a growing preference for a more liberal trading regime: 1820–60, 1860–80 and 1950–73.[17] Prices of primary commodities weakened for a time relative to those of industrial products in the first and the third period and strengthened in the second. The important fact is that, in each case, these changes took place over a number of years, instead of imposing suddenly major adjustment tasks on the countries involved. The steady and continuous improvements in their relative position encouraged landed interests, dominant at the time, to favour trade liberalisation in 1860–80; and industrial and financial interests, in a comparable position of power and influence a century later, to adopt a similar attitude in 1950–73. As pointed out earlier, there was a strong current of opinion in favour of a more open trading regime between 1820 and 1860 also, even though the policy outcomes were rather mixed.

The other three periods present a totally different picture in this respect. With the exception of a few years just before the First World

War, the terms of trade of primary producers deteriorated more or less continuously, and often sharply, between 1880 and 1913. The deterioration was even more dramatic in the period 1914–50 which includes two highly destructive world wars. The years since 1973 have been marked by unprecedented – in terms of both their size and speed – improvements and, later, deterioration in the terms of trade of energy producers; and extremely erratic movements in prices of other primary commodities relative to those of manufactured goods.

Persistent changes of such magnitudes require structural adjustments, and these may take years to achieve. This means that high and rising unemployment levels – characteristic of the 'isolationist' phases[18] – may continue for quite some time, a condition clearly at odds with the assumption of full employment which is, as shown in Chapter 7, of critical importance in the argument for free trade. Not surprisingly, the periods of major shocks to the international system (1880–1913, 1914–50, 1973–) have all been associated, though not the same extent, with retreats into economic insularity. Furthermore, as one would expect, an important characteristic of all three periods has been a determined effort by a growing number of primary producers to industrialise.[19] These efforts, in time, inevitably increase the need of the already industrialised countries to adjust also.

IV

The extent to which an international consensus concerning the objective of long-term economic growth exists in certain periods but not in others constitutes another important difference between the 'internationalist' and 'isolationist' phases. There are two reasons why the existence, or absence, of a world-wide unity of purpose will have such an important influence on the character of the international economy.

First, as emphasised in the earlier chapters, in conditions of economic openness and interdependence no country can achieve its economic policy objective in isolation. Yet individual countries may be forced to attempt precisely that if there is a complete breakdown of international consensus about economic objectives and policies. What happens in this case is that some countries are determined to expand and restructure their economies, while in others entrenched economic interests are equally determined to preserve, by 'fighting inflation', the advantages that they have acquired. Such a glaring incompatibility of policy objectives is most likely to arise in the aftermath of a major shock to the international system. The more dynamic nations will react to the shock by trying to re-establish their fundamental equilbrium. The nations lacking the capacity for change, on the other hand, will pretend that the whole problem is nothing more than a short-term inflationary imbalance of the kind analysed in Chapter 4. The result is general international paralysis and stagnation, as each group, in trying to achieve its objective, will continuously frustrate the other group's attempt to do the same. The only way to avoid this is for each country to insulate its economy against external influences.

Second, these tendencies will be reinforced, in the absence of a lasting national commitment to economic progress, by a reduction in factor mobility without which the long-term adjustment process becomes impossible. Productive capacity, employment and incomes will all decline as labour and capital cling desperately to the old, outdated institutions and activities instead of supporting change and improvement. Consequently, a clear, firm, commitment to economic progress by governments, backed up by appropriate actions, is essential for mobilising the vast resources needed; and also in order to reassure the dynamic forces in world society that it is the new, progressive groups and their ideas that determine economic goals and policies, rather than the long-established, conservative interests whose main preoccupation is with maintaining the *status quo* irrespective of how untenable it may be.

There was a growing determination in the period 1820–60, and even more so between 1860 and 1880, to follow the example provided by Britain's Industrial Revolution.[20] It was in the course of these decades, therefore, that, according to Rostow, most of the leading industrial countries took off into self-sustained growth.[21] The pace of industrialisation speeded up in 1880–1913 when many more countries began to industrialise in earnest. Investment and the rate of technical progress increased significantly[22] and, as Table 9.1 shows, there was a further acceleration in the rate of 'world' economic growth. The pace of economic progress reached exceptionally high levels half a century later, in 1950–73, when there was an even greater and more widely diffused effort to industrialise, improve living standards and, in industrial countries, maintain full employment. Moreover, during the periods 1880–1913 and 1950–73 dominant countries – Britain in the first period and the United States in the second – achieved lower rates of growth than other nations, so that there was a significant equalisation in the levels of industrialisation.[23]

In contrast, a widespread commitment to economic and social progress was absent in the interwar period. The global crisis brought to power in many countries entrenched interests, hostile to the very ideas of change and progress. The main objectives of economic policy in most cases became price and exchange rate stability, combined with efforts to resist rather than promote fundamental changes. Inevitably, the creeping stagnation and nationalism of the 1920s gave way to unparalleled decline, unemployment and disintegration of the world economy in the 1930s. As two historians of international economy have pointed out:

> Confronted by a world-wide depression, no country escaped untouched, and there was consequently a reaction against international economic interdependence. Each nation fell back on its own resources and pursued a policy of fostering internal recovery first and foremost. In such an atmosphere, the regulation of foreign trade and financial transactions was a natural and inevitable development.[24]

The period since 1973 bears once more a very strong resemblance to that between 1914 and 1950 – with attempts by developing countries and some industrial ones to sustain economic growth, or full employment, frustrated by other industrial economies determined to 'fight inflation'. To makes things worse, the economic policy of the worlds's largest economy, the United States, has tended to switch the emphasis from 'growth' to 'inflation', or the other way round, even under the same administration.

Consequently, the current phase in international economic relationships fails to satisfy another important condition on which the classical argument for free trade and economic integration rests. Given the existing levels of international interdependence, there is obviously an important underlying 'harmony of interests' among the nations of the world. Nevertheless, this is not sufficient in itself to avoid an outcome as cataclysmic as that which befell the world in the 1930s, unless it can be translated into a 'harmony' of sustainable economic objectives and policies. There is little sign of this at the moment.

V

Uniformity of national economic objectives and policies can contribute significantly to the international adjustment process by reducing the risks and uncertainties normally associated with a possible move to a new, unfamiliar, environment. *Ceteris paribus*, the result will be, as already mentioned, a much greater migration of labour and capital between countries.

As pointed out in Chapter 6, international movements of population can make, at best, only a very small contribution to solving the problem of fundamental disequilibria. The size and growth of the world population, especially in developing countries, is now far too great for labour migration to be considered a realistic long-term policy option.

Nevertheless, there is little doubt that even relatively small movements of this kind can help if they involve emigration from low to high productivity and income countries – normally those with high land:labour and capital:labour ratios. This is most likely to happen in periods of rapid growth, when the latter's unemployment rates are low and persistent shortages of labour limit their scope for further specialisation and growth. At the same time, movements of skilled labour in the opposite direction, though much smaller in number, can play an important role in the development of less industrialised countries.

The first two columns in Table 9.2 show international migration over the periods analysed in this chapter. To make the figures comparable, immigration levels for each period have been expressed as a percentage of the increase in world population during that period.

There is clearly an important difference in the relative size of international migration before and after 1930. One of the reasons for the change is that by this time most of the empty areas of the world – rich in agricultural land and/or minerals and made increasingly accessible by advances in transport and communications – had been settled. The receiving countries (mainly the United States, Argentina, Australia, Canada and Brazil) took steps, therefore, to restrict the number of immigrants they were prepared to accept. By that time, however, millions of people had moved between and within the continents. Fifty-two million (or 20 per cent of the European population at the beginning of the period) emigrated from Europe between 1840 and 1930, mainly to new temperate countries.[25] Moreover, Lewis puts the number of those who left India and China over the same period, predominantly to work in the tropics, at fifty million.[26] By comparison, according to a rather conservative estimate, 9.5 million people emigrated from developing to industrial countries between 1950 and 1974, not an inconsiderable figure. But

Table 9.2 International movements of population and long-term capital since 1840

	*International immigration**		*Exports of long-term capital from industrial countries (current prices)*	
	Annual averages (000s)	*Immigration during a period as % of increase in world population during the same period*	*Year*	*As % of GNP***
1846–60	332	5.6	1840	3.0–4.0
1860–80	368	5.3	1870	3.8
1880–1910	963	11.3	1913	4.9
1911–30	991	6.2	1929	1.0
1931–40	188	0.9	1938	(negative)
1946–55	436	2.2	1953	0.7
1955–73	766	1.3	1960	1.1
1973–76	848	1.6	1973	0.6
			1979	0.7
			1983	0.4

Notes: *Immigration into US, Canada, Australia, Latin America and other countries.
**GNP: 1840–1913 Britain, Germany, France, Belgium, Netherlands, Sweden and Switzerland only; 1929–83 OECD countries.

Sources: Immigration – 1846–1955 Kuznets (1966); 1955–76 calculated from UN (1979), UN *Demographic Yearbooks*, Kuznets (1966) and Rostow (1978). Capital flows and GDP: 1840–1953 Bairoch (1976a); other years from IMF, *Balance of Payments Yearbooks* and OECD.

the size of population in the sending countries was such that this amounted to no more than 0.5 per cent of their population.[27]

Despite the very large changes in magnitudes, there are again clearly discernible differences between the internationalist and isolationist phases; and the period 1880 to 1913 has again much more in common with the former than the latter. In fact, at no other time has the movement of people been so great as during the decades before the First World War. The earliest two periods also showed considerable rates of international migration. There is, however, an important difference. By far the largest proportion of European emigrants in the first two periods came from Britain and, to a lesser extent, Germany.

In 1880–1913 most of the emigrants came from the low income countries of Southern and Eastern Europe even though British emigrants were still greater in total than those from any other country. Most of this change in favour of the less prosperous regions of Europe occurred in the two decades before the First World War.[28] Many European governments and private organisations encouraged the poor and unemployed to emigrate. Pressure of population on limited agricultural resources in the sending countries and scarcity of labour relative to land, and other employment opportunities, in the receiving countries facilitated this enormous movement of population.

The absolute numbers for international migration in 1950–73, though substantial, are dwarfed by the growth of world population during the period, as can be seen from a comparison of the first two columns in Table 9.2. The other important development in the course of this period was in migration patterns. There was a considerable net movement of people from developing to industrial countries.[29] Even Europe ceased in the 1960s to be a net exporter of population. This change was obviously in the right direction in the sense that it could ease, even if only marginally, the adjustment problems of developing countries.

In contrast to the 'internationalist' phases, international migration slumped in the 1930s in both absolute and relative terms. This was a direct consequence of economic stagnation and high unemployment, which led to very tight immigration controls in the receiving countries.

The figures for 1973–76 in Table 9.2 appear to suggest that economic problems over the past decade have had little effect on international migration. In fact, OECD data on net labour movements reveal a rather different picture.[30] As economic conditions deteriorated in member countries – normally the largest recipients of foreign labour – there was a significant fall in the number of immigrants between 1974 and 1978. The subsequent recovery was modest, as it affected only some of the more affluent countries. So far as the international migration of population is concerned the period since 1973 resembles more the 1930s than any other phase in world economic development since the first half of the nineteenth century.

VI

Turning to long-term capital movements[31] – representing investment abroad from industrial countries net of disinvestments – the pattern revealed in Table 9.2 is very similar to that for the international migration of population. There were, clearly, substantial long-term investments in 1820–60, 1860–80, 1880–1913 and (given the extremely large increases in GNP over the period) in 1950–73. The flow of international investment declined relative to total output in the 1920s; and collapsed, turning into disinvestments, in the 1930s. Finally, the period since 1973 again presents a rather mixed picture. Long-term international investment held up well in the second half of the 1970s and, to a slightly lesser extent, in the early 1980s.

These are the facts. But their real significance cannot be appreciated fully without relating them to two major developments which have taken place since the early part of the nineteenth century: increasing capital intensity of production; and the concentration of a growing proportion of world economic resources within a fairly small number of countries and large firms, as described in Part I. Both these developments have tended to make the entry of new firms and countries into the already established areas of production more and more difficult.

Foreign investment played a relatively small role in the early stages of world industrialisation.[32] The existing techniques of production were simple and labour intensive so that only modest amounts of capital were needed to finance even large projects. All this changed dramatically with the arrival of new technology and industries in the second half of the nineteenth century. According to some estimates, when Britain started to industrialise in earnest, early in the century, 'the capital per workers required was the equivalent of 4–5 months' wages'. A few decades later, '6–8 months' wages were necessary in France; whereas at the end of the century, when Hungary started, the load had risen to 3½ years' wages per worker'.[33] Moreover, apart from the heavy investment required in modern production processes, industrialisation, with its heavy concentration in and around urban centres, is impossible without a complex and capital intensive infrastructure. The construction of such an infrastructure normally makes a huge demand on productive resources, something that is usually beyond the capacity of a developing country to mobilise internally.

Not surprisingly, latecomers to industrialisation became increasingly dependent on inflows of foreign capital. Already in the last quarter of the nineteenth century foreign investment was responsible for financing a substantial proportion of domestic fixed capital formation in many of these countries.[34] Even when it was relatively small it played an important role in their development because it brought with it new ideas, technical expertise and capital equipment.[35]

The role of international investment became particularly important in the new, sparsely populated countries in America and Oceania which were absorbing millions of immigrants, mainly from Europe. Hence, the movement of people was followed by a similar movement of long-term capital. This enabled the new countries to produce the foodstuffs and raw materials increasingly demanded in the capital exporting countries as a result of their industrialisation and population growth. The new countries also assisted industrial development in Europe by providing an important market for its manufactures.

During the first two periods most of these capital flows consisted of loans to governments and investments in transport and communications. After 1870 an increasing proportion of the flows were in the form of direct investment in manufacturing and mining – particularly important in 1950–73. The volume and direction of foreign investment were also influenced after 1870 by the growth of barriers to trade, one of the factors which, no doubt, ensured that a significant proportion of these investments went to European countries.[36]

Furthermore, the investments which took place during the 'internationalist' phases and in 1880–1913 shared a number of important characteristics. First, the relative ease with which bonds could be floated abroad enabled borrowers to finance their long-term projects with long-term loans. Operating in this way, international capital markets reduced the temptation to use short-term credits in order to finance long-term investments, a method of finance which could only increase significantly the risk of default. Second, although there were periods when some countries found it very difficult to raise capital abroad, there was no case during these phases of a sudden and widespread 'drying up' of international financial markets which would have forced a large number of countries to choose between two equally damaging courses of action: default or severe deflation. Third, the rapid growth of world demand and trade during most of these periods made it possible for the output generated by new investments to be exported, earning foreign exchange which could at least be used to service the debts without great difficulty.

What is also quite clear, however, is that all these developments have worked chiefly in favour of high income countries. Traditionally, they have attracted by far the largest share of private international investments, making it much easier for them than the rest of the world to initiate and sustain economic changes and, in this way, correct any disequilibria. This tendency was offset to some extent in the second half of the period 1880 to 1913 when an increasing proportion of foreign investments found their way into Latin America and the less industrialised parts of Europe. The inducement for this came from a combination of the countries' economic potential and barriers to trade. But the most notable offsetting actions took place in the period 1950 to 1973 when official aid and loans were used deliberately, and on a substantial scale, to assist the countries experiencing fundamental disequilibria. It started in the late 1940s with the Marshall Aid given by the United States to West European countries struggling with the enormous problems of post-war reconstruction and adjustments. It then continued with aid – again mainly from the United States, though other industrial countries also participated in this – to developing countries.

It was all quite different in the interwar period.[37] Private long-term loans from the most important international lender, the United States, dried up at the end of the 1920s and were not replaced by official assistance. The world economic slump and protection made it impossible for the borrowers to earn the foreign exchange needed to service the debts. The absence of a co-ordinated effort by the lending countries to reschedule the debts forced many borrowers to raise short-term loans for long-term purposes – a course of action which cannot be sustained for long. An already critical economic situation was made worse by tight monetary policy and high interest rates in the United States, which increased the burden of servicing the debt. Inevitably, many borrowing countries defaulted. Others imposed severe deflationary measures and, as a result, in quite a few cases underwent violent political changes.[38] The breakdown of the international economic order was such that even one of the most industrialised countries, Germany, went through such an ordeal with great long-term cost to itself and the rest of the world.

While many of these problems were avoided in the second half of the 1970s, international developments since 1981 have a good deal in common with those just described. The international bond market is still less important than the market for loan financing, as the potential lenders have been frightened off by fears of inflation. Moreover, the maturities are often not greater than those of bank credits. At the same time, transnational banks, which played such an important role in financing balance of payments deficits and adjustments in the newly industrialised and developing countries, are now very reluctant to lend to these borrowers because of the size of their debts and the problems which they have had in servicing them.

The most important causes of the borrowing countries' difficulties are very similar, therefore, to those which had such devastating effects in the interwar period: the problem of raising long-term loans and, consequently, the use of short- to medium-term credits to finance long-term investments; persistent stagnation in the world economy and selective protection, both of which restrict borrowers' exports; and restrictive monetary policies and high interest rates in the United States and other industrial countries which have increased greatly the burden of debt servicing. However, unlike in the interwar period, *de facto* defaults have been prevented by official loans and widespread rescheduling, frequently on the initiative and with the participation of governments and central banks from industrial countries, and international organisations. Nevertheless, many developing countries have been required to implement highly deflationary policies which have already produced a good deal of political instability in a number of them. (Most of these problems will be analysed in much more detail in Part IV.)

For these reasons, the risk of another disintegration of the world economy, as in 1914–50, remains. In the absence of large-scale international investments and real resource transfers, structural deficit countries are condemned to perpetual stagnation. This means that further participation in the international division of labour, far from providing net benefits, will in fact impose on them unacceptably high net social costs. In the circumstances, the only sustainable long-term course of action realistically open to them, as pointed out in Part II, is to insulate their economies and pursue a policy of national self-sufficiency.

Given the sheer scale and variety of resources required in modern industrialisation, and the inability of most countries to mobilise them internally, international investments and transfers of real resources represent the only way to overcome the absence of an extremely important condition for the establishment and survival of an open international economic system: that of equality of opportunity, or 'perfect competition', to which the classical economists attached so much importance.

VII

The important question to consider now is whether these very large differences in the size of foreign investments reflect significant changes in international financial arrangements between the periods. In other words, has the international financial system operated much more effectively in certain periods than in others and, if so, why?

The world consists of numerous independent, sovereign states, each with its own currency. The right to issue a national currency is regarded, in fact, as an integral part of that sovereignty. In the absence of some arrangement to link all these diverse currencies, it would obviously be impossible for trade to take place between countries except in the form of bilateral balances. Residents of country *A* would sell their produce to those of country *B* and use the proceeds to buy *B*'s goods and services equal to the value of their earnings. *B*'s currency would be of no use to them in their own country or in trade with other nations. Such a trading and payments system would, clearly, be cumbersome and inefficient – giving very little scope for international specialisation and, consequently, for an increase in world output, employment and incomes.

One way to avoid this kind of problem is for the governments of as many countries as possible to come to some formal agreement specifying the types of assets to be used in settling international debts; and the rules of behaviour to be observed when such debts arise. Alternatively, they can accept officially the informal arrangements which have evolved over time at the micro-economic level. Whatever its origin, the real test of efficiency of an international financial system will lie, ultimately, in the extent to which it promotes financial flows in such a way as to reduce, in the long run, global disparities in economic development and income levels. As shown in Part I, the (upward) equalisation of incomes is of critical importance in widening continuously the scope for further increases in international specialisation, production, employment and incomes.

There are four basic requirements without which the system is unlikely to pass this test.

First, there has to be, as already mentioned, a consensus on what constitutes the assets which are generally acceptable in settling international debts. The importance of this is that it enables national monetary authorities to hold these liquid assets as their reserves, which can be used either to finance temporary, unforeseen, balance of payments deficits; or to maintain a certain relationship between their currency and currencies of other countries. The role of the reserve assets can be performed by: (a) a commodity such as gold (as under 'the gold standard'); or (b) the commodity and one or two currencies (as under 'the gold exchange standard' when gold, US dollar and sterling were used for this purpose); or (c) the currency of a major trading nation (as since the early 1970s when the world has for all practical purposes been on 'the dollar standard'); or (d) an internationally created asset (such as the 'Special Drawing Rights' available to members of the International Monetary Fund).

Second, once nation states agree that certain assets can be used as reserve assets, they have also to come to some agreement, or understanding, on the method by which national currencies can be exchanged for these assets and, therefore, for one another.

There are two main options here. Governments can fix the exchange rates within a narrow range and accept the responsibility for maintaining them within that range. If they are successful in this, the exchange risk will virtually disappear and the system become highly integrated. The widespread confidence that the parities can be maintained indefinitely will, in the absence of exchange controls, make national currencies almost perfect substitutes for one another.

Alternatively, if no government is either able or willing to maintain fixed parities the rates may be left to float. Whether such a system leads to international financial and economic distintegration or not will depend on the degree of specialisation already reached; and also on the existence of a large country which accounts for a high proportion of world production, trade and finance.

If there is a high degree of international specialisation and countries are of more or less the same size, they will have a strong incentive to re-establish quickly a regime of fixed rates and clearly specified rules of international behaviour. Otherwise, they would all be confronted with the very high and rising costs imposed on all of them by contraction in the international division of labour caused by the uncertainty and confusion created by floating exchange rates, especially if each country attempted to pursue an independent economic policy.

Many of these problems and the risk of disintegration will still remain even if the level of international specialisation is high and there is a large economy which plays an important role in international exchange. However, it is possible in this case to minimise exchange risks and to avoid major disruptions to the existing international system by using increasingly the large country's currency to perform the role of an international medium of exchange, unit of account and store of value. In other words, the currency comes to play more and more the role of world 'money'; and the country's financial institutions start to fulfil to a considerable extent the role of global financial institutions. If no country is in this position, the result may be a system consisting of a number of financial unions developed around large economies and embracing those countries which have close trading and financial ties with them.

Hence, while a regime of floating exchange rates is likely to discourage international integration by raising exchange risks, it need not reverse it, unless the world consists entirely of small countries which also happen to be at a low level of national and international specialisation.

Third, the stability of an international financial system – essential if there is to be widespread confidence in it – can be maintained only if countries accept certain stabilisation and adjustment rules. This is imperative for the very simple reason that each country's actions will have repercussions well beyond its borders. The most important requirement here is that each country take prompt measures of the kind suggested in Chapter 4 to stabilise its economy if unanticipated external imbalances appear as a result of either inflationary or deflationary policies; and that planned current account imbalances should be offset *ex ante* by securing appropriate inflows of foreign investments.

It is generally accepted that these rules have to be observed in a regime of fixed exchange rates, as governments are normally under an obligation to maintain existing parities. In contrast, it used to be widely held – and still is by many economists – that under floating rates each country is sufficiently insulated from external developments to be able to pursue an independent economic policy. In practice, this is true only of a world of self-sufficient economies in which foreign production and trade account for a negligible share of total output. Where this is not the case, the only way for countries to regain national economic independence is to regress to a more primitive stage of economic development. The overall cost of such a course of action – economic, social and political – is so great that no modern nation state is likely either to embrace it deliberately or, even if it did so, to sustain it for very long. Consequently the fundamental stabilisation and adjustment rules will have to be observed – except perhaps in the very short run – irrespective of whether exchange rates are fixed or floating.

Finally, if people are to have confidence in the reserve assets, their creation in an international financial system has to be based on certain rules and conventions, clearly understood and widely accepted. Excess supply of such assets will progressively weaken the confidence in them and, in this way, first destabilise and then destroy the system. Persistent excess demand, on the other hand, will impose a constraint on the growth of world production and trade and lead, inevitably, to a search for some suitable alternative.

Rapid economic growth and international specialisation are incompatible, therefore, with a system based on a commodity, such as gold, whose supply cannot be controlled easily. The problem of increasing the supply of gold in line with world economic developments and demand is one of the reasons why the gold standard began to give way to a gold exchange standard even before the First World War.[39] The most likely currency to be used for settling international debts under this system will be the currency of the largest and most advanced economy in the world. The country with such an economy is bound to account for a large share of world output and trade, and, consequently, to have financial institutions capable of intermediating internationally. The reliance on the leading country's currency and institutions will spread rapidly if the country also happens to be earning structural surpluses, as this will reduce exchange risks by virtually eliminating the danger that the currency might depreciate.

The most serious weakness inherent in all systems based entirely, or even largely, on the currency of one country is that they can operate only so long as that country enjoys a position of unquestioned economic supremacy and stability. As no country has managed so far to occupy such a position indefinitely, the whole system will become increasingly unstable at the first sign of its relative economic decline, particularly when it becomes clear that the country is finding it difficult to reconcile its internal and external balances. The result will be large-scale movements of short-term funds from the reserve currency into the currencies of the new surplus countries, or even into commodities, as soon as there are signs of economic developments which might lead to its depreciation. This invariably gives rise to uncertainty; uncertainty reduces long-term investment and economic growth; and prolonged economic stagnation leads to more restrictive commercial policies.

This somewhat lengthy digression on the basic conditions needed to enable a global financial system to function effectively is necessary in order to make some sense out of the enormous number of changes which have taken place in the international financial system over the past century and a half. The most important among these – and the extent to which they have influenced the character of each of the six periods – are described briefly in the remainder of this section.

All the essential financial arrangements for a stable international system were present during two of the periods: 1880–1913 ('the gold standard' system) and 1950–73 ('the Bretton Woods System'). In both cases, exchange rates were fixed; gold, sterling and US dollar were used as the reserve assets; their creation was guided by the production of gold and convertibility, at least in settling official debts, of the reserve currencies into gold; and the required stabilisation and adjustment policies were followed by the more industrialised countries. Consequently, the external imbalances of the most active participants in the international system tended to be short-term, small and manageable. Major financial crises were also avoided in both periods because the authorities of the leading countries (mainly Britain before 1914 and the United States after 1950) were willing and able to assist countries with external liquidity problems by performing the function of the 'lender of last resort'.[40]

In their later stages, however, both these periods were characterised by growing uncertainty, flights of short-term capital and concern about the adequacy of the leading countries' reserves.[41] The reasons for this were very much the same: the growth and sophistication of national and international financial markets; and the relative decline of the dominant economy, demonstrated increasingly (a) in its inabilitiy to sustain structural surpluses, and (b) in its incapacity to stabilise the system unilaterally.[42] The Bretton Woods System collapsed at the beginning of the 1970s. The gold standard came effectively to an end with the outbreak of the First World War though, given the underlying problems, it is very doubtful whether it would have survived much longer even without such a lethal shock.

The first two periods, 1820–60 and 1860–80, are quite different from the rest for the very simple reason that the level of financial integration – both national and international – was very low at the time.[43] There was a variety of monetary systems in operation and international payments were predominantly bilateral or triangular in character.[44] The international financial system was bimetallic, with some countries on the gold, some on the silver and others on both these standards. Exchange rates often floated, and there was a good deal of economic instability. France and Britain acted as the stabilisers of the system, but financial crises were frequent. Apart from the interwar years, these were the most unstable periods of world economic development.[45] It is very doubtful, therefore, whether without the pressure of population on land in Europe there would have been either such a strong trend towards more liberal commercial policies; or such an increase in the production and exchange of manufactures for primary commodities – all of which contributed to a significant increase in international integration during the two periods.

The interwar period, on the other hand, represents the worst example of international financial disintegration experienced so far. The First World War had left many countries incapable of reconciling their internal and external balances.[46] On top of this, many European countries had borrowed heavily from the United States during the war and had somehow to obtain foreign exchange to service and repay these debts. German reparations seemed to provide a solution to the problem, in the sense that the countries could use the receipts from Germany in order to pay off their debts to the United States – hence the obsession with this particular question during the 1920s. The snag was that in order to undertake the reparations the Germans had to earn foreign exchange; and no country was prepared to accept a large-scale expansion of German exports to it because of the effect that this might have on the development of its own economy.

The situation was eased for a time by US investments in Europe; and by American and, to a lesser extent, British stabilisation loans to a number of countries in the early 1920s. The drying up of US investments at the end of the 1920s, caused by the great speculative boom at home, plus the failure of the US authorities to counterbalance this with official loans, made it impossible for many countries to solve their adjustment problems within an open international system or, indeed, to honour their external obligations. Given the circumstances, it is hardly surprising that attempts to fix the parities and revive the gold standard rules proved to be short lived. Everyone knew that no country was really in a position to observe them for very long – not exactly the way to inspire confidence in a particular international arrangement!

To make things worse, the supply of gold was inadequate to sustain a major expansion of world activity and trade. This fact was recognised officially at the Genoa conference in 1922 and led many countries to adopt the gold exchange standard. The problem was that with no economy, financial system and currency in a position of pre-eminence (such as Britain, London and sterling enjoyed before 1914) short-term funds kept moving from one financial centre to another, widening further the cracks in an already shaky international financial edifice. Inevitably, the multilateral system of international trade and payments which had evolved during the thirty or so years before 1914 collapsed in the early 1930s into a series of bilateral arrangements and regional, or colonial, monetary systems. At the end of it all, most of those who had lived through the crises of the 1920s and the 1930s had little doubt that it was the incapacity of the nation states to recognise the reality and obligations of their international interdependence *and* to rearrange their relationship accordingly that led to the Second World War.[47]

The latest phase (since 1973) has many similarities with the 1930s: large-scale movements of short-term capital, volatile exchange rates, absence of clear-cut rules concerning either international reserves or stabilisation and adjustment policies. Yet this so-called 'non-system' has not led, so far at least, to international financial disintegration. A very important reason for this probably lies in the exceptionally high degree of international interdependence developed to a large extent spontaneously, at the micro-economic level, over the last thirty years. In the absence of constructive government actions, this has forced the most important agents of this integration – transnational enterprises – to look for ways which would minimise uncertainty and preserve at least some elements of the post-war system. The result has been the phenomenal growth of a centralised international financial market – the Euromarket – which has facilitated both the financing of short-term imbalances and the adjustment of long-term disequilibria. Moreover, as the institutions of the largest national market, that of the United States, have played the most important role in these developments, the world has moved for all practical purposes to a dollar standard, with the Deutschmark, the yen and the European currency unit (within the EEC) in supporting roles.

Equally important in preventing a major international financial crisis has probably been the fact that, although they have made little effort to create a new international order, governments and central banks have been very careful to avoid a collapse of the kind which took place in the early 1930s. The speed with which they intervened in the early 1980s to prevent defaults on international loans provides the best illustration of their anxiety to maintain some sort of an informal order.

The reason why, in spite of this, there is so much uncertainty, confusion and a general impression of a 'non-system' is that all these actions appear to be no more than *ad hoc* responses to particualr international crises. The strength of both the gold standard and the Bretton Woods System was that the countries involved formally accepted and observed certain rules of behaviour in conducting their international economic relationships. In the absence of such arrangements, experience shows that all international systems, or 'non-systems', are bound to remain dangerously unstable.

VIII

In conclusion, what are the main lessons to emerge from this comparison of some of the most important developments in the world economy since the 1820s?

To begin with, international economic performance does not normally, even less regularly, oscillate between 'golden ages' of uniformly rapid progress and blissful tranquility and periods of stagnation and utter chaos; nor is there anything 'automatic' about the outbursts of great instability when they do occur. Many of the problems which have received a good deal of attention since the early 1970s were in fact present in all the periods: persistent internal imbalances and external deficits in some countries and structural surpluses in others; a good deal of real wages ridigity[48] so that short-term balance of payments deficits had to be corrected mainly through changes in domestic activity and absorption; the tendency of export prices and interest rates to move in the same direction in both surplus and deficit countries; the threat of highly destabilising short-term capital flows; and so on.[49] Nevertheless, these problems rarely combine to produce major international crises of the kind experienced in the period 1914 to 1950 and, to a lesser extent, since 1973.

The most important explanation of these differences appears to be the existence – in certain periods but not in others – of international arrangements which promote an orderly stabilisation and adjustment of national economies. The most important among these are, as one might expect, precisely the factors which have been recognised for a long time as being of critical importance for the achievement and maintenance of a free trade regime: the pursuit of similar economic objectives, based on a widespread recognition of the importance of international interdependence; a reasonably balanced growth which avoids major shocks to the system such as those created by a serious disparity in the development of primary and secondary sectors, giving rise suddenly to the appearance of fundamental disequilibria; an efficient international financial system, designed to assist the countries with serious stabilisation and adjustment problems; and a certain degree of international factor mobility, especially of investments from surplus into deficit countries – which may have to take, for some time at least, the form of official transfers.

All these conditions were met between 1950 and 1973, the most successful period so far in terms of both world economic development and integration. Some of them were also present during the first two periods (1820–60 and 1860–80). However, the absence of a well-developed international order was far less disruptive then than in the twentieth century because the world economy was much less integrated and a good deal simpler. Many of the arrangements which make the existence of a stable international system possible were developed during the period 1880 to 1913. But the shocks which forced a number of countries to underake major structural adjustments, as well as the lack of international cooperation to deal adequately with the problems created by the shocks, made this period less internationalist than is generally believed.

The remaining two, isolationist, periods represent clear examples of reversals in the development of a stable and orderly international system. The order developed before 1914 disintegrated completely in the early 1930s. Nothing as dramatic has happened since 1973. But, as already pointed out, many of the arrangements developed after the Second World War have been seriously weakened.

Inevitably, the success or failure of the world community to evolve international relationships and institutions in a way appropriate to the growing size, complexity and interdependence of national economies has been reflected in changes in countries' commercial policies, as described at the beginning of this chapter.

10 Long-term Changes in International Openness and Income Inequality

I

There are two periods, among the six distinguished in the previous chapter, whose rules and conventions of international behaviour inspired a good deal of satisfaction among contemporaries and nostalgia later on: 1880–1913 (the gold standard) and 1950–73 (the Bretton Woods System).

Both historians and economists have tended to attribute this to a widespread appreciation of the benefits derived from the freedom of trade and orderly international relationships maintained during the first period; and the exceptionally rapid and stable economic progress achieved in the second period. However, though very important, these factors do not in themselves explain why a large number of countries attempt to revive an international order once it breaks down, or, alternatively, wish to retain most of its main characteristics in creating a new order. Considerable efforts were made in the interwar period to re-establish the gold standard; and the demise of the Bretton Woods System in the 1970s inspired similar efforts.

The most obvious explanation for such an allegiance to the two systems is that the progress achieved during the periods that they operated must have been fairly widely diffused; and that the countries which shared in this progress have tended to attribute it to the international economic arrangements prevailing at the time.

It is most unlikely, as emphasised earlier, that an independent sovereign state will participate in an international arrangement if the gains from it are distributed in a way which is unsatisfactory from its point of view. What exactly constitutes an 'unsatisfactory economic relationship' is something that cannot be defined with precision, as it will be influenced by the prevailing levels of international cultural and economic integration. If these levels are low, it is possible that countries will take very little notice even of growing disparities in international economic performance and incomes. As international integration intensifies, most countries are likely, for reasons analysed in Chapter 1, to regard increasingly as unsatisfactory – and try to change – any international order which fails to promote economic progress and long-term equalisation of international incomes. Consequently, the distribution of gains from international integration is bound to be one of the key factors in the long-run success and stability of an open system of international economic relationships.

The last important issue to be considered in this, historical, part of the book is, therefore, that of changes in international income disparities since the early nineteenth century. Can they be in any way associated with the developments described in the previous chapter? Have the periods 1880 to 1913 and 1950 to 1973 been significantly different in this respect from the other four periods? What is the relevance, if any, of all this for international openness and the long-term process of integration?

II

The estimates produced by Kuznets and Bairoch, for example, show that the degree of international inequality in economic performance and income was very low at the beginning of the Industrial Revolution. According to Bairoch, in 1800 the level of GNP per capita in the richest countries at the time was less than double the levels prevailing at the other end of the scale. From then on the gap widened rapidly: incomes were 4.5 times higher in the most developed countries in 1860, ten times greater in 1913, eighteen times in 1950 and twenty-nine times by the late 1970s.[1]

These ratios compare per capita income levels in the most advanced industrial countries with those in subsistence economies. If the comparisons are confined to countries which have started to industrialise, in other words countries such as those included in Table 10.1, the ratios, through still high, are much lower. For instance, incomes per head in the four wealthiest countries in 1950 (USA, Canada, Australia and New Zealand) were 10.5 greater than in the poorest four countries (China, India, Kenya and Pakistan). By 1980 the gap had increased slightly: this time incomes in the four richest countries (USA, Canada, Norway and West Germany) were twelve times higher than in the poorest four (Kenya, India, Pakistan and Sri Lanka).[2]

Table 10.1 Coefficients of variation of per capita GNP (per cent)

	25 countries		*53 countries*	
	A	*B*	*C*	*D*
1830	18.2			
1860	34.7			
1880	49.4			
1913	46.8			
1929	47.5			
1938	41.0			
1950	56.0	51.0	64.1	65.2
1973	34.9*	30.9	59.0	61.8
1980	31.2**	29.2	55.6	58.3

Notes: A = Bairoch (1981); B = Summers and Heston (1984); C = all countries: D = Excluding centrally planned economies.
*1970; **1977.
Countries:
Industrial: Australia, Austria, Belgium, Canada, Denmark, Finland, France, West Germany, Iceland, Italy, Japan, Netherlands, New Zealand, Norway, Sweden, Switzerland, UK and USA.
Newly-industrialised: Argentina, Brazil, Greece, Ireland, Israel, Portugal, South Africa, Spain, Uruguay, Venezuela and Yugoslavia.
Developing: Chile, Columbia, Equador, Egypt, India, Kenya, Mexico, Morocco, Nigeria, Pakistan, Paraguay, Peru, Philippines, Sri Lanka, Thailand and Turkey.
Centrally planned: Bulgaria, China, Czechoslovakia, East Germany, Hungary, Poland, Rumania and USSR.
Twenty-five: Australia, Austria, Belgium, Bulgaria, Canada, Denmark, Finland, France, Germany (West Germany), Greece, Italy, Japan, Netherlands, New Zealand, Norway, Portugal, Rumania, South Africa, Spain, Russia (USSR), Sweden, Switzerland, UK, USA and Yugoslavia.
Sources: Bairoch (1981), Summers and Heston (1984). For 1880: Bairoch (1976b), Rostow (1980).

III

The weakness of these, like all, ratios is that they take into account only the extreme values and ignore the rest. More revealing and important are, therefore, the long-term comparisons of inequality of international per capita incomes shown in Tables 10.1 and 10.2. (All the original estimates of incomes are in US dollars at constant prices.) The figures show dispersions around the mean international income,

Table 10.2 Income dispersion within each group and in relation to industrial countries (coefficients of variation, per cent)

	1950	*1973*	*1980*
Within each group			
Industrial countries	34.3	13.9	14.1
Newly industrialised countries	35.3	24.8	20.3
Centrally planned economies	43.4	35.3	34.3
Developing countries	33.1	39.9	40.6
In relation to industrial countries			
Industrial and newly industrialised	47.3	35.6	34.0
Industrial and centrally planned	46.0	29.8	28.6
Industrial and developing	68.7	66.4	63.2

Source: Summers and Heston (1984).

calculated from per capita incomes of the twenty-five countries for which the long-term data are available; and a selection of fifty-three countries which, again, excludes subsistence economies.

Taking, first, the twenty-five countries only, the dispersion of their income levels in 1830 (Table 10.1) – roughly, when the first imitators of the British Industrial Revolution began to industrialise – was similar to that which exists among the newly industrialised countries today (Table 10.2). By 1860, however, international income inequality had gone up sharply, followed by even more rapid growth in the disparities during the second period (1860–80). These changes can probably be explained by two factors. First, by 1880 some countries had achieved substantial economic progress, while others had not even started to industrialise. Second, as pointed out in Chapter 9, the origin and direction of international factor movements during these two periods were clearly in favour of countries with high per capita incomes.

Important changes took place in both these respects during the second half of the next period (1880–1913). For the first time since the beginning of the Industrial Revolution, the growing disparity in international income levels was arrested, even slightly reversed. What is more, this was achieved during a period when per capita incomes were rising at a higher rate than at any time before the Second World War.[3] Only a few of the twenty-five countries had failed by this time, in Rostow's jargon, 'to take off into self-sustained growth'. This very important change was reflected, as described earlier, in an increasing use of restrictive commercial policies by most countries engaged in restructuring their economies; and in a change in the direction of international factor flows in a way favourable to the countries with low per capita income.

A much more pronounced equalisation of international incomes occurred, as can be seen from the first column in Table 10.1, in the interwar period – all of it in the 1930s. The important aspect of this change is that it was the result of a combination of two factors: a *decline* in per capita incomes in many of the most affluent countries, and increases in incomes in poor countries. In other words, economic developments during the 1930s 'affected the less industrialised countries more mildly'.[4]

The equalisation which took place between 1950 and 1973 was quite different in character. The Second World War had affected the twenty-five countries unevenly, leaving their income levels more unequal (Table 10.1) than ever before. By 1973, however, the differences had shrunk to one of the lowest levels on record, with the dispersion comparable to that in 1860. The figures produced by Summers and Heston (second column in Table 10.1) show an even lower dispersion. The same trend is also noticeable if the data for over fifty countries are analysed, though it is less dramatic than the change experienced by the twenty-five countries. Furthermore, Table 10.2 shows that the gap in per capita incomes had narrowed in three out of the four groups, with developing countries as the only exception. The most noticeable equalisation of incomes took place among the eighteen industrial countries. There was also a narrowing of differences in income levels between industrial and the other three groups of countries, with developing countries doing least well in this respect.

All these changes took place during a period of exceptionally rapid increases in world production and incomes from which all four groups benefited, though not equally. Taking the averages for each group, the largest increase in per capita income was achieved between 1950 and 1973 by centrally planned economies (154 per cent), followed by industrial countries (121 per cent), newly industrialised countries (117 per cent) and developing countries (61 per cent). These broad rankings, leaving aside centrally planned economies whose growth was to a large extent generated internally, correspond fairly closely to the direction of international investments and resource transfers during the period. By far the largest volume of private and official investments took place in industrial countries, with newly industrialised countries getting the next largest slice and developing countries trailing behind.

It is difficult to compare developments in the distribution of per capita incomes since 1973 because comparable data are not available beyond 1980. What seems to have happened in the second half of the 1970s is that (as in the 1920s) the narrowing of international income differentials was halted in all the groups, except among newly industrialised countries (Table 10.2). The other interesting – though given the experience in the earlier phases not entirely surprising – development is that a comparison of increases in average incomes per head between 1973 and 1980 gives a rather different ranking from that observed during the preceding period. The largest increase this time was recorded by developing countries (27 per cent), followed by centrally planned economies (14 per cent), newly industrialised countries (13 per cent) and industrial countries (9 per cent).

There are indications, however, that the trend towards lower disparities in international incomes may have been reversed in the first half of the 1980s.[5] Following the debt crisis in 1981–82 many newly industrialised, developing and even some centrally planned economies have been forced to reduce drastically their growth rates. As a result, the growth of per capita income has slowed down in most of them. Some countries have even experienced reductions in their income levels. Lower increases in per capita income are apparent also in industrial countries, though the deceleration has been less pronounced in their case. Taking the period since 1973 as a whole, however, industrial countries appear to have experienced an appreciably lower rate of growth in their per capita income than almost any other group of countries.[6]

IV

As emphasised in Chapter 8, it would be wrong to regard commercial policies and international economic relationships in general as the dominant factor in the development of a country. All economies do not have an equal potential for growth. Even more important, all countries have not shown themselves equally able, ready and willing to absorb the cultural and institutional changes which would have enabled them to industrialise. It would obviously be absurd to attribute the economic success of Japan, the United States, Canada and Australia, or the failure of Argentina, Brazil and China, to the nature and character of *international* economic orders and disorders prevailing over the past century.

At the same time, providing that the willingness to change and a determination to emulate the example of industrial nations exist within a country, international economic arrangements designed to promote economic growth and global specialisation can make a significant contribution to the achievement of these goals. An important conclusion which emerges from the description in the preceding sections is that changes in the world distribution of incomes during different periods are clearly and consistently associated with major developments during each period.

To begin with, liberal commercial policies pursued by countries at different levels of development will, without compensatory movements in the factors of production, invariably increase international income disparities. In other words, such policies will, as the experience in 1820–60 and 1860–80 shows, favour the most advanced economies. Whether they have achieved this status by developing their natural wealth, industrial potential or a combination of the two, their accumulated stock of resources and knowledge gives these countries an enormous competitive advantage over less advanced economies. Consequently, free trade will, in the absence of compensatory factor movements, widen the gap in economic performance and incomes of the two groups.

What makes, *ceteris paribus*, such an international system inherently unstable is the fact that, even if greater international integration makes the newcomers better off in absolute terms, a combination of relative economic stagnation and cultural integration will leave them with serious adjustment problems. They will have no alternative, therefore, but to impose trade restrictions in order to reduce the scale of these problems. This is what happened in the last quarter of the nineteenth century and on a much greater scale in the 1930s.

Second, the cost of international economic crises and disintegration tends to be very high in advanced economies, often even higher than in developing countries, because of the scale of their involvement in the international division of labour. This explains why their incomes increased relatively slowly in the years preceding the First World War and in the second half of the 1970s; and why so many of the most advanced countries experienced actual reductions in their per capital income levels in the 1930s.[7] The maintenance of an open and growing world economy, with an orderly system of international economic relationships is, therefore, very much in the interest of these countries.

Third, three is, of course, a way for the most advanced countries to promote the achievement of such an open system: by investing in the less advanced countries and, in general, assisting them to achieve higher standards of productivity and incomes. The United States, and to a lesser extent some of the other leading industrial countries, pursued such a policy deliberately in the period 1950 to 1973, the only period since the beginning of the Industrial Revolution during which trade liberalisation was accompanied by a widespread reduction in international differences in economic performance and incomes. Both these trends, as already pointed out, were most pronounced among industrial countries. Nevertheless, the experience and behaviour of industrialised nations in this period demonstrate clearly the way that the economic welfare of the whole world could be increased in the long run.

Fourth, the importance of this policy approach is that far from reducing the rate of economic growth in individual countries it accelerates it by enabling them to engage in intra-industry specialisation and trade. This, as explained in Part I, is possible on a significant scale only among countries with high *and* similar efficiency and income levels. Not surprisingly, this kind of trade made its appearance towards the end of the nineteenth century when 'the era of mass consumptions dawned, and several of the major industrial regions began to draw level ... It meshed the European, and indeed the world, economy into an ever tighter network ... as everyone became ever more dependent on everyone else.'[8] All this has become even more true of international developments since the 1950s. Their importance lies in the fact that they demonstrate conclusively that in a dynamic international economy there is no long-term conflict between equality and efficiency. On the contrary, the two reinforce each other and, in this way, generate further improvements in world welfare.

Finally, in dynamic conditions, even an international order which promotes the growth and equalisation of international efficiency and income levels cannot survive indefinitely – unless its rules and conventions are continuously adapted in such a way that they can deal effectively with the problems created by greater integration and interdependence. The Bretton Woods System collapsed in the end because it lacked the provisions needed to cope with such changes.

The problem of institutional adaptation to economic integration will be discussed in Part V. Before doing this, however, it is important to examine some of the unique problems created for the international economy by the energy crisis and its aftermath. Part IV deals with these issues.

Part IV
The Long-term Consequences of the Energy Crisis

The energy crisis of the 1970s and 1980s has added an entirely new dimension to the adjustment problems analysed in earlier chapters. It also provides an important example of the risks involved in an adversarial approach to international economic relationships in a world of highly integrated and interdependent national economies. The continuing tendency to regard international specialisation and exchange as a zero-sum game, in which national economic welfare can be improved only at the expense of other countries, is bound sooner or later to produce an outcome in which everyone is worse off.

There is still considerable disagreement about the nature of developments in the world energy market since the early 1970s and the most likely course of action that can be expected from the producers and consumers over the remaining years of the twentieth century. Some experts are convinced that the real price of oil – the most important primary source of energy – will go up, while others are equally sure that it will fall. The nearest that the two groups seem to come to something resembling a consensus is in recognising that 'the price uncertainty experienced in the 1970s will continue into the 1980s and beyond'.[1]

Yet a widespread agreement about the origin of the energy crisis and the threat which it poses to the development of a stable international economic order is essential because of a number of new elements which it has introduced into the world economy. First, there is the constant threat of another serious imbalance in the energy market, accompanied by another shock to the international system. Second, the most important producers of one of the key primary commodities, oil, have demonstrated their willingness and ability to reduce the growth of oil output to rates which impose a physical constraint on world economic development. Nothing of the kind has happened since the beginning of the Industrial Revolution. Third, the widespread uncertainty concerning the future course of the world economy has changed the behaviour of both savers and investors in a way which prevents the required adjustments and, consequently, threatens an eventual disintegration of the world economy.

The three chapters in Part IV analyse each of these new developments in turn. The analysis will be confined to energy, especially oil, even though price movements of a number of other primary products since the early 1970s[2] *have raised policy issues which are of a rather similar nature. However, although some of these commodities are of strategic importance, none of them has a world-wide 'domain' comparable to that of petroleum.*[3] *Hence, no other primary product has created adjustment problems, or posed a threat to an integrated world economy, on even remotely the same scale.*

11 Origins of the Energy Crisis

I

The most important aspect of the energy crisis is that it has never had anything to do with an actual shortage of energy. The known reserves of oil and other fuels are still substantial. The problem is that most of them can be extracted only at costs which are considerably higher than those prevailing in the 1950s and 1960s.

It was the growing realisation of this fact, combined with a number of important economic and political developments, that led in the 1970s to an abrupt change in the attitude and behaviour of oil and, subsequently, other energy producers. The result was that, within a very short period, the world economic environment was transformed in a way which was both dramatic and unique.

II

In 1971 the official price of crude oil was US$1.26 per barrel, less than double the level ($0.75) at the beginning of the 1960s. Ten years later, at the end of 1981, it stood at $34.00 per barrel, almost twenty seven times higher than the 1971 price. What is more, most of this extraordinary change in the fortune of oil producers was accomplished in two big jumps: between October 1973 and January 1974 the price of crude oil almost quadrupled (from $2.80 to $10.84); and over a similar period at the end of the decade, between October 1979 and January 1980, it went up by more than 40 per cent (from $18.00 to $26.00 per barrel). The collapse of oil prices in 1985–86 was equally dramatic and occurred also within a very short period. Between November 1985 and April 1986 the price of crude oil fell from around $28 to about $15 per barrel. Some of it was traded at even lower prices on the spot market, at $10–$13 a barrel.

The concentration of such large changes in the price of oil since the early 1970s within the three twelve-months periods (1973–74, 1979–80 and 1985–86) is shown in Table 11.1, together with the accompanying volatility in export prices of manufactured goods and other primary commodities. As a result of these, exceptionally wide

Table 11.1 Annual changes in world output, trade and prices, 1963–86

				Prices (in terms of US$)			*Terms of trade*		
		Output	*Trade*	*Manufactures**	*Oil***	*Non-oil primary commodities****	*Industrial countries*	*Developing countries*	
								Oil exporting	*Others*
Average:	1963–72	4.7	8.5	3.0	3.0	2.5	0.3	0.5	–
	1973–86	2.9	4.2	7.2	30.3	7.3	−0.4	12.5	−0.8
Annual:	1973	6.2	12.5	17.7	40.0	53.2	−1.6	11.8	6.1
	1974	0.6	4.5	21.8	225.8	28.0	−11.9	138.4	−5.6
	1975	−0.5	−4.0	12.3	5.1	−18.2	2.7	−5.4	−9.0
	1976	4.9	11.0	–	6.3	13.3	−1.0	5.8	6.0
	1977	4.0	4.7	8.0	9.6	21.2	−1.4	1.0	6.5
	1978	4.5	5.4	15.6	0.4	−5.5	3.9	−10.3	−3.9
	1979	3.3	6.5	14.2	45.9	17.8	−2.8	26.8	−1.2
	1980	2.0	1.7	10.7	63.5	5.9	−6.4	43.8	−5.9
	1981	1.6	0.8	−4.9	9.9	−13.9	−1.2	11.8	−5.3
	1982	0.5	−2.3	−2.5	−4.2	−10.1	2.7	0.1	−2.6
	1983	2.6	2.8	−3.3	−11.7	7.1	2.3	−8.8	0.2
	1984	4.4	8.7	−3.7	−2.1	3.7	1.1	1.1	1.5
	1985	2.9	2.9	1.0	−4.4	−12.2	1.8	−4.2	−1.2
	1986 (est.)	3.1	3.3	14.0	−40.0	12.0	6.7	−37.4	3.6

Notes: * The UN index of unit values of exports of manufactured goods from the major industrial countries.
** The oil export unit value of the oil exporting countries.
*** IMF index of market quotations of non-oil primary commodities.

fluctuations in international prices, the world has experienced over the period unusually large short-term changes in the distribution of income among the three major groups of producers. The terms of trade, shown in the last three columns, have oscillated widely – as each group has tried to improve, or at least maintain, its position relative to the rest of the world.

For instance, industrial countries have reacted to these demonstrations of the newly found market power of oil exporters and other primary producers by reducing their levels of activity. The contractions have inevitably led to sharp reductions in the demand for primary products, as industrial nations are still by far the most important consumers of these commodities. The subsequent weakening of oil and other raw material prices has tended to improve industrial countries' terms of trade during recessions, but at the cost of heavy losses in their output and incomes. Primary producers, on the other hand, have used the opportunities offered by periods of relatively rapid expansion of the world economy to raise prices and thus improve their incomes.

As Table 11.1 shows, the overall effect of the continuous attempts by each of the three groups to exploit its market power at the expense of the rest of the world has been, so far at least, to produce first a large-scale redistribution of world income towards oil producers; and then a much more modest redistribution away from them, mainly in favour of industrial countries. However, the size and short-term volatility of these redistributions have been on a scale which, as will be shown later, has created major adjustment problems in each of the three groups.

III

Like all crises, the energy crisis is the outcome of a number of factors. They had all been in evidence for some time before suddenly combining in 1973 to produce one of the most abrupt and far-reaching peacetime changes in the world economic environment.

To begin with, the exceptionally rapid growth of world output, trade and transport during the 1950s and the 1960s led to a very large increase in demand for energy. The demand for oil increased even faster, as it was cheap relative to other primary sources of energy. World oil production, which was growing very rapidly throughout the period, accelerated from an annual rate of 7 per cent in the 1950s to

Table 11.2 Share of geopolitical regions in world oil production (per cent)

	OECD	*OPEC*	*Centrally planned economies*	*Developing countries*	*World*
A. Shares					
1950	52.9	32.8	8.6	5.7	100.0
1960	38.5	41.8	16.0	3.7	100.0
1973	22.9	54.2	17.7	5.2	100.0
1979	21.8	47.8	22.4	8.0	100.0
1984	27.5	31.8	26.4	14.3	100.0
B. Average annual changes in oil production					
1960/50	3.8	9.8	14.1	1.2	7.2
1973/60	1.2	10.2	8.8	10.9	8.0
1979/73	1.1	−0.2	6.0	9.4	1.9
1984/79	2.1	−11.6	1.0	9.1	−2.6

Sources: International Energy Agency (1982) and British Petroleum (1985).

about 8 per cent between 1960 and 1973 (see Table 11.2). By the early 1970s oil had become, as Table 11.3 shows, the most important source of primary energy in all the major sectors of the OECD economies. In 1973 it accounted for 57.3 per cent of total energy consumption in industrial countries – far more important than coal and gas combined.[1]

The rapid growth in demand for oil, especially in the United States and Japan, had not only created a sellers' market[2] but had also by the early 1970s made industrial countries heavily dependent on oil imports from OPEC. As Table 11.2 shows, OECD share of oil production had fallen from 53 per cent in 1950 to 23 per cent in 1973 – reflecting, in fact, the extent to which the United States had declined in relative importance as an oil producer. Over the same period OPEC's share went up from 33 per cent to 54 per cent.

Moreover, all these changes were taking place during a period in which the political map of the world underwent a major transformation. Numerous countries, including many oil producers, gained political independence in the 1950s and the 1960s. This gave them for the first time the opportunity to use their natural resources in order to develop and modernise their own economies.

The task before them was, and still is, enormous. The gap which they have to bridge to attain the levels of economic development achieved by industrial countries is so wide, and the resources with which to attempt this so limited, that there is a strong feeling of bitterness and resentment towards industrial nations in large parts of the world. This is particularly true of those countries in which backwardness and widespread poverty is attributed by the inhabitants directly to colonial exploitation, mismanagement and support of an indigenous social structure inimical to progress. Not surprisingly, the arrival of national independence has frequently been followed by internal political changes which brought to power groups determined, among other things, to extract some compensation from industrial countries for the problems of development which they had inherited.

Needless to say, this is not an interpretation of history which is widely accepted in industrial countries. On the contrary, the majoirty opinion there seems to be that developing countries are confronted with problems of their own making. Consequently, attempts by primary producers to take advantage of changes in international market conditions in order to extract rents from industrial nations are regarded by the latter as 'blackmail', and so as something to be resisted strongly. The same attitude is also reflected in the reluctance of industrial countries to increase the level of their economic and technical assistance to developing nations. All suggestions for creating a more equitable long-term distribution of wealth through a 'new international economic order'[3] have come so far to nothing.

There is a long-standing tendency, therefore, for the two sides to regard their economic relationships in a typically antagonistic fashion: as a zero-sum game in which each of them can achieve its economic and other objectives only at the expense of the other.

It is essential to bear in mind the strength of these attitudes and the reasons behind them in order to understand properly OPEC's behaviour since the early 1970s. It might be argued, as some experts have done, 'that pre-1973 oil prices were too low to be sustained much beyond the mid-1970s. Similarly, pre-1979 prices were too low to be sustained beyond the mid-to-late 1980s'.[4] However, it is clear from the subsequent international economic developments that the two large increases in the price of oil 'went too far', as the Saudis admitted in 1981,[5] a verdict which would probably not be accepted by the majority of OPEC members. Unlike Saudi Arabia, most of them 'have some combination of large populations, rapid social mobilisation, rising expectations, large revenue needs, low petroleum reserves, and more costly production ... All are worried about depleting their petroleum reserves too quickly'.[6] These worries have played an important role in determining their pricing and output policies since the early 1970s.

There was a considerable oversupply of oil on the world market in

Table 11.3 OECD: share of primary energy sources, sectors and fuels in total final energy consumption*

	Shares				*Average annual % changes*		
	1960	*1973*	*1979*	*1984*	*1960–73*	*1973–79*	*1979–84*
A. Primary energy							
Oil	45.6	57.3	57.1	53.2	6.1	1.2	−3.1
Solid fuels	29.0	12.0	10.6	11.1	−2.5	−0.9	−0.1
Gas	16.8	19.2	18.9	19.9	5.4	1.0	−0.4
Hydro + other	8.5	9.5	8.7	9.0	3.9	−0.5	−0.8
Nuclear	0.1	2.0	4.5	6.8	33.6	16.3	5.6
Total	100.0	100.0	100.0	100.0	3.8	1.2	−1.5
B. Sectors							
Industry	41.3	41.8	39.4	36.5	5.2	0.2	−3.0
Transport	25.3	25.6	27.8	29.7	5.4	2.6	−0.2
Residential/ Commercial	33.4	32.6	32.8	33.8	5.0	1.3	−0.9

C. Fuels		*Solid fuels*	*Oil*	*Gas*	*Electricity*	*Total*
Industry	1960	37.8	29.7	20.1	12.4	100.0
	1973	22.0	41.5	23.4	13.1	100.0
	1979	20.3	43.5	20.9	15.3	100.0
	1984	23.8	34.4	23.5	18.3	100.0
Transport	1960	7.7	91.5	0.1	0.7	100.0
	1973	0.3	99.0	0.0	0.7	100.0
	1979	0.1	99.3	0.0	0.6	100.0
	1984	0.1	99.3	0.0	0.6	100.0
Residential/ Commercial	1960	28.1	36.1	25.0	10.8	100.0
	1973	8.4	44.6	28.8	18.2	100.0
	1979	7.9	37.7	32.4	21.4	100.0
	1984	8.0	31.0	33.7	26.4	100.0

Note: *Shares may not add up to 100 per cent because direct consumption of heat is not shown.
Source: International Energy Agency (1982 and 1986).

1960 when a number of major oil producers formed the Organisation of Petroleum Exporting Countries (OPEC). Faced with the problem of excess supply, oil companies reduced their prices, causing a fall in the revenue of the producing countries. Yet it was apparent even then, as Griffin and Teece point out, that there were substantial economic rents to be earned in the oil market.[7] The marginal cost of producing oil was $0.10 to $0.20 per barrel. At the same time, the retail prices of petrol exceeded $30 per barrel in many parts of Europe because of the high excise taxes collected by governments of the consuming countries. Hence,

> rents were spread quite unevenly between the consuming country's treasury, the international oil companies, and the oil producing countries. The existence of these rents, with a large portion accruing to the consuming countries and the international oil companies, no doubt created considerable resentment in the producing countries. Thus an initial goal of OPEC was to wrest some of these economic rents from the international oil companies and the treasuries of the consuming nations.[8]

The organisation achieved little in the 1960s, except for certain improvements (from the members' point of view) in the system of taxation. However, with the appearance of excess demand in the oil market in the early 1970s, the OPEC governments found themselves in a sufficiently strong position to alter their relationship with oil companies. By assuming control over the production – first through the majority and then full ownership of their most valuable natural resource – pricing decisions also passed to the national authorities. The countries were in a position, therefore, to take full advantage of the sellers' market which developed in 1973 and again at the end of the decade. The price of crude oil quadrupled in 1973–74 and more than doubled in 1979–80.

It is debatable whether OPEC would have felt confident enough first to engineer such huge price increases and then to maintain them at these very high levels for a number of years in the absence of a world-wide consensus in the 1970s that the *real* price of oil could only rise in the long run. The concern for future developments in the oil market was inspired in the 1970s by the then known reserves of petroleum and by expectations that the demand for oil would continue to increase rapidly because the growth of the world economy would do the same. No one expected industrial countries to abandon the objective of full employment and enter a period of prolonged economic stagnation.

Developments in the 1970s have led many people to question these assumptions. The known reserves of oil have increased[9] while the rates of growth have slumped. Nevertheless, there are still many experts, including those with the International Energy Agency, who maintain that whatever may happen to the real price of oil in the 1980s, it is likely to rise, probably sharply, some time in the 1990s.[10] If this happens, the problem, as before, will not be the actual availability of oil, but the likely behaviour of producers and consumers. It is the difficulty of predicting with any certainty the behaviour of the two groups which is causing the uncertainty mentioned in the introduction to Part IV.[11]

IV

Several factors will determine whether problems created by the energy crisis are going to be reduced significantly and permanently in the foreseeable future: the rate of exploration and development of the known reserves of oil and other forms of energy; the number and characteristics of the main oil producers; the extent to which environmental problems and risks associated with certain energy sources are overcome; the behaviour of producers of energy sources other than oil; improvements in the efficiency with which energy is used; and the degree of economic cooperation between energy producing and consuming countries, as well as between members of each of these two very broad and diverse groups.

This is a rather long list; and, to make things worse, considerable uncertainty surrounds developments in each of the factors which it contains. The long-term energy prospects depend on actions of economic agents which, in turn, are determined by what the agents expect the energy prospects to be! Moreover, there are strong indications that these expectations tend to be influenced predominantly by relatively short-term developments in the oil and other energy markets.

Recent changes in the attitude of industrial countries towards exploration and development of their energy resources provide an example of this. The world's potential oil reserves may be substantial. The reserves are of little use, however, unless they are discovered, explored and developed. All this requires considerable investments.

The extent to which such investments are made will depend on current as well as expected prices of oil and other sources of energy. The two large increases in the price of oil in the 1970s and expectations that the real price of oil would rise in the long term encouraged massive efforts to explore and develop high cost reserves of oil and gas, such as those in the North Sea. Considerable efforts were made also to develop other sources of energy.

International preoccupation with long-term energy prospects appears to have weakened appreciably, however, since the first drop in the official price of crude oil early in 1983. For intance, fixed investment in the US oil industry, which almost trebled in volume between 1973 and 1981, has declined continuously since then. Exploration and development of North Sea oil and gas reserves has also been reduced markedly, especially after the collapse of oil prices in 1985–86. The cost of developing these reserves is too high to be profitable at prices prevailing in the first half of the 1980s. Furthermore, the weakening of oil and other energy prices has raised doubts about the long-term profitability of investments in the energy sector.

It is impossible to predict with any certainty how long these doubts and lower investments are going to last. What is certain, however, is that they carry considerable long-term risks. As the International Energy Agency keeps warning: 'Sustained low oil and energy prices could well affect the replacement of oil by other fuels and the development of new energy sources'[12] – making oil importing countries increasingly vulnerable to another sharp rise in prices of the kind experienced in the 1970s.

The ability of oil producers to cause another 'oil shock' either deliberately or accidentally will depend, among other things, on their number and cohesion. Generally, the smaller the number of producers and the more identical are the conditions under which they operate the more similar are likely to be their policy objectives and actions. The emergence of new oil producers outside OPEC (such as the UK, Mexico and Norway) and their insistence on pursuing independent production targets have made an important contribution to the oil glut which developed in the 1980s. The same is true also of the clear division of national interests between the so-called high and low absorbers within OPEC. Obviously, the longer these divisions among the producing countries last the more difficult it will be for them to coordinate their policies in order to engineer another large increase in the price of oil.

There is a strong possibility, however, that the number and the characteristics of major oil producers may change significantly in the 1990s.[13] With the exception of the Soviet Union and Mexico, no country outside OPEC accounts for more than a tiny share of the world's total proved oil reserves; and, on present policies, a high proportion of these reserves is likely to be exhausted by the early to mid-1990s. By contrast, around 60 per cent of the oil reserves known in the mid-1980s were located in five members of OPEC: Saudi Arabia, Kuwait, Iran, Iraq and Abu Dhabi. Iran apart, all of them have very small economies whose domestic development and demand for imports can be met by relatively small volumes of oil output and exports. Furthermore, according to some experts, countries of similar size could replace in the 1990s most of the high-absorbing members of OPEC whose reserves are already low.[14]

There is, of course, no certainty that this will happen. New oil reserves may be discovered in other parts of the world, bringing another group of high-absorbing producers on the international oil market. But if the prediction does materialise the risk is that

> the new lineup may usher in a host of new problems for the oil-thirsty world. An oil producers association dominated by low-absorbing, high-reserve countries faced with limited opportunities for foreign investments and increasing protectionism against their non-oil exports may find its best long-term interest in leaving a large share of oil reserves in the ground. Such a strategy, in turn, might have far-reaching implications... for the stability of oil supplies...[15]

Considerable uncertainty surrounds, therefore, the likely number and characteristics of oil producers towards the end of the twentieth century and the effect that this factor may have on world energy prospects.

The same is true also of the effect that the growing international concern about environmental and safety risks, associated with most of the existing forms of energy, may have on the development of oil substitutes in the foreseeable future. The lower the rate at which the inter-fuel substitution takes place the more vulnerable is the world economy likely to be to another oil shock.

Two environmental issues have become of particular concern in the 1980s. The emission of oxides of sulphur and nitrogen from burning fossil fuels (the so-called 'acid rain') has led to international disputes, especially in Western Europe, because of the damage that methods of power generation in certain countries are believed to have had on agriculture and forestry in the neighbouring countries.[16] It is impossible to predict with any certainty the effect that both domestic and international pressure are likely to have on development of fossil fuel resources in individual countries. However, as the International Energy Agency points out, future production of coal in industrial countries, to take one example, may be 'constrained' by environmental considerations as well as the state of the world economy and the price of oil.[17]

The increasing reliance of many countries on nuclear energy has given rise to even more widespread anxieties. A number of accidents, or near accidents, involving nuclear plants in different countries – culminating in the Chernobyl disaster early in 1986 – have focused international attention on the risks associated with this type of energy. As a result, some countries have delayed construction of their new nuclear plants. Many of the projects have also been cancelled. These developments may have an important effect on the long-term energy balance in the world economy. As can be seen from Table 11.3, nuclear energy has played a major role since 1973 in reducing the dependence of industrial countries on oil.

The only way to avoid serious environmental problems is to develop new, non-polluting forms of energy. This will inevitably take time, at least fifty years according to some estimates.[18] Hence, environmental concern about many of the existing forms of energy and uncertainties surrounding their future development are likely to persist for a long time.

The belief that much greater reliance on the existing sources of energy other than oil will solve problems created by the energy crisis rests on the assumption that the behaviour of their producers cannot possibly resemble that of OPEC. They are far more numerous, their products differ significantly and so also in many cases do conditions under which they operate. It is impossible to organise an effective cartel in these circumstances; and in the absence of cartel arrangements the producers' behaviour is most unlikely to be uniform.

However, experience since 1973 shows that other energy producers are no less inclined than members of OPEC to exploit their competitive strength if the market conditions turn in their favour. The only possible difference is that, realising the extent to which sudden and large price increases could damage their own long-term interests, they might (unlike OPEC) follow a policy of more gradual price increases.

A rough indication of the extent to which all these propositions are valid is provided by the data in Table 11.4. What they show is that prices of coal, gas and electricity have risen consistently and at very high rates since 1973 – though the increases have been spread over a longer period than those of crude oil and oil products. Nevertheless, as the International Energy Agency pointed out, the price of fuels other than oil 'in the course of about four years (1973–77) increased by about the same amount as the initial *increase* in the price of oil'.[19]

Table 11.4 Increases in oil and other fuel prices in the seven largest OECD countries[a] (per cent, per annum)

	Crude oil[b]	*Oil products*[c]	*Coal, gas and electricity*[d]
Average: 1960–73	3.2	2.2	3.2
Over previous year:			
1974	198.3	61.7	28.7
1975	6.6	11.1	25.6
1976	6.8	11.1	15.9
1977	7.1	9.1	19.0
1978	1.2	−0.5	10.5
1979	37.8	30.4	14.2
1980	70.0	40.3	22.5
1981	11.7	30.9	24.6

Notes: [a] USA, West Germany, Japan, UK, France, Italy and Canada.
[b] Nominal price of landed crude oil.
[c] Nominal prices of fuel oil, light oil and gasoline.
[d] Nominal prices of coal, gas and electricity (in both industry and the residential/commercial sector).

Source: International Energy Agency (1982, p. 65).

What is particularly important and revealing about these changes is the fact that they have been engineered by the combined actions of governments and energy producing conglomerates. Realising, as a result of OPEC achievements, the extent of potential rents to be reaped in energy production, all governments favoured increases in energy prices and taxes to conserve their country's energy resources; and to use the prices of energy producing industries as a convenient channel for increasing government revenues in order to sustain the required expenditure levels in conditions of high inflation. Energy producing conglomerates, on the other hand, could always justify higher prices by the high development costs of oil resources outside OPEC; and by the cost of extracting other fuels.

Other things remaining equal, the ability of energy producers to exploit their market power will depend on the growth of world demand for energy. This, in turn, will be determined by the rate of growth of world economy and the speed of improvements in the efficiency with which oil and other sources of energy are used. The importance of the first of these two factors will be analysed in the next chapter. As for the efficiency, a good deal of uncertainty surrounds both the extent to which lasting improvements have taken place since 1973 and the effect that lower oil prices are likely to have on further gains in this respect in the foreseeable future.

The apparent improvements over the past decade in the efficiency with which energy is used (measured by energy consumption per unit of GDP)[20] could easily be misleading. Energy intensity varies from sector to sector. Hence, a change in the composition of total output will have a major effect on the overall energy:output ratio even if the ratios for individual sectors remain exactly the same. A fall in the aggregate ratio which is of a long-term, structural, nature will clearly constitute an improvement in the energy efficiency for the economy as a whole. But this conclusion would be obviously wrong if it was applied to a purely temporary, cyclical, change in the composition of total output.

Given the prolonged stagnation in the world economy, which has had a particularly adverse effect on some of the heavy energy users in capital goods industries, it is at present very difficult to discover whether the observed decline in the energy:output ratio has been caused mainly by structural or by cyclical factors. It takes time to develop new sources of energy; or to replace existing capital stock with stock which uses energy more efficiently. The longer the slow growth of world output persists the longer is this process likely to take, for the very simple reason that the volume of energy saving investment, like the volume to total investment, will be greater when actual and expected levels of demand and output are high.[21] Hence, it is far from clear that the observed changes in the energy:output ratios represent genuine, long-term improvements.

Lower energy prices have added to this the uncertainty about future improvements in this area. As the International Energy Agency points out, 'most investments designed to improve the efficiency of energy use are based on the requirement of relatively short pay-back periods.

A sustained decline in oil (and other energy) prices would worsen the economics of such investments and would slow down further progress in this area'.[22] In other words, while there is little doubt that the short-term price elasticity of demand for energy is low, considerable uncertainty at present surrounds the long-term price elasticity.

V

In addition to all this, there are serious political uncertainties. They are extremely important because political developments will continue for quite some time to play a critical role in determining the energy balance and, thus, the world economic environment.

Most oil producers are highly unstable politically. An internal upheaval could occur at almost any time in one of the major exporters, contributing, like the Iranian revolution, to another serious disturbance in the world economy. Moreover, there has always been a considerable division of opinion about future oil output and prices between the countries with small populations and large reserves, such as those on the Arab Peninsula, and other OPEC members. The former, as the Saudis have stated clearly on several occasions, have never been keen to allow oil prices to rise so high, or so fast, as to encourage a rapid development of substitutes – something that would jeopardise their long-term industrialisation.[23] In contrast, the main concern of the so-called high-absorbing oil producers has always been to maximise their short-term income – an attitude dictated by their mounting economic problems: rapidly growing populations, substantial external debts and, in most cases, small and dwindling oil reserves.

Slow growth of the world economy and demand for oil have exacerbated the latter's problems and made it even more difficult for the two groups to harmonise their policies. Attempts to agree on a common set of economic objectives and policies have not been helped by the fact that two major oil producers, Iran and Iraq, have been at war with each other for most of the 1980s.

For all these reasons, considerable uncertainty surrounds future behaviour of oil producing countries. Yet this is a factor which is bound to have a major effect on the world economy for quite some time. According to the International Energy Agency, oil will still account for almost half of total energy consumption in industrial countries at the end of the twentieth century.[24] Its relative importance in the energy consumption of developing countries is likely to be even greater.

The current position and future behaviour of industrial countries are equally difficult to assess and predict. Japan has been almost unique in persisting since 1973 with major structural changes designed to improve the energy efficiency of the economy and reduce its vulnerability to another energy shock. As for the rest, one of the difficulties in predicting their future prospects is that, as already pointed out, 'we are unsure about ... how much adjustment to the two major price increases has already occurred, and about the effects on demand of changes in GNP growth rates'.[25] To make things worse, there is no consensus among industrial nations about the future course which they wish to pursue either internally or in relation to oil producing countries. There has been no attempt so far to come to an understanding with key oil producers which would minimise the threat of another substantial increase in the price of oil during a period of sustained expansion in the world economy.

Equally serious is the absence of an agreement among industrial countries about their economic objectives and policies. There is a clear division at the moment between the countries which would like to pursue more expansionist economic policies in order to reduce the exceptionally high and rising levels of unemployment; and the countries whose governments are content to continue with a basically deflationary policy in order to avoid another inflationary explosion. As things stand, it is far from clear which group is likely to prevail in the short run, let alone the long run. What is increasingly clear, however, is that – other things remaining the same – either course of action could give rise to another serious crisis in the world economy.

For instance, a rapid and sustained global economic expansion could easily create an energy imbalance in favour of oil producers, causing a series of large increases in oil and other energy prices in the 1990s.[26] Such a development could destabilise politically as well as economically many of the consuming countries, still trying to recover from the shocks experienced since the early 1970s. But the alternative is equally dangerous for both oil producers and consumers. Persistent stagnation of the world economy can lead, as in 1985–86, to a temporary collapse in oil prices. This creates substantial economic problems for high-cost energy producers, slows down the development of oil and other energy resources, discourages energy conservation, and thus prepares the ground for another substantial jump in energy prices at some later date.[27] It is hardly necessary to add that persistent stagnation could also prove to be extremely costly in economic and social terms for oil importing countries.

In many ways, therefore, the world energy balance is potentially far more unstable in the mid-1980s than it was a decade earlier. The danger inherent in such a highly uncertain environment is that it is likely to force energy producers to behave in a way which may prove in the long run to be extremely costly to themselves as well as to the rest of the world. The reason for this is that 'the greater the uncertainty the greater is the incentive to *hold back production*'.[28] To the extent that they do so, they may impose a serious constraint on the growth of the world economy which will ultimately work to their long-term disadvantage also.

12 Economic Consequences of the Energy Constraint

I

One of the most dangerous aspects of the uncertainties described in the previous chapter is that they may perpetuate the energy constraint on the growth of the world economy. The two exceptionally large increases in the price of oil, plus the threat of similar increases, have made it impossible even for industrial countries to reconcile in the short run high employment levels with low inflation rates, and the two domestic objectives with that of external balance. The financial position of many developing countries has deteriorated to such an extent that it reached crisis proportions in the early 1980s.

The present chapter will examine first the existence and seriousness of the energy constraint, using a relatively simple analytical framework.[1] This will be followed by a description of some of the most important economic developments since 1973 and the way that they have affected different groups of countries.

II

In the short term, production levels are limited by the factor of production which is relatively scarce. In the long run, the pace of economic expansion will depend on the rate of growth of this factor and on improvements in the efficiency with which it is used.

This is true, of course, only so long as that particular factor imposes the most serious constraint either on the levels or the growth of a country's productive potential. If the relevant scarcities change significantly, and something else assumes the limiting role, then the attention in judging physical limits to a country's growth will have to switch to this factor. The experience of industrial countries over the last thirty years provides an illustration of such a change.

For almost two decades, until 1973, the upper limit to output expansion in industrial countries was given in the short run by the full employment 'barrier', as their economies were operating persistently at very low rates of unemployment. In the long run, the growth of industrial countries' productive potential was determined, therefore, by the growth of their labour force, labour productivity and changes in the hours of work.[2] This means that so long as the economies were operating at less than full employment the actual rate of growth could exceed for a time the rate of growth of their productive potential. But once the full employment barrier was reached, attempts to grow above this rate inevitably led to an acceleration in the rate of inflation and balance of payments problems.

However, economic developments since 1973 indicate that the growth of output in industrial countries is much more likely to be limited by a rather different barrier, imposed by inadequate supply of energy –mainly oil.[3] It seems reasonable, therefore, that in judging the sustainable rate of growth attention should switch from labour –which has ceased, for the time being, to be the most important limiting factor – to energy.

The energy constrained, or sustainable, rate of growth depends, then, on the expected rate of growth of energy supply and improvements in the efficiency with which this energy is used. However, given that energy, unlike labour, is highly mobile internationally, the concept is meaningful only if applied globally. In theory, a single country could always get more oil, for example, even in the short run, providing that it was prepared to pay a slightly higher price for it than the rest of the world. But with the supply of oil given, it would only be able to do this at the expense of one or more countries which would have to decide now whether to have less oil (and a lower level of activity) or to maintain their supply of oil intact by also offering to pay a higher price for it. Sooner or later, therefore, most countries would be faced again with the dilemma of accepting either a higher level of unemployment or a higher rate of inflation and larger external deficits. In other words, although it is possible for a particular country to escape for a while from the energy constraint the world as a whole cannot do so.

III

The change can be illustrated analytically by treating the world as a single, closed, economy and using the framework encapsulated in the lower half of the graphs employed in Part II.

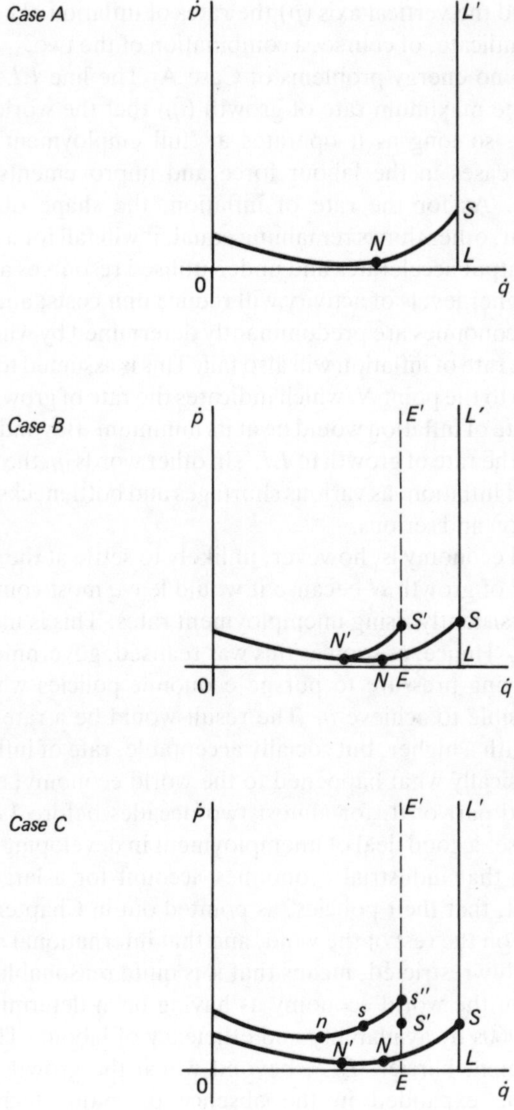

Figure 12.1 Growth and inflation before and after the 'oil shocks'

The three most important cases are shown in Figure 12.1. In each instance, the horizontal axis ($\mathring{q}$) shows the short-term rates of growth of output and the vertical axis ($\mathring{p}$) the rates of inflation. The points on each curve indicate, of course, a combination of the two.

There are no energy problems of Case A. The line LL' indicates, therefore, the maximum rate of growth ($\mathring{q}_l$) that the world economy can achieve, so long as it operates at 'full employment', with the existing increases in the labour force and improvements in labour productivity. As for the rate of inflation, the shape of the curve indicates that, other things remaining equal, it will fall for a time as the growth of output accelerates and under-utilised resources are brought into use. Higher levels of activity will reduce unit costs; and, as prices in modern economies are predominantly determined by what happens to costs,[4] the rate of inflation will also fall. This is assumed to happen in the graph up to the point N, which indicates the rate of growth at which the global rate of inflation would be at its minimum. Beyond this point, the closer is the rate of growth to LL', in other words $\mathring{q}_l$, the higher will be the rate of inflation, as various shortages and bottlenecks tend to be more common and serious.

The world economy is, however, unlikely to settle at the 'non-inflationary' rate of growth N because it would leave most countries with high and persistently rising unemployment rates. This is inevitable as N is below $\mathring{q}_l$. Hence, as soon as this was realised, governments would be under strong pressure to pursue economic policies which would make it possible to achieve $\mathring{q}_l$. The result would be a rate of growth associated with a higher, but socially acceptable, rate of inflation $\mathring{p}_S$.

This is basically what happened to the world economy, at least the industrialised part of it, for almost two decades before 1973. There was, of course, a good deal of unemployment in developing countries. But the fact that industrial economies account for a large share of world output, that their policies, as pointed out in Chapter 2, have a major effect on the rest of the wold, and that international mobility of labour is highly restricted, means that it is quite reasonable to regard the growth of the world economy as having been determined in the 1950s and 1960s by availability and efficiency of labour. There was a full employment barrier, LL', beyond which the growth of output could not be expanded in the absence of major technical and institutional changes which would move the 'barrier' to the right. Any attempt to do so would have simply resulted in an acceleration in the rate of inflation in excess of S.

Suppose now that the largest producers of oil, by far the most important source of energy, decide that it is in their long-term interest to reduce permanently the rate of growth of their output; and that they do this suddenly and to such an extent that the combined rate of growth of energy *and* the efficiency with which energy is used falls below the full employment barrier.[5] In other words, $\mathring{q}_e$ is now lower than $\mathring{q}_l$.

This is illustrated in Case B by the fact that EE' is to the left of LL'. The most obvious consequence of this shift is that if the world labour force and labour productivity continue to grow as before then, *ceteris paribus*, the world will be confronted with a continuously rising unemployment rate. Moreover, increases in the rate of growth of output will now result much more quickly in higher inflation rates. Both the non-inflationary rate of growth (N') and the socially acceptable rate of inflation (S') are well below N and S, the rates attainable before the energy crisis. This means that so long as energy supply and/or the efficiency with which energy is used do not increase sufficiently for EE' to shift to the right and at least equal again LL', all attempts to achieve $\mathring{q}_l$ will only lead in the short run to an acceleration in the rate of inflation along the EE' line. On the other hand, if governments chose the lowest possible rate of inflation as their only policy objective, actual growth rate (N') will be even below $\mathring{q}_e$. This will lead, of course, to an even larger increase in unemployment.

There is a very good reason, however, why changes in the energy market of the kind described here can be expected to have an even more adverse effect on the world economy than Case B suggests. In this particular case, it is assumed that the behaviour of all economic agents – with the exception of oil producers – remains unchanged. Hence, prices will rise sharply now as the rate of growth approaches EE' only because of the rush to replenish energy stocks in anticipation of the forthcoming shortages. At $\mathring{q}_e$, the overall rate of inflation will be exactly the same as before ($S' = S$). The only difference is that the energy barrier has reduced the rate of growth below $\mathring{q}_l$ so that unemployment is rising.

It is most unlikely, however, that the behaviour of economic agents will remain unchanged in these circumstances. Other things remaining equal, repetition of sudden and widespread shortages in a market as important as that for energy will inevitably cause sudden, unanticipated and large increases in prices.

Not surprisingly, a strong element of inflationary expectations, accompanied by a good deal of uncertainty, will be introduced into the world economy. Everyone will expect prices to rise. At the same time, no one will be sure when they are likely to do so, or by how much. The uncertainty will tend to induce economic agents to take steps to protect their incomes. Hence, depending on the price elasticity of demand for their products, firms will either tend to charge higher prices than they would do otherwise or go for shorter contracts so that they can revise prices more frequently. For similar reasons, labour organisations will demand bigger increases in wages and salaries than they would have done in periods of price stability. New contracts will, therefore, tend to embody not only unanticipated past changes in costs and prices but also in many instances a certain additional, precautionary, mark-up in case there is an unexpected increase in prices during the contract period. For reasons explained in Chapter 1, the state of their absolute and relative incomes becomes a preoccupation of economic agents in the process of economic development; and with modern means of transport and communications this has become a world-wide preoccupation, likely to be especially pronounced in periods of large and unanticipated price changes.

The results will be an upward shift in the growth-inflation curve, as in Case C. Consequently, the rate of inflation common before the energy crisis (*S*) can now be achieved only at a rate of growth (*s*) which is even lower than $\mathring{q}_e$. The latter is attainable in this example, unlike in Case B, only if the world is prepared to tolerate an appreciably higher rate of inflation (s''). If, on the other hand, the achievement of the lowest rate of inflation (*n*) becomes the main objective of government policies, the growth of output will be even lower and, consequently, increases in unemployment much higher than in Case B.

The developments illustrated in Figure 12.1 have, therefore, an extremely important implication for economic policy. Removal of the inflationary push brought about by changes in expectations is not going to bring the world back to *S* (Case A) so long as the energy barrier EE' remains. At best, a downward shift in the growth-inflation curve to its original position – say, through very effective prices and incomes policies – would take the economy, other things remaining equal, to S' (Case B), but not further. The only way to enjoy again the growth (unemployment) and inflation rates common before the energy crisis is to push the EE' line to the right at least as far as LL'. If the position of the existing energy producers cannot be changed, this can be achieved only by using different sources of energy and improving significantly the efficiency with which energy is used, a process which, as already pointed out, is likely to take a very long time.

Finally, although serious in its overall effect, the energy constraint will obviously affect individual countries differently. Some of these will have rich energy resources which will enable them to use the large increases in rents to finance restructuring of their economies without domestic sacrifices or balance-of-payments problems. Some will have the benefit of national unity and flexible institutions, making it possible for them to achieve similar results in the long run by pursuing a successful industrial policy. They may be also able to sustain more rapid growth in the short run through a prices and incomes policy.[6] Smaller countries, or countries which have not existed for very long as independent political entities, may find it easier to respond to external developments in this way.[7] There is usually a strong and widespread feeling of vulnerability to external threats and shocks in such countries, making it relatively easy to achieve a national consensus without which large-scale economic adjustments are impossible.

In contrast, countries which lack adequate energy resources and/or are deeply divided into powerful sectarian interests will be condemned to long-term stagnation. Entrenched interests and ossified institutions will make it extremely difficult for them to escape problems of the kind illustrated in Case C. Unfortunately for the rest of the world, this group is likely, for reasons analysed by Olson, to include some of the largest and most advanced economies. Given the extent to which they dominate the world economy, their stagnation will inevitably impose a serious constraint in conditions of international integration and interdependence on the adjustment efforts even of the most dynamic economies. This is another reason why it may take the whole world a long time to solve the economic problems created by the energy crisis.

IV

Although they are relatively easy to define theoretically, neither $\mathring{q}_l$ nor $\mathring{q}_e$ is easy to quantify. The reasons for this are partly conceptual and partly statistical.

As explained earlier, the energy crisis had nothing to do with an actual shortage of either oil or any other primary source of energy. It was the direct result of a decision to reduce output and exports made by a small number of dominant oil producers. Moreover, these decisions, based on certain criteria about the real price of oil and national revenues, are not unalterable. This means that so long as the producers deliberately maintain a fairly large margin of spare capacity (as OPEC have done since 1973), they can as easily increase the volume of their output in the short run (shift *EE'* in Figure 12.1 to the right) as they can reduce it further. Consequently, it is very difficult in these circumstances to determine the size of $\mathring{q}_e$, the energy constrained rate of growth ('the energy barrier').

For similar reasons, $\mathring{q}_l$ cannot be regarded as a labour-constrained rate of growth of the productive potential when there are large pools of unemployed and underemployed labour, such as those which have existed since 1973 even in industrial countries. In these conditions, $\mathring{q}_l$ represents the minimum rate which has to be attained in order to keep the existing rate of unemployment constant, rather than the rate which cannot be exceeded in the short term.

Attempts to quantify the two rates are complicated further by data problems. For instance, in the case of $\mathring{q}_e$ it is difficult to establish whether observed changes in energy efficiency are of a temporary or permanent nature. Data inadequacies make it also difficult to produce reliable estimates of the underlying rate of labour productivity growth – one of the key variables in determining the size of $\mathring{q}_l$ – even for countries with highly developed statistical services. An estimate of this kind for the world as a whole would be, therefore, of little value.

Nevertheless, it is possible to get at least a very rough idea of the size of 'world' $\mathring{q}_l$ and $\mathring{q}_e$ by analysing the position of OECD countries. For although these countries do not comprise 'the world', they account for 75 per cent of world GNP, and for a similar proportion of world fixed investment[8] and oil consumption.[9] Inevitably, economic policies and developments within OECD countries will have a very significant effect on the rest of the world, as was shown in Chapter 2. Furthermore, this is a reasonably homogeneous group of countries for which most of the relevant data are available.

The rate of growth of the 'productive potential' at a given rate of unemployment can be defined as:

$$\mathring{q}_l = \mathring{l} + \mathring{q/l} + \mathring{h},$$

where

$\mathring{q}_l$ = annual rate of growth needed to keep the rate of unemployment constant,
$\mathring{l}$ = annual rate of growth of labour force,
$\mathring{q/l}$ = annual growth of labour productivity,
$\mathring{h}$ = annual changes in standard weekly hours of work.

Data are readily available for two of these variables. Between 1973 and 1984 total labour force in OECD countries increased at an average annual rate of 0.8 per cent.[10] Over the same period, standard weekly hours are estimated to have declined by about 0.7 per cent per annum.[11]

The problem, as usual, is to get an estimate of the underlying rate of productivity growth. There is normally a close relationship between the growth of output and growth of productivity. The main reason for this is that rapid and sustained growth of demand and output tends to encourage rapid and sustained growth of investment, which normally embodies technical advances. Slow growth tends to do exactly the opposite.

Since the mid-1970s output growth has not only slowed down appreciably in industrial countries but also fluctuated much more than before. The result has been a substantial fall in the rate of growth of new investment (see Tables 12.1 and 12.2). This would normally suggest a marked decline in the underlying growth of productivity. However, OECD and other reports suggest that, as a result of slow growth and widespread squeeze on profits, most of these new investments have been used to reduce costs by improving productivity of all inputs, including labour. Important technical advances since the early 1970s, regarded by some historians as the 'Fourth Industrial Revolution',[12] also appear to have been predominantly labour-saving in character.

These developments suggest that the underlying growth of productivity in OECD countries need not have slowed down all that much since the 1960s. The observed relationship between output growth in industrial economies and their unemployment rates leads to a similar conclusion. In the 1960s, the underlying growth of productivity in these economies was 4 per cent per annum.[13] Given annual rates of growth of the labour force (0.8 per cent) and decline in the hours of work (0.7 per cent), a 4 per cent rate of growth of productivity would imply $\mathring{q}_l$ for OECD economies of 4.1 per cent (0.8 + 4.0 – 0.7). In other words, other things remaining equal, that is the rate of growth that they would have to achieve and sustain in order to keep unemployment constant. In fact, unemployment has declined in these countries on two occasions since 1973 (1977–79 and 1984–85) when they have managed to sustain for two or more years an average rate of growth of slightly over 3.5 per cent. That would suggest an underlying rate of productivity growth since 1973 of around 3.5 per cent per annum, giving $\mathring{q}_l$ of 3.6 per cent per annum (0.8 + 3.5 – 0.7).

How does this particular rate compare with that of the 'energy constrained rate of growth' ('the energy barrier') over the same period? The latter rate can be defined as

$$\mathring{q}_e = \mathring{e} + \mathring{q}/e,$$

where

$\mathring{q}_e$ = annual rate of growth of energy constrained output,
$\mathring{e}$ = annual rate of growth of energy supply,
$\mathring{q}/e$ = annual changes in energy efficiency.

The simplest way to estimate $\mathring{q}_e$ is to concentrate on oil. It has been, after all, at the centre of the energy crisis. Moreover, oil is the only source of energy in which OECD countries were not self-sufficient, as a group, over the period analysed here – a fact which made them so vulnerable to reductions in OPEC's production and exports.[14]

Between 1973 and 1984 world oil production fell by 6.3 per cent, equivalent to an annual rate of −0.6 per cent. Oil supply outside OPEC increased by 54.5 per cent. But, given its relative size, this was more than offset by a deliberate reduction in OPEC output of 40.9 per cent.[15] At the same time, the apparent efficiency with which oil was used improved in OECD countries at an annual rate of 3.7 per cent.[16] These figures give an energy constrained rate of growth of 3.1 (3.7 − 0.6) per cent per annum, which is appreciably lower than the OECD constant unemployment rate of growth of 3.6 per cent.

Clearly, the difference in the two growth rates has been sufficiently large since 1973 to make it impossible for OECD countries to maintain full employment levels to which they had become accustomed in the 1960s – unless OPEC could be persuaded to reverse its policy stance. New and existing oil producers outside the cartel were simply not large enough to fill the gap left by cuts in its exports.

Problems created by the difference between $\mathring{q}_l$ and $\mathring{q}_e$ are even more serious, in fact, than the preceding analysis indicates. The reason for this is that the analysis has so far ignored inflationary effects of the difference. As shown in the previous section, unless OPEC is prepared to accommodate increases in world demand for oil, attempts by OECD countries to achieve a rate of growth close to $\mathring{q}_l$ will inevitably lead in the short run to an acceleration in their rates of inflation.

The OECD Secretariat estimated at the end of the 1970s that a shortfall in oil supplies of two million barrels per day would increase the price of oil by some 30 per cent. This would add within a year 2–3 percentage points to OECD inflation rates, depending on the degree of adjustment in other prices and wages.[17] According to a subsequent OECD study, each of the two large increases in oil prices (in 1973–74 and 1979–80) 'directly raised the OECD general price level by about 2 percentage points relative to what it would have been otherwise. And the induced wage/price spiral multiplied this figure several-fold over the following few years'.[18]

Consequently, industrial countries found themselves after 1973 in the invidious position of having to choose between substantially higher inflation if they tried to achieve a rate of growth close to $\mathring{q}_e$ (*EE'* in Figure 12.1); or substantially higher unemployment if they settled for a rate of growth below $\mathring{q}_e$ (to the left of *EE'*). As the analysis below shows, their preference underwent a significant change over the period: from a qualified support for the first option in the latter part of the 1970s to a total commitment to the second option early in the 1980s. These changes have had far-reaching economic and financial effects not only on industrial countries but also on the rest of the world, including members of OPEC.

V

With the overall rate of growth of a highly integrated world economy reduced by the energy constraint, it is difficult to see how any group of countries could have improved its economic performance since the early 1970s in absolute terms, except in the very short run. As shown in Chapter 2, stagnation in any one area will affect adversely everyone else, though not equally. Even in this environment some countries, or groups of countries, may experience an important *relative* improvement in their levels of development and international competitiveness.

Tables 12.1 and 12.2 illustrate the familiar story of deterioration in global economic performance since 1973 and the extent to which it has been accompanied by increasing instability. Because of the size of their economies, the most important, from a global point of view, has been the sharp deterioration in economic performance of industrial countries. Their overall rate of growth has been halved, with the growth of per capita incomes, investment and trade showing an even more marked decline. Not surprisingly, the average unemployment

Table 12.1 Economic performance of the major groups of countries before and after the 'oil shocks'

	Industrial countries		Oil exporting countries		Other developing countries	Centrally planned economies[a]
GDP, average annual growth (%)		Unemployment[b]	Total	Excluding oil		
1968–73	4.7	3.2	8.5	n.a.	6.4	6.5[c]
1974–78	2.6	4.9	5.7	10.3	5.5	5.4[c]
1979–84	2.3	7.1	1.2	4.0	3.6	3.0[c]
GDP per capita, average annual growth (%)						
1968–73	3.9		6.7		4.0	2.8[c]
1974–78	1.7		6.4		3.4	2.9[c]
1979–84	1.4		−0.4		1.3	n.a.
Gross fixed investment, average annual growth (%)						
1968–73	5.4		14.1[d]		8.3	8.0[e]
1974–78	0.4		18.0		6.1	2.5[f]
1979–84	2.2		2.7		1.4	1.6
Consumer prices, average annual increase (%)						
1968–73	5.3		5.5		11.2	0.5[c]
1974–78	9.5		16.6		26.5	1.5[f]
1979–84	7.0		18.0		33.4	5.2
Exports, average annual growth (%)						
1968–73	10.6		8.9		8.3	10.0
1974–78	4.8		0.2		4.9	6.5
1979–84	4.1		−6.6		7.4	4.2

Imports, average annual growth (%)				
1968–73	10.4	12.4	8.4	11.2
1974–78	3.1	23.6	4.6	8.3
1979–84	3.3	1.8	3.2	2.6
Current account balances, billions of SDRs, annual averages				
1968–73	7.4	2.4	−7.8	n.a. (0.5[h])
1974–78	−3.8	24.5	−24.8	−3.0[g] (−4.5[h])
1979–84	−24.0	25.9	−55.7	−2.8[g] (9.4[h])
Long-term capital balances, billions of SDRs, annual averages				
1968–73	−8.4	0.8	9.7	n.a.
1974–78	−13.2	−0.6	25.6	n.a.
1979–84	−25.9	−0.9	51.9	n.a.
Basic balances of payments, billions of SDRs, annual averages				
1968–73	−1.0	3.2	2.0	n.a.
1974–78	−16.9	24.0	0.9	n.a.
1979–84	−49.9	25.0	−3.7	n.a.

Notes: a Bulgaria, Czechoslovakia, the German Democratic Republic, Hungary, Poland, Rumania and USSR.
b Per cent of the labour force.
c Net material product.
d 1970–73.
e 1971–75.
f 1976–80.
g 1979–83, billions of US dollars.
h Trade balance only, in billions of US dollars.

Sources: IMF: *World Economic Outlook*, UN: *Economic Survey of Europe*, UN: *Economic Bulletin for Europe*, IMF (1984a), IMF (1984b), IMF (1982a), World Bank (1985) and Summers and Heston (1984).

Table 12.2 The energy crisis and increasing instability of the world economy

	Coefficient of variation between different years, per cent				
	Industrial countries	*Oil exporting countries*		*Other developing countries*	*Centrally planned economies*
Growth of GDP		*Total*	*Excluding oil*		
1968–73	25.5	18.8	n.a.	40.6	21.5
1974–78	92.3	84.2	26.2	16.4	13.0
1979–84	78.3	133.3	40.0	27.8	36.7
Growth of gross fixed investment					
1968–73	59.6	45.4		62.6	n.a.
1974–78	2,400.0	116.7		95.1	n.a.
1979–84	200.0	255.6		385.1	106.2
Increases in consumer prices					
1968–73	24.5	60.0		47.3	n.a.
1974–78	26.3	14.4		10.9	n.a.
1979–84	30.0	25.6		23.1	76.9
Current account balances					
1968–73	33.8	70.8		39.7	n.a.
1974–78	363.2	82.0		20.6	n.a.
1979–84	53.3	156.8		30.5	n.a.
Long-term capital balances					
1968–73	44.0	125.0		28.9	n.a.
1974–78	65.9	1,250.0		24.2	n.a.
1979–84	43.2	2,044.0		24.7	n.a.

Source: Calculated from the sources quoted in Table 12.1.

levels in 1979–84 were more than double the levels in 1968–73. The prolonged stagnation of these countries – relative to their productive potential – has enabled them to reduce their inflation rates in the 1980s, not least by depressing world commodity prices. Nevertheless, the inflationary pressures in the industrialised part of the world were still noticeably higher in the first half of the 1980s than before 1973.

In addition, it was common for industrial countries, as a group, to run persistent current balance of payments surpluses before 1973, even at full employment. As these were exceeded only slightly by net outflows of long-term capital, industrial countries were virtually balancing their basic balance of payments over a complete cycle. In contrast, since 1973 many of these countries have been more or less permanently in deficit on their current account while, at the same time, increasing their net long-term lendings to the rest of the world – with the result that there has been a sharp deterioration in their basic balance. The balance, a deficit of about 50 billion SDRs per annum in 1979–84, represents no more than a fraction of 1 per cent of the countries' average annual GDP over the period. None the less, given its unequal distribution among the countries, it has been sufficiently large in absolute terms to create considerable financial and exchange rate problems.

It is quite remarkable how well the developing countries, other than oil exporters, managed to weather the storm caused by the first oil shock. Their overall and per capita growth rates were only slightly lower in 1974–78 than in 1968–73. As a result, the annual expansion of their fixed investments also held up extremely well. All this was sustained during a period in which the growth of their trade declined significantly – though, overall, changes in trade volumes worked slightly to their advantage: as the growth of imports fell by a little more than that of exports, other things remaining equal, they should have experienced an improvement in their balance of payments. However, as shown in Table 11.1, the size of oil price increases was such that it produced a sharp decline in developing countries' terms of trade and, consequently, a substantial deterioration in their current account balances (Table 12.1).

The reason that this deterioration did not create serious financing problems for the group as a whole lies in the fact that it was offset by a corresponding increase in inflows of long-term capital into developing countries, so that their combined basic balances remained in surplus. In other words, developing countries managed to sustain their economic expansion between 1973 and 1979 by increasing their borrowing of long-term capital abroad. This explains why, despite an unequal distribution of basic balances among the countries, there was no international debt crisis in the second half of the 1970s.

The second oil shock, on the other hand, had an extremely adverse effect on these countries. Their terms of trade deteriorated even more seriously than after the first shock, increasing significantly the size of their current account deficits – despite the fact that between 1979 and 1984 they achieved a remarkable improvement in their export performance and a further reduction in the growth of their imports. To make things worse, the increase in long-term borrowing that they were able to achieve during this period was insufficient to cover the deficits, so that their basic balances became negative. There was no alternative this time, therefore, but to reduce their annual rates of economic development much more drastically than in the second half of the 1970s. Even this was not sufficient, however, to dispel the doubts which developed in 1981–82 about the countries' solvency, giving rise for the first time since the beginning of the 1930s to a serious international debt crisis, and threatening to condemn most of these countries to perpetual economic stagnation.

Nothing illustrates better the extent of international economic interdependence in the 1980s than the fact that even the relatively closed and tightly controlled centrally planned economies have been unable to escape the consequences of the energy crisis.

There are a number of problems in comparing their economic performance before and since 1973 with those of other countries. The data about centrally planned economies are not always readily available, even for some of the key economic indicators. For example, they do not publish balance of payments statistics.[19] What is more, even when available, the data may not be comparable to those for other countries. The rates of growth shown under GDP in Table 12.1 refer, in their case, to net material product only.

Nevertheless, despite the differences, what emerges quite clearly from Tables 12.1 and 12.2 is that the recent experience of centrally planned economies has not been fundamentally different from that of industrial and developing countries other than oil exporters. Like these two groups, centrally planned economies have also undergone a sharp decline in the growth of their output, investment and trade. At the same time, they have had a substantial acceleration in their rates of inflation. Furthermore, in common with other oil importing countries, the economies of Eastern Europe – though not the USSR – experienced a deterioration in their external accounts. Like developing countries, they suffered only a small deceleration in their growth rates in the second half of the 1970s. Similarly, their external deficits during the period were financed by borrowing heavily abroad. As a result, like a number of developing economies, some East European countries – notably Poland and Rumania – became by the early 1980s unable to service their external debts. The debts were eventually rescheduled, but at the cost of severe domestic deflation.

Perhaps the most surprising revelation to emerge from the data set out in Tables 12.1 and 12.2 is the extent to which, since the end of the 1970s, oil exporting countries have been affected adversely by the response of the rest of the world to the problems created by their pricing policies. So far in the 1980s, they have experienced a far worse deterioration in their economic performance than any other group of countries. No other group has had such a dramatic slump in the growth of its output and investment. Oil exporters are also unique in having suffered collectively – and this is particularly true of the exporters with high incomes per head – a continuous fall in their per capita incomes between 1979 and 1984.[20] They have also experienced a very sharp acceleration in their inflation rates since 1973.

Nor is their external position as satisfactory as the balance of payments averages in Table 12.1 indicate. What the averages, influenced by the huge surpluses in 1979–81, fail to reveal is the fact that since 1981 oil exporting countries, as a group, have been continuously in deficit on their current balance of payments. In fact, with the exception of Saudi Arabia and the small surplus countries on the Arab Peninsula, oil exporters have been running high deficits both on their current and basic balances, much more so than before 1973. It is hardly surprising, then, to find a number of OPEC members (Algeria, Venezuela, Nigeria, Indonesia and Ecuador) among the countries with heavy external debts; or to discover that many oil exporters have slumped heavily in their credit ratings on international capital markets.[21] Overall, their economic performance since 1973 has been far less favourable than that which they managed to achieve between 1968 and 1973 – though their levels of output and income per head are, of course, much higher.

The most important reason for this is that the relative economic stagnation in the rest of the world has had a dramatic effect on oil exports and, therefore, on the general economic performance of oil exporting countries. The effect has come about in two ways. First, there has been a decline in the world demand for oil as well as an increase in oil output outside OPEC. Second, as a result of this, the key exporters within OPEC decided to cut their production and exports sharply in order to prevent a slump in world oil prices.

VI

It is clear from the preceding analysis that the two large increases in the price of oil, both of which took place over very short periods, have created serious economic problems not only for the rest of the world but for the oil exporting countries themselves. As OPEC have discovered at considerable cost to themselves in the 1980s, it is in no one's interest to destabilise a highly integrated international economic system.

The first increase in the price of oil could, possibly, have been justified on grounds of the long-established incapacity of the international community to deal even with major problems, no matter how damaging they threaten to be, until they reach crisis proportions. Given the extremely rapid growth before 1973 of demand for oil, a finite resource, it could be argued that it was less costly for the world to be warned about the impending energy crisis sooner rather than later; and there is little doubt that the four-fold increase in the price of oil did shake the world out of complacency concerning the future supply and cost of energy. A steady, gradual, increase in its real price from then on would have therefore benefited both oil importing and oil exporting countries in the long term. The former would have had the time to deal with a manageable problem of substituting alternative sources of energy for oil and of restructuring their economies; and a recovery of the world economy of the kind which appeared to be in progress towards the end of the 1970s would, if sustained,[22] have enabled members of OPEC to make progress towards achieving their long-term goals.

Although they differ in many respects, oil exporting countries share a number of common objectives: rapid economic growth in order to achieve a sustainable and reasonably equitable increase in per capita incomes and standards of living; diversification of their productive base in anticipation of the eventual exhaustion of their oil reserves; and price stability.[23]

As pointed out in the last section, since 1979 their overall rate of growth has slumped to below that of the other three groups of countries; they have experienced a persistent decline in their per capita incomes; the rate of growth of their sectors other than oil has slumped from an average of 10.3 per cent in 1974–78 to 4.0 per cent in 1979–84; and they have experienced a more serious rate of inflation since 1973 than either industrial or other developing countries. The last development is attributable directly to an unsustainable surge in economic activity after 1973 which strained greatly the countries' administrative and institutional capacities, apart from giving rise to physical bottlenecks following an explosion in rising expectations and demand for consumer goods and services. A more moderate, but stable and sustainable rate of development could have avoided this. On all counts, therefore, oil producing countries have been far less successful in achieving their stated policy objectives since 1979 than they were before 1973.

Yet this outcome was avoidable for the very simple reason that it was predictable. Given the heavy dependence of all OPEC countries on the revenues from oil exports to achieve their policy objectives, the enormous increase in their development programmes after 1973 was clearly going to make them even more dependent on the major importing countries. The acceleration in their development programmes was sustainable only so long as they could maintain a high level of foreign exchange earnings – which they could not, possibly, hope to achieve in the absence of high levels of demand for oil abroad. The latter are determined chiefly, at least in the short to medium term, by the rates of output growth in the importing, especially industrial, countries; and these are unlikely to be maintained at high levels in the face of sharply mounting structural problems caused by huge increases in the price of oil every few years. Inevitably, the second round of large increases in oil and other energy prices has produced a situation in which all countries are growing well below their productive potential, accumulating economic and social problems as the aspirations of their citizens become increasingly frustrated. International interdependence has quite simply reached such a high degree that it requires no particular foresight to conclude that another large increase in oil prices would produce an outcome even more damaging to *all* concerned than the two experienced so far.

At the same time, the existence, or even the threat, of a constraint to growth through the inadequate supply of a commodity with a global domain, such as oil, limits the choice of broad economic strategies open to national – particularly industrial – economies in a way which is historically unique. Traditionally, for reasons analysed in the preceding chapters, an unfavourable change in global economic environment has tended to encourage individual countries to reduce their dependence on other economies by protective measures in trade and finance. This partially insulates their economies from external developments, and thus enables them to pursue independent economic policies appropriate to the specific problems that they are experiencing.

The existence of the energy constraint ensures that such a strategy, if adopted universally, would be no more successful in returning industrial countries – given their weight in the world economy – to the levels of activity and employment common before 1973 than a harmonised attempt to expand their economies within the existing, integrated framework. This is true even if one ignores the fact that a collective return to autarkic policies by industrial countries would now almost certainly create large structural problems in each economy:

serious shortages and bottlenecks in certain sectors and overcapacity in others. So long as the energy constraint remains, a synchronised attempt by all countries behind protective barriers designed to bring each of them back to full employment and low inflation would soon result in the reappearance of the problem that aggregate $\mathring{q}_l > \mathring{q}_e$. In other words, global changes in commercial policy are irrelevant in these circumstances. Irrespective of the character of international commercial regimes, one country may be able to escape the constraint. The world as a whole cannot.

Whatever they might be tempted to do, nation states have really little choice now but to attack the constraint within an internationally integrated framework. The problem is that it has not affected all of them equally, and this has given rise to different policy needs and preferences even within each of the groups analysed earlier. Not unnaturally, the priority attached to a particular policy objective will depend on the nature and size of a country's underlying economic difficulties and the extent to which these are hurting the most powerful socio-political groups within the country. Hence, some industrial countries have tried to reduce their unemployment levels while others have concentrated on keeping inflation low at whatever cost. Some OPEC countries have been determined to maximise the short-term rents from oil while others, taking a longer-term view, have tried to achieve a more realistic pricing policy. To make things worse, few countries in either group have been consistent in their attitudes and policies.

The result has been widespread uncertainty, exacerbated by a financial outcome which has made a world-wide recovery even more difficult to achieve than it would have been otherwise.

13 Financial Effects of the Energy Crisis

I

The financial effects of the energy crisis have received at least as much attention since the first oil shock as the effects described in the previous two chapters. The size of the balance of payments imbalances caused by sudden changes in the price of oil, the 'recycling' of OPEC surpluses and the debt crisis have all been analysed in considerable detail.

The widespread preoccupation with these three issues is not difficult to understand. The large current account surpluses and deficits began to appear in exactly the same year, 1973, which saw the final breakdown of the Bretton Woods System. It was far from clear at the time, therefore, that the existing institutions, national or international, could cope with such a major shock to established global economic and financial relationships. As it turned out, the 'recycling' problem was solved in the 1970s thanks in part to the ingenuity with which transnational banks utilised and developed further the opportunities provided by the euromarkets. The debt crisis of the early 1980s assumed menacing proportion mainly because of the threat which it presented to the liquidity, even solvency, of these banks – the very institutions whose actions in the 1970s had prevented a total collapse of the international economic order developed after the Second World War. A sudden retreat from international intermediation by the banks, either voluntary or enforced, would have left a vacuum which no country or international organisation was in a position to fill. There was a real threat, therefore, that the world would experience a repetition of the financial breakdown which took place for very similar reasons at the end of the 1920s.

The attention which these problems have received from economists, bankers and policy makers has, undoubtedly, been responsible for avoiding a far more serious economic crisis than the one which the world has actually experienced since the early 1970s. Yet, in spite of all these efforts, little has been done to solve the underlying problems. As shown in the preceding chapters, they are still there; and the main reason for this is that the international community has deliberately refused to accept the fact that the energy crisis has given rise to a number of long-term economic and financial issues – all highly interrelated and none, therefore, capable of being solved in isolation.

First, there is the economic problem caused by the need to adjust to higher energy prices and the continuous threat of a physical constraint to world economic growth. Second, there is the financial problem which has to be solved successfully before the world can deal with the economic problem. This requires a cooperative effort between the new international savers (confined to a few oil exporting countries) and the rest of the world. Third, there is the institutional problem: the need to develop new, or strengthen existing, financial institutions capable of intermediating globally so that the required adjustments can take place as speedily and efficiently as possible.

The first issue was discussed in the last two chapters and the third will be considered in Part V. The analysis in the remainder of this chapter will concentrate on the reasons behind the failure to find a satisfactory solution to the financial consequences of the energy crisis and the threat to the survival of a highly integrated international system posed by this failure.

II

In one important respect the energy crisis is quite different from the more customary shocks to the international system, such as those caused by world wars or revolutionary technical advances: under certain conditions, it could keep recurring at very short intervals over a long period. The price elasticity of demand for oil is very low in the short run. Most of the world's oil reserves are concentrated in a relatively small number of countries. So long as these countries can sustain their cartel arrangements, they are in a position to manipulate the world oil supply in such a way as to engineer frequent, large increases in the price of oil and, consequently, massive redistribution of world income in their favour. Hence, a major task confronting the rest of the world since 1973, unchanged by the collapse of oil prices in 1985–86, has been to come to some sort of arrangement with OPEC which would discourage it from using its monopoly power to create continuous international crises by raising, and keeping, its prices at the levels which impose impossible short- to medium-term adjustment problems on the oil importing countries.

Providing that such an arrangement had been made between the two groups of countries, the long-term solution to the adjustment problems caused by higher oil and other energy prices would have been no different, in principle, from the approach adopted so successfully in the international reconstruction programme after the Second World War.

As already pointed out, the large increases in the price of oil in 1973/74 and 1979/80 caused a massive redistribution of world income. A large proportion of this income went to a relatively small number of OPEC countries with low import propensities – in other words, high propensities to save. The resource transfer from the rest of the world to OPEC, implied by the redistribution, could not be achieved, therefore, through trade. The surplus OPEC members were simply in no position to absorb such a volume of imports in the short to medium term. The problem was now to find an adequate outlet for these savings; and a relatively small number of large market economies were the only areas of the world that could provide investment opportunities on the scale required.

Consequently, the key to solving the adjustment problems created by the crisis – without large transitional costs in terms of lost output and high unemployment – rested on the ability of these two groups of countries to arrange a smooth transfer of financial and real resources. Under such an arrangement, OPEC would have lent its surpluses on a long-term basis to industrial countries, partly by financing capital formation in these countries and thus acquiring a small share in the ownership of their fixed assets. In return, industrial countries would have been able to finance their current account deficits for as long as it took them to adjust their economies to the threat of an energy constraint to their future growth. They would also have been in the position to continue lending to the rest of the world.

The end result of such an orderly arrangement of the financial and real transfers between oil exporting and importing countries would have been higher rates of growth and activity levels in all countries. It is most unlikely, of course, that world expansion would have been as rapid as before 1973 – for the very simple reason that OPEC would never have increased its output at the rates which would have brought the price of oil down to anywhere near its pre-1973 levels. But the rate of expansion of the world economy could have been fast enough to avoid the deep and prolonged recessions experienced since the early 1970s.

The main reason why the apparently rational solution described above has never even been attempted is that the leading industrial countries, especially the United States, have persistently refused to accept the fact that increases in the price of oil and income redistribution in favour of OPEC were of more than a very temporary nature. Instead of coming to some sort of agreement with OPEC, the United States seemed determined to make every effort to break it up. There were even threats in the mid-1970s that the US marines might be sent to occupy the Arab oil fields and ensure a continuing supply of cheap oil! The fact, highlighted by the oil shocks, that at the rates of demand and supply common before 1973 the world would run out of the known, low cost, oil reserves within a few decades was conveniently forgotten. Nor did industrial countries seem prepared to consider the possibility that, with the price of oil and levels of demand back to their pre-1973 levels, no alternative sources of energy would be developed in time for the world to turn to when oil ran out!

Given the extent of international integration and interdependence, once the United States and other major industrial countries decided to treat the whole problem as being nothing more than a matter of short-term disequilibrium to be corrected by deflation, other countries had little alternative but to do the same. Instead of developing an international approach to what was clearly a global problem, each country was left to cope with its own current account deficits. In most cases, this consisted of short-term external borrowing and deflation. The relatively small number of developing countries and centrally planned economies which chose the alternative policy option of borrowing abroad and restructuring at home managed to persist with their expansionary policies until after the second oil shock. Then, for reasons to be discussed later, they too were forced to undertake extremely severe deflations of their economies.

III

The refusal of the industrial countries to accept that the problems created by the energy crisis are of a long-term nature is difficult to justify on economic grounds. Their behaviour is quite easy to understand, however, from a political point of view. For the United States and other major industrial countries to accept that the real price of oil will rise in the long term would amount, in effect, to an explicit admission of their economic dependence on the half-a-dozen small oil exporting countries; and to do that is to accept political constraints which normally go with economic dependence. No industrial country, especially a major one, has been prepared to contemplate this – even though they have all been aware of the fact that a refusal to come to some arrangement with the key oil exporters involves considerable welfare costs to themselves as well as to the rest of the world.

The problem is, in fact, the outcome of another consequence of the energy crisis: the division between dominant and surplus economies, which is quite unique.

Traditionally, the world's dominant economies have belonged to the countries with persistent structural surpluses, providing the rest of the world with both short- and long-term capital. They have also tended to share a number of other important characteristics.

First, such economies have a large and highly diversified productive capacity, well in excess of their domestic demand for goods and services. They, therefore, need external markets in order to export this surplus – the only way in which they can utilise fully their productive potential. Hence, the continuous search for export markets, and the state of these markets, play an important role in the economic strategy and foreign policy of these countries. The large size of the dominant economies ensures that they account for a large proportion of world output, trade and investments – so that their policies have a major impact on the rest of the world.

Second, thanks to their high productivity, income and consumption levels, dominant economies tend to have a high propensity to save. This makes it possible for them to finance the growth of their investments (domestic and foreign) and exports without the need to resort to the policies which would depress their domestic demand and, consequently, jeopardise their own long-term growth.

Third, the capacity to generate a large volume of savings gives rise to the development of an advanced financial system, capable of channelling them into short and long-term investments, both at home and abroad.

Fourth, as the dominant economies normally operate close to the frontiers of technology, the rate of their economic growth depends on the pace of advances in technical knowledge and the organisation of economic activity. They have, therefore, both the capacity and the need to generate such changes. Equally, it makes the rest of the world highly dependent on these countries – as its own economic progress will depend on its ability to acquire from them a wide range of goods and services, as well as their technical and organisational knowledge.

Fifth, the high level of specialisation achieved by the dominant economies makes them both able and willing to absorb a large quantity of imports from the rest of the world. In this way, they come to provide the largest and most important market for other countries' exports. These exports are of special importance to developing countries. They provide the means for acquiring the essential products and knowledge from dominant economies without which it is virtually impossible for these countries to industrialise.

Sixth, the combination of competitive advantage enjoyed by dominant economies and their need for access to other countries' markets tends to encourage most of their economic agents to favour a high degree of international openness and integration as the means for sustaining a continuous improvement in their own incomes.

Seventh, their ability to earn persistent structural surpluses, combined with the leading role which they play in the world economy, enables them to pursue consistent long-term policies. *Ceteris paribus*, they are under no pressure to change their policies in order to reconcile their internal and external balances. The general realisation that they are in such a position creates a widespread confidence in the existing international economic order, which is in many ways an extension of the order prevailing within the dominant economies.

Finally, the world's dominant economies also invariably happen to be the world's dominant military and political powers, shaping the course of world events.

There is little doubt that these characteristics, normally associated with a dominant *and* surplus economy, describe closely the position and behaviour of the UK before 1914 and the United States between the end of the Second World War and the second half of the 1960s. In fact, as a group, industrial countries still exhibit all these characteristics except one: the ability to run persistent structural surpluses.

The change was analysed in the previous chapter for the group as a whole. It is also confirmed if one analyses the experience of individual countries in the 1980s. The only major industrial economy which has expanded rapidly enough to achieve a significant reduction in its rate of unemployment, the United States, has also been running record deficits on its current balance of payments. Most of the other major economies have been experiencing current account surpluses over the same period, achieved invariably at the cost of low increases in output and rising unemployment. In this respect, the most important industrial countries, apart from the US, are behaving very much like the UK in the 1920s: maintaining their financial independence and, through this, their international influence by sacrificing productive capacity and employment at home.

As emphasised earlier, the only group of countries which is now capable of running balance-of-payments surpluses in periods of rapid growth consists of a few tiny oil exporting economies: Saudi Arabia, Kuwait, the United Arab Emirates, Libya and Iraq. (Among industrial countries only Japan, Switzerland and Norway seem capable of running structural surpluses.)

This is, however, the only characteristic which the group shares with the traditional dominant, surplus economies. Both individually and combined these are very small countries with underdeveloped economies and financial systems, dependent almost entirely for their prosperity on exports of a single commodity – oil. They are of negligible importance as markets to the rest of the world. Nor do they possess any new technical or organisational skills which other countries are anxious to acquire. Their international standing and influence rests entirely, therefore, on their ability to manipulate the supply and price of oil, which can last, barring technical advances which would make oil obsolete as a source of energy, only as long as their reserves of oil.

Even their ability to use this policy weapon – the sole source of their balance of payments surpluses – depends on the actions of industrial countries and, to a lesser extent, of other oil producers. A reduction in the rate of growth of the world economy, combined with higher output by the marginal oil producers, can quickly wipe out those countries' surpluses, as happened in the 1980s.

In this important respect, the position of the six surplus oil producers is totally different from that enjoyed by the surplus countries which were sufficiently large to dominate the world economy for a time. As Table 13.1 shows, irrespective of fairly large fluctuations and changes in the world economy between 1870 and 1914, the UK did not have a single deficit on its current balance of payments over this period. In the 1920s, when its current account surpluses were achieved only at the expense of stagnation and unemployment at home, it was obviously in no position to continue with its earlier role of chief supplier of capital to the rest of the world. With the exception of a few years in the 1950s, the US earned consistently current account surpluses in the 1920s and between 1948 and 1967. From then until 1973 its capacity to finance other countries' deficits, without imposing intolerable strain on its own economy, declined sufficiently fast to create a number of international financial crises, culminating in the final breakdown of the Bretton Woods System in 1973. The role of stabilising the world economy and providing capital for long-term

Table 13.1 Current balances of payments (BP) and unemployment (U) in dominant-surplus countries since 1870

	Mean	*Highest*	*Lowest*	*Coefficient of variation (%)*
UK				
1870–1914				
BP (£m)	79.9	235.0	10.5	65.9
U (%)	4.5	11.4	0.9	55.6
1921–30				
BP (£m)	104.3	201.0	−18.0	69.2
U (%)	12.4	15.2	10.6	14.5
1931–39				
BP (£m)	−60.0	23.0	−250.0	132.2
U (%)	16.7	22.5	11.3	25.7
USA				
1919–30				
BP (US$bn)	1.2	3.8	0.4	83.3
U (%)	4.7	11.7	1.4	63.8
1931–39				
BP (US$bn)	0.3	1.1	−0.1	133.3
U (%)	19.3	24.9	14.3	18.1
1948–67				
BP (US$bn)	2.1	6.8	−1.8	109.5
U (%)	4.8	6.8	2.9	25.0
1968–73				
BP (US$bn)	0.5	7.1	−5.8	840.0
U (%)	4.6	5.8	3.4	21.7
1974–84				
BP (US$bn)	−13.7	18.1	−101.6	240.1
U (%)	7.4	9.5	5.5	17.6
INDUSTRIAL COUNTRIES				
1968–73				
BP (US$bn)	7.9	13.0	4.7	40.5
U (%)	3.1	3.6	2.6	12.9
1974–84				
BP (US$bn)	−20.9	15.3	−61.0	111.0
U (%)	6.1	8.7	3.5	26.2
*OPEC**				
1973–78				
High absorbers				
BP (US$bn)	2.1	24.0	−16.3	604.3
Low absorbers				
BP (US$bn)	24.9	39.6	12.6	42.7

Table 13.1 *cont.*

	Mean	*Highest*	*Lowest*	*Coefficient of variation (%)*
1979–84				
High absorbers				
BP (US$bn)	−0.3	11.0	−14.3	852.1
Low absorbers				
BP (US$bn)	25.2	92.4	−14.2	172.6

Note: *High absorbers: Algeria, Ecuador, Gabon, Indonesia, Iran, Nigeria and Venezuela. Low absorbers: Iraq, Kuwait, Libya, Qatar, Saudi Arabia and the United Arab Emirates.
Sources: Mitchell (1975), Mitchell and Deane (1962), *The Economist* (1985), OECD (1985), IMF (1984c) and Bank of England.

growth could have been performed by the combined strength of industrial countries between 1968 and 1973, though not since.

The apparent inability of the dominant countries to reconcile their internal and external balances without financial support from the key oil producers, the equally apparent inability of the latter to achieve their policy objectives without assistance from industrial countries, and the continuing refusal of the two sides to come to some sort of agreement which would help them overcome these problems, have had far-reaching financial effects. By giving rise to a degree of uncertainty about the future course of the world economy without parallel since the end of the 1920s, the energy crisis has had a profound effect on the behaviour of international savers and investors.

IV

Even in reasonably stable and predictable times economic decision makers will be anxious to have adequate provisions of liquid assets, as well as easy access to borrowing facilities that they can use if, or when, the need arises. This enables them to respond rapidly to changes in the environment in which they operate. 'Liquidity', as Hicks put it, 'is freedom. When a firm takes action that diminishes its liquidity, it diminishes its freedom; for it exposes itself to the risk that it will have diminished, or retarded, its ability to respond to future opportunities'.[1]

The same is also basically true of countries. A country whose reserves of internationally liquid assets are small and whose credit standing on international financial markets is low will also find it extremely difficult 'to respond to future opportunities'. Even more important, it will be in no position to minimise the short-term costs to its economy of adverse developments abroad. Consequently, all national monetary authorities hold a certain amount of foreign exchange, as a buffer against temporary, unforeseen external shocks.

This preoccupation with liquidity is likely to become particularly intense in periods of growing economic instability and widespread uncertainty about future prospects. In these circumstances, both lenders and borrowers will continue to be aware of a whole range of alternative outcomes to any particular course of action, but without being able to attach objective probabilities to any of them. Hence, both will become reluctant to commit a significant proportion of their resources to projects which have long gestation periods. At the same time, there will be a tendency for decision makers at all levels to develop, as a matter of prudence, a strong preference for fairly liquid assets.

These trends have been increasingly in evidence since the early 1970s. Of course, there was already a growing instability and uncertainty in the international economy even before the energy crisis, as the US became patently incapable of managing the international system and there was no other country, or international institution, capable of undertaking this role. However, the energy crisis intensified the uncertainty by giving rise to a division between the surplus and dominant countries which was far more serious than the problems created by the relative decline of the US economy in the 1960s. Some of the prominent characteristics and behaviour of the 'new savers' contributed further to this.

The vast amount of oil revenues accumulated by OPEC after 1973 was owned by governments, not private individuals. The main policy objective of those governments has been to maximise social welfare by using these revenues, either immediately or at some later date, to develop their economies – rather than to treat them, following the example of industrial countries, as investible surpluses to be employed for the purpose of generating long-term income from abroad.[2] Given the objective, it was inevitable that their main preoccupation – and in this respect their behaviour is not different from that of institutional investors – has been with short-term accessibility, safety and returns on their assets. This is reflected in the disposition of OPEC surpluses.

Most of the earnings have been held in the form of short-term assets, mainly eurocurrency deposits in industrial countries' banks.[3]

This pattern of behaviour was reinforced further by the fact that oil exporters have so little in common with the traditional surplus countries. As the opportunities for long-term investment in these countries are very limited, they have tended to place most of their investments abroad in a small number of industrial economies. In doing this, they have often encountered hostility and institutional obstacles (rules and regulations) which have prevented them from investing on the scale, or in the sectors, which they have regarded as being particularly attractive (manufacturing, banking, insurance and agriculture).[4] An important reason for the resentment was almost certainly the origin of their surpluses: the fact that they were obtained by exploiting OPEC's monopoly power rather than as a result of technical and organisational advances from which, eventually, other countries could also hope to benefit. Moreover, to the extent that they have tried to increase their direct investment abroad, they have lacked, apart from capital, all the other ingredients which the recipient countries have come to value most from such investment – especially technical and managerial expertise, and access to the world's largest export and financial markets.

The uncertainty about longer term developments in the world economy has also had a significant effect on the behaviour of those making fixed investments, many of whom, like transnationals, happen to be large savers. Annual growth of such investments has declined sharply since the early 1970s in industrial and centrally planned economies; and in the rest of the world since the early 1980s. Inevitably, this has been reflected in the volume of international direct investments. Inward direct investment into industrial countries declined sharply during and immediately after the 1975 and 1982 recessions.[5] Developing countries had a similar experience in the early 1980s. In their case, the relative importance of direct investment as a source of external funds fell markedly over this period.[6] Moreover, a large proportion of direct investment since the mid-1970s has reflected the underlying uncertainty in the international economic environment. Many of these investments were used to diversify market and currency risks[7] and to finance projects with very short payback periods.[8]

These developments reflect the fact that low levels of activity, high interest rates and uncertain long-term prospects have made it more profitable to acquire and hold financial rather than real assets. Direct investment may be more attractive as a hedge against inflation, but it is less liquid and, consequently, carries a greater risk. It has become prudent, therefore, even for companies such as transnationals, responsible for most of international direct investments, to keep a high proportion of their vast financial assets in a fairly liquid form, instead of committing them to large-scale fixed investments.

The result has been a huge volume of highly liquid and diversified (by type and currecy) assets held by both official institutions and private enterprises. The great advantage of such arrangements, from the point of view of individual holders, is that it enables them to stabilise their income as well as to reduce the risk of losses in the real value of the assets. The problem from a broader point of view, national or international, is that as the scope for diversification increases so also will the volume of international flows of short-term capital, especially in an unstable and highly integrated world economy. The greater the instability the more will this capital be moved around in search of a relatively safe refuge. Hence, every change, actual or expected, in a country's short-term policies and prospects will be reflected quickly in the demand for its currency.

It is impossible to estimate the exact size of these flows for the whole world. However, it is clear from the available data that they are huge and, what is more, that they have grown enormously in recent years. For instance, according to one estimate, foreign exchange turnover on the US market, the largest in the world, amounted to $33.5 billion a day in 1983, almost a sevenfold increase since 1977 when the corresponding figure was $5 billion per day.[9] As the same study shows, 'non-financial institutions' such as transnational corporations played a far from negligible role in the growth of these transactions.

Inevitably, exchange rate fluctuations have increased greatly since the early 1970s.[10] The fact that they have done so much more in nominal than in real terms, indicates that international investors have been interested mainly in exploiting short-term differences in the macro-economic policies of industrial and other countries.[11] In other words, short-term capital movements have continued to reflect, as in earlier periods,[12] stagnation and uncertainty in the world economy. In doing this, as their size and volatility have grown, they have made even more unmanageable the very same problems which prompted them in the first place.

V

The overall effect of all these developments has been to introduce a number of important innovations and changes in the structure of international finance. These changes are highly relevant because, while solving the financing problems created by the energy shocks, they have made the world economy vulnerable to serious financial disturbances of a rather different kind.

To begin with, loan financing became much more important than bond financing. Up to 1973 eurocurrency credits featured less prominently in international capital markets than external bonds. For instance, between 1970 and 1972 their average share of the market was only 39 per cent. The relative importance of the two forms of finance fluctuated a good deal over the following six years (1973–78), but eurocurrency credits became considerably more important, accounting, on average, for 57 per cent of the total. Their share increased further after 1979, to 67 per cent or more.[13] It was only in the mid-1980s that international bonds recovered some of the lost ground, satisfying more than 40 per cent of the demand for finance on international capital markets.[14]

These changes can be explained to some extent by the types of borrower who had relatively easy access to the two forms of finance. Traditionally, as risks of investing in them are appreciably lower, industrial countries have featured much more prominently in international bond markets, taking up two-thirds or more of the funds borrowed in this way.[15] Not surprisingly, the revival of the international bond market in 1984 coincided with the return of borrowers from industrial countries, especially from the United States and Japan. Yet, even in the case of industrial countries, most of their external borrowing after 1979 (on average almost 60 per cent of the total) was in the form of eurocurrency credits. Loans of this kind accounted for over 90 per cent of external borrowing by developing countries and centrally planned economies.[16]

Another important development over this period, implied in the preceding analysis, has been a very strong preference of both lenders and borrowers for euromarkets. It is not simply that eurocurrency credits have become since the early 1970s the most important form of international finance. Since 1980, eurobonds (the bonds underwritten by a number of banks and issued simultaneously in several national markets) have also become a much more important source of external funds than foreign bonds (raised on domestic bond markets to which foreigners are allowed access).[17]

Apart from a large reduction in the real value of official loans to developing countries – until 1973 their most important source of external funds – caused by industrial countries' own financial problems, the main reasons for the great appeal of euromarkets since 1973 have been very much the same as those which gave rise to the phenomenon in the first place. The lenders avoid the risk that their assets might be seized or frozen by an unfriendly government, or, alternatively, that they might, at some future date, be restricted in their choice of profitable investments by economic stagnation at home combined with restrictions on lending abroad. The banks – the most important intermediaries in the process – escape the various controls that their central banks impose on them, especially in periods of monetary stringency, by increasing their operations outside the area of the central bank's jurisdiction. The result is that they can lend on more favourable terms, something that, naturally, appeals to the borrowers. Besides, by raising their capital on euromarkets rather than foreign bond markets, the borrowers can escape the tight entry requirements which are usually required in the latter. All these opportunities have been exploited brilliantly by the banks' capacity for innovation.[18]

However, it would be difficult to argue that the phenomenal growth of euromarkets since 1973 has been entirely against the will of national governments and central banks. After all, by far the highest proportion of eurocurrency credits and international bonds, especially eurobonds, has been raised by central governments and other public bodies.[19] The authorities appear, therefore, to have been very active in utilising the freedom enjoyed by euromarkets in order to preserve some independence in their policy making – at least from direct intereference by other governments, or the International Monetary Fund.

Nevertheless, this freedom has had a fairly high price attached to it. New forms of international lending and borrowing have been accompanied by important changes in the conditions attached to them –notably in terms of their maturity distribution.

Loans raised in euromarkets have been predominantly of a short- to medium-term nature. Over 40 per cent have had maturities of less than seven years and only a slightly higher proportion have been with maturities of seven to ten years. Eurocurrency credits with maturities of over ten years have accounted for less than 8 per cent of the total. Moreover, maturities of eurocurrency credits have fluctuated a good deal since the early 1970s.[20]

Maturities of international bonds, on the other hand, have been both more stable and longer. For instance, around 17 per cent of the total volume of capital raised in this way on international markets between 1974 and 1981 had maturities of over fifteen years or longer.[21] Nevertheless, even here, over 40 per cent of the bonds issued over the period had maturities of a medium- to short-term nature, with almost a quarter of all the bonds having maturities of less than five years.[22]

The overall effect of changes in international finance with heavy reliance on eurocurrency credits, especially by developing countries, has been to reduce markedly the average maturities of medium to long-term debts. The average for the major borrowers fell from 17.2 years in 1972 to 12.7 years in 1981.[23] The average maturity of foreign debts incurred by some of the largest borrowers was even lower: 9.7 years in the case of Brazil and 8.7 years in the case of Mexico.[24] As the World Bank has pointed out: 'For many countries, the shortening of maturities was not a deliberate policy ... Often they faced a choice between borrowing short term or not borrowing at all, since commercial creditors were no longer willing to lend longer term'.[25] Many of these loans were raised, however, not for the purpose of financing short-term balance of payments deficits but in order to undertake fixed investments with long gestation periods.

The mismatch since 1973 between the periods over which international loans have had to be repaid and the years which it takes the new investments, financed with these loans, to become productive does not seem to have a historical precedent. Before 1914 most international borrowing was in the form of bonds with very long maturities. Even maturities of 'up to ninety-nine years were not uncommon'.[26] At least half of the foreign bonds issued in the United States in the 1920s had average maturities of twenty years.[27] Average maturities of new public debt commitments in the 1960s were eighteen years.[28] For reasons to be discussed in the next section, the mismatch which appeared after 1973 was to contribute a good deal to the problems encountered by both lenders and borrowers in the early 1980s.

Banks tried to overcome the apparent discrepancy between the lenders' strong liquidity preference and the borrowers needs by coming up with a number of innovations. Two of these have had a particularly important bearing on subsequent events.

First, there was the rapid growth of syndicated loans, as banks tried to minimise their risks by acting together: borrowing short and lending longer term.[29] This type of maturity transformation and lending increased very sharply in the late 1970s and early 1980s. Suddenly, in

1981–82, banks' perception of risks changed dramatically when they discovered that a number of heavy borrowers were unable to service their debts. The volume of syndicated loans has declined sharply since then, especially to certain regions of the world; and the maturities of these loans have also declined significantly.[30]

Second, there has been a sharp increase since the mid-1970s in the proportion of developing countries' foreign debt obtained at floating interest rates. In 1974 loans of this kind accounted for about 16 per cent of developing countries' public debt. By 1980 the proportion had risen to a third and three years later, in 1983, it was over 40 per cent of the total.[31] As usual, the average conceals the fact that in a number of cases the proportion of floating debt was higher than this in the early 1980s. This is particularly true of a number of developing countries which have experienced extremely serious debt problems: Venezuela (81.4 per cent), Mexico (74.0 per cent), Nigeria (67.2 per cent), Brazil (66.0 per cent) and Argentina (53.6 per cent).[32]

The practice of lending at floating interest rates has not been confined to eurocurrency credits. The revival of bond lending in the first half of the 1980s coincided, among other things, with a rapid increase in the relative importance of floating rate notes.[33]

In summary, the importance of the developments and innovations described briefly in this section is that they enabled banks to attract short-term deposits, solving in this way the problem of 'recycling' – in other words, the problem of short-term balance of payments financing. At the same time, the changes have created conditions that could easily lead to a major financial crisis if a sufficiently large number of countries borrowed heavily for the purpose of long-term adjustments. There would be the risk in this case of a significant mismatch between the lenders' preference for liquidity in conditions of economic stagnation and uncertainty and the borrowers' need for investments, many of which are likely to have long gestation periods. Inevitably, it was the desire of a number of countries to finance their long-term investments by heavy borrowing abroad, and the problems which they experienced in servicing these debts, that created in the early 1980s a major 'debt crisis'.

VI

Much has been written in recent years about the size of external debts accumulated since the early 1970s by developing countries. As Table 13.2

Table 13.2 External debt of non-oil developing countries: its size and maturity distribution, 1973–84

		Ratios of debt to		*Maturity (per cent of total debt)*		
				Short-term	*Long-term*	
	Total debt (US$ bn)	*Merchandise exports*	*Exports of goods and services*		*To official creditors*	*To private creditors*
1973	130	1.6	1.2	13.8	39.2	47.0
1974	161	1.4	1.1	14.3	37.3	48.4
1975	191	1.7	1.2	14.1	36.6	49.3
1976	228	1.7	1.3	14.5	36.0	49.5
1977	291	1.7	1.3	18.2	34.4	47.4
1978	343	1.7	1.3	17.5	35.0	47.5
1979	406	1.6	1.2	16.3	33.5	50.2
1980	490	1.5	1.2	19.0	32.2	48.8
1981	578	1.7	1.3	19.7	30.6	49.7
1982	655	2.0	1.5	20.2	30.2	49.6
1983	694	2.1	1.6	16.3	31.8	51.9
1984	731	2.0	1.5	14.2	33.0	52.8

Sources: Dillon, Watson and Kincaid (1985, p. 2) and IMF, *World Economic Outlook*.

shows, the total debt increased by about two and a half times between 1973 and 1978; and more than doubled in the following six years. The debt:exports ratio has gone up from about 1.5 in 1973/74 to 2.0 in the first half of the 1980s; or, if annual exports of both goods and services are taken into account, from around 1.1 in 1973/74 to 1.5 in 1982/84.

Taken on their own, the figures in the first three columns of Table 13.2 may seem large, even alarming. However, compared with similar ratios for earlier periods, especially the levels of external debt common before the First World War, they appear to be anything but excessive. For instance, in 1913 quite a few countries had debt:exports ratios of positively staggering proportions compared to those observed in the 1980s: Canada 8.6, South Africa 6.3, Latin America 5.2, Australasia 4.8 and Russia 4.8.[34] India (2.4), Japan (2.3) and China (2.2)[35] had the smallest debts, on this criterion, among the countries listed by Lewis. yet, by present day standards, all three had fairly large debt:exports ratios.

As the international system before 1914 was not permanently in a state of crisis,[36] it is difficult to attribute the debt crisis of the early 1980s simply to the size of developing countries' external debts.

Whatever their size, foreign debts present no serious problem so long as a number of important conditions are satisfied. The loans have to be used in such a way as to generate net income. Moreover, in order to service the debt, the borrower has to be in a position to convert some of this income into foreign exchange through exports. This particular task will obviously be easier if enough of the income generated by investments from a foreign loan materialises during the lifetime of the loan – which is why it is important that investments with long gestation periods should be financed with long-term loans.

Countries which rely on short-term borrowing for this purpose expose themselves to the risk that the foreign loans may not be 'rolled over' for as long as is necessary to complete the relevant investment projects; or that the loans may be 'rolled over' on much less favourable terms, affecting significantly the longer-term viability of the investments in progress. The borrowing country can be certain of avoiding problems of this kind only as long as it is in a position to pay the interest on its loans regularly so that the lenders have no reason to doubt in its ability to do so in the future.

The important point here is that this 'ability' depends on more than the country's own actions. As already mentioned, a country must be able to earn foreign exchange in order to service its debts. It can only do this through exports; and what happens to its exports will depend to a significant extent on current and future economic policies and demand in its export markets. This seems to be obvious enough. Yet it was the widespread neglect of this inevitable consequence of international economic integration that lay at the centre of the debt crisis which developed so rapidly in the early 1980s.

There is little doubt that the energy crisis added significantly to the adjustment and financing problems of developing economies, especially the more dynamic and advanced members of this group of countries. According to Cline, who attempted to quantify this contribution: 'The single most important exogenous cause of the debt burden of non-oil developing countries is the sharp rise in the price of oil in 1973–74 and again in 1979–80.'[37]

This is actually a rather incomplete explanation of the problem. What it neglects is the fact that many developing countries (especially the so-called 'newly industrialised countries') and centrally planned economies deliberately adopted, after the first oil shock, the long-term adjustment strategy described earlier in this chapter: they borrowed abroad even more heavily than before in order to continue the expansion and modernisation of their economies.

As the official, concessional, loans were inadequate for the purpose (Table 13.3), developing countries borrowed increasingly on commercial terms from private creditors, consisting predominantly of industrial countries' banks. The latter were, of course, more than happy to find an outlet for the huge oil surpluses deposited with them, as well as for the excess savings from industrial countries[38] which were experiencing a significant reduction in the growth of their fixed capital formation. The practice of syndicated loans appeared to reduce considerably the risk that individual banks were facing in lending so heavily to developing economies. Besides, investments in many of these economies appeared to promise considerably higher returns than those in leading industrial countries.[39]

The relatively high returns were only one of the factors indicating to the rest of the world that many of the borrowers were remarkably successful in the pursuit of their long-term strategy. As shown in Chapter 12, developing countries sustained the growth of their fixed investments and output in the second half of the 1970s extremely well. What is more, the success of their adjustment policies was also reflected in the fact that, unlike in the years before 1973, the volume of their exports was growing more rapidly than the volume of imports. This was particularly true of the newly industrialised countries.[40]

Table 13.3 Total resource flows to developing countries by major types of flow, 1970–84*
US$ bn at 1983 prices and exchange rates

	1970–74	*1975–78*	*1979–84*
I Official development assistance	24.04 (41.6)	30.28 (33.9)	34.74 (37.1)
II Grants by private voluntary agencies	2.28 (4.0)	1.94 (2.2)	2.21 (2.4)
III Non-concessional flows	31.57 (54.5)	57.23 (63.9)	62.32 (60.6)
1 Official or officially supported	10.55 (18.3)	19.24 (21.4)	20.84 (22.2)
2 Private	21.01 (36.2)	38.0 (42.4)	41.48 (38.4)
(a) Direct investment	7.81 (13.8)	13.75 (15.5)	11.58 (12.3)
(b) Bank sector	9.07 (20.9)	21.48 (23.9)	29.14** (25.3)
(c) Bond lending	0.84 (1.5)	2.78 (3.0)	0.76 (0.8)
Total resource flows	57.89 (100.0)	89.45 (100.0)	99.27 (100.0)

Notes: *Percentage shares of total flows are shown in parenthesis.
**Bank sector figures include, for the last two years of this period, considerable amounts of rescheduled short-term debt.
Source: OECD revision of the data published in OECD (1984, p. 28).

Worries about the potential shortage of oil and other raw materials further increased the flow of capital to developing countries.

Not surprisingly, few people seemed to show great concern about the size of international debts even during and immediately after the second oil shock. Certainly the international organisations most closely involved in monitoring economic and financial developments in the world appeared to exude nothing but calm and a sense of satisfaction at the way that existing financial arrangements were functioning. For instance, the Bank for International Settlements reassured the international community in 1979 by stating confidently: 'We know from experience that even large current account imbalances can be financed without too much trouble by the international banking community.'[41] It was not, of course, alone in believing this. The World

Bank and OECD, two highly respected international organisations, expressed similar views at the time.[42] Two years later, in 1981, the IMF could still conclude its review of the international financial scene by observing that 'the overall debt situation ... does not give cause for alarm'.[43] Yet it was only a few months later in that same year that the international financial community found itself in the middle of the worst debt crisis since the early 1930s!

The sudden change had little to do with the behaviour of developing countries, many of which attempted to continue with more or less the same policies as before.[44] Its main cause is to be found in major policy changes in some of the key industrial countries around 1980, and the widespread failure to realise the effect that they would have on developing countries and, through them, on the long-term viability of industrial countries' own financial sectors. In other words, the origin of the debt crisis can be traced to a general failure to appreciate the extent and consequences of international economic integration. To make things worse, the appearance of the surplus oil producers had helped obscure the fact that the energy crisis had not altered the basic relationship between developing and industrial countries. The former were still in the position of dependent, deficit, economies, while the latter continued to enjoy the status of dominant-'surplus' countries, even though a large part of their international lending consisted now of investible funds that they were channelling into developing countries on behalf of the surplus oil producers.

The second oil shock coincided with, or was soon followed by, important changes of governments and policies in a number of large industrial countries, notably the United States. Suddenly, 'the fight against inflation' became not just a major policy objective but, for the first time since the Second World War, virtually the only policy objective. The new governments seemed to show little concern for the welfare costs that could result from their pursuit of such a narrow policy objective. Consequently they adopted, with banks and other financial institutions as their most vociferous supporters, an even more uncompromisingly deflationary approach to the second oil shock than had their predecessors. The result was a sharp and prolonged world-wide recession in 1980–83. Moreover, as the emphasis was put now on highly restrictive monetary policies (in the belief that they represented the most effective means of bringing inflation under control) both nominal and real interest rates were raised and maintained at exceptionally high levels.

The effect of these changes on output, investment and employment in industrial countries and the rest of the world soon became apparent. After all, exports account for a significant share of total output in many developing countries; and, as was shown in Chapter 2, industrial countries still take over 60 per cent of their exports. Economic stagnation in industrial economies was bound, therefore, to have an adverse effect not only on the growth of developing countries but also on their capacity to meet their external obligations.

The subsequent development of an international debt crisis was the inevitable result of a combination of factors. Some of them have featured in all crises of this kind in the past. Others were a direct result of the innovations and changes described in the previous section.

First, stagnation in industrial countries led to a deterioration in the export earnings of developing countries: the slower growth of their exports in volume terms was exacerbated by a sharp fall in prices.

Second, as a high and increasing proportion of developing countries' external borrowing consisted of floating interest and short-term loans (with maturities of less than one year), deflationary policies in industrial countries were bound not only to reduce the ability of developing countries to acquire foreign exchange, but also to increase, at the same time, their debt service charges. The heavy reliance of the United States and other major industrial countries on tight monetary policies with high interest rates made this unavoidable. As a result of this, according to the World Bank: 'Interest obligations on foreign debt increased by as much as 5 per cent of GDP for some of the major borrowers.'[45]

Third, as these problems accumulate, the borrowers' ability to service their debts depends critically on the lenders' willingness to 'roll over' the existing loans and grant new ones, and on the conditions on which they are prepared to do so. The trouble is that, as mentioned earlier, lenders may refuse to continue lending if there is any doubt about the borrowers' capacity to meet their future obligations; and in times of financial crisis it is precisely this capacity that is in question. Moreover, as the crisis spreads and lenders begin to panic about the extent to which it is threatening their own liquidity, even solvency, they may become reluctant to extend loans even to countries which are not experiencing serious servicing problems.

This is precisely what happened in 1981–82. Once Poland and Mexico had highlighted the difficulties that heavy borrowers were experiencing, and transnational banks had realised the extent of their exposure in these countries,[46] it became extremely difficult for developing countries to continue borrowing on international financial markets – except on terms which would make their position even more untenable. It was at this point that the banks and their central banks were confronted with the possibility of wholesale defaults by developing countries: not because they wanted it but because they had no alternative.

The danger of a major collapse of the international financial system, with potentially disastrous consequences for both developing and industrial countries, was avoided at the last moment thanks to the intervention of the latter's central banks and international organisations. A whole series of impromptu arrangements were initiated with governments of the countries with serious debt problems, leading to an eventual rescheduling of the debts. There were only thirteen reschedulings in 1981. By 1983 the number had gone up to thirty-one (involving twenty-one countries). A similar number of reschedulings were also made in 1984. (This compares with only seventeen debt reschedulings, involving seven countries, in the period 1955–70; and about thirty reschedulings in the whole of the 1970s.)[47]

The increasing involvement in debt rescheduling of official institutions explains the recovery in relative importance of official, especially concessional, loans shown in Tables 13.2 and 13.3; and the decline in the proportion of short-term debt which can be seen in the fourth column of Table 13.2. It also accounts for the sharp decline in the growth of output and investment in developing countries described in Chapter 12 – as this was one of the conditions demanded by industrial countries and international organisations in order to approve debt reschedulings.

For the time being, therefore, the debt crisis has ceased to be an immediate policy issue. Yet the underlying problems remain. As argued in Part II, economic policies which perpetuate or, even worse, increase fundamental disequilibria are untenable, except in the short term. This means that so long as the uncertainty and stagnation which have plagued the world economy since the early 1970s remain, the risk of another, possibly even more serious, debt crisis also remains.

Part V
The Main Prerequisites for a Stable International Economic System

The concept of the 'division of labour' represents one of the oldest as well as one of the most fundamental ideas in economics. The Greeks – notably Thucydides, Plato and Aristotle – attached considerable importance to it, mainly because of its political effects. They discussed at some length the process by which the size of a country determined the extent to which its citizens could specialise and, in this way, increase the efficiency, wealth and power of the state. Their treatment of the concept already contained all the ingredients which, centuries later, Adam Smith was to use so effectively in order to turn the division of labour into, as Schumpeter put it, 'the engine' of economic progress.[1]

The advantages of economic specialisation have been appreciated, therefore, for a long time. At the same time, economists and other social scientists have been aware also of its social costs. Socieites progressively lose their cohesiveness, as they become split into classes and special interest groups. In addition, there is the danger of a possibly 'dehumanising' effect in forcing people to perform narrowly specialised, increasingly simplified tasks.

There is, however, one important aspect of specialisation to which few economists have paid much attention: the relationship between different stages of the division of labour and those changes in the organisation of production and distribution without which an increasingly integrated economic system cannot function effectively. In fact, it is no exaggeration to say that these changes represent a precondition for the survival of such a system. The institutions and organisational forms which function successfully at one level of economic development can easily become a serious obstacle to stability and further progress at the next level. The dynamics of managing an economic system are, therefore, as important as the dynamics of the system itself, for the simple reason that the two are inextricably linked.

As Cipolla observed in his review of the reasons for the economic decline of a number of countries and empires: 'Ways of doing things are strategically important in determining the performance of society. If the necessary change does not take place and economic difficulties are allowed to grow, then a cumulative process is bound to be set into motion that makes things progressively worse. Decline enters then into its final, dramatic stage.'[2]

Dangers of something like this happening will be particularly great in a world of constant and rapid changes, some of which are bound to produce large discontinuities. This is why all dynamic economies tend from time to time to experience crises of differing severity and duration – invariably caused by delays in institutional reorganisation and behavioural adaptation to major and lasting changes in the economic environment. Hence, the greater the changes the more likely they are, in a highly integrated economy, to give rise to uncertainty and stagnation. No economic agent (individual, firm, government) will now be sure how the other agents are likely to react in the new circumstances, especially as the changes will never affect all of them equally.

The result is a period of economic stagnation. Even when everyone knows what ought to be done to reverse the process few people are prepared to take the initiative. The cost of taking the necessary action is judged to be so high, when risk premia are added, that in all but a few cases it is expected to exceed anticipated benefits. The crisis will be resolved only when new institutions are created, reducing risk premia to such an extent as to make required adjustments both possible and worthwhile. In other words, the crisis is resolved only when a new economic order is created – an order based on flexible but generally acceptable and widely observed rules and conventions.

This applies equally at all levels of economic decision making: micro-economic, national and international. It is for this reason that there are important parallels in economic developments within each of the three levels and the evolution in methods of policy co-ordination to which they give rise.

The three chapters in Part V analyse various ways of organising economic activity at a high level of integration and interdependence; the most important duties and obligations that soveriegn nation states, whose economies are highly interdependent, have to accept if they are to realise their economic objectives; and, finally, country groupings most likely to form an optimum policy area.

14 Economic Progress and Economic Organisation

I

As economic processes become more and more specialised and divided, people inevitably become increasingly separated, both geographically and in their understanding of each other's problems, aspirations and skills. It is, therefore, in the very nature of the continuous specialisation and segmentation of production and distribution processes that they increase the problem of communication and, thus, the risk of failure. The ability to achieve a particular economic objective depends increasingly on the compatibility and timing of a vast number of seemingly unrelated actions carried out by a large number of people. Yet most of these people frequently have no idea that they are working towards the same goal for the very simple reason that they are not even aware of each other's existence! To complicate matters further, no objective can be attained unless it is, first of all, accepted by those whose participation is essential for its realisation.

For all these reasons, the division of labour is bound to create a good deal of uncertainty; and under these conditions 'the actual execution of activity becomes in a real sense a secondary part of life; the primary problem or function is deciding what to do and how to do it'.[1] In other words, in an uncertain world it becomes essential to find ways of: (a) securing agreement about the type of action required to deal with unanticipated events; and (b) ensuring that those involved in the activities which form part of an integrated chain in the wealth-creating process have some idea of what other groups participating in the same chain are doing, as well as of what they intend to do.

It is preoccupations of this kind that give rise to different forms of administrative control, the main aim of which is to reduce uncertainty and the risk of failure. As the size and complexity of the production chain grows, those in charge of various economic entities within the chain will try to minimise uncertainty by assuming control over an increasing number of factors which are of strategic importance in the pursuit of their long-term objectives. The form that this control takes, and the flexibility with which it responds to the needs for co-ordination created by technical and economic change, will determine in the end the success or failure of an economic strategy. It is for this reason that the organisation of economic activity will have an important effect on economic performance;[2] and continuous success in economic performance will, eventually, require a reorganisation of economic activity. Under dynamic conditions, the very success in solving a problem and attaining a particular objective will give rise to new problems and, consequently, new objectives.

This is why there are important similarities at all levels of economic activity in the evolution of their economic organisation. Each of them ('micro' and 'macro') represents a particular form of *collective* action, the only way in which economic activity can take place once people begin to specialise so that different individuals and groups perform different tasks.

II

Organisational problems which result from the complexity and uncertainty created by the division of labour are apparent already at the level of the 'firm', the micro-economic unit of collective action. The firm accomplishes its objectives through a fairly intricate division of labour which in many ways represents a microcosm of modern industrial society. Hence, an understanding of developments in its internal organisation, of the structure of its industry, and of the way that these two determine the pattern of its behaviour, makes it easier also to appreciate the evolution that much more complex forms of economic organisation, such as those at the national and international levels, have to take.

New industries usually start with a relatively large number of producers, all offering slightly different varieties of the same type of product. However, with time, some of them will prove to be much more resilient than others as a result of their engineering, marketing, financial or managerial superiority. Consequently, they will expand their operations both by internal growth and by taking over their less successful competitors. The increase in the scale of output of successful companies will be accompanied by increased specialisation within them, within the industry in which they operate and within the industries closely related to it. The reason for this is that the 'capacity to buy depends upon the capacity to produce', or in other words, 'the division of labour depends in large part upon the division of labour'.[3] As the proliferation and complexity of production grows, the number of functions that have to be performed in order to ensure the success of the production process (engineering, research and development, marketing, finance and others) multiply. The problem of co-ordinating these numerous activities becomes acute.

It is in the process of such changes that personal contacts will give place increasingly to impersonal, legal contracts. This becomes essential in order to ensure the required flow of goods and services which the firm needs if it is to achieve its objectives. However, the success of the contractual arrangements will depend on the frequency with which transactions between different producers take place; the extent to which these transactions depend on long-term investment made especially for the purpose; and the uncertainty to which such transactions are subject.[4] The greater the uncertainty the more difficult it becomes to incorporate a wider range of possible outcomes into a contract so that it remains acceptable to the parties over a long period. The alternative is short-term contracts, which would make the contractual arrangements much more flexible. Their most serious disadvantage, however, is that they make long-term corporate planning and, consequently, long-term investment decisions extremely difficult.

These problems multiply as the complexity of an industry increases and different stages of production are carried out by a multitude of highly specialised, independent producers. For instance, there is the growing problem of obtaining information about the past performance and future intentions of individual enterprises. More and more time has to be spent in bargaining. The risk that contracts might not be fulfilled, or that they might not be completed on time, increases. At the same time, there is a lack of machinery for resolving quickly the conflicts between different organisations.

The result of all these complications is an increase in delays, uncertainty and, therefore, production costs. Even worse, from the point of view of a firm, these developments restrict its freedom of action, its ability to respond rapidly to the changes and shocks which take place continuously in a dynamic environment.

It is in order to avoid many of these problems that, as the division of labour increases, firms will begin to 'internalise' more and more of the functions and production processes which are of strategic importance for the achievement of their objectives.[5] That is, internal organisation and planning will take the place of market exchange. The integration of different activities within one firm harmonises the interests – or at least reconciles the differences, by fiat if necessary – and in this way makes it possible for the firm to initiate innovations and changes, as well as to react promptly to changes introduced by its competitors.

How far the process can continue will depend to a significant extent on the development and efficiency of the system of transport and communications. Writing in the 1930s Austin Robinson suggested that uncertainty would limit the size of a firm because communications – and, thus, a quick response to unforeseen developments – would be more difficult in a large than in a small firm.[6] The immense progress in this area since then, especially since the 1950s, has reduced greatly the 'uncertainty barrier' to the growth of firms. In fact, recent developments in transport and communciations have enabled firms to internalise not only different types of activity but also activities located in different regions of a country as well as in different parts of the world. This is, as Buckley and Casson[7] have pointed out, one of the reasons for the phenomenal growth of transnational enterprises since the 1950s. In other words, industrial firms, banks and other corporate entities have been able to grow by exploiting the large size of the world market – while, at the same time remaining in full control of their 'ownership specific' advantages, notably their technical, financial and managerial superiority.

Another development which has enabled firms to diversify their activities across industries and countries has been the evolution of the multidivisional structure of organisation, a result of the growth of individual firms described above.[8] Beyond a certain level of growth and specialisation in a firm, managerial diseconomies of scale set in. Those responsible for running the enterprise have to make an increasing number of highly complex decisions, while at the same time becoming more and more removed from the levels of, say, the production and marketing processes at which these decisions have to be implemented. If the hierarchical structure is highly centralised, the efficiency of the whole enterprise will be reduced by the inevitable delays and mistakes, as the problems which require attention, and the subsequent decisions, pass through numerous levels of the hierarchy. The shortcoming is particularly serious in a rapidly changing and uncertain environment when top management is required to deal with all sorts of novel problems which require prompt decisions and actions. The cost of overcentralisation is reduced greatly by decentralising the decision-making process along divisional lines.

However, functions which firms rarely, if ever, decentralise are those that involve fixed capital expenditure above a certain nominal sum. The main reason for this is that the decisions made about 'the long-term uses of capital are both the means and the determinants of the directions the overall enterprise will be taking. It is a matter of the prospective best use of the corporation's capital resources in which the planning horizon involves a decade or more ... No division has the appropriate scope or the time perspective to make these decisions'.[9] In other words, the board of directors of a modern corporation is concerned with the long-term strategy of the enterprise, not its day-to-day management and administration. As the responsibilities become narrower, down the hierarchical structure of a corporation, the time horizons of the decision-making process also becomes shorter.

The main advantage of this kind of executive division of labour is that it enables a firm to 'internalise' a large number of different activities, and in this way to co-ordinate them within a coherent, long-term strategy which reduces at least some of the uncertainty and risks that its decision makers have to face. The firm becomes able, therefore, to react speedily to a changing environment. This ensures its survival as well as its long-term success and growth. At the same time, its subdivisions also derive an important advantage from these arrangements by 'being able to draw on the overall resources of the corporation [so] that the division can, if its case is strong, get more capital than it would generate internally were it an autonomous enterprise. Indeed, from the common fund it may be able to obtain more funds than it would acquire in the market and on more favourable terms'.[10]

III

However, while one firm can internalise some highly integrated operations, both across industries and national frontiers, it cannot internalise all of them. The huge scale of most modern industries, managerial diseconomies, the limited resources at the disposal of a firm and anti-monopoly legislation combine to ensure this. Hence, most modern industries will tend to end up with a fundamentally oligopolistic structure:[11] a few large enterprises surrounded by numerous entities of small to medium size highly dependent on one or two of the 'giants'. This means that although internalisation may solve the problem of co-ordination within a firm, it still leaves a good deal of uncertainty concerning the behaviour of other firms in the same industry.

Consequently, oligopolists have had to develop a number of alternative ways of co-ordinating their activities to enable them to attain their corporate objectives. In each case, a general realisation and acceptance of their interdependence is the most important precondition for co-ordinating their corporate strategies.

All oligopolists are aware of the fact that, given the overall economic environment, the most as well as the least favourable course of action open to each of them depends on actions taken by his rivals. It would not make sense, therefore, to provoke them into actions detrimental to all members of the industry. This is why oligopolists will be careful to avoid doing something that promises short-term gains at the cost of breaking the accepted code of behaviour within the industry thus increasing uncertainty and, with it, the problem of achieving their own long-term objectives.

The emphasis is, therefore, on achieving a long-term competitive advantage rather than on gains of a purely short-term nature. Price competition, in which all oligopolists can engage at short notice, and from which none of them can gain any lasting advantage, will be avoided. Oligopolistic competition instead relies heavily on various 'non-price' factors which involve long-term improvements in the firms' technical, marketing, financial and managerial performance. It is in this way that each of them hopes to acquire certain 'ownership specific' advantages which, unlike short-term price changes, cannot be reproduced easily by his rivals.

The success of oligopolists' attempts to co-ordinate their activities in a way which is beneficial to each and, therefore, all of them will depend critically on two factors. First, the more comparable are the levels of efficiency (in other words, the cost conditions) attained by oligopolists the more similar are also likely to be their price preferences and, consequently, their patterns of behaviour. Second, the smaller the number of oligopolists in an industry the better they are likely to be informed about their rivals' prices, output and profits – which, again, reduces the risk that any one of them will act in a way which is detrimental to everyone's interest. In other words, the more similar the conditions under which oligopolists operate the greater the chances that they will act in such a way as to maximise their own as well as the industry's profits.

There are a number of alternative methods used by oligopolists to co-ordinate their actions. What they all have in common is that, by accepting in the management of their own firms certain rules of behaviour which restrict each firm's autonomy, oligopolists end up, in fact, managing both the short-term behaviour and the long-run progress of their industry. That is, in accepting constraints imposed by their interdependence, oligopolists surrender a certain degree of their corporate independence. But, in return, they acquire an important influence over the allocation and use of productive resources considerably wider than those which are under their direct control!

Cartels provide the most obvious example of this. In establishing a cartel oligopolists reach an open, formal agreement about overall output and prices. However, the success of this joint strategy depends on *each* of the members: (a) accepting a price that brings all of them the highest return obtainable without encouraging new entrants which could destroy the cartel's cohesion; and (b) adjusting their output, if demand conditions change, in such a way that the agreed price can be sustained.

An awareness of oligopolistic interdependence and the extent to which each oligopolist's actions can influence developments in his industry are equally important, though less apparent, in those cases in which cartels are either difficult to organise or forbidden by law. In the absence of such an awareness both formal and informal attempts by firms in an industry to co-ordinate their actions will be broken by 'chiselling' (price undercutting).

On the other hand, once interdependence is recognised and accepted, firms will strive to observe certain generally desirable rules of behaviour which minimise uncertainty within their industry. Where one firm is dominant it will act as the 'leader', indicating by its own behaviour the course of action that the rest of industry should take in response to external developments. In the absence of a clear leader, the largest firms in an industry can alternate in providing similar signals.

Whatever the form that oligopolistic co-ordination within an industry takes its key aspect remains the same: by accepting that orderly pricing is in their common interest, firms will adjust output and stocks to prevailing prices and *not* the other way round. But the real significance of the oligopolistic type of behaviour is that it forces firms to recognise their interdependence and, consequently, to look for lasting solutions to their problems, instead of engaging in competitive skirmishes which result in transient gains for some of them and long-term losses for all.

IV

However, reduction of uncertainty and risk within an industry is not enough to guarantee its long-term progress. This can still be impeded – given the interdependence of various sectors of an economy – by uncertainty to which developments outside the industry give rise. One of the tasks of national economic management is, therefore, to promote *inter*-sectoral co-ordination of activity by reducing uncertainty in ways which are external to individual sectors but internal to the economy as a whole.

National economies are much more diverse and, therefore, much more complex – both in economic and social terms – than a firm or industry. Yet the basic policy issues concerning their levels and patterns of activity, and methods of organisation required to deal with them, are not fundamentally different in the three cases. In fact, as the size of firms increases and the activities in which they engage become more and more diversified, their problems of organisation and management become similar to those experienced at the macro-economic level.

One of the reasons for this is that there is a common factor which ensures that both modern firms and modern states attach so much importance to 'growth'. In most modern industries, firms have to grow in order to preserve their corporate identity. It is much more difficult for outsiders to take over a large than a small firm. The process of 'internalising' productive activities plays an important role in this by giving a firm the resources needed to deal with outside threats.

For similar reasons, given the threat of foreign interference and domination, usually associated with economic backwardness in an increasingly industrialised world, most countries will make an effort to industrialise in order to preserve their national identity by strengthening the capacity to defend their soveriegnty. Hence, once a country starts to industrialise, its major trading and territorial rivals will have no alternative but to do the same. The longer they delay their industrialisation the greater will become the gap between them and their more dynamic rivals. As a result of this, the rate of their economic growth will have to be appreciably higher than that of the leading rival if they are to re-establish the *status quo ante* within a reasonable period of time. As explained in Part II, rapid and sustained recovery of this kind is not something that developing and declining economies can achieve easily.

Modern industrial processes rely heavily on increasing returns to scale, in other words, on mass production. The two key features in this process are the division of human labour and the heavy use of machines and tools in the production process. The first presents great problems of organisation and management: (a) in processing and absorbing highly complex information; and (b) in co-ordinating and controlling a wide range of highly interdependent activities. The heavy dependence of modern production processes on fixed capital creates the need for large volumes of investment in education and in productive facilities – as both skilled labour and productive capital stock are in short supply in the early phases of industrialisation.

Not surprisingly, the state will tend to play a very important role in the early stages of economic development, irrespective of whether the means of production are owned privately or collectively. One reson for this is that it has the power to create – by fiat if necessary – the consensus for change without which the desired economic transformation cannot take place. Moreover, in many cases, only the state can mobilise scarce national resources and channel them into the sectors which will produce the fastest rate of grwoth. This will be achieved by 'internalising' within the state apparatus (that is, by bringing within government control) the power to direct the generation of savings and allocation of investment.[12] In some cases, a particular outcome will be ensured by public ownership of the means of production. In others, governments will use fiscal and monetary policies, and the whole legislative framework available to them, in order to obtain the distribution of income which produces a large volume of savings – most of which will then find their way into the infrastructure, education and basic industries.

The highly centralised, 'planned', form of national economic management can produce a high rate of investment and growth for some time. Technical change is one of the ways in which the volume of new investment, in which it is embodied, raises the productive potential of an economy. At the same time, the change generates a more complex division of labour which, in turn, requires organisational adaptations in order to increase productive efficiency to the levels required by the new technology. At this point, those responsible for national economic management face problems akin to those which directors of a firm experience when the size and complexity of its operations reach the level at which managerial diseconomies set in. The economy simply becomes too complex for a centralised body to co-ordinate its numerous operations, especially in times of rapid or unforeseen changes.[13]

The only way to avoid the rigidities and inefficiencies which centralisation produces at higher levels of development is to decentralise the decision-making process. The exact form that such decentralisation takes will be influenced greatly by the degree of social cohesion which exists in a country. In the end, it is this factor that will determine not only the future path of an economy but also the means by which the desired results are achieved, or whether they are achieved at all.

In the countries which have attained a high degree of social cohesion governments and the representatives of industry, finance and labour unions play a role not dissimilar to that of the board of directors in a large corporation. The institutional framework within which they operate is not designed to 'direct' or 'administer' the economy. Its main purpose is to promote sectoral co-ordination either by a combination of income and price policies (designed to minimise the uncertainty about future movements in costs and prices and, thus, promote investment by reducing the risk premia);[14] or by industrial policies (the aim of which is to assist new investment, as well as technical and organisational changes, in both new and declining industries).[15]

In other words, national economic management in such economies consists of bringing key economic sectors together in order to enable them to co-ordinate their actions in a way which promotes rapid adjustments to both internally generated changes and external shocks. As in the case of a multidivisional firm, the economy as a whole benefits from the direction provided by a widely accepted long-term strategy; and firms in key sectors gain from being able to acquire larger financial resource, and on more favourable terms, than they could obtain on the market in the absence of such a strategy. It is for this reason that, thanks to their ability to produce a flexible and broadly co-ordinated response, 'corporate economies' are much more successful in dealing with large external shocks than either their 'planned' (highly centralised) or 'market' (high decentralised) counterparts.

As 'market' economies lack the cohesion to develop a corporate form of organisation, their governments will try to use the combined weight of the sectors which they control directly to provide the kind of economic leadership which is analogous to that of the dominant firm in an oligopolistic industry. By altering its revenue, as well as its current and capital expenditure, a government will signal to the rest of the economy the 'required' short-term response to economic changes which are taking place either inside or outside the country. Moreover, the government also hopes to influence in this way the long-term development of the economy by stabilising the level of effective demand. The macro-economic management of a 'market' economy has, therefore, two purposes: to maintain high levels of output and employment in the short run; and to reduce uncertainty and, thus, make firms and industries more confident and optimistic about future economic prospects. Hence, if successful, stabilisation policies should increase the volume of private investment and, in this way, the long-term rate of economic growth.

Sectoral interdependence is recognised in this form of macro-economic management by the importance which is attached to price stability: the 'signals' are given in terms of quantities, not prices. This also increases the effectiveness of the 'multiplier' process. Changes in the aggregate propensity to consume, or save, will have much greater impact if prices are stable – so that the adjustment to changes in the volume of demand has to be made in quantitative terms (such as stocks, output, investment and employment).

This is, of course, the most important organisational aspect of the Keynesian attempt to improve the performance of market economies by using their government sector to provide a form of intersectoral co-ordination and, in this way, raise their investment and employment levels. A 'free-for-all' competitive approach can be dangerously counterproductive in an oligopolistic environment; and, as pointed out earlier, the structure of most modern economies is, basically, oligopolistic.

V

The main weakness of even the most successful Keynesian and 'corporate' approaches to national economic management is that their effectiveness diminishes progressively as a country becomes integrated into the world economy and its economic agents begin to receive signals from their own as well as from other governments, often of a conflicting nature.

Yet, under dynamic conditions, the opening up of an economy is inevitable in the long run. As its national division of labour reaches higher stages of specialisation, limitations imposed by the size of the domestic market will become a serious barrier to further progress. More and more tradeable sectors will, therefore, require free access to the much larger world market in order to utilise fully economies of scale. The impetus that trade liberalisation gives to international specialisation will expand each country's exports *and* imports relative to its total national output – making all of them increasingly dependent on developments in the rest of the world.

In this way, the division of labour will lead to a spread of oligopolistic economic relationships from industry to national and, ultimately, international levels. Consequently, the extent to which a country can achieve its main objectives will depend on its own as well as other countries' actions. In an interdependent world economy, the level and stability of effective demand, output, investment and employment become inevitably international, rather than purely national, problems. Nevertheless, most countries, especially those of medium and large size, are likely to refuse to accept the constraint which these changes place on their ability to pursue independently their national objectives and policies. After all, this is what they have always done. Their ideology and institutional framework have evolved, therefore, for the specific purpose of preserving and promoting their national interests, frequently at the expense of other countries.

As a result, international economic integration, especially when it is rapid, will tend to create conditions which resemble those that occur in an industry before the firms comprising it develop a code of behaviour that recognises their interdependence and uses it to mutual advantage. The structure of the industry at this stage is such that it consists of firms of different sizes. None of them is sufficiently large to dominate it. However, several firms have grown to such a size that each of them can have an appreciable effect on the market for the industry's products and thus on its competitors. The problem at this stage is that the firms have not yet learned to appreciate the real significance of their interdependence. Each continues, therefore, to pursue its own objectives independently, irrespective of the effect that they might have on its competitors, in the belief that it will be able to increase and sustain its share of the market even in the short run. The result is a period of cut-throat competition damaging to all.

'Beggar-my-neighbour' policies are the international equivalent of this type of competition. Underestimating the extent to which they are dependent on one another, each country tries to solve its economic problems at the expense of other countries. As the latter invariably retaliate, no one solves anything and everyone is worse off in the long term!

There are at least three reasons why, *ceteris paribus*, rapid international integration may lead to a beggar-my-neighbour type of competition and general economic stagnation. First, as levels of efficiency and incomes vary considerably from country to country, the nature and size of their problems and policies will also vary a good deal. It will be impossible, in the circumstances, to achieve a co-ordinated policy response spontaneously. Second, the task of achieving an international consensus on any important issue will be made even more difficult by the fact that as the number of participants in the international division of labour increases their understanding of other countries' economic positions and likely policy responses is likely to diminish. The larger a group the more difficult it is to reconcile the members' needs, objectives and actions. Third, structural changes which destabilise national economies are usually followed by government actions which define the rules and encourage modes of behaviour consistent with the new economic environment. More specifically, governments may allow, or even encourage, mergers and takeovers in one or more industries, making it easier for the remaining firms both to rationalise existing capacity and to create new one. It is also easier for a relatively small number of firms to foresee the consequences of their own actions as well as those of their competitors, something that should normally prevent costly outbursts of cut-throat competition. No one can perform such a role in relation to sovereign nation states.

Hence, if nation states wish to maintain and improve their economic welfare within an economically integrated framework, they have to organise their relationships in a way which enables them to achieve these objectives. They can do this only if (like firms within an oligopolistic industry) they accept that genuine political independence – the power to take actions irrespective of their effect on other countries and irrespective of developments in the rest of the world – diminishes progressively with every increase in international economic integration.

The way that countries react to limitations which international integration imposes on their sovereignty will determine the character and future progress of the world economy. There are, at least in theory, a number of arrangements that can be used to ensure that they co-ordinate their actions and, in this way, achieve mutually desirable goals. Virtually all of them closely resemble the forms of collective action employed by firms within a large, multi-product oligopolistic industry.

VI

To begin with, two or more countries with highly integrated economies can merge into a political union. The union provides their economic agents, already highly interdependent, with a uniform framework of institutions, rules, regulations and macro-economic policies. The uniformity reduces the uncertainty and risks normally associated with incompatible institutional arrangements and conflicting policies. The change enables economic agents to pursue their long-term objectives, instead of devoting all their energies and resources to ensuring short-term survival in an uncertain, crisis-ridden environment.

There are two serious obstacles to such a solution of international economic problems in the 1980s, one political, the other economic.

Sovereign nation states are reluctant to lose their national identity, invariably a matter of great national pride, born in a different age and nurtured ever since in the struggle for collective survival. In other words, the reluctance has a practical side: the safeguard and promotion of specific national needs and aspirations which may become impossible within a larger political union. The dream of a 'United States of Europe' is as far from realisation in the mid-1980s as it was in the 1950s when the European Economic Community, around which the 'States' were to evolve, was created. For similar reasons, not one of the attempts to create a 'United Arab Republic' has survived for very long.

However, even if changes in political organisation of this kind were possible, the nature and complexity of contemporary international economic relationships are such that it is very doubtful that political unions involving a few countries, whatever their other merits, would provide an optimum policy area. They would do little, for instance, to improve the existing, informal 'arrangements' between a large economy and its small 'dependencies'. In this case, the small countries are too dependent on the large country, despite their political independence, to have institutions and policies which are radically different from its own. The relationship which they have evolved corresponds, therefore, to that of the dominant country model analysed in Section VIII. Political unions involving countries with large economies are more likely to create an optimum policy area. However, for reasons to be analysed in Section IX, the resistance to such an arrangement is likely to be very strong, as their nationals will tend to regard the political and economic costs of such a union as being far greater than any foreseeable benefits.

VII

For a long time after the start of the Industrial Revolution, the most common method of achieving a political union was by military conquest (a violent equivalent of industrial 'takeover') rather than by peaceful negotiations. In this way, the country with sufficient military power could 'internalise' factors which were of strategic importance for its economy but happened to lie outside its frontiers. The purpose of such an action, as the mercantilists had been quick to recognise, was to minimise the uncertainty and costs of economic development by ensuring adequate supplies of foodstuffs and raw materials, and securing captive markets for the country's surplus products. Although economic factors were not the only reason for colonialism, it is considerations of this kind that provided the main driving force behind colonial expansion.[16]

However, as no nation has ever been big enough, or strong enough, to conquer the whole world and keep it permanently subjugated, a country adopting this strategy will, sooner or later, come into conflict with other countries determined to pursue the same course of action. Abundant supplies of raw materials and foodstuffs are available only in certain parts of the world; and there are relatively few potential colonies with a large capacity to absorb imports. National conflicts and wars become, therefore, an inevitable outcome of the 'colonialist' strategy for dealing with unpredictable externalities on a global scale.

The military resolution of international economic conflicts involves high human and material costs at all levels of development. With industrialisation, the costs become prohibitive. The growth of a country's technical and productive potential inevitably increases its capacity to invent and manufacture highly destructive weapons. The main purpose for making these weapons is to deter other countries from threatening a country's 'vital interests' – including attempts on their part to secure exclusive access to foreign raw materials, foodstuffs and markets. The immense human and material costs of the two world wars demonstrate better than any analytical argument the awesome power for mutual destruction available to highly industrialised nations.

Moreover, the process which makes the cost of military conflict among industrial countries prohibitive gives rise also to the need to look for alternative solutions to problems of general interest. As countries industrialise, their economic structures and institutions become increasingly similar.[17] The first is the product of a growing resemblance in their tastes and factor prices, and ensures that most of each industrial country's trade is with other industrial countries. Most of their investments abroad are also located in the industrialised part of the world. This, obviously, reduces the need for, as well as the feasibility of, the military option open to an industrial country for 'internalising' strategic economic factors located in other industrial countries. The growing institutional and behavioural similarity helps also to avoid the risk of accidental conflicts by ensuring that the reactions of different countries to a particular change in the economic environment, though far from uniform, become more predictable.

The irrelevance of the colonial model applies also to the relationship between industrial and developing countries. The rivalry among industrial nations – between and within the 'capitalist' and 'socialist' blocs – protects developing countries from conquest by an industrial power. At the same time, the international division of labour makes industrial countries increasingly dependent on raw materials and energy sources, many of which are produced by less developed countries, while the latter can industrialise only with the help of the industrial countries' technology, expertise and capital.

Consequently, as the energy crisis has shown, there is an increasing need for a co-ordination of economic activities not only between industrial nations but also between industrial and developing countries. The colonial model does not provide a realistic solution to this problem – even if one ignores the ethics of military conquest.

VIII

There is an alternative arrangement, however, under which a country can assume effective control and management of the world economy without resorting to military conquest. It achieves this position as a result of its size, resources and more rapid economic advance than the rest of the world. In the long term, these advantages combine to create a productive potential so large, relative to those of other nations, that the country dominates world output and trade for the simple reason that it accounts for a large share of each. Its financial sector plays a similar role in international finance. In other words, the country develops all those characteristics normally associated with a structural surplus, dominant economy of the kind described in Chapters 5 and 13.

Once a country achieves this position of pre-eminence in international economic affairs, its domestic and external policies are bound to have a major effect on output and employment in the rest of the world in both the short and the long terms. Other countries will, therefore, have to respond to these policies and, in doing so, they will (collectively) influence the dominant country's ability to achieve its own economic and other objectives. Hence, willy-nilly, to the extent that it tries to ensure the stability and growth of its own economy, the dominant country will find itself managing the world economy as well.

There is no evidence that in the nineteenth century the British Government and the Bank of England ever set out to manage the international system in order to promote world economic welfare. Their actions were prompted purely by the pursuit of national self-interest. Yet, as the British economy was both much more industrialised than the rest of the world and very open, these actions could not avoid having a major effect on the stability and growth of the world economy. Britain accounted for a large share of world output, and London was the most important international financial centre. At the same time, the country was dependent on imports of food and raw materials and the limited size of its domestic market forced British industry to rely heavily on exports. This introduced a high degree of complementarity and interdependence between the British economy and the rest of the world, making it possible for the country to 'manage', by accident rather than design, the world economy.

The US position after the Second World War was quite different. Unlike their British counterparts, the Federal Government and the Federal Reserve Board of Governors undertook the task of managing the international economy consciously. They were forced to act in the late 1940s by the apparent inability of the International Monetary Fund and the World Bank to assist European countries in their urgently needed post-war reconstruction[18] which, in turn, resulted in the growing threat of political upheaval in Western Europe. This was clearly against US long-term interests.[19] Subsequent US policies – fiscal, monetary and commercial, as well as Marshall Aid and other assistance to industrial and developing countries made, for almost quarter of the century, a major contribution to the unprecedented stability and growth of the world economy.

Although many experts have tended to look back with nostalgia to the periods of British and American domination, there are, in fact, serious long-term weaknesses in an international economic order which depends largely on the correct perception of self-interest and benevolence of one country. Unlike a dominant firm in an industry, a dominant country cannot prevent other sovereign states from developing their economies. Indeed, many of those actions which enhance its own long-term economic welfare and political influence, such as exports of capital and technical knowledge, also assist economic development in other countries. These changes in the relative performance and position of countries may result in the long term either in the emergence of a new dominant economy which has neither the institutions nor the global perception of self-interest to manage the international economy, or in a world in which no economy is capable of performing such a task.

The first problem appeared after the First World War when the UK became incapable of managing the international system and the US was unprepared and unwilling to do so. The adverse effect that this period of 'transition' in international economic relationships had on the world economy was described in Chapter 9. The important lesson to emerge from the interwar experience, so far as the organisation of international economic activity is concerned, is that the presence of a dominant economy does not necessarily guarantee the existence of an international order which promotes global economic welfare. On the contrary, the world economy is likely to go through a period of great instability and crises until the new dominant power becomes able and willing to 'manage' the system.

The absence of a dominant economy, and the unlikelihood of any one country ever again being in a position to assume such a role, is a development which has become apparent since the late 1960s. The decline of US economic influence, brought about by rapid economic progress in other countries, signifies therefore the end of a particular and long-lasting phase in world economic history, the phase during which an international economic order could be imposed by a dominant power. Given the current configuration of international economic and political relationships, it is inconceivable that another country could 'manage' world economy in the 1980s in the way that it was managed for a time accidentally by Britain and deliberately by the United States.

IX

As international economic integration has reached a very high level in the 1980s, and no single country appears to be in a position to 'manage' the system, some form of supranational organisation seems to be the only way to ensure the required co-ordination of global economic activity without which the maladjustments accumulated since the early 1970s cannot be solved. The problem is that a 'supranational' framework of economic institutions cannot function effectively unless it is backed up by a similar form of organisation at the political level – in other words, a world government. Such a government is needed to decide on global priorities and then let the various institutions initiate and oversee their translation into practice. Using modern means of transport and communications, the whole edifice could be constructed in such a way as to replicate at the international level the institutional framework developed in various forms in advanced economies.

In theory, all this is both rational and feasible. What is more, modern technology has probably reached a level at which such a framework of global institutions could operate successfully. The problem, as usual, is that, whatever the level at which they evolve, institutions can function effectively only if they reflect accurately existing power relationships. At the international level, this means that a supranational form of organisation can be developed only if nation states, especially large ones, become convinced that loss of national independence and sovereignty will increase their economic welfare, influence and power. Moreover, as absolute improvements in these respects are unlikely to be regarded as advantageous if they are spread unequally, each nation will also have to be convinced that it will not enjoy any of these gains to a lesser extent than other nations. These two conditions are extremely important under a system operated by supranational institutions because, having given up its sovereignty, no nation has the means with which to reverse a deterioration in its position, either absolute or relative.

As no form of global economic and political authority could possibly guarantee either of these conditions, it is unrealistic to expect nation states to surrender their sovereignty to a supranational world authority. It is not simply a matter of historic traditions and cultural differences. What is at stake is nothing less than their ability to influence events in a way which is in the interest of powerful political groups within each country.

Citizens of a small country, tied economically to a large neighbour, may not lose much, apart from their national pride, in a process of transferring sovereignty to a supranational authority. Those of a large country are in a quite different position. They know from experience that the size of the country and the resources at their disposal give them an important advantage in international negotiations and bargaining. The demise of the nation state would deprive them, therefore, of an important advantage. Hence, even if small countries were willing to surrender their sovereignty to a 'world government', large countries would be most unlikely to do so in the foreseeable future; and their refusal to participate in supranational organisations would deprive the latter of any ability to deal effectively with global economic problems.

It was because of its inability to overcome these fundamental problems that the much more modest attempt made at Bretton Woods in 1944 failed to create a system of stable and sustainable international economic relationships. Two of the three organisations originally planned, the International Monetary Fund and the International Bank for Reconstruction and Development (the 'World Bank'), were established at Bretton Woods, but they were given totally inadequate resources to assist member countries with their stabilisation and adjustment problems.[20] Not surprisingly, the two have proved time and again to be in no position to provide more than marginal assistance in situations in which a large number of countries find it increasingly difficult to reconcile their internal (high levels of employment and low rates of inflation) and external (balance of payments) balances: in the post-war reconstruction period, in assisting developing countries and in dealing with the effects of the two oil shocks.[21] The third institution planned at Bretton Woods, the International Trade Organisation (with the task of promoting international economic integration through trade and of stabilising world commodity prices) never materialised. It was superseded by GATT, a much more modest organisation.

Hence, although a good deal has been written about the 'Bretton Woods System', or even the 'IMF System',[22] the simple fact is that the system created at Bretton Woods has never operated in the form intended by its founders. The important organisational point, normally overlooked, is that although major world powers were to play an important role in the institutions created at Bretton Woods *none* of them was intended to manage the system on its own. The main purpose of creating the supranational organisations was to avoid the risks associated with world dependence on changes in the attitude and policies of a single country. The intention behind the institutional framework created at Bretton Woods was, therefore, that major policy decisions were to be taken collectively, in a way not dissimilar to that employed in a 'corporate economy'.

The problem was that there was one country, the United States, which had both the resources and institutions to help other nations with the stabilisation and development of their economies; and, as any other country would have done in similar circumstances, it was not prepared to let some supranational organisation disburse the resources on its behalf. Instead, when it did decide in 1947 to play an active role in international economic affairs it did so unilaterally and in its own national interest.

However, in doing this, the United states embraced the two guiding principles of the Bretton Woods System which, after all, it had helped formulate: the spirit of international co-operation and the desire for some form of centralised co-ordination of international economic activity. Both were examplified, among other things, in a rigid adherence to fixed exchange rates. But in realising these 'Bretton Woods objectives', the United States bypassed international organisations and became directly involved in the international stabilisation and adjustment process.

As a result, the post-war international economic system was managed not 'supranationally' as intended at Bretton Woods, but by one country, according to the principles of the dominant economy model described earlier. In other words, the system was managed, in effect, by the US Treasury, the US Federal Reserve and the US Department of Commerce according to the rules laid down by the US Government. It would be more appropriate, therefore, to call the international system which operated so successfully from the late 1940s until the beginning of the 1970s the 'Washington System'.

X

In conclusion, like firms and industries, countries operating in an internationally integrated environment have to evolve a system of organising their activities according to some generally recognised and acceptable set of principles and rules. In other words, they have to establish a code of behaviour appropriate to their level of interdependence if they are to achieve and sustain a desirable level of economic welfare.

There are a number of ways both formal and informal in which nations can organise their relationships in order to reduce the risks and uncertainties inevitably present in a dynamic economic environment. With one exception (see the next chapter), all the major possibilities were considered in the second part of this chapter and found wanting. In fact, not one of them appears to provide a realistic, viable model of organising international economic activity in the 1980s.

The political union of a few countries is neither feasible nor adequate to provide an optimum policy area. The colonial solution, even if it were morally acceptable, would lead to military conflicts which could engulf the whole world. Its peaceful alternative, the dominant country model, is unworkable for the simple reason that no country is in a position to undertake such a role. Finally, as nation states are not prepared to give up sovereignty, a supranational solution to international economic problems – managed by what Immanuel Kant called a universal, cosmopolitan state[23] – is even more utopian.

There seems to be no answer to the central question in contemporary international economic relationships: how to reconcile the fact that while economic problems are becoming increasingly international the only form of organisation available for dealing with them remains national? The next chapter analyses some of the key conditions that have to be satisfied, and the ways in which this might be done, if current economic problems are to be solved within an organisational framework in which the nation state continues to be the only viable decision-making unit.

15 Policies Compatible with an Integrated World Economy

I

The analysis in the previous chapter leads to two important conclusions. First, continuous economic progress requires constant adaptation and change in economic organisation as well as in the rules and conventions which guide economic behaviour. This applies to all phases of economic development and to each level of economic activity. Second, with greater international integration and interdependence, the character of the world economic environment has become distinctly oligopolistic in the last quarter of the twentieth century. International economic developments are dominated by the objectives and policies of a relatively small number of large industrial nations and, to a lesser extent, a few oil producers. However, while each of them can have a perceptible influence on the growth and stability of other economies, none is large enough to impose a particular economic order on the rest of the world and manage the international economy accordingly. Equally, no sovereign state is willing to hand over to a supranational authority the right to determine its economic objectives and policies.

The only to achieve a stable system of international relationships under these conditions is for individual countries, especially those with large and advanced economies, either to agree formally on a mutually satisfactory code of behaviour or to accept one tacitly. In other words, stability of the international economic system depends now critically on the ability and willingness of individual countries to pursue policies which are compatible with their national economic objectives *and* with the objectives and policies of other countries.

This involves the acceptance of certain obligations and rules of behaviour. The problem is that, even if accepted formally, neither will be effective unless countries with highly integrated economies treat their *de facto* interdependence as an irreversible development which severely reduces the ability of all of them to act independently.

As explained in Chapter 1, a country may control the rate at which it increases its economic ties with other nations. However, once it begins to specialise and participate actively in international exchange, it can retreat into economic insularity only at the cost of lower long-term productivity and income levels. Whatever their short-term merits, in the long run autarkic policies are irreconcilable with a continuously developing economy. Consequently, if they fail to accept this fact and to evolve a stable interantional economic order, countries with dynamic economies will be confronted again and again with the problem of forging a code of behaviour appropriate to a high level of international economic interdependence. It happened in the nineteenth century, in the interwar period and, again, in the 1970s and 1980s.

The main reason for the repeated failure to develop a lasting international economic order has always been the same. In refusing to recognise the long-term costs of international economic disintegration, sovereign nation states have failed time and again to ensure collectively that no country participating in the international division of labour feels that it would improve its economic welfare by retreating into autarky.

This has nothing to do with altruism. Even in an oligopolistic system, a successful firm can take over a weak competitor. It can also increase its share of the market by driving such competitors out of business. In contrast, for reasons described in the previous chapter, a country with a successful economy cannot annex countries with much less advanced economies; and if it is unable to do this, it cannot 'drive them out of business' and take over their markets either. Unlike firms, countries with serious economic problems do not 'fold'. They adopt protective policies; and, if either a large country or a large number of small countries is forced to resort to such policies, the result will be international economic disintegration. As pointed out in Chapter 10, the consequence of such disintegration will be particularly adverse in advanced economies because of their highly developed and complex level of specialisation.

II

Suppose now that, although none of them is prepared to give up its sovereignty, nation states accept that the costs associated with international economic disintegration make their interdependence irreversible. What exactly should they do collectively to establish a successful and lasting global economic order under these conditions?

The answer is relatively simple (though far from easy to put into practice!): they should observe in dealing with each other some of the basic rules and regulations which they have evolved within their own borders to promote economic progress and political unity. The experience of industrial countries, especially those with federal constitutions, is particularly relevant in this respect.

The reason for this is not simply that the world economy represents an aggregate of national economies, with industrialised nations responsible for by far the largest proportion of that aggregate. Much more important in the present context is the fact that all industrial countries experience within their borders problems which are not dissimilar to those observed at the international level. Yet economic disintegration and political upheavals happen extremely rarely in these countries.

Modern nation states normally contain within their borders a number of different regions with different levels of productivity and income. Moreover, uneven regional growth will give rise in time to structural problems for exactly the same reasons as those observed internationally: permanent shifts in demand patterns which favour some regions at the expense of others; technical changes in products and production methods which give a significant competitive advantage to certain regions; and the discovery of new, or the exhaustion of old sources of raw materials. Furthermore, inter-regional differences may increase over time as a result of cumulative progress in some regions and stagnation in others, a process usually exacerbated by factor movements.[1]

The danger which arises out of the tendency towards unequal development is that, if left unchecked, it threatens the very *raison d'être* of a modern nation state. The state, after all, is no more than a special type of organisation developed, often as a result of violent struggle, for the purpose of maintaining the security of its borders and unity within them. Behaviour within the organisation is guided by rules and laws, and enforced, if necessary, by the full power of the state. Experience shows, however, that rules and laws are effective only so long as they are widely accepted. Coercion never produces a lasting solution. The stability of a national economic order is determined, therefore, by the extent to which the majority of citizens are convinced that it is organised in a way which is more likely to promote their long-term interests than any available alternative.

Over the last hundred years, all industrial countries have gone through a number of structural changes and readjustments in their economies. They have also, without exception, evolved institutions, rules and conventions which reflect, to some extent at least, the changing power relationships within their economies and societies.

The main purpose of all these changes has been to safeguard and promote national economic integration and political unity.

The critical question, to be considered in the remainder of this chapter, is whether some of the key approaches to economic management adopted by governments at the national level can be reproduced internationally while, at the same time, leaving the basic policy-making unit, the nation state, intact.

III

The first precondition for achieving a stable economic order is that there should be one set of clearly defined, widely supported and consistent objectives – and a set of policies compatible with them. At the national level, these are formulated and pursued by central government.

For example, from the end of the Second World War until the 1970s, all industrial countries set their macro-economic policies in terms of the three most important aspects of fundamental equilibrium (see Chapters 3 and 5): full employment (which, given the growth of their productive potential, determined the required rates of growth, both short and long term); a socially acceptable rate of inflation; and a balance on their extenral transactions. In addition, all of them also aimed at a more equitable distribution of income and wealth.

Three of the four objectives reflected the strong aspirations of individuals and groups within the countries and were, therefore, judged to be essential not only for increasing economic welfare but also for enabling those countries to achieve a high degree of social cohesion and political stability. The remaining objective – the balance of payments – was a recognition of the constraints imposed on a country's ability to achieve internal balance by its limited resources, as well as by the policies and objectives of other countries.

Furthermore, the pursuit of these objectives also performed an important role in the management of complex national economic systems, with highly decentralised decision-making processes. First, it facilitated the co-ordination of countless economic activities by providing a yardstick for judging the likely timing and character of short-term stabilisation policies. Second, the resolve to use the vast national resources which modern governments can mobilise for the purpose of achieving their objectives reduced uncertainty and increased confidence about future economic developments and prospects. The result was exceptionally rapid economic growth both in industrial countries and in the rest of the world. Third, the more successful were the countries in achieving their objectives the easier it became to transfer resources from the individuals and regions that were clearly gaining from rapid economic change to those that were affected adversely by the process. This enabled the latter to adjust and, consequently, continue to participate in the national division of labour.

Implicit in the last point is something that has been of critical importance for the establishment and survival of a stable economic order. Central governments may produce one set of uniform policy objectives which apply to the country as a whole. But this is never also true of their policies. On the contrary, differences in family and regional incomes, and the capacity for development, are taken into account in highly selective policies – designed specifically to discriminate between individuals, sectors and regions.

The important question now is whether something similar can be achieved at the international level in conditions in which there is neither a world government nor a dominant economy. The answer depends obviously on the extent to which national governments are willing and able to act collectively in such a way that the sum total of their actions is exactly the same as if there were a single, effective world economic authority. More specifically, a stable international economic order can be created and maintained only if individual countries set identical policy objectives but, at the same time, arrange their economic relationships in such a way that they can pursue policies which differ in important respects, discriminating in favour of the countries and regions with lower efficiency and income levels.

These two requirements are as inseparable at the international level as they are in the pursuit of national policy objectives, and for exactly the same reason. Contrary to the belief of many economists, countries do not have different 'national preferences' in the sense that, according to the conventional wisdom, some prefer 'high inflation' while others are prepared to tolerate 'higher unemployment'. As a result of global cultural integration, there is little doubt that there is a strong pressure now in virtually all parts of the world for continuous improvements in economic welfare. Most countries are also hoping to reach eventually the sort of affluence enjoyed by nations with the highest efficiency and income levels. No country with an open economy can achieve and/or sustain such a level of economic development without attaining fundamental equilibrium; in other words, without being able to reconcile in the long term the objectives listed at the beginning of this section. A country which can accomplish only one policy objective at a time is demonstrating far less its 'preference' than the fact that it is in fundamental disequilibrium.

Thus, it would be relatively easy for all countries with highly interdependent economies to agree on the same macro-economic policy objectives. This would produce one set of common, global policy targets with exactly the same effect as if there were a single world government. The problem is that the commitment would mean little in practice if it required the countries also to pursue identical policies – unless they all happened to enjoy full employment, exactly the same efficiency and income levels *and*, in addition, were able to achieve further improvements in economic welfare at exactly the same rates! As neither of the last two conditions is ever likely to be satisfied in a dynamic world economy, a sustainable international economic order has to allow for the differences by enabling countries to pursue policies which are different but compatible.

IV

One area in which international openness and integration leave very little scope for differences of this kind is that of monetary policy. Other things remaining equal, actual or anticipated changes in a government's monetary stance will invariably trigger off short-term capital movements either into or out of the country's currency, depending on the nature of the new policy stance relative to those adopted elsewhere. Consequently, unless other governments also change their monetary policies in the same direction, international capital will sooner or later confront the government with a difficult choice. If it wants to keep its exchange rate stable, in order to avoid the destabilising effects of exchange rate variations, it will have to revert quickly to the original policy. If, on the other hand, it is determined to pursue an independent monetary policy, it will have to let its exchange rate appreciate/depreciate, irrespective of the adverse effects that this is likely to have either on its trade and employment (appreciation) or inflation (depreciation).

If a significant number of countries behave in this way, there will inevitably be an increase in the uncertainty and risks in all those activities associated with international specialisation and exchange. No one will be sure now about future levels of exchange rates; and, if economic agents lack confidence in the existing means for settling international debts, they are bound to reduce the volume of international transactions. To the extent that they do this, they will slow down, or even reverse, the growth of world output, employment, productivity and income. Increases in the production of goods and services will improve the standard of living only if they can be exchanged efficiently; and this cannot be accomplished in a complex modern economy if there is a widespread lack of confidence in 'money', the asset used in settling debts. Independent monetary policy and currency instability are, therefore, inimical to the functioning and further progress of an integrated economic system.

The problems which they pose are solved in every sovereign state by the existence of a single currency and a single monetary authority. The task of the latter is to issue the currency and control credit conditions in order to promote price stability and thus, *ceteris paribus*, confidence in the currency. The fact that there is only one type of money which is legally accepted for settling debts within the country increases its utility both as a medium of exchange (by eliminating costs associated with currency conversion) and as the store of value (by making it acceptable in exchange for all goods and services within the country). In addition, the absence of regional currencies eliminates completely the danger of destabilising interregional capital flows promoted by either speculative or precautionary considerations. Nor is there any reason for regions to accumulate 'exchange reserves' in order to facilitate specialisation and exchange within the country. Monetary arrangements within the economy, therefore, satisfy the needs created by its current level of development, and, at the same time, also make easier further increases in the division of labour.

The lesson from this for the international economy is obvious enough: the more closely integrated and interdependent national economies become the greater is the need for them to create a similar monetary framework globally.

The simplest way of doing this, employed successfully in the past, is to peg national currencies to each other. To the extent that the parities are fixed and generally regarded as unalterable, the effect is exactly the same as if there is a single world currency. A system of fixed rates has, therefore, the attraction of reconciling the illusion of national monetary independence with the need for a stable, generally acceptable means for settling international debts.

However, for a regime of fixed parities to perform effectively –within the highly integrated international financial system of the

1980s – the functions normally associated with monetary union, it is necessary to do more than simply 'fix' the rates of exchange. Currencies have, in fact, to be perfectly convertible. This is possible only if there is complete confidence that international debts will be settled now and in the future ('spot' and 'forward') at exactly the same rates of exchange. Any deviation from this condition, any expectation or even suspicion that it will not be met in future, will inevitably lead to large, highly destabilising capital flows, making it extremely difficult and costly to sustain the system.

The extent to which currencies can be fixed in such a way that they are almost perfectly convertible, without causing losses in economic welfare in the countries concerned, will depend on a number of factors. For example, exchange rates can be fixed and sustained within very narrow margins if external disequilibria are small and of a purely temporary nature. In other words, rigidly fixed parities will be possible to implement when all countries are in fundamental equilibrium and observe strictly the short-term stabilisation rules described in Chapter 4. If, for whatever reason, they are unable and/or unwilling to observe the rules or, more likely, if some of them are in fundamental disequilibrium, their current account deficits will have to be covered by adequate inflows of long-term capital. Alternatively, the structural deficit countries will have to resort to extensive import controls. Nor is this all. Even the short-term disequilibria of the kind described in Chapter 4 can give rise to highly destabilising international capital flows. The flows can be avoided, or kept to a minimum, only if national financial systems are either rudimentary or highly insulated by means of rigorously enforced exchange controls. The alternative is to have adequate swap arrangements among central banks, promptly activated whenever needed to counteract private flows. Finally, a poorly developed system of international transport and communications will also act as an effective barrier to capital flows, by making it very risky to move funds from one currency into another.

This rather long list leads to an important conclusion: the chances of establishing a lasting regime of fixed exchange rates will tend to diminish progressively with every increase in international integration and interdependence. In other words, the regime is likely to become progressively less viable as the need for it grows!

That, of course, is precisely the problem with which the international community has been confronted in the last quarter of the twentieth century. Enough evidence was presented in the earlier chapters to show that not one of the conditions listed above is satisfied in the 1980s. Serious structural problems are in growing evidence even in industrial countries. Those in the rest of the world are, potentially, huge. International money and capital markets have proliferated and become highly sophisticated – culminating in the development and extremely rapid growth of the euromarkets. The scope for international transfers of capital is enormous, and the spread of transnational enterprises makes it virtually impossible to control them.

As a result of all these changes, even industrial countries have found it impossible to participate in a system of fixed exchange rates. The last serious attempt which they made in this respect at the end of 1971, as part of the Smithsonian Agreement, survived for just a little over a year.[2] (Some countries, like the UK, were forced by large-scale outflows to let their currencies float within months of signing the Agreement.) The integration of international financial markets has increased greatly since then, and so also have the prevalence and size of fundamental disequilibria experienced by many countries.

For all these reasons, a system of fixed exchange rates could be sustained realistically in the 1980s only if governments imposed draconian restrictions on international capital flows and other transactions involving foreign exchange. That, however, would be completely at odds with the main reason for setting up such a system in the first place: to promote world economic development within an internationally integrated framework.

This leaves the creation of a monetary union – with a single, common currency – as the only feasible solution to international financial instability reflected in the widely floating exchange rates since the early 1970s.

The main objection to the idea of a common international currency is that it would require a world central bank to issue the currency and conduct the monetary policy, two important aspects of national sovereignty that no country is prepared to abandon. This is a formidable obstacle. It has been responsible for the failure of all proposals which have tried to establish a highly centralised, unitary, global monetary system such as that developed nationally first in Europe and, subsequently, in many other countries of the world.[3]

In fact, this particular problem could be overcome by creating an international equivalent of a decentralised central banking structure such as the Federal Reserve System of the United States. The main attraction of such a system is that it is designed specifically to provide the benefits of central banking facilities and co-ordination in a large and highly decentralised banking system. Under this arrangement, central banks within each country would continue to look after its business and credit conditions and ensure that the overall system is responsive to them – in the same way that each of the twelve Federal Reserve Banks within the US system is responsible for its own region.[4]

At the same time, national central banks would become, to a much greater extent than they are today, national as well as international institutions. Each of them would now represent the interests and views of its own country as well as participate in determining an international credit policy. In this way, countries would exchange the right to issue separate national currencies, which is of little practical significance in an internationally integrated system, for the right to issue the international currency and control its supply – something which is of greater practical significance in such a system. But to perform this function effectively and to mutual benefit, countries would have first of all to achieve collectively that unity of purpose and action made possible within each of them by the existence of a single political authority, the national government. They would be able to do this only if their governments accepted (as no outside power can force them to do so) the preconditions for the creation of a stable international economic order described in the first three sections of this chapter.

This kind of consensus is also essential if members of an international monetary union are to agree on a common international currency, normally a controversial and difficult decision. Basically, there are two possibilities here: to internationalise one of the existing national currencies or to create a completely new unit of account. Whichever option is selected, its general acceptance would depend on the ability of governments to overcome certain emotional and practical obstacles.

The attachment which most people feel towards their national currency is partly a matter of familiarity and partly a reflection of the fact that every currency represents an important, visible sign of a distinct national identity. Each is issued by a separate national authority, each looks different and, in most cases, each also has a different name which enables everyone to associate it immediately with its country of origin.

The practical problem concerns the choice of an international unit of account. It is likely to be particularly difficult if a number of economies involved in the formation of a monetary union happen to be of roughly equal size. There will be no natural candidate in this case for 'internationalisation', as none of the national currencies will be used significantly more in international transactions than the others.

Considerations of national prestige and the reluctance to let any of the rivals reap the benefits normally associated with seigniorage[5] will tend to produce a stalemate. The alternative, a completely new currency, lacks the appeal of familiarity and, consequently, the liquidity enjoyed even by the existing national units of account. Not surprisingly, it has never commanded much support.

As it happens, the world has in the 1980s not only a ready-made institutional model that could be adapted globally (the US Federal Reserve System) but also a currency which has been used for decades as an international reserve asset: the US dollar. A great variety of financial assets are denominated in it. It is also the currency in which most of the world's primary commodities are priced. Its pre-eminence has evolved naturally from the fact that it is the 'money' of the world's largest national economy. For all these reasons, the US dollar has been widely used since the 1940s as an international medium of exchange, unit of account and store of value in a way that none of the artifically created, purely accounting 'reserve assets', such as the Special Drawing Rights and the European Currency Unit, could be.

However, if the 'US dollar' were to be transformed into the 'international dollar', it would be essential to transform also the US Federal Reserve System into an International Federal Reserve System. Central banks of the countries which joined the Monetary Union would then form, with the US Federal Reserve Banks, the pillars of the System – with an International Board of Governors and an International Open Market Committee at the top. The formation of a global monetary authority of this kind would be imperative in order to ensure that the United States could not claim something that would be unacceptable to other countries: the benefits (seigniorage) that normally accrue to those in sole control of a currency which is used universally.

It would also remove one of the major objections to such a monetary union: that it would result in a revival of US economic and political hegemony over the rest of the world. Under the arrangement suggested here the US would lose as much sovereignty over its currency as other countries – even though the dollar would replace other national monetary units. Its monetary authorities would now have to share the responsibility for controlling the supply of international dollars with other members of the system. Moreover, although the US Federal Reserve System would provide the foundations for creating an international central banking organisation of the same type, the monetary policy and other functions associated with central banking would be performed jointly by its Federal Reserve Banks and other countries' central banks. (To make the system manageable, central banks of countries below a certain size could be grouped on a regional basis, creating Reserve Banks which would represent individual groups rather than countries.) Given that there are significant disparities in regional levels of economic development and structure within the United States, it is far from certain that the twelve US Federal Reserve Banks would act as a monolithic 'US bloc'. It is much more likely, in fact, that in the formulation of overall monetary policy they would side with other members' central banks according to the similarity of their interests.

The objection that if the Board of Governors of the International Federal Reserve Bank is located in Washington, or in the capital of any other major industrial country, it will be influenced by the government of that country could be met by situating it in a neutral, small state such as Switzerland. It should not be too difficult, in fact, to transform the Bank for International Settlements in Basle into the International Federal Reserve Board. The Bank is already widely regarded as the nearest equivalent to a Central Bankers' Bank, with regular monthly meetings at which the governors and other senior officials of major industrial countries' central banks discuss world economic and monetary developments. The committee for supervising international banks is also located there.

Hence, technically, there is no great problem in taking the world's economic and financial integration to its logical end – a common currency and a common central bank – while maintaining national control over international monetary policy.

The relative ease with which a monetary union of the kind described above could be achieved does nothing, however, to remove the most serious objection to it, expressed by numerous economists: that it would exacerbate the existing inequalities in productivity and income levels.

The argument is simple enough. A complete monetary union eliminates balance of payments problems. But it does nothing to remove the existing, or prevent future, disparities in regional productivity and income levels. On the contrary, it will increase these disparities by depriving the countries with lower productivity and income levels of the ability to alter their exchange rates and in this way improve their competitive position. To make things worse, the monetary policy pursued by the union is likely to ignore their problems. It will be designed specifically to serve either the majority or the 'average' interests.

This traditional objection to a complete monetary union has two important weaknesses: it assumes that countries with highly integrated economic and financial systems can pursue independent monetary policies, and that changes in exchange rates are sufficient to solve the problems associated with fundamental disequilibria. The analysis and evidence in the preceding chapters show clearly that neither of these assumptions is valid.

At the same time, the objection draws attention to an extremely important issue, discussed at length in Parts II and III. A highly integrated economic system cannot survive in the absence of policies, pursued jointly by all members, which facilitate fundamental adjustments within the system. Creation of a monetary union with a common currency represents one of the ultimate steps in establishing complete economic integration. It removes an important obstacle to international specialisation.

But in order to ensure that this specialisation takes place and leads to widely diffused improvements in global economic welfare, it has to be accompanied by additional policies. Their main characteristic ought to be flexibility, making it possible to use them to discriminate between individuals, sectors and regions – something that monetary policy cannot do.[6] Its main function is to ensure that credit conditions within a country, or a monetary union, are conducive to non-inflationary economic growth; and in an economy in which there were automatic tendencies towards speedy adjustments and income equalisation this would be sufficient. This is, of course, precisely what modern economies lack, as a result of large inequalities in the concentration of economic power within them and thus in their ability to adjust. Hence, additional policy instruments have to be employed to compensate for the growing lack of flexibility.

V

Capital and labour markets are the key areas within a monetary union to which selective policies may have to be applied if the two factors of production are to promote rather than obstruct the long-term adjustment process. As emphasied in Part II, international factor movements – mainly those of capital – play a critical role in this process. But there is no guarantee that a high degree of international factor mobility will do anything to reduce the existing disparities in employment, productivity and income levels. On the contrary, it may make them even wider.

It has already been pointed out that one of the attractions of a monetary union is that it removes the need to worry about the balance of international payments. This, however, does not solve the problem of internal imbalances.

It is generally assumed in international economics that the problem can be solved 'automatically', without any 'interference' from government, if the factors of production are allowed to move freely between countries in search of higher incomes. In other words, international adjustments will be achieved and the disparities in factor incomes will be kept low if labour is allowed to migrate from the countries where unemployment is high (and wages low) to those where it is low (and wages high), and if international investment is allowed to move in the opposite direction in search of higher profits. This is why some economists regard a high degree of international factor mobility as the most important precondition for setting up a monetary union.[7] In its absence, so the argument runs, the union will collapse because it will be incompatible with the maintenance of full employment.[8]

The main flaw in this argument is not that it overestimates the importance of factor mobility but, rather, that it ignores the possibility that the mobility may not produce the expected result.

For instance, the situation of countries with rising unemployment will not improve if emigration of their labour force is accompanied by capital outflows. Yet the prevalence of economies of scale in modern production processes is virtually certain to ensure such an outcome. These economies can be exploited only if markets are large which, *ceteris paribus*, gives an advantage to high income countries. As explained in Parts I and II, it is for this reason that, in the absence of exchange controls, international investment will tend to move from low income/high unemployment countries to those where unemployment is low and incomes high. In conditions of increasing returns to scale, higher wages do not necessarily mean higher unit costs and lower profits. The latter are much more likely to prevail in low-wage economies.

Labour mobility need not produce long-term equilibrium either. If differences in employment and income levels between countries are sufficiently large for the benefits of migration to exceed by a clear margin the costs, the flood of immigrants may be on such a scale as to impose serious economic and social costs on the high income countries. If the emigrants contain a high proportion of highly skilled labour, their departure will exacerbate the adjustment difficulties of the low income countries also.

All modern governments are familiar with these problems because they exist within their borders, as a result of interregional differences in employment, productivity and income levels. They also know from experience that a high degree of interregional factor mobility will not reduce these disparities unless prompted by regional policies especially designed for this purpose.

The extent and character of these policies has tended to vary from country to country, depending on their economic and political system, and on the size and urgency of the interregional adjustment problems. In countries where economic activity is rigidly controlled and planned from the centre, the government has also controlled interregional movements and the allocation of both investment and labour. In contrast, market economies have usually tried to influence labour mobility by means of financial incentives and disincentives; and the location of investment by a combination of incentives and direct controls which reduce the choice of locations in which to expand, or reallocate, productive capacity. There is little doubt that these measures are at least partly responsible for the fact that regional income inequalities never reach the size of those observed internationally.[9] Finally, in times of a major war, when large-scale restructuring of the economy has to be achieved over a short period and when the need for national harmony of interests is particularly great, even market economies resort to widespread controls and central direction of resource allocation.[10]

Controls of this kind are obviously inconceivable internationally. The process of economic decision making is even more diffused at this level than in market economies. Moreover, no government would be able to control capital flows within a complete monetary union. The only way to influence at least some of the flows under these conditions is to use a combination of incentives and disincentives to encourage investment in those parts of the union where unemployment is rising and to discourage it in the areas of rapid growth and labour scarcity. This is, of course, what national governments have been doing as part of their regional policies. The difficulty at the international level is that the same effect would have to be achieved by a number of national governments co-ordinating their investment policies very closely. Judging by national experience, the feasibility and success of such co-operation would depend chiefly on the ability of governments in the more successful countries to persuade their compatriots that this is in their long-term interest, something that is likely to be particularly difficult in times of slow growth and rising unemployment.

Nevertheless, co-operation of this kind would be essential. Unlike capital controls, those on labour immigration could, and no doubt would, continue indefinitely even within a monetary union, for reasons mentioned earlier. Moreover, even in those cases where controls of this kind did not apply (as at present within the European Economic Community), linguistic, cultural and social factors would combine to reduce international labour mobility. This means that, as within countries, if labour would not be moved from declining to prosperous regions, ways would have to be found to move capital in the opposite direction. In the absence of these movements, the union's survival would be threatened in the long term by an accumulation of economic, social and political difficulties in countries with an above-average proportion of declining regions.

Investment guarantees by governments and government backed institutions, plus various incentives and disincentives might be of some assistance in this respect. However, it is unlikely that they would be effective in stimulating private investment in declining regions on the required scale if differences in economic performance and prospects between these and the more prosperous areas were large and growing. Direct intergovernmental transfers of resources would be needed in these circumstances; and to achieve such transfers, there would have to be a high degree of fiscal co-operation between governments.

Hence, it is this co-operation, more than anything else, that is likely to determine the feasibility and the long-term survival of an international monetary union. As it is the high degree of international economic and financial interdependence that makes the creation of such a union necessary, this is tantamount to saying that international fiscal co-operation is the key factor in determining the feasibility and the long-term survival of a highly integrated international economy. The larger the differences in employment, productivity and income levels between the countries linked in this way the more this is likely to be the case.

VI

Not surprisingly, the critical importance of inter-state fiscal co-operation and resource transfers is something of which countries with federal constitutions tend to be particularly aware. Their experience shows that the development of an effective method for spreading widely the economic benefits of integration is a major factor in 'the formation and holding together of the unions'.[11]

The most important function performed by fiscal policy nationally is to prevent the accumulation of economic and social problems to an extent which threatens the very existence of a nation state. It is no coincidence that separatist movements tend to flourish in regions with income per head well below those prevailing in the rest of the country. The longer this difference continues the more likely are an increasing number of people to become convinced that the existing system of the national economic and political integration is against their interest. Quebec in Canada, Northern Ireland and Scotland in the United Kingdom, the Walloon regions of Belgium, the Basque region in Spain – all with strong separatist movements – share one important characterstics: they represent the least prosperous areas within their country. Finally, if interregional inequalities are allowed to become wide, attempts to reduce them may produce strong separatist movements in richer regions also, in protest against a growing fiscal burden which the existing economic and political union places on them.

As international differences in employment and income levels are far greater than those which exist within countries, the problem of maintaining the cohesiveness of an internationally integrated system is bound to be much more serious than anything experienced nationally.

This inevitably makes fiscal co-operation the most difficult area of economic policy in which to reconcile the demands made by international economic integration with those of national political sovereignty. In conditions of interdependence, it requires, more than any other aspect of economic management, a careful assessment of the interaction between international and national economic welfare and the extent to which policy makers have to promote the former in order to achieve the latter. The success in reconciling the two will depend chiefly on the degree to which their national social preferences coincide: for a country's fiscal policy is as much a reflection of its social philosophy and preferences as of its economic capabilities and needs.[12]

This kind of consensus is particularly important in the conditions analysed here: a monetary union in which all member governments maintain their autonomy to tax, spend and borrow. Without the consensus, members of the union would find it impossible either to take effective stabilisation measures in the short run or to pursue coherent adjustment policies in the long run.[13]

As explained in Parts I and II, short-term stabilisation measures tend to become increasingly ineffective, even counterproductive, if pursued in isolation by an open, internationally integrated economy. Hence, a high degree of collaboration among governments in formulating their macroeconomic policies is essential if they are to achieve their short-term objectives.

The need for such collaboration becomes even greater within a monetary union. Monetary policy is now determined centrally by all member countries. At the same time, there is no central authority to ensure that individually determined fiscal policies are compatible. The outcome depends entirely, therefore, on how far member governments can reconcile their objectives and policies. If they succeed, each country will benefit from the combined effects of domestic and foreign multipliers. If they fail, these same multiplier effects will ensure that the overall inflationary or deflationary result of changes in autonomously determined fiscal stances turns out to be much greater than the sum total of individually taken actions (see Chapter 2). In other words, there will be considerable 'overshooting' or, if governments try to avoid this, 'undershooting' in actual levels of aggregate demand within the union, generated by changes in member countries' fiscal policies.

The risk of this will be increased if there are significant differences in member countries' taxation and social policies, as these differences may force governments to rely much more on discretionary stabilisation measures (Keynesian demand management) than they would do if their economies were insulated from external developments. The reason for this is that reliance on such measures is normally reduced in national economies by the existence of a whole range of automatic stabilisers created by social and other legislation. The stabilisers consist of progressive taxation, and unemployment and other benefits designed to provide at least an adequate standard of living for the less fortunate members of society. Their macro-economic effect is to raise government revenue during cyclical recoveries (dampening the growth of private demand) and to lower it, while increasing government expenditure, in recessions (stimulating private demand). Both these effects may be seriously diminished if countries have significantly different social preferences and fiscal policies, making it necessary for governments to make frequent changes in their fiscal policy in order to influence the level of aggregate demand in their economies.

The differences would also make it very difficult to generate long-term adjustments within the union. Automatic stabilisers perform two additional functions, apart from reducing the magnitude of cyclical fluctuations within an economy: they redistribute income among individuals, households and regions, and in the process of so doing also assist the adjustment process in the regions experiencing high unemployment. It is estimated, for instance, that as much as one-half to two-thirds of a short-term loss of income caused by a fall in a region's export sales tends to be offset in industrial economies through public finance.[14] This redistribution, as mentioned earlier, is generally regarded as a major factor in maintaining the unity of a country. It does so by ensuring that 'small, poor and peripheral regions [are] generously aided by the centre'.[15]

Even more important for the long-term stability of a monetary union is the interregional transfer of resources for adjustment purposes which this income redistribution makes possible. Apart from labour migration, changes in the composition of industrial output play a major role in reducing regional income inequalities. To the extent that this process is not accomplished autonomously at the micro-economic level, regional governments have to take steps to make their regions more attractive to new industries by improving their infrastructure. Furthermore, the governments might also be required to subsidise for a time the development of 'infant' industries within the region; and to introduce measures which enable the existing industries to modernise their products and production methods.

Budgetary constraints will obviously prevent regional authorities from promoting such changes. The reason for this emerges clearly even from a very brief examination of the main components of a budget and the extent to which different methods of financing it are applicable to regional governments within a country and to national governments within an international monetary union. The most important components of a budget consist of:

$$G + D - T - F = b\,[+m - e]$$

where G = public sector expenditure on goods and services and transfer payments; D = interest payments on outstanding government bonds held by the public; T = taxes; F = intergovernmental equalisation grants; b = borrowing from the public (in other words, changes in public holdings of government bonds); m = changes in the monetary base; and e = changes in foreign exchange reserves.

A region cannot change either m or e (both of which are determined by central government) in order to finance an increase in G. Hence, if F remains unchanged, an increase in regional public expenditure has to be financed either by higher taxes (T) or increases in borrowing from the public (b). Their size will be determined by the volume of extra expenditure that regional authorities need to finance on their own, without outside assistance. If the additional expenditure is small or of a temporary nature, there will be no problem in obtaining the necessary finance. But if the region has serious adjustment problems and finds it difficult to attract private capital, G is likely to rise over time, as the region tries to avoid a permanent decline in its economic welfare.

This will be possible only if the regional authorities can raise additional revenue and/or borrow on a substantial scale over a long period. Neither is easy to achieve. A large T, permanently higher than in other regions, may drive away both skilled labour and capital, making it even more difficult to solve adjustment problems in the declining region. A large b, obtained at commercial rates of interest, may lead to a similar outcome as taxes have to be raised to service the debt. Hence, in the absence of interregional equalisation grants, such a region would find it virtually impossible to escape from a vicious circle of permanent decline. In other words, the great advantage of F is that it reduces the need for both T and b, making the interregional adjustments and income equalisation easier.

One of the most serious weaknesses of all internationally integrated systems is that they lack such a safety mechanism to bind them together. Moreover, once they join a monetary union governments cannot use either foreign exchange reserves or money creation to escape, at least temporarily, from a budget constraint. Both m and e are managed centrally, and a majority decision is required to change either.

Hence, if a stagnant economy needs to raise G for restructuring purposes, it has no alternative but to increase T or b, or both, with the risk of triggering off the adverse factor movements described above. The risk is even greater here than in the case of a region because, in the absence of intergovernmental transfers, a booming economy will be able to reduce T and b, making it even more attractive to international capital and highly skilled labour. The subsequent widening of the gap in income levels in the two groups of countries – through cumulative progress in one case and stagnation in the other – will inevitably increase tensions and distintegrating tendencies within the union.

The important point (implicit in the preceding analysis) is that, although in a system of national management of the international economy each country retains, in principle, the right to pursue an independent fiscal policy, the scope for doing this is very limited in practice. As usual, if differences in the level of economic performance are small and if social preferences and policies are similar, lack of very close co-operation between governments need not impose serious strains on international economic relationships. But if these differences are large and growing the strains are not only unavoidable but also likely, sooner or later, to lead to a breaking point.

The only way to avoid this is for governments of independent sovereign states participating in the monetary union to agree on a system of intergovernmental 'equalisation grants', the purpose of which would be to reduce differentials in the fiscal capacity and performance of governments within the union.[16] This can be achieved only if the governments concerned can resolve satisfactorily a number of issues, some mainly political and some technical: the degree to which they ought to equalise their budgetary capacities, which will depend on the standard which they chose for deciding the size of intergovernmental transfers; the method of making the transfers; the measurement of governments' fiscal capacity; and the measurement of each government's expenditure needs and the cost of providing them.[17]

Given the existing differences in economic performance and social preferences even among industrial market economies, it is inconceivable that a complete monetary union of the kind described earlier in this chapter could survive for very long in the absence of a speedy and genuine effort to develop an effective system of intergovernmental transfers. It is for this reason that a satisfactory resolution of fiscal issues is probably the most important requirement for a sustainable economic order in conditions of international integration.

VII

So far, the analysis in this chapter has implied, in a highly simplified fashion, that the success and long-term viability of an internationally integrated system depend entirely on the willingness and ability of national governments to co-operate in achieving certain macro-economic policy objectives. This is obviously important. But it is not enough. The preceding analysis has ignored the one institution which has been instrumental in linking national economies to their present level of interdependence and over which no single government has adequate control: the transnational enterprise. It is the growth and behaviour of transnationals which has been largely responsible for the need to create a new international economic order and, if such an order is established, it is their actions that are likely to play an important role in its ultimate success or failure. Given the vast resources at their disposal and the highly intricate way in which they have linked national economies, an important precondition for creating a stable international economic order consists therefore of ensuring that the future behaviour of transnationals is compatible with the achievement of overall national and international policy objectives.

As emphasised in Part I, the world as a whole has benefited greatly from the technical and managerial advances which large enterprises in general and transnationals in particular have made possible. There is little doubt that in many sectors of a modern economy they provide the most efficient form of organising the production of goods and services on a global scale. By concentrating large resources within one enterprise they can avoid costly cut-throat competition and the waste of productive resources (in the form of excess capacity) common in highly competitive industries, as well as remove many of the uncertainties and risks which present a serious obstacle to economic progress.

At the same time, the vast market power at their disposal creates another risk: they may abuse the power and in doing so give rise to important social costs. Their operations can cause serious misallocation of resources, widen national and international income inequalities, and retard the technical and other changes needed for long-term improvements in economic welfare.

It is in order to avoid the risks associated with the concentration of market power that the growth of industrial concentration has been followed in many countries by legislative measures against restrictive practices and other forms of 'monopoly' power. Economic reasons apart, this legislation also reflects the need to prevent the emergence of serious conflicts of interest between large corporations and the rest of the community which might threaten the unity and political stability of the state. The rapid increase in the power and influence of transnationals has made it necessary to enact similar measures on a global scale; and the only way in which this can be done realistically is for countries to harmonise their attitudes and behaviour towards these enterprises.

There are two obstacles to achieving such a harmonisation. First, the large economic resources at their disposal and the fact that they operate in a number of different countries have given transnationals considerable political influence. Second, in spite of this, most of them still seem to have failed to grasp the importance of their own role in the creation of a stable international economic order, and the fact that the establishment of such an order may well be imperative for their own long-term survival.

The growth in their size and their ability to influence economic, social and political relationships within and between countries appear to have done little to change the way in which even the largest transnationals formulate their main policy objectives. The supreme goal is still basically that of profit maximisation – expressed in the narrow, accounting terms of private costs and benefits. This, after all, is what those whose capital is invested in these enterprises expect the management to achieve.

Not surprisingly, if the micro-economic rules of the game are defined in these terms, those running transnationals will do their best to prevent, weaken or avoid any laws, rules and regulations which limit their ability to achieve the ultimate corporate objective. Many of them have been very active, therefore, in ensuring that the countries in which they operate are run by political parties that owe their success, even their position as a major political force, to the financial and other support which they receive from transnationals. Quite a few governments in industrial and other market economies fall into this category. This explains why the governments of many industrial countries have been so reluctant to take an active part in any attempt to develop a uniform and effective set of rules and regulations in this area.

Leaving aside problems which such an attitude creates for the ability of these governments to achieve their national objectives, the failure to evolve and enforce a univeral code of industrial behaviour could prove to be extremely costly in the long term to transnationals themselves.

This conclusion is consistent with the analysis and evidence presented in the preceding chapters. Since the mid-1970s, the internationalist ideal has been undergoing probably one of its most serious trials. High and in many cases increasing levels of unemployment, inflation rates and external deficits, and large international debts, cannot persist indefinitely. Sooner or later, governments will be forced to take steps leading to the solution of these problems. If they cannot do this collectively they will resort, as in the past, to unilateral action.

Policies designed to deal only with national problems cannot succeed unless individual economies can be insulated; and the only way to do this effectively now is to emasculate transnationals, even break them up. In fact, if they were to make effective international co-operational impossible, national management of the international economy would in the end also require government action of this kind. Consequently, generally accepted obligations and rules of behaviour which are observed both by governments and transnationals, and which contribute to the creation of a stable international economic order, are as much in the long-term interest of transnational enterprises as of the countries in which they operate.

Very broadly, there are three important areas in which governments need to co-ordinate tightly their actions towards transnationals.

The first of these is political. A stable international economic order is impossible if transnationals – and this applies to both domestic and foreign enterprises[18] – fail to respect the socio-political preferences and aims of the countries in which they operate. In would, of course, be naive to expect these enterprises to refrain, any more than other vested interest groups, from lobbying for economic and social policies, and (where these exist) political parties which are likely to advance their interests. But this is quite different from either direct or indirect actions by the corporations which are intended to overthrow a government, or to cause fundamental changes in the political system of a country. Yet there are many examples of transnational enterprises providing direct support in the past to those elements in a country's population which were working actively towards these ends. Moreover, some of them have often tried to destabilise and weaken democratically elected governments by providing strong opposition to measures (such as welfare provisions, industrial democracy, or prices and incomes policies) which, by maintaining its social cohesion and political stability, may be essential for a country's long-term economic progress.

The most effective way of avoiding these problems would be for all governments to agree not to come to the aid of one of their own enterprises whose assets in a foreign country were nationalised because of its interference in the country's social and political processes. Political interference by transnationals could also be avoided if all nations agreed on the rules which would determine the compensation of a country's nationals if their assets abroad were nationalised for any reason other than the one just mentioned; and on the sanctions from the international community that would follow if these rules were not observed.

Prevention of large-scale tax evasion by transnationals is another area in which national governments need to co-operate closely. The creation of a complete monetary union would make it impossible for transnationals to influence, as they can do at present, many aspects of economic policy (monetary, exchange rate, commercial) and in this way a country's ability to achieve its economic objectives. But they would still be in a position to have a major impact on a country's performance through its fiscal policy, the one area in which governments would retain the autonomy to tax and spend according to what they judge to be their national interest. The greater the autonomy the greater would be the scope for transnationals to use their internal transfer pricing to maximise net profits by transferring a large proportion of income from countries with high to those with low taxes. Their gain, however, could turn out to be a major loss for some of the countries in which they operate, as the transfers would increase disparities in international performance and incomes.

For instance, if they engage in tax evasion through transfer pricing, transnationals will inevitably reduce the amount of savings available to a country with relatively high taxes. If the country happens to have an excess of domestic savings over investment at full employment there is no problem, apart from the question of equity. But if it has structural problems and needs to increase the level of saving in order to finance new investments required to restructure the economy, the tax-evading action by transnationals will aggravate its adjustment problems. According to the analysis in Chapter 5, other things remaining equal, lower savings will result in lower investment and, therefore, a lower rate of growth, opening up further in the long term the gap between the country with structural problems and the more successful countries.

There are two reasons for this. By avoiding relatively high taxes in this particular country, transnationals will, *ceteris paribus*, increase the tax burden of its other residents, including domestic enterprises. As a result, the ability of purely national firms to expand and modernise their productive capacity will diminish. At the same time, the government's ability to increase revenue to an extent that would compensate it for the losses caused by transnationals is likely to be limited by the rising resentment from residents against further increases in taxation, and the fear of even greater flights of capital abroad. Consequently, the government will be even less able than before to help domestic firms realise their investment plans.

Various schemes for ensuring that transnationals cannot escape their tax liabilities have been proposed by, among others, the United Nations, the OECD and the EEC Commission.[19] Their main problem is that tax evasion is very difficult to detect if it takes place in the course of numerous, perfectly routine transactions within a large multiproduct enterprise. Hence, the only way to avoid the wider economic consequences of such evasion is to develop an effective system of international intergovernmental transfers. After all, taxes which escape one government will accrue in one form or another to some other government.

The relative, even absolute, decline of an economy can be accelerated further if transnationals misuse their oligopolistic power by engaging in restrictive practices[20] – the third area in which governments need to harmonise their policies.

Transnationals have the resources to produce rapid changes in the existing patterns and levels of international economic development. However, their size and command over productive resources can also provide a serious obstacle to such changes. They can do this in two ways: through their internal investment policies and by exploiting differences in national laws concerning the concentration of economic power and restrictive practices.

The behaviour of the subsidiaries and affiliates of a transnational enterprise is invariably subject to restrictions imposed by the parent company. This is necessary in order to ensure that they operate in a way which is consistent with its global strategy of maximising profits and growth, and of minimising risks. These considerations will dictate which of them are allowed to expand and which to contract, or even close down. It will also decide their product range and which markets they are to serve. In addition, the overall strategy will determine which of them will use the most up-to-date products and production methods available to the company. They will under no circumstances be allowed to compete against one another.

As these subsidiaries are located in different countries, the restrictions involved in global strategies of the parent companies, far from assisting, may well retard the economic progress of a country in which they are located – making it increasingly difficult for the country to maintain fundamental equilibrium.

> Its industry may be prevented from producing goods for home consumption or export, which it is capable of producing competitively. Where production for home consumption is involved, the country may have to import products which could be made domestically at lower cost. It may, furthermore, be prevented from importing products from the lowest cost sources, with consequent adverse effects upon domestic price levels and productive efficiency.[21]

Nevertheless, the country will be unable to take on its own effective measures against such practices because of the threat that they could make its position even worse. If other countries refrain from taking similar steps, the measures will discourage inward investment as well as encourage disinvestment, as transnationals operating within the country switch their operations abroad where they can pursue their global strategies unimpeded.

Furthermore, by integrating vertically various stages of production, transnationals may acquire access to raw materials, components and distribution networks – making it very difficult for new firms to be established anywhere on a competitive basis. If this is not enough, they can reinforce these 'barriers to entry' through predatory pricing, lowering their prices in a particular market to such an extent that potential competitors are driven out of business. As soon as this is accomplished, prices can be raised again up to the level required by the global profit-maximising strategy.

A country may take steps to outlaw any of these practices within its borders. But it can do little to prevent them if they originate outside its territory. For instance, it is in no position to forbid concentration of control of strategic primary products within a few companies or, once this happens, to do anything to ensure that the companies do not exploit their market power by restricting output and raising prices. Measures of this kind could be taken only with full co-operation of all the countries concerned. For similar reasons, short of imposing strict quantitative controls on trade, it would be unable to stop companies located abroad from pursuing, through imports, a policy of predatory pricing. Lower import prices can always be justified as being nothing more than a reflection of greater efficiency and lower unit costs abroad. Alleged differences in efficiency, rather than corporate global strategies, can be also used to explain why some companies charge widely differing prices in different countries for an identical product.

For all these reasons, national management of the international economy, to be effective in avoiding problems analysed earlier in this chapter, requires a harmonisation of 'anti-trust' policies.

VIII

The final issue with which internationally integrated economies have to come to grips with is that of stabilising the terms of trade between primary and industrial products. This is required in order to avoid highly destabilising shocks to the international economy of the kind analysed in Part IV.

Historically, major international economic crises appear to have coincided with periods of either acute shortages or surpluses of primary commodities: in the 1870s, in the period between the two world wars and since 1973. On each occasion, developments in the primary sector gave rise to a significant redistribution of world income and, in this way, triggered off large-scale changes in world demand and production patterns. The crises have erupted because major changes in the existing productive structures, more often than not, involve institutional as well as economic adjustments and, normally, these can be made only over a long period.

Realising the dangers (economic, social and political) inherent in a sudden appearance of large-scale discontinuities, all industrial countries have tried to prevent them by means of 'commodity stabilisation' policies. The method used for this purpose has tended to vary from country to country. The aim, however, has always been to achieve one or all of the following: (a) to minimise the effects of fluctuations in primary product prices on costs and prices in the rest of the economy, as these could affect adversely investment and economic growth; (b) to avoid inflationary and deflationary spirals in the economy to which large swings in the distribution of national income would inevitably give rise; (c) to avoid large interregional differences in income and the tensions which they could create; and (d) to ensure a steady and reliable supply of primary products, many of which play a strategic role in modern industrial economies.

The main problem in organising effective commodity stabilisation schemes internationally is that there is no one capable of enforcing a particular agreement, a particular course of action. Governments can employ schemes of this kind within their country by either persuading or coercing both consumers and producers to accept them on the grounds of national security and well-being. Internationally, the schemes can be introduced and, once launched, achieve the desired result only if the countries concerned are convinced that they are in their long-term interest.

If the international community needed a major shock to remind it of this fact, the energy crisis has provided it by inflicting high economic and social costs on oil consuming countries and on most of the producers as well. Moreover, it has demonstrated clearly the possibility that, in the absence of international co-operation, crises of this kind could occur again and again in the future. In addition, since the early 1970s many other primary producers have shown that they too can respond quickly to increases in world economic activity by raising their prices sharply; and consumers have, in turn, reminded producers of their ability to depress these prices through deflation.

Hence, this is another area of global interdependence which requires international co-operation if a stable world economic order is to be created. The important condition for success here is that actions designed to prevent the recurrence of another oil or similar 'shock' to the international system should be confined in coverage and scope to those areas within which they can realistically be expected to achieve their main objective.

First, where necessary, an international commodity scheme – managed by an international board consisting of the most important produces and consumers of a strategically important primary product – should ensure its adequate long-term supply by stabilising producers' earnings. This is essential in order to provide them with both the incentive and the means to undertake necessary investment. The scheme should not be confused with international income redistribution, or be used to enable a developing or declining economy, if one of them happens to be a major producer, to undertake its long-term adjustments. Intergovernmental fiscal transfers and loans, or private investment guaranteed by governments of surplus countries are the correct way to deal with these wider problems if the country is unable to attract private long-term investment.

Second, the schemes should only cover those actual or potential imbalances which have important international repercussions in the market for a particular commodity. The imbalances internal to a country should be the responsibility of that country. If they create adjustment problems which require international assistance, the assistance should be provided with measures which facilitate foreign investment or intergovernmental co-operation of the kind suggested above. Any attempt to enlarge primary product stabilisation schemes for this purpose will inevitably condemn them to failure from the start.

Third, given the wide-ranging effect that oil has on the world economy, international initiatives designed to deal with problems that it poses must be separated from the schemes whose purpose is to stabilise markets for other primary commodities.

Taking 'commodities' first, one of the two broad policy approaches can be adopted: stabilisation of the price of a particular commodity; or stabilisation of the producers' export earnings through compensatory financing.[22]

The main problem with price stabilisation schemes is that, far from reducing disequilibria in a particular commodity market, they may actually exacerbate them. If producers' interests gain the upper hand in negotiations and the price is set too high relative to the price that would be obtained in the absence of such a scheme, demand for the commodity will fall while output will rise. The result will be excess supply – all those 'mountains' and 'lakes' of unsold products which have made the EEC Common Agricultural Policy one of the costliest, most irrational and least defensible schemes of its kind ever designed. If, on the other hand, consumers' interests prevail and the price is set too low demand will increase while, at the same time, output will decline. The result will be excess demand, making it impossible to maintain a particular price. Either way, therefore, a policy which aims to keep primary commodity prices stable will sooner or later become unsustainable.

It is for this reason that compensatory financing schemes are much more promising. They allow prices to fluctuate according to prevailing market conditions and then compensate producers, according to some previously agreed but renegotiable formula, if they suffer a loss of income as a result of the fluctuations.

The main features of what could become a highly successful scheme for compensatory financing can be already found, in fact, in the STABEX (Stabilisation Fund for Exports) programme operated by the EEC countries under the Lomé Convention, as well as in some of the proposals put forward by Sweden and Germany.[23] Its success would depend on the extent to which it managed to incorporate a number of important elements. It would have to be limited to a number of key commodities. Otherwise, the financial resources required for the purpose could easily exceed the total that the consuming countries would be willing to contribute. The scheme should cover only those commodities where a high proportion of total output enters international trade. Problems associated with the commodities consumed predominantly within producing countries are internal to these countries and, consequently, do not require an international commodity stabilisation programme. Equally, such schemes should not be confused with balance of payments corrections and adjustments for which, as already emphasised, other means of international assistance should be found. Moreover, the compensatory finance schemes should be limited to low income countries, as they lack resources to stabilise incomes of key primary producers. More advanced countries have both the means and the institutions to achieve this objective internally.

The exact details of such a scheme would depend on the bargaining skill and strength of the most important producing and consuming countries. But it would almost certainly have to incorporate a number of important features. It would be used to compensate the export earnings of the producers of a particular commodity if they fell below the average for the preceding four or five years (in other words, over a period covering a full business cycle). Some of the financing could be provided in the form of loans and some (going to very low income producers) as grants. Repayments of loans would take place only when export earnings exceeded this average. Furthermore, some of the loans could be interest free, except when subsequent earnings exceeded the average by a certain percentage for more than one year. The scheme could stipulate from the outset, therefore, the interest to be charged (the market rate or some rate below it) in such cases.

A compensatory financing scheme could, in this way, fulfil several important functions: it could stimulate an adequate supply of certain strategically important commodities without encouraging overproduction in those cases where there is a clear long-term decline in international demand; it could discourage overproduction in high cost sources of supply; and, with the threat of interest rate charges on export earnings well above the stipulated average, it could discourage excessive short-term profit maximisation which could prove to be against the producers' as well as consumers' interests, for reasons mentioned earlier.

Finally, it is hardly necessary to point out that the extent to which a commodity stabilisation scheme achieves these ends will depend ultimately not only on understanding and co-operation between consuming and producing countries but also on the general economic climate. Even the best scheme is bound to fail if it is pursued in isolation, especially in the absence of other policies considered in this chapter. For instance, no scheme can survive if consuming countries, through persistent deflation of their economies, depress primary producers' incomes to such an extent as to require increases in the fund allocated for compensatory financing beyond levels which they are prepared to contribute. Moreover, the longer this situation persists the more likely it is to increase long-term instability in international commodity markets.

Schemes of the kind described above would be much more difficult to apply in the case of oil. The huge increase in its nominal and real price in 1973/74 and 1979/80, and the subsequent falls, would make it very difficult for producers and consumers to agree on the period whose average should be used as the yardstick.

At the same time, oil has a much more important influence on the world economy than any other primary product. Moreover, it is a finite resource which could be exhausted in the foreseeable future, in the absence of an appropriate increase in alternative sources of energy and their more efficient use. A rate of growth equal to that of the productive potential in industrial countries alone would probably be sufficient to ensure this outcome.

For all these reasons, a policy is required which will encourage an adequate supply of oil, a continuous development of (preferably non-polluting) substitutes and a more efficient use of all the existing sources of energy. Furthermore, events since 1979 ought to have made it clear to industrial *and* oil producing countries that the energy crisis has proved to be extremely costly to both groups and disastrous for the developing countries which have no oil. The future of the world economy depends, therefore, among other things, on how far the two sides can develop rational, lasting rules of behaviour.

Probably the most reasonable base for achieving these objectives lies in stabilising annual changes in the real price of oil within a certain range. Oil price rises – relative to those of, say, manufactures – above the ceiling would require increases in the volume of oil production. Conversely, a fall in the real price below the floor of the range would be the signal that oil output should be reduced. Industrial countries would be required to share the responsibility for stabilising the price by either reducing or increasing their levels of activity. As another precaution against future 'shocks', the agreement could also specify the maximum annual increases in oil output that the main producers would be either able or willing to achieve.

An agreement of this kind would, of course, be far from easy to put in practice. Which prices would be used? How long would the real price of oil have to move in a particular direction before somebody had to take action? Who exactly would be required to take it, oil producers or industrial nations? Which countries should bear the main burden of adjustment? On the other hand, it is difficult to see how, in the absence of such rules to guide their actions, both oil consuming and producing nations can escape the extremely serious constraint imposed on their economies by the energy crisis. Given the high level of international interdependence, problems created by the crisis affect all of them – irrespective of whether they have oil or not.

IX

The most important conclusions contained in this rather long chapter can be summarised as follows.

So long as the only effective institutional framework for formulating and executing macro-economic policies exists within independent nation states, it is the extent to which these states are able and willing to co-operate that will determine the long-term viability of existing international economic relationships. More specifically, the experience of countries which have coped successfully with problems created by economic integration and interdependence within their own borders suggests that the future course of international specialisation and openness will depend largely on how far, collectively, they succeed in developing a code of behaviour which they observe nationally.

To begin with, they have to be in complete agreement about their major policy objectives. At the same time, their policies must be compatible with the level of interdependence that they have reached, as well as with economic conditions prevailing within individual countries.

Next, they have to agree on one or more assets, acceptable to all, to be used in settling international debts. This is essential for the stability and further progress of a highly developed and integrated global economic system. In theory, this means either that exchange rates will have to be rigidly fixed and maintained or that the world will have to accept a single asset as representing 'world money'. In practice, the more advanced national financial systems are and the more closely they are linked the more difficult will it be to sustain a regime of fixed parities. International financial stability will come to depend increasingly, therefore, on how far individual countries are prepared to give up that part of their sovereignty which is concerned with the creation and management of national currencies and form a monetary union.

As such a union would do nothing to solve the internal adjustment problems of individual countries, its establishment would require members of the union to evolve a system of incentives and disincentives to encourage the movement of private long-term capital towards developing and declining economies. Even more important to ensure smooth and adequate economic adjustments within the union, and a reasonably equal distribution of gains from the membership, they would have to agree on substantial intergovernmental fiscal transfers similar to those which exists in most countries, especially those with federal constitutions. Close fiscal co-operation represents one of the key factors in the survival and further progress of highly integrated economic systems.

Even if they were willing to co-operate in this way, governments would be able to do so only to the extent that they could mobilise the support and resources within their countries. To do this effectively, they would have to harmonise their policies towards transnational enterprises – the one form of micro-economic organisation whose actions can turn into failure even the most imaginative scheme for intergovernmental fiscal co-operationa and adjustment policies.

Finally, to avoid sudden and large shocks to the international system, such as the energy crisis, a stable international economic order requires effective 'commodity stabilisation' schemes as well as close co-operation between oil producing and consuming countries.

This is a formidable list of policy requirements, much more demanding than anything that nation states have been so far prepared even to contemplate seriously. The strong implication behind this list is that a highly integrated international economic system can survive only if nation states can reconcile their political independence with the development of a complete economic union. The further they are from achieving such a union the more unstable the system is likely to be.

As shown in the preceding chapter, the division of labour and economic progress in general depend, among other things, on the evolution of appropriate forms of economic organisation, both at the micro and macro-economic levels. This means that if the division of labour exceeds the ability of existing institutions to cope with the problems which it creates – or to adapt accordingly – it will invariably revert to a lower level of specialisation and interdependence. Long-term economic progress is incompatible with prolonged or growing uncertainty and instability.

16 The Optimum Policy Area

I

The last chapter left one very important question unanswered: what exactly is the 'area' (meaning the grouping of independent national entities) most likely to enable its constituent units to pursue effectively the policies needed to achieve and sustain a high level of economic welfare? In other words, what is an optimum policy area in the 1980s?

The earlier analysis has shown that the nation state becomes increasingly ineffective as an independent policy-making unit with the growth of international integration and interdependence. However, although this is now true of virtually every country in the world – it is not true of all of them equally. Some are much more open and integrated into the world economy than others. They are not all under the same pressure, therefore, to search for international solutions to their national problems. This suggests that the world as a whole may not be an optimum policy area either. So, what is?

Mundell[1] was the first economist to raise formally, in the early 1960s, the question of 'optimum currency areas' – by which he meant areas within which exchange rates should be fixed. His answer, and the same is true also of all the contributors in the debate that followed, was determined by what he regarded to be the most important *single* factor that would make it possible for countries to reconcile their internal and external balances. In Mundell's analysis only a high degree of capital and labour mobility could accomplish this.

McKinnon, on the other hand, argued that it was the extent of openness of individual economies that determined an optimum currency area because it imposed a limit on their ability to pursue relevant economic policies in isolation.[2] Ingram[3] and Scitovsky[4] used a similar criterion to decide whether a currency area was optimal or not – only in their case it was the extent of financial (rather than 'real') integration that mattered. Kenen took a somewhat different view. His main concern was with a country's ability to adjust with minimum cost to shocks originating abroad.[5] Hence, he argued that an optimum currency area should consist of countries with highly diversified economies. Finally, according to Haberler[6] and Fleming[7] only countries with similar inflation rates and similar policy preferences should join a currency union.

All these writers have something interesting to say. In many cases their analysis provides an important, though limited, insight into the seriousness of a particular obstacle to greater international economic specialisation. The problem, as numerous critics have pointed out, is that the analysis which uses a single criterion to establish what constitutes an optimum currency area is too restricted in scope. As such, it cannot provide an adequate assessment of the costs and benefits which arise from an economic union.

That can be done only if a number of important issues, such as those described in the last chapter, are considered together. This will be attempted briefly in the sections that follow in relation to specific suggestions for closer international monetary unions and economic co-operation in general. To emphasise the difference between this broader approach and the single criterion method used traditionally, the analysis will be concerned throughout with optimum *policy* areas.

II

Policy requirements for a stable international economic order were analysed in the last chapter in relation to countries which form an open and highly integrated system of economic and financial relationships. This implies a high degree of interdependence, the main characteristic of a predominantly oligopolistic environment.

The stability of oligopolistic relationships depends to a large extent on two factors (see Chapter 14). First, it is greater the smaller is the number of countries involved. This makes it easier for each of them to realise the extent of its dependence on the others. The smallness of the group also enables each member to become familiar with the aspirations, difficulties and institutions of the others. Consequently, they are in a position to anticipate each others' needs and actions and thus evolve policies which are sufficiently compatible to improve the economic welfare of all.

Second, countries are more likely to evolve a stable international economic order if they operate under similar conditions – in other words, if their efficiency and income levels as well as their socio-economic preferences are alike. The similarities reduce the need for fiscal transfers. They also make the transfers easier to accomplish because countries with similar economic and social preferences are likely to have similar political systems and, therefore, to pursue very similar fiscal policies. In addition, the closer are the economic conditions and institutions prevailing in different countries the smaller will be the *net* factor movements between them. This ensures that, even in the absence of exchange and other controls, international migration of capital and labour will not impose serious costs on any one of them.

Providing that these conditions are satisfied, there is no reason for highly integrated economies to reduce their interdependence by imposing restrictions on trade and factor movements. A complete monetary union is, therefore, sustainable – facilitating further the international division of labour by ensuring financial stability.

These are some of the main conclusions of the last two chapters. How far would certain international monetary and economic unions of the kind frequently advocated since the early 1970s satisfy these conditions? By considering this question it is possible to get some idea of what might constitute international 'optimum' policy arrangements in the 1980s.

III

It is sometimes suggested that developing countries could solve some of their most pressing problems and achieve more rapid progress if they acted together as a united 'Third World bloc'. There are obviously occasions when, by synchronising their policies, developing countries could force industrialised nations to assist them more adequately in the effort to develop and modernise their economies. For instance, they could threaten to default *en masse* on their foreign debts, or use the first opportunity to create another energy crisis.

The problem, as the energy shocks and the debt crisis have demonstrated, is that not all of them would benefit from such actions. Other things remaining equal, many developing countries would in fact lose heavily. Moreover, even the clear 'winners' would not be able to sustain their gains in the long term because of counter-actions taken by industrial countries. Suggestions for a 'Third World bloc' have to be based, therefore, on something much more sustainable: long-term advantages that would enable all its members to improve their economic welfare more effectively in such a grouping than they could do either in isolation or as members of some other bloc.

One possible advantage could stem from the fact that a 'Third World bloc' would consist of economies with similar efficiency and income levels, similar problems and needs. This should provide its members with a strong incentive to combine their resources in order eventually to attain the same goal: a level of productivity and income comparable to those which exist in the most industrialised nations. In principle, at least, it should therefore be relatively easy for them to achieve a 'harmony of interests' and thus be able to follow similar and/or compatible policies. Providing that they reach and maintain such a level of co-operation, they might even be able to evolve in the long run a high level of international division of labour without becoming in the meantime heavily dependent on industrialised countries.

The relatively small differences in living standards and international competitiveness among developing countries could, in theory, provide a 'Third World bloc' with another advantage. So long as most of their international exchange took place within the bloc, developing countries could avoid the large internal and/or external imbalances common at present. The existing disparities in their efficiency and income levels are too small to cause serious adjustment and financing problems in the less economically advanced and competitive members of the bloc. As a result, it might not be essential to establish a close fiscal union, something that would be difficult to achieve under any circumstances.

Although all these propositions seem to be reasonable enough, on closer examination the 'advantages' turn out to be illusory rather than real.

First, one of the difficulties in creating a viable 'Third World bloc' is that all developing countries have much closer economic links with industrial economies than with one another. As pointed out in Chapter 1, this is one of the reasons why various attempts to create economic unions among them have failed to live up to expectations. Their level of specialisation is invaribly too low for the volume of intra-union trade to be of much relevance, compared to the volume of trade in which each member is engaged with countries outside the union – predominantly those in the highly industrialised 'North'. This is also the only part of the world from which a developing country can obtain an adequate supply of the resources without which it would be unable to industrialise. Hence, each of them is much more anxious to develop close links with industrial countries than with other developing economies.

Second, it is far more difficult to achieve a 'harmony of interest' among developing than among industrial nations. The former are not only much more numerous and less integrated economically but also, in a number of important respects, much more heterogeneous. Some developing countries have yet to 'take off into self-sustained growth'. Others, such as the newly industrialised countries, are well on the way to challenge the supremacy of industrialised countries in many areas of economic activity. There is a wide gap in the resources, needs and the capacity for further economic development between these two groups.

In addition, many of the more advanced 'Third World' countries are likely to have similar resources and, consequently, try to develop competitive rather than complementary industries. When this happens, barriers to trade between developing countries will be as high, if not higher, than the barriers between them and industrial countries.

The problem of achieving similar objectives and compatible policies within a 'Third World bloc' would be exacerbated further by the fact that different developing countries tend to depend heavily on different industrial economies. As a result, each developing country will adjust its policies according to what is happening in the industrial country with which it has close trading and financial links – rather than in response to developments and needs within the bloc. These differences would also make it impossible for such a bloc to establish a monetary union (even if the countries could agree on its institutional aspects) unless industrial countries developed it first.

Finally, as they all have large adjustment needs, for a long time no country belonging to a 'Third World bloc' would be in a position to export capital, and technical and managerial expertise on a scale that would make a significant contribution to the development of the less industrialised members of the bloc. All these resources would have, therefore, to be obtained from outside the bloc – from industrial countries' governments and/or transnational enterprises. These are additional reasons why members of a 'Third World bloc' would be likely, for quite some time, to give much higher priority to developing a mutually beneficial code of behaviour with industrial countries than among themselves.

In summary, an economic union consisting of developing countries only would come nowhere near fulfilling the required conditions for an optimum policy area.

IV

The breakdown of the Bretton Woods System and the fear of yet another return to beggar-my-neighbour policies has led some experts to suggest the formation of regional (or continental) monetary unions, or blocs. The idea is that the unions would evolve around a major country recreating, in effect, the dominant country model on a smaller, regional scale. Thus, for instance, there could be an American bloc around the United States, a West European bloc around West Germany (and the EEC), a South Pacific bloc around Japan, and an East European bloc around the Soviet Union.[8] Other countries could then attach themselves to one of these blocs according to the closeness of their economic relationships and socio-political preferences. In this way, regional blocs would prevent a return to highly damaging economic nationalism. Moreover, they could also be used as the first step in any attempt to rebuild a new and viable international economic order.

There is, of course, nothing revolutionary about the idea of 'regional monetary unions'. They have always existed in one form or another. Small economies inevitably develop very close links with a large neighbour. One of the consequences of this is that many of them will keep their currencies fixed to that of the region's dominant country. What those who expect to see even closer intraregional economic and financial relationships have in mind is that, confronted with growing uncertainty and threats of international economic disintegration, countries within each region will tend to strengthen their ties further, at the expense of those with the rest of the world. They are, after all, much more dependent on each other than on economies in other regions. Moreover, they would be in a much better position to deal with adverse international developments as a bloc than if they tried to cope with them in isolation.

The most apparent advantage that a regional bloc would enjoy, compared to a single national economy, is that its productive capacity would be far more diversified. Consequently, it would be much less vulnerable to outside shocks and changes in economic policy. Even an increase in barriers to trade and factor movements between the blocs would still leave each member country in the position to benefit from international specialisation, especially as any loss of the markets outside the bloc would now be compensated by an increase in intra-bloc trade and division of labour.

A traditionally high degree of interdependence among economies of a region inevitably makes it extremely difficult for any one of them to pursue effectively independent monetary, exchange rate or commercial policies. The success of each country's stabilisation and adjustment policies depends to a great extent, therefore, on the explicit, or at least tacit, support of its neighbours – especially that of the region's dominant economy. In the circumstances, it makes sense for all of them to ensure financial stability within the region by forming a monetary union.

What makes such a union both advantageous and feasible is the fact that countries within a region normally have long experience of pursuing similar economic objectives and policies. Close historical links would have left them little alternative.

These are considerable advantages. But would they be sufficient to turn regional blocs into optimum policy areas? The answer depends on two factors: the strength of a region's economic ties with other regions and the ability and willingness of members of such a bloc to co-operate in solving its internal problems.

Taking interregional links first, there seems little doubt that greater attempts at regional insularity cannot now escape many of the frustrations which make national economic policies sub-optimal when pursued in isolation.

For example, the formation of regional monetary unions might reduce international financial instability, but it would not eliminate it. Most of the highly destabilising international capital flows involve the currencies of the countries around which some of the largest regional blocs are supposed to evolve: the US dollar, the Deutschmark and the Japanese yen. Hence, the establishment of monetary unions within each region would not eliminate exchange rate fluctuations, though they would be now interregional.

The fluctuations would happen irrespective of whether each region had a common currency or whether all countries maintained their national currencies but fixed them to that of the region's dominant currency. A movement of capital from, say, the West European to the American bloc would, *ceteris paribus*, lead to the depreciation of European currencies relative to those of members of the American bloc. The depreciation would generate inflationary pressures within Europe (and, other things remaining equal, in other regions), especially if prices of the world's key primary commodities continued to be fixed in US dollars. At the same time, those members of the American region whose exports to the rest of the world have high price elasticities of demand would be affected adversely by the appreciation.

Nor would the instability end there. Some European countries would continue to be much more dependent on trade with the American bloc than others. As a result, they would experience stronger inflationary pressures, making it increasingly difficult for them to maintain either a fixed exchange rate relative to other members of the European union or, if the price elasticities of their exports and imports were low, their output and employment levels. For similar reasons, the appreciation would not affect all countries in the American region equally. Hence, other things being equal, the longer the interregional differences in policies persisted the more difficult it would become to maintain intra-regional consensuses for a particular macro-economic policy stance. To avoid this, something would have to be done to help certain countries eliminate the economic and social costs imposed on them by their membership of the union.

Furthermore, without developing special relationships with influential outsiders, such as the key oil producers, to promote their mutual long-term interests – the creation of regional blocs would do nothing to remove the threat of further shocks, like the energy crisis, to the international system.[9]

The main policy dilemma confronting individual blocs in their external relationships would not, therefore, be fundamentally different from that experienced at present by individual countries: would a bloc be better off retreating behind protective barriers or promoting interregional arrangements of the kind suggested in the last chapter?

Equally important are some of the problems that regional blocs would have to solve internally in order to remain viable in the long term.

A regional bloc would consist of countries at very different levels of development, often with significant differences in their income and efficiency levels. Its stability and long-term survival would depend, therefore, on developing intra-bloc arrangements which would not only prevent the gaps from widening but also facilitate their reduction in the long term. If low income countries were unable to attract sufficient long-term private investment, they would require a combination of official investment, officially guaranteed private investment and official transfers from the more affluent members of the bloc to enable them to tackle at least their most urgent economic and social problems.

The creation of an effective regional economic union would in most cases, therefore, require substantial capital outflows from the more industrialised members of the union. Their volume would depend on the size of regional disparities in the level of economic development. The larger the disparities the greater would be demands made on the dominant country and other affluent members of the union to assist the catching up process within the region – and the stronger would be the resentment within these countries towards such assistance.

The resentment might be fuelled also by the knowledge that pressure of this kind would be greater on some dominant countries than on others (assuming that each took responsibility for economic stability and adjustments within its region). Given the variations in efficiency and income levels within different blocs, the Germans, for example, would have to undertake a much smaller transfer of resources to ensure the stability of a West European bloc than the Americans and the Japanese would have to provide within their blocs. On the other hand, unequal generosity by the dominant and other structural surplus countries in their region would almost certainly encourage less advanced countries to seek closer ties with members of other blocs. Significant differences in socio-political preferences and systems within a region would produce a similar result. Hence, over a long period it might be far from easy to achieve and, in particular, to maintain the required 'harmony of interests' and unity of purpose within regional economic unions.

Assuming that socio-political differences are not irreconcilable, the long-term viability of a regional monetary union would depend also on something that has been ignored in the last chapter and, so far, in this one: the extent to which countries are able to pursue different commercial policies. As shown in Parts II and III, there are broadly three ways to sustain the stability of an international economy in which important differences exist in the capacity of individual countries to achieve and/or maintain fundamental equilibrium: through international factor mobility (and related resource transfers), through barriers on trade and factor movements,[10] or through a combination of the two. The extent to which these policy alternatives are employed will vary over time with the size of structural imbalances in the world economy and the willingness of structural surplus countries to assist the deficit countries in their adjustment efforts – something that is, after all, also in their own interest.[11]

Hence, if intra-regional differences in efficiency and income levels are such that neither the dominant nor the other surplus countries within a particular region can realistically be expected to provide sufficient transfers of resources over time, internal cohesion of a partial monetary union can still be maintained by varying national trade and other controls according to the ability of each country to achieve and maintain fundamental equilibrium. That is, the need to achieve financial stability and promote further economic progress within the region could be met by a system of fixed exchange rates instead of creating a common regional currency. Currencies in each region would be pegged to that of the dominant economy and, in this way, to each other.

At the same time, structural deficit countries would be allowed to retain controls on their foreign trade and payments with other countries within their bloc as well as those in other regions. The level of these controls would depend on the seriousness of a country's difficulty in reconciling its internal and external balances and the volume of foreign assistance that it could obtain for its stabilisation and adjustment needs. This means that under dynamic conditions countries would have to accept an obligation to increase the openness of their economies with improvements in international competitiveness, and to allow other countries to raise their barriers to trade and capital flows, without the risk of retaliation, if their long-term position deteriorated seriously and they were unable to attract adequate inflows of long-term capital.

Arrangements of this kind would reduce to manageable proportions the size of short- to medium-term disequilibria in developing and declining economies. They would also reduce to realistic proportions the volume of financial and other assistance that the dominant and other surplus countries would have to provide within their region in order to ensure its long-term viability.

Nevertheless, even these arrangements would not be sufficient to turn individual regional blocs into optimum policy areas. The economic ties between members of different regions, especially their dominant economies, are now too great to allow the almost complete regional self-sufficiency which would be required for that. Moreover, all regions have strong links with certain key primary producers, such as oil exporters. In other words, although they are more self-sufficient than individual countries, no region is large enough in the 1980s to deal effectively in isolation with what are, basically, global trading and financial problems, or to prevent the emergence of another oil shock.

V

Despite the doubts expressed at the beginning of this chapter, the analysis since then seems to lead to the conclusion that once economic problems assume global proportions there is really only one optimum policy area: the world. There simply does not appear to be any other level at which some of the most pressing problems of our time can be solved. The loss of welfare to which international integration can give rise in certain cases can be avoided if all industrial and other surplus countries join forces to provide the means for adequate resource tranfers. The energy constraint can be removed by co-operation between energy producers and consumers and careful national development of primary resources and their substitutes. The abuse of corporate power can be prevented by developing mutually consistent national strategies towards transnational enterprises, involving countries at different levels of development and situated in different parts of the world. Complete or partial monetary and fiscal unions can be established by carefully taking into account differences in income levels and the ideological preferences of the countries concerned. Hence, there does not seem to be any single grouping of countries capable of dealing with all these problems adequately in isolation.

At the same time, although many of the contemporary economic problems are too large for even the largest economy to solve on its own, and some of them would turn even a bloc of countries into a sub-optimal policy area – few affect all countries of the world either directly[12] or equally.

The problem of controlling destabilising short-term capital flows is much more acute in industrial countries than in the rest of the world. In fact, the solution has to be found by relatively few industrial nations with large real and financial sectors, not by the whole world. The operations of transational enterprises can create serious policy difficulties in industrial and some developing countries, but not everywhere. Again, it is a group of countries – though, admittedly, a large one – that constitutes the optimum policy area in this respect. The key to long-term stabilisation of oil and other important commodity prices lies in a mutually satisfactory arrangement between a small number of large industrial consumers and the producers.

The question of economic unions has much wider implications. Nevertheless, even in this case different policy solutions have to be applied to different groups of countries if the world as a whole is to be an effective policy area. Adjustment and stabilisation problems created by international integration in a dynamic environment affect every single country. But the effects can vary significantly. Some countries can gain considerably. Others may suffer heavy losses in employment and income. It is for this reason that countries should never be required to harmonise their commercial policies unless they happen to be at similar levels of efficiency and incomes; or, unless surplus countries are prepared to guarantee transfers of real resources which enable deficit countries to achieve long-term external equilibria by opening up their economies and co-operating closely with other countries.

This implies that in future, as in the past, different financial and other arrangements should apply to different countries.

An economic (complete monetary) union should be formed only by countries which are able to satisfy three important conditions. First, their economies ought to be integrated and interdependent to such a degree that they have little alternative but to seek international solutions to their national problems. Second, they ought to be sufficiently industrialised and competitive internationally to sustain complete openness of their economies without incurring long-term losses in economic welfare. Third, they ought to be willing and able to come to the assistance of any member experiencing problems of this kind – to ensure that they do not develop into a long-term disequilibrium that would destabilise the whole union.

Clearly, only industrial market economies are capable at present of satisfying all these conditions, though not even all of them are in the position to join such a union. Some (Switzerland, Sweden and Austria) might be reluctant to do so because of the risk that the union would compromise their political neutrality. Some (for example Scandinavian countries) might prefer to stay out because membership of the union could make it difficult for them to pursue their highly advanced social policies. Some (for example Italy) might find it wiser not to join the union because their level of efficiency and income is still not sufficiently high to make it possible for them to compete or attract capital on equal terms with the most advanced members of the union. Lastly, some (for example the UK) may have reached such an advanced stage of relative economic decline that the long-term cost of belonging to such a union would be too high.

Nevertheless, all these and other countries could enjoy the benefit of international financial stability and growth by forming a partial monetary link with the main group. They could peg their exchange rates to that of the union's currency, while maintaining controls on international trade and payments according to the rules described in the previous section. In the short run, these controls would vary with a country's level of efficiency and income relative to that of the union. In the long term, controls on international transactions would be altered with changes in a country's international competitiveness.

This means that any country which reaches efficiency and income levels similar to those enjoyed by members of the economic union, and has socio-political preferences and institutions similar to theirs, should be able to join the union. Equally, any country already in the union, whose membership imposes serious long-term economic and other costs on its own residents – which other members are unable or unwilling to help rectify – should be able to leave the union. An arrangement of this kind would be essential not only for the benefit of this country but for the stability of the whole union.

VI

Co-ordinated national economic mangement can solve international problems provided that nation states recognise and accept as irreversible the fact that they will inevitably cease to be an optimum policy area as they become linked to other economies through the international division of labour – even though they may still remain the most important policy-making unit. In return, like all decision-making entities within an oligopolistic environment, they acquire control over developments which extend well beyond their frontiers.

Economic nationalism is still strong precisely because international safeguards against the harmful effects of global integration and interdependence are so weak. The main reason for this is, of course, political. It lies in the failure of most nation states – or more accurately, the dominant interests within them – to come to terms with a world in which, largely as a result of their own actions, developments over the past three decades have altered significantly their ability to influence in isolation the course of events in their own countries.

The creation of adequate safeguards against the undesirable consequences of international economic integration is essential for more than the survival of a multilateral system of trade and payments. Given the close connection in all human societies between economic and political developments, and between these developments and wars, there is a serious risk that the longer global economic conflicts of interest remain unresolved the more likely they are to escalate into civil wars, or even a global military conflict.[13] As pointed out in Chapter 9, many contemporary observers drew attention to a close correlation between severe economic deflations and revolutions in the interwar periods.[14] The architects of the Bretton Woods System in the 1940s were equally convinced that it was the failure of the international community to co-operate during the preceding two decades that led to the Second World War.[15]

The speed with which the national institutional frameworks can be adapted to manage the international economy may well determine, therefore, much more than the future prosperity of mankind. Managed carefully, and for the benefit of all concerned, international economic integration can enhance greatly the welfare of mankind; mismanaged, in the pursuit of narrow self-interest, if may easily put at risk its very existence.

In case this conclusion appears to be unnecessarily gloomy and dramatic, it is worth remembering that the disintegration of an international system caused by inappropriate forms of economic and political organisation is nothing new. There is sufficient archaeological evidence to indicate that conflicts between continuously increasing economic specialisation and integration and an institutional framework resistant to change have been the main reason for the collapse of many early states and civilisations.[16] If these relatively simple agricultural civilisations declined and disintegrated because they could not evolve institutions capable of coping with constant change, what is there to prevent the highly complex industrial civilisation evolved over the last two centuries from coming to a similar end for exactly the same reason? The framework of economic objectives, policies and institutional arrangements considered in this book provides probably the minimum requirement for avoiding such an outcome.

Notes and References

Part I International Economic Integration

1. Roberts (1980, p. 919).
2. 'In the sense of *combining separate economies* into larger economic regions the word integration has a very short history ... It has not been used anywhere in the old, chiefly historical, literature on the economic amalgamation of the nation state, nor in the literature on customs unions, including the *Zollverein*, nor in the literature on international trade before the 1940s. No subject index of any book that I know on international economics prior to 1953 contains the entry "integration"' (Machlup, 1977, p. 3. The emphasis is in the original).

1 The Process of International Economic Integration

1. Seers and Vaitsos (1980, p. 2).
2. Ibid.
3. The concepts are applicable, of course, at all levels of economic activity: sectoral, regional, national and international.
4. Observing the very limited success which the USSR and its East European allies have had in the attempt to integrate their economies, Brabant (1980, p. 6) makes the obvious, yet frequently ignored, point that: 'It is certainly not an inevitable sequence of events that the acceptance of a political document on integration with that name will almost automatically entail the emergence of the relevant economic processes.'
5. Balassa's definition of economic integration which is often quoted in the literature is, therefore, quite inadequate. According to him, 'as a process, it encompasses measures designed to abolish discrimination between economic units belonging to different national states; viewed as a state of affairs, it can be represented by the absence of various forms of discrimination between national economies' (Balassa, 1962, p. 1). A little later, Balassa links economic integration with trade liberalisation in even stronger terms: 'The removal of trade barriers in a free trade area, for example, is an act of economic integration' (ibid., p. 2n). Not necessarily! As argued above, it is simply 'an act' of opening up the economy, which may or may not lead to integration!
6. The Council for Mutual Economic Assistance comprising the USSR and its East European allies, better known as 'Comecon'.
7. See the relevant chapters in El-Agraa (1982).
8. Consideration of the national interest will normally make governments act with a good deal of caution when liberalising their commercial policies. It is for this reason that, as the CMEA ('Comecon') experience shows, international economic integration will proceed very slowly when it is controlled tightly from the centre. (See, for instance, Brabant 1980, Schiavone 1981 and Lavigne 1975 for a discussion of the CMEA

problems.) Disagreements about resource allocation are also likely to be frequent, as all of them may want to introduce certain new industries, or refuse to contract those which they had developed at considerable cost behind protective barriers. Cf. Berend (1971), El-Agraa (1982).

9. According to one student of economic developments in the EEC, US transnationals have contributed more to the rapid economic integration of the member states than have their own firms (Pelkmans 1983, p. 18).
10. As a closed economy is not exposed to continuous shocks and changes from the outside, its rate of economic progress will be dictated by its own inventiveness and institutional adaptability. An open economy will be in a similar position *only* if it is one of the pace-setters, in other words, one of the countries which generate changes in tastes, products and production techniques to be followed by the rest of the world. Otherwise, its economic welfare (employment and incomes) will be influenced significantly, for reasons to be discussed in later chapters, by the rate at which it absorbs, relative to the rest of the world, technical and institutional advances made in other countries.
11. In other words, the attitudes and patterns of behaviour which Duesenberry (1949) observed and analysed within the United States, become increasingly apparent on a global scale.
12. The importance of this relationship is discussed in some detail in Panić (1978).
13. Panić (1976), Hirsch and Goldthorpe (1978), Courchene (1980).
14. See Wright (1984) for a description of the British experience since the end of the nineteenth century.
15. Cf. Kuznets (1966, pp. 311 and 315).
16. Lewis (1955) provides an excellent analysis of these factors.
17. Even at the end of the 1960s, a decade in which so much was done to liberalise international trade, the degree of protection was greater and, consequently, the extent of international specialisation was smaller in standardised goods than in either primary or differentiated products. Cf. Hufbauer and Chilas (1974).
18. Cf. Bairoch (1976a), Maizels (1963), Kuznets (1967), Green and Urquhart (1976).
19. Hirschman (1945, p. 146).
20. Robertson (1938).
21. Hicks (1953).
22. Mundell (1957).
23. It is for this reason that a large country with high per capita incomes will often tend to adopt such technical advances originating abroad much more quickly than the nations which have made them.
24. As Dunning (1983) shows, this has been the case throughout this century, the period for which reasonably comparable data are available.
25. See Linder (1961).
26. Cf. Chandler (1977), Scherer (1980). Increasing returns to scale can be observed in most modern activities, though the scope for achieving them varies, often significantly, between different industries. See Pratten (1971).

27. See, for instance, Krugman (1980) and Lancaster (1980).
28. As Marshall pointed out, external economies consist of 'the many various economies of specialised skill and specialised machinery, of localised industries and production on a large scale', the 'increased facilities of communication of all kinds', trading expertise and so on (Marshall [1920] 1956, pp. 267 and 365–6).

2 International Economic Integration and Interdependence

1. Cf. Dornbusch and Krugman (1976), OECD (1973). Both studies show export prices to be determined much more by domestic costs than by competitors' prices, which is exactly what one would expect in a world of heterogeneous goods and services.
2. See, for instance, Kravis and Lipsey (1971, 1978), Isard (1977).
3. Surveys of the relevant literature are provided by, among others, Aliber (1978), Argy (1981) and Llewellyn (1980).
4. Kuznets (1966, p. 302).
5. See also Kuznets (1964 and 1966).
6. Maizels (1963) includes an analysis of the characteristics of small countries' trade.
7. The very high averages for Group III in the upper part of the table and Group V in the lower part are the result of Belgium's exceptionally high trade ratio for 1979. Incidentally, of the countries included in Table 2.1 two – Libya and Saudi Arabia – are excluded because of the lack of comparable data.
8. Page (1979, p. 166).
9. Ibid. See also the table on p. 169.
10. Kuznets (1964, p. 56).
11. The group of centrally planned economies in Table 2.4 includes USSR, Bulgaria, Czechoslovakia, East Germany, Hungary, Poland and Rumania.
12. The table refers only to trade in goods. However, if similar data were available for services they would no doubt show very much the same picture, as this type of trade also tends to be determined predominantly by the level of economic development. Cf. Sapir and Lutz (1981). For an analysis of the difficulties which developing countries are experiencing in developing trade among themselves and their dependence on industrial countries see Havrylyshyn and Wolf (1981).
13. See Fortune (1972) on the important role which income equalisation plays in the growth of trade.
14. Grubel and Lloyd (1975), Aquino (1978), Giersch (1979). See also Balassa (1986) for an attempt to quantify the relative importance of a number of factors in the development of intra-industry trade.
15. Aquino (1978).
16. Cf. Kuznets (1964), Aquino (1978). It inevitably takes some time before developing countries reach the level of industrialisation which enables them to specialise in a wide range of products and production methods. At the same time, inter-industry trade may remain impor-

tant for those industrial countries, such as Canada and Norway, which are rich in certain natural resources.

17. See, for instance, Scherer (1980), Prais (1976). The changes in industrial, national and international forms of organisation caused by technical advances are discussed in Part V.
18. Cf. Aquino (1978), Grubel and Lloyd (1975).
19. Kuznets (1966). Sen (1984) contains a survey of the relevant empirical literature as well as an analysis of the reasons for these similarities.
20. See, for instance, Pryor (1972) and Hughes (1976).
21. According to Dunning (1981a, p. 436): 'intra-industry and intra-firm direct investment tends to be greatest in the sectors in which [transnational corporations] possess the type of ownership advantages which is best exploited internally rather than by way of licensing, management contracts, franchise and technical service agreements etc'. He also found evidence that 'patterns of direct investment may lag those of trade' (ibid., p. 434).
22. Cf. Stopford, Dunning and Haberich (1980), United Nations (1978 and 1981), Stopford and Dunning (1983).
23. See, for instance, Frobel, Heinrichs and Kreye (1980). There is certainly evidence that the industries in which transnationals are active show not only the highest levels of intra-industry international direct investment and trade but also the highest levels of intra-firm trade. Cf. Dunning and Pearce (1981), Dunning (1981a) and, particularly, Casson and Associates (1986).
24. Lack of relevant information makes it impossible to do more than speculate about this at the moment. Nevertheless, there is a fairly strong possibility that international integration in recent decades has been accompanied by a certain amount of economic disintegration within countries, as transnationals have altered the spatial distribution of their activities within and between countries.
25. Compare, for instance, indicators of the extent of intra-industry trade in different industries estimated by Grubel and Lloyd (1975) and Aquino (1978) with the data on intra-firm trade in Helleiner (1981) and Casson and Associates (1986).
26. Batchelor, Major and Morgan (1980, pp. 90–91).
27. Quoted in United Nations (1985, p. 117).
28. Dunning and Pearce (1981, p. 132). See also Sen (1984, pp. 233–40) for a survey of the evidence on the importance of intra-firm trade in a number of countries.
29. Cf. United Nations (1985, pp. 117–18).
30. Quoted in Sen (1984, p. 236).
31. Cf. Helleiner (1981, p. 28) from which this and the other figures in the paragraph were taken.
32. Ibid., p. 34.
33. See Panić and Joyce (1980) and Panić (1982) for an analysis of certain aspects of the UK's experience in this respect.
34. Goldsmith (1969). Furthermore, with the exception of centrally planned economies, long-term financial developments in different countries follow broadly similar lines (Goldsmith, 1966). This finding is

similar to the one made by Kuznets (1966), which showed the growing long-term similarity of different countries' industrial structures.

35. Kenen (1976, p. 20).
36. Ibid.
37. Whitman (1969).
38. See, however, World Bank (1985, p. 60) for estimates of the importance of foreign credit in total credits of a number of developing countries. See also Goldsmith (1966).
39. OECD (1982a, p. 8).
40. Cooper (1968), Mills (1976), Walter (1985).
41. Hawkins (1972).
42. Cf. Kuznets (1966).
43. Goldsmith (1969).
44. Bloomfield (1968), World Bank (1985).
45. See Grubel (1979), Dunning (1981a).
46. Goldsmith (1969).
47. Ibid, p. 399.
48. Larsen, Llewellyn and Potter (1983, pp. 49–50).
49. Ibid., Hickman and Schleicher (1978), Fair (1982).
50. Larsen, Llewellyn and Potter (1983, p. 68). This means, as the authors point out, that 'the model's properties could be inappropriate in simulation conditions approaching full capacity utilisation' (ibid.).
51. See also Cline and Associates (1981).
52. Cf. Goldstein and Khan (1982).
53. Ibid.
54. The OECD model of financial 'linkages' and exchange rates is described in some detail in Holtham (1984).
55. Larsen, Llewellyn and Potter (1983, p. 66).
56. This point is emphasised in Hickman and Schleicher (1978).

Part II The Nature, Causes and Elimination of International Economic Instability

3 The Concept of Fundamental Equilibrium

1. See, for instance, Kindleberger (1969), Veil (1975) and Thirlwall (1980).
2. The concern with financing external imbalances would also disappear if the whole world started to use a common currency. There would be no balance of payments problems in this case, though the adjustment problems would remain. Global monetary union would still raise, therefore, a number of important policy issues in the international economy. These are discussed in Part V.
3. Cooper (1966, p. 384).
4. See Hodjera (1969) and Veil (1975) for comparisons of the relative stability of different measures of the balance of payments.
5. Thirlwall (1980, p. 10).
6. Veil (1975) and IMF (1977).
7. See Nurkse (1947) and, especially, Meade (1951) for a discussion of the

need to reconcile internal and external balances, even though their definitions are not exactly the same as that given here.

8. It is far from easy to establish whether an economy is in fundamental equilibrium or not; and it certainly cannot be done on the basis of its performance over one or two years. The judgement can be formed only after examining the relevant data covering at least one full cycle in order to take into account cyclical and seasonal factors, both in the economy and in the rest of the world. Otherwise, it is easy to confuse temporary developments for underlying, fundamental, strengths and weaknesses, and vice versa.
9. Solomon (1982, p. 12).
10. This is, of course, Harrod's 'natural rate of growth' (Harrod, 1948). The term seems, however, much less appropriate than the one used in the text, as there is nothing 'natural' either in the long-term growth of labour or in the rate and character of technical progress.
11. Nurkse (1947), Meade (1951).
12. Machlup (1958).
13. Machlup (1973, p. 189).
14. Ibid.

4 Short-term, or Cyclical, Disequilibria

1. The exact magnitude of the impact will depend on the respective sizes of the two countries. This qualification will be ignored, however, in the analysis that follows because it does not alter the conclusion.
2. The analysis in the remainder of this section represents a geometric illustration of the multiplier process with foreign trade repercussions. Algebraic derivations of equilibrium under these conditions are available in every modern textbook on international trade.
3. Two options are open to *B* here. First, it can devalue its currency. If the relevant trade elasticities are high enough, this will reduce its imports and increase its exports, helping to restore the internal and external balances. But this would exacerbate the economic contraction in *A*, as its exports would fall and imports rise. Anticipating this, it is very likely that *A* would also devalue its currency in order to re-establish the initial parity. There has been no change, after all, in *A*'s policy objectives: its recession and external surplus are unanticipated, not planned. With *A*'s devaluation, the two countries would be back where they started, with the problem which prompted *B*'s action still unresolved. In addition – and this could be very serious – the exchange rate changes would almost certainly destroy confidence in the existing international financial order based on fixed parities. The result would be constant flights of capital between *A* and *B* (for precautionary and speculative reasons) in response to purely temporary changes either in actual economic developments and policies or in expectation of such developments. Second, *B* could impose import controls. However, as this would increase deflationary tendencies in *A*, it would almost certainly retaliate again. The result would be a reduction in the international division of labour, forcing both countries to restructure their economies accor-

dingly. A short-term, cyclical, problem would be turned, in this case, into a long-term, structural, one of the kind analysed in the next chapter. That is why a prompt action by *A* is essential here to reconcile internal and external balances in *both* countries.

4. See, for instance, estimates of the relevant elasticities in Magee (1975), and Artus and Young (1979).

5 Fundamental, or Structural, Disequilibria

1. The term 'structure' is used here, and in the rest of this book, to mean the 'composition' (in other words, a given distribution) of factor inputs and outputs at a point of time; and 'structural change' to denote permanent alternations in such distributions over a period.
2. This is an analytical simplification. There may be many standardised products with income elasticities of demand greater than unity. The important point is that these elasticities will normally be lower than income elasticities of demand for new or improved products ('luxuries'); and that the predominance of one or other group in the structure of production and trade of open economies may, *ceteris paribus*, affect the rate of its long-term development. The assumption in the text (that one group has income elasticity of demand greater than unity while the other group's elasticity is lower than unity) helps to explain one of the main reasons why some countries experience fundamental disequilibria under certain conditions.
3. Rostow (1960).
4. The recent experience of some of the small oil-rich countries (Saudi Arabia and Kuwait) is quite exceptional. Although apparently running structural surpluses they obviously have little in common with the countries described here. The importance of this for eliminating fundamental disequilibria will be discussed in Part IV.
5. The only important exception to this will be a structural surplus country which is losing the capacity for continuous advance and change so that it is on the way to becoming a declining economy. The long-term development of structural deficit countries will represent, therefore, a potential threat, as it is likely to make the economy even less competitive internationally. However, a country in this position has really ceased to be a genuine surplus country and, consequently, should not be included in the group considered here.

6 The Long-term Adjustment Process: Major Policy Options

1. The *status quo* policy option is normally advocated by those who confuse long-term adjustment problems with those of short-term correction or stabilisation by concentrating on a country's external balance – ignoring in the process both its activity and employment levels, as well as developments in the rest of the world. This particular analytical approach makes sense only in the case, described in Chapter 4, of a small country experiencing short-term disequilibria. It has nothing to do, therefore, with the long-term, fundamental disequilibria

experienced by interdependent economies.

2. This tendency can be observed clearly within countries, as there are no institutional obstacles to factor movements between regions. See, for instance, Borts and Stein (1964).
3. Cf. International Monetary Fund (1944), Article IV, Section 5A. The Article actually recommends 'devaluation' – a step reduction in the value of one currency relative to others – under the system of fixed exchange rates. Devaluation tends to be generally regarded now as a less effective policy instrument in the adjustment process than currency depreciation under floating rates. There are two main reasons for this. Devaluation may be delayed for too long, increasing adjustment problems; and, when it does eventually take place, it may be inadequate to solve the problems which have accumulated through the delay. See, for instance, Friedman (1953) and Meade (1955).
4. Currency appreciation (or revaluation) is expected to produce exactly the opposite results.
5. For a more detailed analysis, see Johnson (1958 and 1972), Corden (1977 and 1982), Artus and Young (1979) and McKinnon (1981).
6. The origin and magnitude of these problems are discussed in Part IV.
7. In a highly specialised international economy very few countries are so 'small' that changes in their competitiveness will remain unnoticed by their trading partners. For instance, small industrial countries often account for a large share of world trade in certain manufactured goods even though their overall share of world trade in manufactures is less than 3 per cent. Cf. Panić and Rajan (1971).
8. See Brown, Enoch and Mortimer-Lee (1980) for a survey of the relevant literature.
9. Cf. Goldsbrough (1981).
10. Exchange rate depreciation tends to give rise in the short run to a deterioration in the current balance of payments. Cf. Spitaller (1980).
11. The fear of exchange rate losses also appears to cause transnationals to overreact frequently. Cf. Robbins and Stobaugh (1973). Given the vast resources at their disposal, this would explain the apparent tendency of exchange rates to 'overshoot' – that is, to move much further in a particular direction than seems to be necessary according to the available information.
12. This is why so often 'when the current account gets bad the capital account gets worse' (Dornbusch 1980, p. 173).
13. The volume and instability of international capital flows will increase under the regime of floating exchange rates unless countries synchronise their macro-economic policies. See Bryant (1980).
14. The interwar experience showed clearly that international financial markets would tend to be very sceptical of the proposition that exchange rate changes could produce lasting adjustments in an economy. Cf. Nurkse (1944).
15. This is particularly true of quantitative controls. Tariffs may not be as effective. If they are not indexed and the domestic rate of inflation is more rapid than inflation in other countries, the original level of protection which they offer can quickly be eroded.

16. These and other aspects of protection are analysed in considerable detail by Corden (1971 and 1974).
17. A country may now also be prevented from imposing administrative controls by its membership of GATT, or a trading block such as the European Economic Community. This need not prevent it, however, from resorting to restrictive measures which are not covered by GATT regulations, such as the so-called 'voluntary export controls'. This explains, in fact, why such measures, rather than administrative protection, have been on the increase since the early 1970s.
18. Bhagwati (1974).
19. See, for instance, Armstrong and Taylor (1978).
20. Cf. Committee on the International Migration of Talent (1970).
21. Pearce (1976).
22. The inability to do so may arise if the countries' capital markets are insufficiently developed to perform their function internationally. Kindleberger (1981) offered this as one of the explanations for West Germany's tendency to have persistent surpluses on its basic balance of payments in the 1960s and early 1970s.
23. In practice, this is not, strictly speaking, correct. The adoption of advances in production techniques and organisation by developing countries is unlikely to get very far without some movement of skilled labour from *S* to *D*. For centuries, this has been an important factor in the development of new industries (cf. Rapp, 1975). In fact, even declining economies may find, when they try to restructure and modernise their industries, that they are short of people possessing the latest technical and organisational skills. Complaints of this kind are common in the United Kingdom.
24. See, for instance, Ingram (1956 and 1957) and Meier (1953).
25. Dunning (1981b) discusses at some length the relationship between different stages of development and international capital flows.
26. World Bank (1985, p. 47) contains a brief description of the international debt cycle hypothesis.
27. This adjustment process assumes that *S* retain their capacity to adapt to technical and other developments. The assumption is important because, under dynamic conditions, a rapid transformation in *D* combined with no changes in *S* would eventually reverse their positions: *D* would start earning structural surpluses and *S* would (as relatively declining economies) become structural deficit countries.
28. Hartland (1949) provides both an interesting and instructive analysis of the role played by public funds in the inter-state adjustment process within the United States.

Part III Phases in International Economic Integration since the 1820s

7 The Doctrine of Free Trade: Internationalism or Disguised Mercantilism?

1. Schumpeter (1963, p. 517).
2. List ([1841] 1885, p. 178). Hamilton had made the same point at the end of the eighteenth century. Cf. Hamilton ([1791] 1934, p. 238).

3. Schumpeter (1963, p. 351n).
4. Smith ([1776] 1937, pp. 437–38).
5. Schumpeter (1963), Heckscher (1955) and Spengler (1960).
6. Smith ([1776] 1937, p. 435).
7. Ibid., pp. 436–37.
8. Ibid., p. 435.
9. Ibid., pp. 435–36.
10. Ricardo ([1822] 1951a, p. 263).
11. Ibid., p. 264.
12. Mill ([1848) 1965, p. 594).
13. It can be shown that, even within the basic analytical framework adopted by the classical and neo-classical economists, in the absence of solidarity and co-operation special interests would benefit from exploiting their advantages. A country enjoying the position of a monopolist or monopsonist would benefit from protection even if other countries retaliated. The proposition made by Bickerdike (1906) was rediscovered by Lerner (1934) and elaborated subsequently by a number of economists.
14. Cf. Heckscher (1955) and Spengler (1960).
15. List ([1841] 1885).
16. Keynes ([1933] 1982).
17. Smith ([1776] 1937, p. 431).
18. Ibid., pp. 430–31.
19. Ibid., p. 429.
20. Brebner (1962, p. 260).
21. Ibid., p. 252.
22. Mill ([1848] 1965, p. 918).
23. Ibid., p. 919.
24. See Hamilton ([1791] 1934).
25. List ([1841] 1885).
26. Marshall (1923, p. 761).
27. Ibid, p. 762.
28. Cf. Lipsey and Lancaster (1956), Haberler (1950) and Ozga (1955).
29. Hume ([1752] 1969).
30. Mill ([1848] 1965, p. 504).
31. Quoted in Wilson (1949, p. 154).
32. Cf. Wilson (1949 and 1951) and Wallerstein (1980).
33. Keynes (1936, pp. 348–49).
34. Cf. Wilson (1949), Spengler (1960), Kenwood and Lougheed (1971).
35. Cf. Kuznets (1965, 1966) and Bairoch (1976a).
36. Heckscher ([1919] 1949) and Ohlin (1933).
37. Cf. Kuznets (1965, 1966).
38. Lydall (1979).
39. Heckscher ([1919] 1949, p. 291).
40. Myrdal (1956 and 1957).
41. Robbins (1952, pp. 10–11).
42. Smith ([1776] 1937, p. 352).
43. Marshall ([1920] 1956, p. 633).
44. Marshall (1923, p. 760).

45. Ibid.
46. See also Semmell (1970).
47. Jeremy (1977).
48. Smith ([1776] 1937, p. 625).
49. Ibid., p. 346.
50. Ibid., p. 347.
51. Ibid., p. 346.
52. Ricardo ([1817] 1951b, pp. 136–37). Italics are not in the original.
53. Ricardo ([1810–11] 1951c, p. 274). Almost a century later, Joseph Chamberlain employed exactly the same argument in advocating protection. Free trade would lead to industrial decline in Britain, which would affect differently the manufacturers (who could live on income from their investments abroad) and the workers (who did not have such a source of income). See Kaldor (1978, p. 236).
54. Mill ([1848] 1965, p. 746).
55. Ibid., p. 749.
56. Marshall ([1903] 1926, p. 408).
57. Marshall (1923, p. 4).
58. Ibid., p. 5.
59. Harrod (1972, p. 397).
60. See Keynes ([1924] 1981a).
61. Keynes ([1931] 1981b).
62. Keynes (1936).
63. Sideri (1970). Compare his findings with the analysis in Ricardo ([1817] 1951b, ch. VII).
64. Schumpeter (1963, p. 376).
65. Wilson (1949, p. 161).

8 Changes in International Competitiveness and National Commercial Policies

1. Keynes (1936, p. 383).
2. Quoted in Semmell (1970, p. 207).
3. Schumpeter (1963, pp. 370–76).
4. Machlup (1977, pp. 106–108).
5. Kenwood and Lougheed (1971, pp. 74–6).
6. Kindleberger (1978a, p. 58).
7. Ibid.
8. See, for instance, Pollard (1981, ch. 7).
9. Similar considerations also forced President Roosevelt to abandon the *laissez-faire* policies on which he had been elected in 1932. Cf. Dalton (1974).
10. Quoted in Gerschenkron (1966a, pp. 65–6).
11. Helleiner (1973).
12. Pincus (1977).
13. Capie (1983a).
14. As explained earlier, the flow of long-term capital from surplus to deficit countries will not remove the latter's need to restrict imports in order to develop new industries and contract the old ones at a socially

acceptable rate. But they will reduce the countries' need to impose additional barriers to trade in order to economise on the very limited reserves of foreign exchange.

15. International comparisons of per capita incomes give rise to many difficulties of their own, especially the estimates of incomes in less developed countries or for earlier periods in history. Cf. Bairoch (1976b), Kravis, Heston and Summers (1978) and Maddison (1982).
16. See Capie (1983a).
17. Cf. Balassa (1965). The same is true also of the rankings of individual industries within a country, particularly at broader levels of aggregation. See Guisinger and Schydlowsky (1971).
18. Bloomfield (1959, pp. 58–9).
19. The United States moved into a surplus at the beginning of this century. Cf. Mitchell (1983).
20. Page (1979, p. 166).
21. Rostow (1978, p. 51).
22. Cain and Hopkins (1980, pp. 467 and 472).
23. Ibid., p. 473. Britain's import duties increased throughout the first quarter of the ninteenth century, reaching the peak in the first half of the 1820s. Cf. Imlah (1958, pp. 121 and 160).
24. Cain and Hopkins (1980, p. 465).
25. Cf. Davis (1979).
26. Cain and Hopkins (1980, p. 477). See also Kindleberger (1978, pp. 50–1). The suggestion that the cost to Britain of free trade in terms of lost output indicates that the policy was magnanimous rather than the deliberate pursuit of a goal that the manufacturers believed to be in *their* long-term interest (McCloskey 1980) confuses the actual outcome with the one intended by British businessmen and politicans.
27. Capie (1983a, p. 24). See also Bairoch (1976a, pp. 172 and 174), Maizels (1963).
28. Cf. Imlah (1958, p. 166).
29. Cain and Hopkins (1980, p. 484).
30. Maddison (1982).
31. Cain and Hopkins (1980, p. 485).
32. See, for instance, Capie (1983b).
33. Cf. Balassa (1967).
34. Cf. Page (1979), OECD (1985).
35. Rostow (1978, p. 51).
36. Bairoch (1976b).
37. Ibid., Rostow (1980).
38. Perkins (1981).
39. Bairoch (1976a, p. 139).
40. Borchardt (1973).
41. Mitchell (1975, p. 801).
42. Sen (1984, p. 171).
43. Borchardt (1973).
44. Mitchell (1975), Green and Urquhart (1976), Bairoch (1976a).
45. Borchardt (1973), Webb (1980).
46. Pollard (1981, p. 262).

47. Glismann and Weiss (1980).
48. Maddison (1982, pp. 174 and 206).
49. Glismann and Weiss (1980).
50. Kindleberger (1984, p. 369).
51. Maddison (1982, pp. 174 and 206).
52. Glisman and Weis (1980), Pollard (1981, p. 302).
53. Glisman and Weiss (1980).
54. Maizels (1963, p. 141), Morgan (1971).
55. Studies of changes in the US commercial policy over the past century reveal similar underlying attitudes and trends (cf. Hawke 1975, Anderson 1972). The early Japanese experience was, for various reasons, rather different. However, they have also exercised a good deal of control over their trade and capital flows since the interwar period (Ozaki, 1972). The relaxations over the last two decades have come, partly, as a result of the extraordinary success and growing confidence of Japanese industry and, partly, in response to strong international pressure.

9 Historical Parallels in the Evolution of International Economic Relationships

1. There is, of course, nothing new in this. The nature of mercantilist policies varied from country to country according to the severity of its economic problems and changes in world economic and political developments. Cf. Spengler (1960).
2. Different phases in the world economic development are discussed in Bairoch (1976a), Rostow (1978) and Maddison (1982). Commercial policies during this period are described in Bairoch (1976a), Kenwood and Lougheed (1971) and Pollard (1981). OECD (1985) provides a detailed analysis of the more recent changes.
3. Kenwood and Lougheed (1971, p. 80).
4. See, for instance, Gourevitch (1977).
5. Pollard (1981).
6. Capie (1983a).
7. Kenwood and Lougheed (1971), Bairoch (1976a), Capie (1983a).
8. Grassman (1980) obtained a declining share of trade to total output (at current prices) for most of this period, for almost all the countries in his sample. However, these results differ from those at constant prices (cf. Capie 1983a) which, like Table 9.1, show an increase in overall economic integration over the period. The discrepancy implies that prices of tradeables declined more rapidly during this period than those of non-tradeables.
9. Maizels (1963, p. 80).
10. Textiles and clothing were still by far the most important commodity group in international trade before the First World War. Cf. Maizels (1963, p. 163).
11. Cf. League of Nations (1927), Pollard (1981).
12. See League of Nations (1943), Nurkse (1944), Lewis (1949) and Kindleberger (1973).

13. Henderson (1955, p. 291).
14. Cf. Anderson (1972).
15. Maizels (1963, p. 141).
16. OECD (1985).
17. Cf. Lewis (1952), Rostow (1978 and 1985), Spraos (1980).
18. Cf. Mitchell (1975 and 1983) and Maddison (1982).
19. See Rostow (1978, 1980 and 1985) and Pollard (1981).
20. Supple (1973), Kindleberger (1978a), Lewis (1978a), Pollard (1981) and Gerschenkron (1966b).
21. Rostow (1978 and 1980).
22. Cf. Landes (1969), Lilley (1973) and Maddison (1982).
23. Bairoch (1976a) and Rostow (1980).
24. Kenwood and Lougheed (1971, p. 210).
25. United Nations (1979, p. 1).
26. Lewis (1978a, p. 14).
27. United Nations (1979, p. 5).
28. See, for example, Bairoch (1976a, p. 113).
29. Cf. United Nations (1979). The benefits may have been offset to some extent, however, by the increasingly selective way in which foreign labour was admitted into industrial countries. A high proportion of the immigrants have been young and with various occupational skills.
30. Cf. OECD (1983a).
31. These data are normally difficult to compile so that most of the time they are neither readily available nor very reliable. In many cases, the figures include, because of the lack of data and the problem of separating different types of capital flows, short-term capital movements.
32. Berrill (1963).
33. Pollard (1981, p. 221).
34. Bloomfield (1968).
35. Berrill (1963, p. 287).
36. Cf. Bairoch (1976a, ch. V).
37. Cf. Nurkse (1944), Kindleberger (1973), Kenwood and Lougheed (1971).
38. Contemporary writers had little doubt about the close relationship between deflation and revolution. See de Cecco (1985, p. 64n) for some relevant references.
39. Triffin (1964).
40. This fact has received a good deal of attention in recent years, notably from Kindleberger. (See Kindleberger 1978b, Kindleberger and Laffargue 1982.) However, as Moggridge (1982) has pointed out, an international arrangement of this kind, though important, is quite inadequate on its own to deal with major disturbances to the global economic system, such as those which took place in the period 1914 to 1950.
41. See Bloomfield (1963), Triffin (1964), Argy (1981), Grubel (1984), Solomon (1982).
42. See, for instance, Saul (1960) and Argy (1981).
43. Cf. Kindleberger (1984).

44. Kenwood and Lougheed (1971, ch. 6).
45. Cf. Maddison (1982, p. 91).
46. See Nurkse (1944), Kindleberger (1973), Kenwood and Lougheed (1971), Pollard (1981).
47. Gardner (1975, 1980).
48. The United Kingdom is one of the few European countries which have escaped the more violent forms of discontent so common over the last two centuries. Nevertheless, even there: 'The wave of strikes for higher wages in 1825, the peak years of the Chartist movement in 1839–42 and 1847–8, the rioting which accompanied the passing of the Second Reform Act of 1867, and the strikes, demonstrations and unrest of the immediate pre-war [1914–18] years are all, in part at least, a consequence of [adverse movements in real incomes of] the working classes' (Burnett 1969, p. 205). This was also the main reason for outbursts of discontent which the country experienced in the 1920s and 1970s.
49. Ford (1962), Bloomfield (1963), Scammell (1965), Triffin (1968).

10 Long-term Changes in International Openness and Income Inequality

1. Bairoch (1981, p. 8). See also Bairoch (1976b), Kuznets (1965 and 1966) and Rostow (1980).
2. These figures have been calculated from the estimates of per capita income given in Summers and Heston (1984).
3. Cf. Bairoch (1976b), Maddison (1982).
4. Bairoch (1981), p. 11).
5. Cf. World Bank (1986, pp. 45 and 154).
6. Ibid.
7. See, for instance, Rostow (1980, p. 288–93).
8. Pollard (1981), pp. 270–71).

Part IV The Long-term Consequences of the Energy Crisis

1. Griffin and Teece (1982, p. 213).
2. Enoch and Panić (1981).
3. See Cooper (1968) and Allen (1976) for a definition of 'international domain'.

11 Origins of the Energy Crisis

1. This is even more true of developing countries where oil 'provides nearly 65% of commercial energy supplies... Coal is used to a considerable extent only in India and Korea which have indigenous supplies' (International Energy Agency 1982, p. 154).
2. 'The period 1960 to 1973 marked a substantial change in the environment facing OPEC... Gradually, there was a shift from a market characterised by oversupply to one characterised by excess demand with virtual disappearance of excess productive capacity outside the OPEC countries' Griffin and Teece (1982, p. 6).

3. See, for instance, Bhagwati (1977) and Independent Commission on International Development Issues (1980). (The latter work is much better known as 'The Brandt Report'.)
4. Gately (1984, p. 1113).
5. Quoted in Moran (1982, p. 113).
6. Ibid., pp. 116–17.
7. Griffin and Teece (1982, p. 4).
8. Ibid.
9. See, for instance, Odell (1981 and 1985). The actual size of the world's oil reserves is of little economic significance if analysed in isolation. Its importance can be assessed only if it is related to the growth of demand for oil (which depends on the composition and rate of expansion of world output) as well as to the other factors analysed in this chapter. Depending on the assumptions which one makes about each of these factors, the conventional oil reserves could either last well into the next century or disappear within the next few decades. A number of alternative possibilities are examined in Energy Modelling Forum (1982).
10. Cf. International Energy Agency (1982 and 1986). See also Gately (1984).
11. Griffin and Teece (1982) contains both optimistic and pessimistic assessments of the world's energy prospects.
12. International Energy Agency (1986, p. 84).
13. Amuzegar (1983, p. 93).
14. Ibid.
15. Ibid.
16. See, for instance, International Energy Agency (1986, pp. 105–15).
17. Ibid., p. 72.
18. OECD-Interfutures (1979, p. 26).
19. International Energy Agency (1982, pp. 65–6).
20. International Energy Agency (1986) provides the most up-to-date estimates of these changes.
21. Cf. Jenne and Cattell (1983).
22. International Energy Agency (1986, p. 83).
23. See, for instance, Moran (1982, p. 113).
24. International Energy Agency (1986, p. 67).
25. Gately (1984, p. 1105).
26. Cf. International Energy Agency (1985 and 1986).
27. This is why even the 'optimists' tend to warn against complacency. Cf. Griffin and Teece (1982, p. 219).
28. Pindyck (1982, p. 184). See also Pindyck (1981).

12 Economic Consequences of the Energy Constraint

1. See also Hicks (1977).
2. This is, basically, Harrod's 'natural rate of growth' (Harrod, 1948). For estimates of the growth of productive potential using this analytical framework see, for instance, Okun (1962), Godley and Shepherd (1964) and Black and Russell (1969).
3. Estimates of the growth of the US productive potential before and after the first oil shock show this quite clearly. Cf. Rasche and Tatom (1977).

4. This comes clearly out of the surveys of relevant literature such as those by Silberston (1970) and Blair (1972). See also Cowling (1983) and Sylos-Labini (1984).
5. Oil is, of course, only one of a number of primary sources of energy. Yet a sudden change of policy by the largest oil producers can have this effect in the short run for three reasons: oil accounts for over 50 per cent of the world's energy consumption, far ahead of any alternative source of energy; the elasticity of interfuel substitution is very low in the short run; and the efficiency with which energy is used can be improved significantly only in the long term as a result of technical changes.
6. See Goldthorpe (1984).
7. Olson (1982).
8. Cf. IMF (1984c). The IMF world totals do not include the USSR, most European centrally planned economies and Indonesia. Nevertheless, they give a fairly good indication of the extent to which OECD countries dominate world output and investment.
9. International Energy Agency (1986, p. 38). OECD share of total world demand for oil was 83.0 per cent in 1973, 79.4 per cent in 1979 and 75.0 per cent in 1984.
10. OECD (1982b).
11. Ibid.
12. See, for instance, Rostow (1985).
13. Cf. OECD (1970).
14. Cf. International Energy Agency (1986, pp. 150–57).
15. Ibid., p. 38.
16. Ibid., p. 139.
17. OECD (1979a, p. 62). In 1979 2mbpd was equivalent to an 8 per cent shortfall in OECD oil imports and a 5 per cent shortfall in oil supply.
18. Larsen and Llewellyn (1983, p. 5). See also OECD (1986, pp. 164–65).
19. See IMF (1984c and 1986) for recent estimates of current account balances of East European countries and the USSR.
20. Cf. World Bank (1985, p. 148).
21. Cf. the March and September issues of the *Institutional Investor*.
22. For reasons to be analysed in Part V, a removal of the energy constraint would not, on its own, be sufficient to guarantee a rapid and sustainable growth of the world economy. But it would make an important contribution towards achieving this end.
23. Amuzegar (1983, pp. 9–10).

13 Financial Effects of the Energy Crisis

1. Hicks (1979, p. 94).
2. See Amuzegar (1983).
3. Cf. IMF (1982b, p. 165) and World Bank (1985, p. 89).
4. Amuzegar (1983, pp. 70–1).
5. Watson, Keller and Mathieson (1984, p. 50).
6. Cf. World Bank (1985, pp. 4 and 21).
7. Group of Thirty (1984, p. 21).
8. Ibid., p. 39.

9. Andrews (1984, p. 38).
10. IMF (1984d). See also Argy (1981).
11. There were also substantial flights of capital from some developing countries, including several (Venezuela, Argentina and Mexico) with heavy external debts. Cf. World Bank (1985, p. 64).
12. This was certainly true of the first decade of this century (Bloomfield, 1963); and even more so of the interwar period (Nurkse, 1944).
13. Dennis (1984, p. 138).
14. Bank for International Settlements (1985, p. 110).
15. Dennis (1984, pp. 140–41) and Watson, Keller and Mathieson (1984, p. 37).
16. Dennis (1984, p. 142).
17. Cf. Dennis (1984, p. 177) and Watson, Keller and Mathieson (1984, p. 37).
18. See, for instance, Dufey and Giddy (1981) and Bank for International Settlements (1986).
19. Dennis (1984, pp. 160 and 178).
20. Dennis (1984, p. 164) and Watson, Keller and Mathieson (1984, p. 7).
21. Dennis (1984, p. 194).
22. Ibid.
23. World Bank (1985, p. 79).
24. Ibid.
25. Ibid.
26. Ibid., p. 13.
27. Ibid.
28. Ibid., p. 4.
29. See Bond (1985) for an analysis of the syndicated credit market between 1972 and 1984.
30. World Bank (1985, pp. 118–19).
31. Ibid., p. 21.
32. Ibid., p. 155.
33. Dennis (1984, p. 179) and Bank for International Settlements (1985, p. 122).
34. Lewis (1978b, p. 34).
35. Ibid.
36. Kindleberger (1978b and 1985).
37. Cline (1984, pp. 8–9).
38. Llewellyn (1984, p. 54).
39. World Bank (1985, p. 42).
40. Cf. OECD (1979b) and Balassa, Barsony and Richards (1981).
41. Bank for International Settlements (1979, p. 178).
42. Cf. World Bank (1979) and OECD (1979b).
43. IMF (1981, p. 11).
44. World Bank (1985, pp. 55–6).
45. World Bank (1985, p. 55).
46. See, for instance, Cline (1984, ch. 2).
47. World Bank (1985, p. 4).

Part V The Main Prerequisites for a Stable International Economic System

1. Schumpeter (1963, p. 188).
2. Cipolla (1970, p. 13). He goes on to describe some of the consequences.

> When needs outstrip production capability, a number of tensions are bound to appear in the society. Inflation, excessive taxation, difficulties in the balance of payments are just a small sample of the whole series of possible tensions …[as]… the conflict among social groups becomes bitter because each group tries to avoid as much as possible the necessary economic sacrifices. As the struggle grows in bitterness, co-operation among people and social groups fades away, a sense of alienation from the commonwealth develops, and with it group and class selfishness.

The result of allowing cumulative decline to go too far is that: 'In environments characterised by lack of co-operation among social groups … all efforts towards renewal can only develop in the unpleasant direction of compulsion' (ibid., p. 14).

Although Cipolla's description of the problems of economic decline is very familiar in the second half of the twentieth century, his comments refer, in fact, to the experience of Rome, Byzantium, Italy, Spain and the Netherlands, as well as to those of the Arab, Ottoman and Chinese empires.

14 Economic Progress and Economic Organisation

1. Knight (1921, p. 268).
2. See, for instance, Chandler (1962 and 1977) and Davis and North (1971).
3. Young (1928, p. 533). 'The rate at which any one industry grows will be conditioned by the rate at which other industries grow, but since the elasticities of demand and of supply will differ for different products, some industries will grow faster than others' (ibid., p. 534).
4. See Williamson (1975 and 1979) and Klein, Crawford and Alchian (1978).
5. Coase (1937). See also Williamson (1971) and Arrow (1975).
6. Robinson (1935). See, however, Schwartzman (1963) for an attempt to test empirically the relationship between uncertainty and firm size. The tests produced rather inconclusive results.
7. Buckley and Casson (1976).
8. Williamson (1975 and 1981).
9. Hefleblower (1960, p. 13).
10. Ibid.
11. Cf. Shepherd (1970), Scherer (1980) and Devine, Lee, Jones and Tyson (1985).
12. Governments of highly industrialised countries with 'market' economies will react in exactly the same way in times of war when national

security requires that big structural changes are made within a short period.

13. This is precisely the problem that the Soviet and other centrally planned economies have tried to solve since the 1950s. Cf. Nove (1964), Šik (1967) and Horvat (1982). The optimism expressed by some mathematical economists (cf. Kantorovich, 1965) that the higher stages of economic development make it possible to perfect advanced planning and accounting techniques, enabling central planners to simulate and execute ideal economic processes, has not been justified in practice.
14. An incomes policy cannot be expected to solve the problem of uncertainty and inflation caused in an open economy by external developments. However, as the Austrian experience has shown it can reduce them significantly even in this case by avoiding economic and social costs of constant confrontation between powerful economic interests. See, for instance, Spitaller (1973) and OECD (1981 and 1983b).
15. The classic example of this is provided by the extraordinary transformation of the Japanese economy since the early 1950s. Throughout this period, 'the government's industrial policies functioned as a safety valve so that firms could boldly pursue aggressive programmes within a secure environment' (Nakamura 1981, p. 66). The knowledge that, if necessary, they could rely on support from government and banks to see them through difficult transitional phases of their development, enabled Japanese firms 'to make daring investments in plant and technology' (ibid, p. 83) which were to give them subsequently such a strong competitive edge internationally. See also Magaziner and Hout (1980), Shinohara (1982) and Magaziner and Reich (1982).
16. For instance, in his recent study of colonialism between 1870 and 1945, Fieldhouse (1981, p. 77) concludes that

    if one attempts to generalise about the characteristic and special consequences of colonialism one basic fact stands out. Every aspect of imperial policy was intended to 'open up' the dependencies to economic development by market forces, relying on the dynamics of the capitalist system in an 'open economy' to transform 'backward' into 'modern' societies. At the same time it was generally hoped to tie the colonial economies to that of each metropolis and thus, by social engineering, to wrench each from its geographical setting and integrate it into an imperial economy.

17. Observing this, Shonfield (1965, p. 378) concluded that: 'The important discovery of the postwar period is that ownership is of itself much less important than either revolutionary proletarian or conservative burgeois philosophy alleged.' See also Dalton (1974).
18. Cf. Mason and Asher (1973, pp. 105–7 and 124–35).
19. See, for instance, Acheson (1969) and Kennan (1967).
20. Spero (1981) provides a highly pertinent account of the early post-war developments.
21. See, for example, MacBean and Snowden (1981).

22. Argy (1981).
23. Kant ([1784], 1984).

15 Policies Compatible with an Integrated World Economy

1. Armstrong and Taylor (1978), Commission of the European Communities (1977a and 1977b) and Borts and Stein (1964).
2. See, for instance, Solomon (1982).
3. This is, of course, the main reason why Keynes' idea of an international Clearing Union (a world central bank) was rejected in the 1940s. (See His Majesty's Government, 1943.) Its chances of success would, almost certainly, be even smaller now.
4. See Board of Governors of The Federal Reserve System (1974), Whittlesey (1963), and D'Arista (1971).
5. This particular issue is analysed, for example, in Grubel (1984).
6. This does not mean, of course, that a particular monetary policy will have a uniform effect on all regions within a country. The regional impact of changes in monetary policy can vary significantly from region to region, depending on the institutional organisation and location of its financial sector as well as on the economic performance of different regions. See Miller (1978) for some estimates of these effects on different parts of the United States.
7. Mundell (1961) provides one of the best known arguments in favour of this proposition.
8. Cf. Meade (1957), Scitovsky (1957) and Corden (1972).
9. Cf. Williamson (1965) and Kuznets (1965 and 1966).
10. See, for instance, Milward (1977, especially ch. 4).
11. Commission of the European Communities (1977a, p. 40). It is for this reason that political scientists have devoted a good deal of attention to the problem of stability of federal systems. See, for example, May (1969).
12. That is why although the proportion of national income devoted to social security is, in general, positively related to the level of income, important differences in the development of the welfare state are often found even among countries with similar per capita income levels and economic and political systems. Cf. Wilensky (1975).
13. A system of fixed exchange rates (such as the gold and the gold-exchange standards) is also dependent for its long-term survival on the strength of such a consensus.
14. Commission of the European Communities (1977a, p. 35).
15. Ibid., p. 32.
16. This is, of course, similar in principle to the assistance that the US government provided to so many countries after the Second World War. It enabled industrial economies damaged by the war to adjust rapidly without the recourse to unsustainable inflation financing through *m*.
17. See Commission of the European Communities (1977b).
18. It is a mistake to believe that a country's 'domestic' transnationals are more likely to act in its national interest than their 'foreign' counterparts. These enterprises, whether of domestic or foreign origin, are interested primarily in maximising their profits. It makes little difference to them,

ceteris paribus, where these profits are generated. As one writer put it: 'Chauvinism is alien to the international firm. Money, as long as it is useable, is fungible. The home grown variety has no advantage over the foreign type. Operating investment decisions are not likely to be based on ideological or nationalistic grounds' (Rubin 1970, p. 183).

19. See for instance, Robinson (1983) which brings together and describes many of these proposals and 'guidelines'.
20. OECD (1977) provides a description of some of the forms in which this misuse manifests itself more frequently.
21. Ibid., p. 18.
22. Attempts to stabilise commodity prices through international commodity agreements of one kind or another have been attempted on many occasions. Only a relatively small number of such agreements have ever been reached, even fewer have got anywhere near achieving their desired objective. See Gordon-Ashworth (1984) for a description of many of these schemes and reasons for their failure.
23. See Twitchett (1981), Sengupta (1980), MacBean and Snowden (1981) and Rangarajan (1978).

16 The Optimum Policy Area

1. Mundell (1961).
2. McKinnon (1963).
3. Kenen (1969).
4. Ingram (1973).
5. Scitovsky (1958).
6. Haberler (1970).
7. Fleming (1971).
8. There is, of course, a parallel here in the development of national political institutions: from city states to feudal kingdoms, and ultimately, the modern nation state. The important difference is that the political progression towards larger policy-making units was achieved in most cases through military conquest.
9. There would also be serious conflicts of interests and tensions between the blocs if key oil producers decided to join a particular regional grouping.
10. This refers to general protection. However, as emphasised in Part III, even when general restrictions are not necessary, specific controls may be required to enable a country to develop new industries or to reconstruct and rationalise old ones.
11. It is assumed here that deficit countries are both willing and able to undertake structural adjustments. This, of course, is not always the case. However, the assumption is essential in any analysis which focuses on the effects of changes in international economic relationships and policies.
12. The most obvious issues in this category are the energy crisis and the collapse of the international financial system.
13. Historically, periods of unusually large numbers of international and civil wars have tended to coincide. Cf. Small and Singer (1982).
14. de Cecco (1985, p. 64n).

15. Gardner (1975 and 1980).
16. Cf. Renfrew (1984, ch. 13).

Bibliography

ACHESON, D. G. (1969) *Present at the Creation: My Years in the State Department* (New York: Norton).
ALIBER, R. Z. (1978) 'The Integration of National Financial Markets: A Review of Theory and Findings', *Weltwirtschaftliches Archiv*, Band 114, Heft 3.
ALLEN, P. R. (1976) 'Organisation and Administration of a Monetary Union', *Princeton Studies in International Finance* (Princeton: Princeton University Press).
AMUZEGAR, J. (1983) 'Oil Exporters' Economic Development in an Interdependent World', *IMF Occasional Paper No. 18* (Washington, DC: IMF).
ANDERSON, J. E. (1972) 'Effective Protection in the US: a Historical Comparison', *Journal of International Economics*, February.
ANDREWS, M. D. (1984) 'Recent Trends in the US Foreign Exchange Market', *Federal Reserve Bank of New York Quarterly Review*, Summer.
AQUINO, A. (1978) 'Intra-Industry Trade and Inter-Industry Specialisation as Concurrent Sources of International Trade in Manufactures', *Weltwirtschaftliches Archiv*, Band 114, Heft 2.
ARGY, V. (1981) *The Postwar International Monetary Crisis* (London: Allen & Unwin).
ARMSTRONG, H. and TAYLOR, J. (1978) *Regional Economic Policy* (Oxford: Philip Allan).
ARROW, K. J. (1975) 'Vertical Integration and Communications', *Bell Journal of Economics*, Spring.
ARTUS, J. R. and YOUNG, J. H. (1979) 'Fixed and Flexible Exchange Rates: a Renewal of the Debate', *IMF Staff Papers*, December.
BAIROCH, P. (1976a) *Commerce Extérieur et Développement Economique de l'Europe au XIX Siècle* (Paris: Ecole des Hautes Etudes en Sciences Sociales).
BAIROCH, P. (1976b) 'Europe's Gross National Product: 1800–1975', *Journal of European Economic History*, Fall.
BAIROCH, P. (1981) 'The Main Trends in National Economic Disparities since the Industrial Revolution', in P. Bairoch and M. Levy-Leboyer (eds), *Disparities in Economic Development since the Industrial Revolution* (London: Macmillan).
BALASSA, B. (1962) *The Theory of Economic Integration* (London: Allen & Unwin).
BALASSA, B. (1965) 'Tariff Protection in Industrial Countries: an Evaluation', *Journal of Political Economy*, December.
BALASSA, B. (1967) *Trade Liberalisation Among Industrial Countries* (New York: McGraw-Hill).
BALASSA, B. (1986) 'Intra-Industry Specialisation: A Cross-Country Analysis', *European Economic Review*, February.
BALASSA, B., BARSONY, A. and RICHARDS, A. (1981) *The Balance of Payments Effects of External Shocks and of Policy Response to These Shocks*

(Paris: Organisation for Economic Co-operation and Development).
BANK FOR INTERNATIONAL SETTLEMENTS (1979) *Forty-Ninth Annual Report* (Basle).
BANK FOR INTERNATIONAL SETTLEMENTS (1985) *Fifty-Fifth Annual Report* (Basle).
BANK FOR INTERNATIONAL SETTLEMENTS (1986) *Recent Innovations in International Banking* (Basle).
BATCHELOR, R. A., MAJOR, R. L. and MORGAN, A. D. (1980) *Industrialisation and the Basis for Trade* (Cambridge: Cambridge University Press).
BEREND, I. (1971) 'The Problem of Eastern European Economic Integration in a Historical Perspective', in I. Vajda and M. Simai (eds), *Foreign Trade in a Planned Economy* (Cambridge: Cambridge University Press).
BERRILL, K. (1963) 'Foreign Capital and Take-off', in W. W. Rostow (ed.), *The Economics of Take-Off into Sustained Growth* (London: Macmillan).
BHAGWATI, J. (ed.) (1974) *Illegal Transactions in International Trade: Theory and Measurement* (Amsterdam: North-Holland).
BHAGWATI, J. (ed.) (1977) *The New International Economic Order: the North–South Debate* (Cambridge, Mass.: MIT Press).
BICKERDIKE, C. F. (1906) 'The Theory of Incipient Taxes', *Economic Journal*, December.
BLACK, S. W. and RUSSELL, R. R. (1969) 'An Alternative Estimate of Potential GNP', *Review of Economics and Statistics*, February.
BLAIR, J. M. (1972) *Economic Concentration: Structure, Behaviour and Public Policy* (New York: Harcourt, Brace, Jovanovic).
BLOOMFIELD, A. I. (1959) *Monetary Policy under the International Gold Standard: 1880–1914* (New York: Federal Reserve Bank of New York).
BLOOMFIELD, A. I. (1963) 'Short-Term Capital Movements Under the Pre-1914 Gold Standard', *Princeton Studies in International Finance* (Princeton: Princeton University Press).
BLOOMFIELD, A. I. (1968) 'Patterns of Fluctuations in International Investment Before 1914', *Princeton Studies in International Finance* (Princeton: Princeton University Press).
BOARD OF GOVERNORS OF THE FEDERAL RESERVE SYSTEM (1974) *The Federal Reserve System: Purposes and Functions*, 6th ed, (Washington, DC: Board of Governors of the Federal Reserve System).
BOND, I. D. (1985) 'The Syndicated Credit Markets', *Bank of England Discussion Paper No. 22* (London: Bank of England).
BORCHARDT, K. (1973) 'Germany 1700–1914', in C. M. Cipolla (ed.), *The Fontana Economic History of Europe. vol. 4. The Emergence of Industrial Societies* (Glasgow: Fontana-Collins).
BORTS, G. and STEIN, J. (1964) *Economic Growth in a Free Market* (New York: Columbia University Press).
BRABANT, J. M. (1980) *Socialist Economic Integration* (Cambridge: Cambridge University Press).
BREBNER, J. B. (1962) 'Laissez-Faire and State Intervention in Nineteenth Century Britain', in E. M. Carus-Wilson (ed.), *Essays in Economic History*, vol. III (London: Edward Arnold).

BRITISH PETROLEUM (1985) *BP Statistical Review of World Energy*, June.
BROWN, R. N., ENOCH, C. A. and MORTIMER-LEE, P. D. (1980) 'The Interrelationship between Costs and Prices in the United Kingdom', *Bank of England Discussion Paper No. 8* (London: Bank of England).
BRYANT, R. C. (1980) *Money and Monetary Policy in Interdependent Nations* (Washington, DC: Brookings Institution).
BUCKLEY, P. J. and CASSON, M. (1976) *The Future of Multinational Enterprise* (London: Macmillan).
BURNETT, J. (1969) *A History of the Cost of Living* (Harmondsworth, Middlesex: Penguin Books).
CAIN, P. J. and HOPKINS, A. G. (1980) 'The Political Economy of British Expansion Overseas, 1750–1914', *Economic History Review*, November.
CAPIE, F. (1983a) 'Tariff Protection and Economic Performance in the Nineteenth Century', in J. Black and L. A. Winters (eds), *Policy and Performance in International Trade* (London: Macmillan).
CAPIE, F. (1983b) *Depression and Protection: Britain between the Wars* (London: Allen & Unwin).
CASSON, M. and Associates (1986) *Multinationals and World Trade* (London: Allen & Unwin).
CHANDLER, A. D. (1962) *Strategy and Structure: Chapters in the History of the Industrial Enterprise* (Cambridge, Mass.: MIT Press).
CHANDLER, A. D. (1977) *The Visible Hand: The Managerial Revolution in American Business* (Cambridge, Mass.: The Belknap Press of the Harvard University Press).
CIPOLLA, C. M. (1970) 'Introduction', in C. M. Cipolla (ed.), *The Economic Decline of Empires* (London: Methuen).
CLINE, W. R. (1984) *International Debt: Systematic Risk and Policy Response* (Washington, DC: Institute for International Economics).
CLINE, W. R. and Associates (1981) *World Inflation and the Developing Countries* (Washington, DC: The Brookings Institution).
COASE, R. H. (1937) 'The Nature of the Firm', *Economica*, November.
COMMISSION OF THE EUROPEAN COMMUNITIES (1977a) *Report of the Study Group on the Role of Public Finance in European Integration. vol. I. General Report* (Brussels: EEC).
COMMISSION OF THE EUROPEAN COMMUNITIES (1977b) *Report of the Study Group on the Role of Public Finance in European Integration. vol. II. Individual Contributions and Working Papers* (Brussels: EEC).
COMMITTEE ON THE INTERNATIONAL MIGRATION OF TALENT (1970) *The International Migration of High-Level Manpower: its Impact on the Development Process* (New York: Praeger Special Studies in International Economics and Development).
COOPER, R. N. (1966) 'The Balance of Payments in Review', *Journal of Political Economy*, August.
COOPER, R. N. (1968) *The Economics of Interdependence* (New York: Columbia University Press).
CORDEN, W. M. (1971) *The Theory of Protection* (Oxford: Oxford University Press).
CORDEN, W. M. (1972) 'Monetary Integration', *Princeton Essays in*

International Finance (Princeton: Princeton University Press).
CORDEN, W. M. (1974) *Trade Policy and Economic Welfare* (Oxford: Oxford University Press).
CORDEN, W. M. (1977) *Inflation, Exchange Rates and the World Economy* (Oxford: Clarendon Press).
CORDEN, W. M. (1982) 'Exchange Rate Protection', in R. N. Cooper, P. B. Kenen, J. B. de Macedo and J. van Ypersele (eds), *The International Monetary System Under Flexible Exchange Rates* (Cambridge, Mass.: Ballinger).
COURCHENE, T. J. (1980) 'Towards a Protected Society: the Politicization of Economic Life', *Canadian Journal of Economics*, November.
COWLING, K. (1983) 'Excess Capacity and the Degree of Collusion: Oligopoly Behaviour in the Slump', *Manchester School*, December.
DALTON, G. (1974) *Economic Systems and Society* (Harmondsworth, Middlesex: Penguin Books).
D'ARISTA, J. W. (1971) *Federal Reserve Structure and the Development of Monetary Policy*, Staff Report, House Committee on Banking and Currency (Washington, DC: US Congress).
DAVIS, L. A. and NORTH, D. C. (1971) *Institutional Change and American Economic Growth* (Cambridge: Cambridge University Press).
DAVIS, R. (1979) *The Industrial Revolution and British Overseas Trade*, (Leicester: Leicester University Press).
DE CECCO, M. (1985) 'The International Debt Problem in the Interwar Period', *Banca Nazionale del Lavoro Quarterly Review*, March.
DENNIS, G. E. J. (1984) *International Financial Flows: a Statistical Handbook* (London: Graham & Trotman).
DEVINE, P. J., LEE, N., JONES, R. M. and TYSON, W. J. (1985) *An Introduction to Industrial Economics*, 4th edn, (London: Allen & Unwin).
DILLON, K. B., WATSON, C. M. and KINCAID, G. R. (1985) 'Recent Developments in External Debt Restructuring', *IMF Occasional Paper No. 40* (Washington, DC: IMF).
DORNBUSCH, R. (1980) 'Exchange Rate Economics: Where Do We Stand?', *Brookings Papers on Economic Activity*, No. 1.
DORNBUSCH, R. and KRUGMAN, P. (1976) 'Flexible Exchange Rates in the Short Run', *Brookings Papers on Economic Activity*, No. 3.
DUESENBERRY, J. S. (1949) *Income, Saving and the Theory of Consumer Behaviour* (Cambridge, Mass: Harvard University Press).
DUFEY, G. and GIDDY, I. H. (1981) 'The Evolution of Instruments and Techniques of International Financial Markets', *SUERF Series 35A* (Tilburg: Societé Universitaire Européenne de Recherches Financières).
DUNNING, J. H. (1981a) 'A Note on Intra-Industry Foreign Direct Investment', *Banca Nazionale del Lavoro Quarterly Review*, December.
DUNNING, J. H. (1981b) 'Explaining the International Direct Investment Position of Countries: Towards a Dynamic or Developmental Approach', in *International Production and the Multinational Enterprise* (London: Allen & Unwin).
DUNNING, J. H. (1983) 'Changes in the Level and Structure of International Production: the Last One Hundred Years', in M. Casson (ed.), *The Growth of International Business* (London: Allen & Unwin).

DUNNING, J. H. and PEARCE, R. D. (1981) *The World's Largest Industrial Enterprises* (Farnborough: Gower Press).

ECONOMIST, THE (1985) *Economic Statistics 1900–1983* (London: The Economist Publications).

EL-AGRAA, A. M. (ed.) (1982) *International Economic Integration* (New York: St Martin's Press).

ENERGY MODELLING FORUM (1982) *World Oil* (Stanford: EMF).

ENOCH, C. A. and PANIĆ, M. (1981) 'Commodity Prices in the 1970s', *Bank of England Quarterly Bulletin*, March.

FAIR, R. C. (1982) 'Estimated Output, Price, Interest Rate, and Exchange Rate Linkages Among Countries', *Cowles Foundation Paper 545* (Yale University).

FIELDHOUSE, D. K. (1981) *Colonialism 1870–1945* (London: Weidenfeld & Nicolson).

FLEMING, J. M (1971) 'On Exchange Rate Unification', *Economic Journal*, September.

FORD, A. G. (1962) *The Gold Standard, 1880–1914* (Oxford: Oxford University Press).

FORTUNE, J. N. (1972) 'Income Distribution as a Determinant of Imports of Manufactured Consumer Commodities', *Canadian Journal of Economics*, May.

FRIEDMAN, M. (1953) 'The Case for Flexible Exchange Rates', in *Essays in Positive Economics* (Chicago: University of Chicago Press).

FROBEL, F., HEINRICHS, J. and KREYE, O. (1980) *The New International Division of Labour* (Cambridge: Cambridge University Press).

GARDNER, R. N. (1975) 'Bretton Woods' in M. Keynes (ed.), *Essays on John Maynard Keynes* (Cambridge: Cambridge University Press).

GARDNER, R. N. (1980) *Sterling-Dollar Diplomacy in Current Perspective: The Origins and Prospects of Our International Economic Order*, New expanded edn, (New York: Columbia University Press).

GATELY, D. (1984) 'A Ten-Year Perspective: OPEC and the World Oil Market', *Journal of Economic Literature*, September.

GERSCHENKRON, A. (1966a) *Bread and Democracy in Germany* (New York: Howard Fertig).

GERSCHENKRON, A. (1966b) *Economic Backwardness in Historical Perspective* (Cambridge, Mass: Belknap Press of Harvard University Press).

GIERSCH, H. (ed.) (1979) *On the Economics of Intra-Industry Trade* (Tubigen: J. C. B. Mohr-Paul Siebeck).

GLISMANN, H. H. and WEISS, F. D. (1980) 'On the Political Economy of Protection in Germany', *World Bank Staff Working Paper No. 427* (Washington, DC: World Bank).

GODLEY, W. A. H. and SHEPHERD, J. R. (1964), 'Long-Term Growth and Short-Term Policy', *NIESR Economic Review*, August.

GOLDSBROUGH, D. J. (1981) 'International Trade of Multinational Corporations and its Responsiveness to Changes in Aggregate Demand and Relative Prices', *IMF Staff Papers*, September.

GOLDSMITH, R. W. (1966) *The Determinants of Financial Structure* (Paris: Organisation for Economic Co-operation and Development).

GOLDSMITH, R. W. (1969) *Financial Structure and Development* (New

Haven: Yale University Press).
GOLDSTEIN, M. and KHAN, M. S. (1982) 'Effects of Slowdown in Industrial Countries on Growth in Non-Oil Developing Countries', *IMF Occasional Paper No. 12* (Washington, DC: IMF).
GOLDTHORPE, J. (ed.) (1984) *Order and Conflict in Contemporary Capitalism* (Oxford: Clarendon Press).
GORDON-ASHWORTH, F. (1984) *International Commodity Control: a Contemporary History and Appraisal* (London: Croom Helm).
GOUREVITCH, P. A. (1977) 'International Trade, Domestic Conditions and Liberty: Comparative Responses to the Crisis of 1873–1896', *Journal of Interdisciplinary History*, Autumn.
GRASSMAN, S. (1980) 'Long-Term Trends in Openness of National Economies', *Oxford Economic Papers*, March.
GREEN, A. and URQUHART, M. C. (1976) 'Factor and Commodity Flows in the International Economy of 1870–1914: a Multi-Country View', *Journal of Economic History*, March.
GRIFFIN, J. M. and TEECE, D. J. (eds) (1982) *OPEC Behaviour and World Oil Prices* (London: Allen & Unwin).
GROUP OF THIRTY (1984) *Foreign Direct Investment, 1973–87* (New York: Group of Thirty).
GRUBEL, H. G. (1979) 'Towards a Theory of Two-Way Trade in Capital Assets', in H. Giersch (ed.), *On the Economics of Intra-Industry Trade* (Tubingen: J. C. B. Mohr-Paul Siebeck).
GRUBEL, H. G. (1984) *The International Monetary System*, 4th edn, (Harmondsworth, Middlesex: Penguin Books).
GRUBEL, H. G. and LLOYD, P. J. (1975) *Intra-Industry Trade* (London: Macmillan).
GUISINGER, S. and SCHYDLOWSKY, D. M. (1971) 'The Empirical Relationship between Nominal and Effective Rates of Protection', in H. Grubel and H. G. Johnson (eds), *Effective Tariff Protection* (Geneva: GATT and Graduate Institute of International Studies).
HABERLER, G. (1950) 'Some Problems in the Pure Theory of International Trade', *Economic Journal*, June.
HABERLER, G. (1970) 'The International Monetary System: Some Recent Developments and Discussions', in G. N. Halm (ed.), *Approaches to Greater Flexibility of Exchange Rates* (Princeton: Princeton University Press).
HAMILTON, A. ([1791] 1934) 'Report on Manufactures', in *Papers on Public Credit, Commerce and Finance* (New York: Columbia University Press).
HARROD, R. F. (1948) *Towards a Dynamic Economics* (London: Macmillan).
HARROD, R. F. (1972) *The Life of John Maynard Keynes* (Harmondsworth, Middlesex: Penguin Books).
HARTLAND, P. (1949) 'Interregional Payments Compared with International Payments', *Quarterly Journal of Economics*, August.
HAVRYLYSHYN, O. and WOLF, M. (1981) 'Trade Among Developing Countries: Theory, Policy Issues, and Principal Trends', *World Bank Staff Working Paper No. 479* (Washington, DC: World Bank).
HAWKE, G. E. (1975) 'The United States Tariff and Industrial Protection in the Late Nineteenth Century', *Economic History Review*, February.

HAWKINS, R. J. (1972) 'Intra-EEC Capital Movements and Domestic Financial Markets', in F. Machulp, W. S. Salant and L. Tarshis (eds), *International Mobility and Movement of Capital* (New York: National Bureau of Economic Research).
HECKSCHER, E. ([1919] 1949) 'The Effect of Foreign Trade on the Distribution of Income', in A.E.A., *Readings in the Theory of International Trade* (Philadelphia: Blackiston).
HECKSCHER, E. (1955) *Mercantilism*, 2 vols. (London: Allen & Unwin).
HEFLEBLOWER, R. B. (1960) 'Observations on Decentralisation in Large Enterprises', *Journal of Industrial Economics*, November.
HELLEINER, G. K. (1981) *Intra-Firm Trade and Developing Countries* (London: Macmillan).
HELLEINER, K. F. (1973) *Free Trade and Frustration: Anglo-Austrian Negotiations, 1860–70* (Toronto: Toronto University Press).
HENDERSON, H. D. (1955) *The Interwar Years and Other Papers* (Oxford: Clarendon Press).
HICKMAN, B. G. and SCHLEICHER, S. (1978) 'The Interdependence of National Economies and the Syncrhonisation of Economic Fluctuations: Evidence from the LINK Project', *Weltwirtschaftliches Archiv*, Band 114, Heft 4.
HICKS, J. R. (1953) 'An Inaugural Lecture', *Oxford Economic Papers*, June.
HICKS, J. (1977) *Economic Perspectives: Further Essays on Money and Growth* (Oxford: Clarendon Press).
HICKS, J. (1979) *Causality in Economics* (Oxford: Basil Blackwell).
HIRSCH, F. and GOLDTHORPE, J. H. (eds) (1978) *The Political Economy of Inflation* (London: Martin Robertson).
HIRSCHMAN, A. O. (1945) *National Power and the Structure of Foreign Trade* (Berkeley: University of California Press).
HIS MAJESTY'S GOVERNMENT (1943) *Proposls for an International Clearing Union*, Cmnd. 6437 (London: HMSO).
HODJERA, Z. (1969) 'Basic Balances, Short-Term Capital Flows and International Reserves of Industrial Countries', *IMF Staff Papers*, November.
HOLTHAM, G. (1984) 'Multinational Modelling of Financial Linkages and Exchange Rates', *OECD Economic Studies*, Spring.
HORVAT, B. (1982) *The Political Economy of Socialism* (Oxford: Martin Robertson).
HUFBAUER, G. C. and CHILAS, J. G. (1974) 'Specialisation by Industrial Countries: Extent and Consequences', in H. Giersch (ed.), *The International Division of Labour: Problems and Perspective* (Tubingen: J. C. B. Mohr-Paul Siebeck).
HUGHES, A. (1976) 'Company Concentration, Size of Plant, and Merger Activity', in M. Panić (ed.), *The UK and West German Manufacturing Industry 1954–72* (London: National Economic Development Office).
HUME, D. ([1752] 1969) 'On the Balance of Trade', in R. N. Cooper (ed.), *International Finance* (Harmondsworth, Middlesex: Penguin Books).
IMF (INTERNATIONAL MONETARY FUND) (1944) *Articles of Agreement of the International Monetary Fund* (Washington, DC: IMF).
IMF (1977) *Balance of Payments Manual*, 4th edn, (Washington, DC: IMF).

IMF (1981) 'External Indebtedness of Developing Countries', *Occasional Paper No. 3* (Washington, DC: IMF).

IMF (1982a) *International Financial Statistics – Supplement on Trade Statistics* No. 4 (Washington, DC: IMF).

IMF (1982b) *World Economic Outlook* (Washington, DC: IMF).

IMF (1984a) *International Financial Statistics – Supplement on Output Statistics* No. 8 (Washington, DC: IMF).

IMF (1984b) *International Financial Statistics – Supplement on Balance of Payments* No. 7 (Washington, DC: IMF).

IMF (1984c) *World Economic Outlook* (Washington, DC: IMF).

IMF (1984d) 'Exchange Rate Volatility and World Trade', *IMF Occasional Paper No. 28* (Washington, DC: IMF).

IMF (1986), *World Economic Outlook* (Washington, DC: IMF).

IMLAH, A. H. (1958) *Economic Elements in the Pax Britannica* (Cambridge, Mass.: Harvard University Press).

INDEPENDENT COMMISSION ON INTERNATIONAL DEVELOPMENT ISSUES ('The Brandt Report') (1980) *North–South: A Programme for Survival* (London: Pan Books).

INGRAM, J. C. (1956) 'Capital Imports and the Balance of Payments', *Southern Economic Journal*, April.

INGRAM, J. C. (1957) 'Growth and Canada's Balance of Payments', *American Economic Review*, March.

INGRAM, J. C. (1973) 'The Case for European Monetary Integration', *Princeton Essays in International Finance* (Princeton: Princeton University Press).

INTERNATIONAL ENERGY AGENCY (1982) *World Energy Outlook* (Paris: Organisation for Economic Co-operation and Development).

INTERNATIONAL ENERGY AGENCY (1985) *Energy Policies and Programmes of IEA Countries – 1984 Review* (Paris: Organisation for Economic Co-operation and Development).

INTERNATIONAL ENERGY AGENCY (1986) *Energy Policies and Programmes of IEA Countries – 1985 Review* (Paris: Organisation for Economic Co-operation and Development).

ISARD, P. (1977) 'How Far Can We Push the Law of One Price?', *American Economic Review*, December.

JENNE, C. A. and CATTELL, R. K. (1983) 'Structural Change and Energy Efficiency in Industry', *Energy Economics*, May.

JEREMY, D. J. (1977) 'Damming the Flood: British Government's Efforts to Check the Outflow of Technicians and Machinery, 1780–1843', *Business History Review*, Spring.

JOHNSON, H. G. (1958) 'Towards a General Theory of the Balance of Payments', in *International Trade and Economic Growth* (London: Allen & Unwin).

JOHNSON, H. G. (1972) 'The Case for Flexible Exchange Rates, 1969', in *Further Essays in Monetary Economics* (Cambridge, Mass.: Harvard University Press).

KALDOR, N. (1978) 'The Nemesis of Free Trade', in *Further Essays in Applied Economics* (London: Duckworth).

KANT, I. ([1784] 1984) 'Idea for a Universal History with a Cosmopolitan

Purpose' in H. Reiss (ed.), *Kant's Political Writings* (Cambridge: Cambridge University Press).

KANTOROVICH, L. V. (1965) *The Best Use of Economic Resources* (Cambridge, Mass: Harvard University Press).

KENEN, P. B. (1969) 'The Theory of Optimum Currency Areas: an Ecclectic View', in R. A. Mundell and A. K. Swoboda (eds), *Monetary Problems in the International Economy* (Chicago: University of Chicago Press).

KENEN, P B. (1976) 'Capital Mobility and Financial Integration – a Survey', *Princeton Studies in International Finance* (Princeton: Princeton University Press).

KENNAN, G. F. (1967) *Memoirs, 1925–50* (Boston: Little, Brown).

KENWOOD, A. G. and LOUGHEED, A. L. (1971) *The Growth of the International Economy, 1820–1960* (London: Allen & Unwin).

KEYNES, J. M. ([1924] 1981a) 'A Drastic Remedy for Unemployment: Reply to Critics', in *The Collected Writings of J. M. Keynes*, vol. XIX, (London: Macmillan).

KEYNES, J. M. ([1931] 1981b) 'Unemployment and Protection', in *The Collected Writings of J. M. Keynes*, vol. XX, (London: Macmillan).

KEYNES, J. M. ([1933] 1982) 'National Self Sufficiency', in *The Collected Writings of J. M. Keynes*, vol. XXI, (London: Macmillan).

KEYNES, J. M. (1936) *The General Theory of Employment, Interest and Money* (London: Macmillan).

KINDLEBERGER, C. P. (1969) 'Measuring Equilbrium in the Balance of Payments', *Journal of Political Economy*, November–December.

KINDLEBERGER, C. P. (1973) *The World in Depression, 1929–1939* (London: Allen Lane).

KINDLEBERGER, C. P. (1978a) *Economic Response: Comparative Studies in Trade, Finance and Growth* (Cambridge, Mass.: Harvard University Press).

KINDLEBERGER, C. P. (1978b) *Manias, Panics and Crashes: a History of Financial Crises* (New York: Basic Books).

KINDLEBERGER, C. P. (1981) 'Germany's Persistent Balance of Payments Disequilibrium Revisited', in *International Money* (London: Allen & Unwin).

KINDLEBERGER, C. P. (1984) *A Financial History of Europe* (London: Allen & Unwin).

KINDLEBERGER, C. P. (1985) 'Historical Perspective on Today's Third World Debt Problem', in *Keynesianism vs Monetarism and Other Essays in Financial History* (London: Allen & Unwin).

KINDLEBERGER, C. P. and LAFFARGUE, J. P. (eds) (1982), *Financial Crises: Theory, History and Policy* (Cambridge: Cambridge University Press).

KLEIN, B., CRAWFORD, R. A. and ALCHIAN, A. A. (1978) 'Vertical Integration, Appropriable Rents and the Competitive Contracting Process', *Journal of Law and Economics*, October.

KNIGHT, F. H. (1921) *Risk, Uncertainty and Profit* (Boston, Mass.: Houghton Mifflin).

KRAVIS I. B. and LIPSEY, R. E. (1971) *Price Competitiveness in World Trade* (New York: National Bureau of Economic Research).

KRAVIS, I. B. and LIPSEY, R. E. (1978) 'Price Behaviour in the Light of Balance of Payments Theories', *Journal of International Economics*, May.

KRAVIS, I. B., HESTON, A. and SUMMERS, R. (1978) *International*

Comparisons of Real Product and Purchasing Power (Baltimore: Johns Hopkins University Press).

KRUGMAN, P. (1980), 'Scale Economies, Product Differentiation and the Pattern of Trade', *American Economic Review*, December.

KUZNETS, S. (1964) 'Quantitative Aspects of the Economic Growth of Nations: IX. Level and Structure of Foreign Trade – Comparisons for Recent Years', *Economic Development and Cultural Change*, October.

KUZNETS, S. (1965) *Economic Growth and Structure* (London: Heinemann Educational Books).

KUZNETS, S. (1966) *Modern Economic Growth* (New Haven: Yale University Press).

KUZNETS, S. (1967) 'Quantitative Aspects of the Economic Growth of Nations: X. Levels and Structure of Foreign Trade – Long-Term Trends', *Economic Development and Cultural Change*, January.

LANCASTER, K. (1980) 'Intra-Industry Trade Under Perfect Monopolistic Competition', *Journal of International Economics*, May.

LANDES, D. S. (1969) *The Unbound Prometeus: Technological Change and Industrial Development in Western Europe from 1750 to Present* (Cambridge: Cambridge University Press).

LARSEN, F. and LLEWELLYN, J. (1983) 'Simulated Macroeconomic Effects of a Large Fall in Oil Prices', *OECD Working Paper No. 8* (Paris: Organisation for Economic Co-operation and Development).

LARSEN, F., LLEWELLYN, J. and POTTER, S. (1983) 'International Economic Linkages', *OECD Economic Studies*, Autumn.

LAVIGNE, M. (1975) 'The Problem of Multinational Socialist Enterprises', *ACES Bulletin*, Summer.

LEAGUE OF NATIONS (1927) *Tariff Level Indices* (Geneva: League of Nations).

LEAGUE OF NATIONS (1943) *Quantitative Trade Controls* (Geneva: Legaue of Nations).

LERNER, A. (1934) 'The Diagramatic Representation of Demand Conditions in International Trade', *Economica*, August.

LEWIS, W. A. (1949) *Economic Survey, 1919–1939* (London: Allen & Unwin).

LEWIS, W. A. (1952) 'World Production, Prices and Trade, 1870–1960', *Manchester School*, May.

LEWIS, W. A. (1955) *The Theory of Economic Growth* (London: Allen & Unwin).

LEWIS, W. A. (1978a) *The Evolution of the International Economic Order* (Princeton: Princeton University Press).

LEWIS, W. A. (1978b) *Growth and Fluctuations, 1870–1913* (London: Allen & Unwin).

LILLEY, S. (1973) 'Technological Progress and Industrial Revolution, 1700–1914', in C. M. Cipolla (ed.), *The Fontana Economic History of Europe. vol. 3. The Industrial Revolution* (Glasgow: Fontana-Collins).

LINDER, S. B. (1961) *An Essay on Trade and Transformation* (New York: John Wiley & Sons).

LIPSEY, R. G. and LANCASTER, K. (1956) 'The General Theory of the Second Best', *Review of Economic Studies*, vol. XXIV.

LIST, F. ([1841] 1885) *The National System of Political Economy* (London: Longmans).
LLEWELLYN, D. T. (1980) *International Financial Integration: the Limits of Sovereignty* (London: Macmillan).
LLEWELLYN, D. T. (1984) 'Modelling International Banking Flows: an Analytical Framework', in J. Black and G. S. Dorrance (eds), *Problems of International Finance* (London: Macmillan).
LYDALL, H. (1979) *A Theory of Income Distribution* (Oxford: Clarendon Press).
MACBEAN, A. I. and SNOWDEN, P. N. (1981) *International Institutions in Trade and Finance* (London: Allen & Unwin).
MACHLUP, F. (1958) 'Equilibrium and Disequilibrium: Misplaced Concreteness and Disguised Politics', *Economic Journal*, March.
MACHLUP, F. (1973) 'Exchange Rate Flexibility', *Banca Nazionale del Lavoro Quarterly Review*, September.
MACHLUP, F. (1977) *A History of Thought on Economic Integration* (London: Macmillan).
MADDISON, A. (1982) *Phases of Capitalist Development* (Oxford: Oxford University Press).
MAGAZINER, I. C. and HOUT, H. M. (1980) *Japanese Industrial Policy* (London: Policy Studies Institute).
MAGAZINER, I. C. and REICH, R. B. (1982) *Minding America's Business: the Decline and Rise of the American Economy* (New York: Harcourt, Brace, Jovanovic).
MAGEE, S. P. (1975) 'Prices, Incomes and Foreign Trade', in P. B. Kenen (ed.), *International Trade and Finance: Frontiers for Research* (Cambridge: Cambridge University Press).
MAIZELS, A. (1963) *Industrial Growth and World Trade* (Cambridge: Cambridge University Press).
MARSHALL, A. ([1903] 1926) 'Memorandum on the Fiscal Policy of International Trade', *Official Papers of Alfred Marshall* (London: Macmillan).
MARSHALL, A. ([1920] 1956) *Principles of Economics*, 8th edn, (London: Macmillan).
MARSHALL, A. (1923) *Industry and Trade* (London: Macmillan).
MASON, E. S. and ASHER, R. E. (1973) *The World Bank since Bretton Woods* (Washington, DC: The Brookings Institution).
MAY, R. J. (1969) *Federalism and Fiscal Adjustment* (Oxford: Clarendon Press).
McCLOSKEY, D. N. (1980) 'Magnanimous Albion: Free Trade and British National Income, 1841–1881', *Explorations in Economic History*, July.
McKINNON, R. I. (1963) 'Optimum Currency Areas', *American Economic Review*, September.
McKINNON, R. I. (1981) 'The Exchange Rate and Macroeconomic Policy: Changing Postwar Perceptions', *Journal of Economic Literature*, June.
MEADE, J. E. (1951) *The Theory of International Economic Policy. vol. I. The Balance of Payments* (Oxford: Oxford University Press).
MEADE, J. E. (1955) 'The Case for Variable Exchange Rates', *Three Banks Review*, September.
MEADE, J. E. (1957) 'The Balance of Payments Problems of a Free Trade

Area', *Economic Journal*, September.

MEIER, G. E. (1953) 'Economic Development and the Transfer Mechanism: Canada, 1895–1913', *Canadian Journal of Economics and Political Science*, February.

MILL, J. S. ([1848] 1965) *Principles of Political Economy*, J. M. Robson (ed.), (London: Routledge & Kegan Paul).

MILLER, R. J. (1978) *The Regional Impact of Monetary Policy in the United States* (Lexington, Mass: Lexington Books).

MILLS, R. H. (1976) 'The Regulation of Short-Term Capital Movements in Major Industrial Countries', in A. K. Swoboda (ed.), *Capital Movements and their Control* (Leiden: A. W. Sijthoff).

MILWARD, A. S. (1977) *War Economy and Society, 1939–1945* (London: Allen & Unwin).

MITCHELL, B. R. (1975) *European Historical Statistics, 1750–1970* (London: Macmillan).

MITCHELL, B. R. (1983) *International Historical Statistics: the Americas and Australasia* (London: Macmillan).

MITCHELL, B. R. and DEANE, P. (1962) *Abstracts of British Historical Statistics* (Cambridge: Cambridge University Press).

MOGGERIDGE, D. E. (1982) 'Policy in the Crises of 1920 and 1929', in C. P. Kindleberger and J. P. Laffargue (eds) (1980), *Financial Crises: Theory, History and Policy* (Cambridge: Cambridge University Press).

MORAN, T. (1982) 'Modelling OPEC Behaviour: Economic and Political Alternatives', in J. M. Griffin and D. J. Teece (eds), *OPEC Behaviour and World Oil Prices*, op. cit.

MORGAN, A. D. (1971) 'Imports of Manufactures into the United Kingdom and Other Industrial Countries, 1955–69', *NIESR Economic Review*, May.

MUNDELL, R. A. (1957) 'International Trade and Factor Mobility', *American Economic Review*, June.

MUNDELL, R. A. (1961) 'A Theory of Optimum Currency Areas', *American Economic Review*, September.

MYRDAL, G. (1956) *An International Economy* (New York: Harper).

MYRDAL, G. (1957) *Economic Theory and Underdeveloped Regions* (London: Duckworth).

NAKAMURA, T. (1981) *The Postwar Japanese Economy: its Development and Structure* (Tokyo: University of Tokyo Press).

NOVE, A. (1964) *Economic Rationality and Soviet Politics* (New York: Praeger).

NURKSE, R. (1944) *International Currency Experience* (Princeton: League of Nations).

NURKSE, R. (1947) 'Domestic and International Equilibrium', in S. E. Harris (ed.), *The New Economics* (New York: Alfred A. Knopf).

ODELL, P. R. (1981) 'International Energy Issues: the Next Ten Years', in P. Tempest (ed.), *International Energy Options: an Agenda for the 1980's* (London: Graham & Trotman).

ODELL, P. R. (1985) 'Back to Cheap Oil?', *Lloyds Bank Review*, April.

OECD (1970) *The Growth of Output, 1960–1980* (Paris).

OECD (1973) 'The International Transmission of Inflation', *OECD Economic Outlook*, July.

OECD (1977) *Restrictive Business Practices of Multinational Enterprises* (Paris).
OECD (1979a) *Economic Outlook*, July.
OECD (1979b) *External Indebtedness of Developing Countries: Present Situation and Future Prospects* (Paris).
OECD (1981) *Integrated Social Policy: a Review of Austrian Experience* (Paris).
OECD (1982a) *Controls on International Capital Movements* (Paris).
OECD (1982b) '28½ Million Unemployed', *OECD Observer*, March.
OECD (1983a) *Labour Force Statistics, 1970–81* (Paris).
OECD (1983b) *Economic Survey of Austria* (Paris).
OECD (1984) *External Debt of Developing Countries* (Paris).
OECD (1985) *Costs and Benefits of Protection* (Paris).
OECD (1986) *Economic Outlook*, May.
OECD-INTERFUTURES (1979) *Facing the Future* (Paris).
OHLIN, B. (1933) *Interregional and International Trade* (Cambridge, Mass.: Harvard University Press).
OKUN, A. M. (1962) 'Potential GNP: its Measurement and Significance', *Proceedings of the American Statistical Association*.
OLSON, M. (1982) *The Rise and Decline of Nations* (New Haven: Yale University Press).
OZAKI, R. S. (1972) *The Control of Imports and Foreign Capital in Japan* (New York: Praeger).
OZGA, S. A. (1955) 'An Essay in the Theory of Tariffs', *Journal of Political Economy*, December.
PAGE, S. A. B. (1979) 'The Management of International Trade', in R. Major (ed.), *Britain's Trade and Exchange Rate Policy* (London: Heinemann Educational Books).
PANIĆ, M. (1976) 'The Inevitable Inflation', *Lloyds Bank Review*, July.
PANIĆ, M. (1978) 'The Origin of Increasing Inflationary Tendencies in Contemporary Society', in F. Hirsch and J. H. Goldthorpe (eds), *The Political Economy of Inflation* (London: Martin Robertson).
PANIĆ, M. (1982) 'International Direct Investment in Conditions of Structural Disequilibrium: UK Experience since the 1960s', in J. Black and J. H. Dunning (eds), *International Capital Movements* (London: Macmillan).
PANIĆ, M. and JOYCE, P. L. (1980) 'UK Manufacturing Industry: International Integration and Trade Performance', *Bank of England Quarterly Bulletin*, March.
PANIĆ, M. and RAJAN, A. H. (1971) *Product Changes in Industrial Countries Trade: 1955–1968* (London: National Economic Development Office).
PEARCE, D. (1976) *Environmental Economics* (London: Longman).
PELKMANS, J. (1983) 'The Community's Vivid Core: Integration Processes in Industrial Product Markets', Paper presented at the Seventh World Congress of the International Economic Association in Madrid, mimeographed.
PERKINS, J. A. (1981) 'The Agricultural Revolution in Germany, 1850–1914', *Journal of European Economic History*, Spring.
PINCUS, J. J. (1977) *Pressure Groups and Politics in Antebbelum Tarrifs* (New York: Columbia University Press).

PINDYCK, R. S. (1981) 'The Optimal Production of an Exhaustible Resource when Price is Exogenous and Stochastic', *Scandinavian Journal of Economics*, June.
PINDYCK, R. S. (1982) 'OPEC Oil Pricing, and the Implications for Consumers and Producers', in J. M. Griffin and D. J. Teece (eds), *OPEC Behaviour and World Oil Prices*, op. cit.
POLLARD, S. (1981) *Peaceful Conquest: the Industrialisation of Europe, 1760–1970* (Oxford: Oxford University Press).
PRAIS, S. J. (1976) *The Evolution of Giant Firms in Britain* (Cambridge: Cambridge University Press).
PRATTEN, C. F. (1971) *Economies of Scale in Manufacturing Industry* (Cambridge: Cambridge University Press).
PRYOR, F. L. (1972) 'An International Comparison of Concentration Ratios', *Review of Economics and Statistics*, May.
RANGARAJAN, L. N. (1978) *Commodity Conflict* (London: Croom Helm).
RAPP, R. T. (1975) 'The Unmaking of the Mediterranean Trade Hegemony: International Trade Rivalry and Commercial Revolution', *Journal of Economic History*, September.
RASCHE, R. H. and TATOM, J. A. (1977) 'Energy Resources and Potential GNP', *Federal Reserve Bank of St Louis Review*, June.
RENFREW, C. (1984) *Approaches to Social Archaeology* (Edinburgh: Edinburgh University Press).
RICARDO, D. ([1822] 1951a) *The Works and Correspondence. vol. IV. Pamphlets and Papers 1815–1825*, P. Sraffa (ed.), (Cambridge: Cambridge University Press).
RICARDO, D. ([1817] 1951b) *On the Principles of Political Economy and Taxation*, P. Sraffa (ed.), (Cambridge: Cambridge University Press).
RICARDO, D. ([1810–11] 1951c) 'Notes on Bentham' in *The Works and Correspondence. vol. III. Pamphlets and Papers 1809–1811*, P. Sraffa (ed.), (Cambridge: Cambridge University Press).
ROBBINS, L. (1952) *The Theory of Economic Policy* (London: Macmillan).
ROBBINS, S. M. and STOBAUGH, P. B. (1973) *Money in the Multinational Enterprise: a Study of Financial Policy* (New York: Basic Books).
ROBERTS, J. M. (1980) *History of the World* (Harmondsworth, Middlesex: Penguin Books).
ROBERTSON, D. H. (1938) 'The Future of International Trade', *Economic Journal*, March.
ROBINSON, E. A. G. (1935) *The Structure of Competitive Industry* (Cambridge: Cambridge University Press).
ROBINSON, J. (1983) *Multinationals and Political Control* (Aldershot: Gower).
ROSTOW, W. W. (1960) *The Stages of Economic Growth* (Cambridge: Cambridge University Press).
ROSTOW, W. W. (1978) *The World Economy: History and Prospects* (London: Macmillan).
ROSTOW, W. W. (1980) *Why the Poor Get Richer and the Rich Slow Down* (London: Macmillan).

ROSTOW, W. W. (1985) 'The World Economy Since 1945: a Stylised Historical Analysis', *Economic History Review*, May.
RUBIN, S. J. (1970) 'The International Firm and National Jurisdiction', in C. P. Kindleberger (ed.), *The International Corporation* (Cambridge, Mass.: MIT Press).
SAPIR, A. and LUTZ, E. (1981) 'Trade in Services: Economic Determinants and Development Related Issues', *World Bank Staff Working Paper No. 480* (Washington, DC.: World Bank).
SAUL, S. B. (1960) *Studies in British Overseas Trade, 1870–1914* (Liverpool: Liverpool University Press).
SCAMMELL, W. M. (1965) 'The Working of the Gold Standard', *Yorkshire Bulletin of Economic and Social Research*, May.
SCHERER, F. M. (1980) *Industrial Market Structure and Economic Performance*, 2nd edn, (Chicago: Rand McNally).
SCHIAVONE, G. (1981) *The Institutions of Comecon* (London: Macmillan).
SCHUMPETER, J. A. (1963) *History of Economic Analysis* (London: Allen & Unwin).
SCHWARTZMAN, D. (1963) 'Uncertainty and the Size of the Firm', *Economica*, August.
SCITOVSKY, T. (1957) 'The Theory of the Balance of Payments and the Problem of a Common European Currency', *Kyklos*, Fasc. 1.
SCITOVSKY, T. (1958) *Economic Theory and Western European Integration* (London: Allen & Unwin).
SEERS, D. and VAITSOS, C. (eds) (1980) *Integration and Unequal Development: The Experience of the EEC* (New York: St Martins Press).
SEMMELL, B. (1970) *The Rise of Free Trade Imperialism* (Cambridge: Cambridge University Press).
SEN, G. (1984) *The Military Origins of Industrialisation and International Trade Rivalry* (London: Frances Pinter).
SENGUPTA, A. (ed.) (1980) *Commodities Finance and Trade* (London: Frances Pinter).
SHEPHERD, W. G. (1970) *Market Power and Economic Welfare* (New York: Random House).
SHINOHARA, M. (1982) *Industrial Growth, Trade, and Dynamic Patterns in the Japanese Economy* (Tokyo: University of Tokyo Press).
SHONFIELD, A. (1965) *Modern Capitalism* (Oxford: Oxford University Press).
SIDERI, S. (1970) *Trade and Power: Informal Colonialism and Anglo-Portuguese Relations* (Rotterdam: Rotterdam University Press).
ŠIK, O. (1967) *Plan and Market Under Socialism* (New York: International Arts and Sciences Press).
SILBERSTON, A. (1970) 'Surveys of Applied Economics: Price Behaviour of Firms', *Economic Journal*, September.
SMALL, M. and SINGER, J. D. (1982) *Resort to Arms: International and Civil Wars, 1816–1980* (Beverly Hills: Sage Publications).
SMITH, A. ([1776] 1937) *An Inquiry into the Nature and Causes of the Wealth of Nations*, E. Cannan (ed.), (New York: Modern Library).
SOLOMON, R. (1982) *The International Monetary System, 1945–81*, 2nd edn, (New York: Harper & Row).

SPENGLER, J. J. (1960) 'Mercantilist and Physiocratic Growth Theory', in B. F. Hoselitz (ed.), *Theories of Economic Growth* (New York: Free Press).

SPERO, J. E. (1981) *The Politics of International Economic Relations*, 2nd edn, (London: Allen & Unwin).

SPITALLER, E. (1973) 'Incomes Policy in Austria', *IMF Staff Papers*, March.

SPITALLER, E. (1980) 'Short-Run Effects of Exchange Rate Changes on Terms of Trade Balance', *IMF Staff Papers*, June.

SPRAOS, J. (1980) 'The Statistical Debate on the Net Barter Terms of Trade Between Primary Commodities and Manufactures', *Economic Journal*, March.

STOPFORD, J. M. and DUNNING, J. H. (1983) *Multinationals: Company Performance and Global Trends* (London: Macmillan).

STOPFORD, J. M., DUNNING, J. H. and HABERICH, K. O. (1980) *The World Directory of Multinationals*, vol. I (London: Macmillan).

SUMMERS, R. and HESTON, A. (1984) 'Improved International Comparisons of Real Product and its Composition, 1950–80', *Review of Income and Wealth*, June.

SUPPLE, B. (1973) 'The State and the Industrial Revolution, 1700–1914', in C. M. Cipolla (ed.), *The Fontana Economic History of Europe. vol. 3 The Industrial Revolution* (Glasgow: Fontana-Collins).

SYLOS-LABINI, P. (1984) *The Forces of Growth and Decline* (Cambridge, Mass.: MIT Press).

THIRLWALL, A. P. (1980) *Balance of Payments Theory and the United Kingdom Experience* (London: Macmillan).

TRIFFIN, R. (1964) 'The Evolution of the International Monetary System: Historical Reappraisal and Future Perspectives', *Princeton Studies in International Finance* (Princeton: Princeton University Press).

TRIFFIN, R. (1968) *Our International Monetary System: Yesterday, Today and Tomorrow* (New York: Random House).

TWITCHETT, C. C. (1981) *A Framework for Development: The EEC and the ACP* (London: Allen & Unwin).

UNITED NATIONS (1978) *Transnational Corporations in World Developments: a Re-examination* (New York: United Nations).

UNITED NATIONS (1979) *Trends and Characteristics of International Migration Since 1950* (New York: United Nations).

UNITED NATIONS (1981) *Transnational Banks: Operations, Strategies and their Effects on Developing Countries* (New York: United Nations).

UNITED NATIONS (1985) *Transnational Corporations in World Development – Third Survey* (London: Graham & Trotman).

VEIL, E. (1975) 'Surpluses and Deficits in the Balance of Payments: Definition and Significance of Alternative Concepts', *OECD Occasional Studies*, July.

WALLERSTEIN, I. (1980) *The Modern World System II: Mercantilism and the Consolidation of the European World Economy, 1600–1750* (London: Academic Press).

WALTER, I. (1985), *Barriers to Trade in Banking and Financial Services* (London: Trade Policy Research Centre).

WATSON, M., KELLER, P. and MATHIESON, D. (1984), 'International

Capital Markets-Developments and Prospects', *IMF Occasional Paper No. 31* (Washington, DC: IMF).

WEBB, S. B. (1980) 'Tariffs, Cartels, Technology and Growth in the German Steel Industry, 1879–1914', *Journal of Economic History*, June.

WHITMAN, M. N. (1969) 'Economic Openness and International Financial Flows', *Journal of Money, Credit and Banking*, November.

WHITTLESEY, C. R. (1963) 'Power and Influence in the Federal Reserve System', *Economica*, February.

WILENSKY, H. (1975) *The Welfare State and Equality* (Berkeley: University of California Press).

WILLIAMSON, J. G. (1965) 'Regional Inequality and the Process of National Development: a Description of the Patterns', *Economic Development and Cultural Change*, July.

WILLIAMSON, O. E. (1971) 'The Vertical Integration of Production: Market Failure Considerations', *American Economic Review – Papers and Proceedings*, May.

WILLIAMSON, O. E. (1975) *Markets and Hierarchies* (New York: The Free Press).

WILLIAMSON, O. E. (1979) 'Transactions-Costs Economics: the Governance of Contractual Relations', *Journal of Law and Economics*, October.

WILLIAMSON, O. E. (1981) 'The Modern Corporation: Origin, Evolution, Attributes', *Journal of Economic Literature*, December.

WILSON, C. (1949) 'Treasure and Trade Balances: The Mercantilist Problem', *Economic History Review*, vol. II, no. 2.

WILSON, C. (1951) 'Treasure and Trade Balances: Further Evidence', *Economic History Review*, vol. IV, no. 2.

WORLD BANK (1979) *World Development Report* (Washington, DC: World Bank).

WORLD BANK (1985) *World Development Report* (New York: Oxford University Press).

WORLD BANK (1986) *World Development Report* (New York: Oxford University Press).

WRIGHT, J. F. (1984) 'Real Wage Resistance: Eighty Years of the British Cost of Living'. *Oxford Economic Papers – Supplement*, November.

YOUNG, A. (1928) 'Increasing Returns and Economic Progress', *Economic Journal*, December.

Index of Names

Index of Subjects